ISAIAH ROGERS

ISAIAH ROGERS

Architectural Practice in
Antebellum America

James F. O'Gorman

Research by Denys Peter Myers and
James F. O'Gorman

Foreword by Earle G. Shettleworth Jr.

University of Massachusetts Press
Amherst and Boston

Copyright © 2015 by University of Massachusetts Press
All rights reserved
Printed in the United States of America

ISBN 978-1-62534-122-8 (paper); 121-1 (hardcover)

Designed by Dennis Anderson
Set in Adobe Garamond Pro by House of Equations, Inc.
Printed and bound by Sheridan Books, Inc.

Library of Congress Cataloging-in-Publication Data

O'Gorman, James F.
Isaiah Rogers : architectural practice in antebellum America / James F. O'Gorman ;
research by Denys Peter Myers and James F. O'Gorman ; foreword by Earle G. Shettleworth Jr.
    pages cm
Includes bibliographical references and index.
ISBN 978-1-62534-122-8 (pbk. : alk. paper) —
ISBN 978-1-62534-121-1 (hardcover : alk. paper)
 1. Rogers, Isaiah, 1800–1869. 2. Architects—United States—Biography.
 3. Architectural practice—United States—History—19th century. I. Title.
NA737.R585 O49 2015
720.92—dc23
[B]
2014027579

British Library Cataloguing-in-Publication Data
A catalogue record for this book is available from the British Library.

Frontispiece: Boston Merchants' Exchange, Boston, Massachusetts, 1840–43.
State Street front. Courtesy Bostonian Society.

Note: All drawings and buildings are by Isaiah Rogers or
his office unless otherwise credited.

To the memory of
John O'Gorman and Catherine (Kitty) Tobin,
James P. O'Gorman and Mary Scully,
Paul J. O'Gorman and Dorothy Hogan.
From Tipperary to Missouri

What is the best approach? Perhaps a daybook of the artist's life.
				Edward Weston

CONTENTS

	Foreword by Earle G. Shettleworth Jr.	xi
	Preface	xiii
	Introduction	1
1	Marshfield and Boston, 1800–1834	13
2	New York and Boston, 1834–1841	52
3	Boston and New York, 1841–1848	89
4	Cincinnati, 1848–1852	143
5	Louisville and Cincinnati, 1852–1861	177
6	Cincinnati and Washington, D.C., 1861–1869	215
	Afterword	231
	Appendix: Chronological List of Buildings and Projects	241
	Notes	257
	Index	277

FOREWORD

THIS BOOK would not exist without the research of the late Denys Peter Myers. At the beginning of my sophomore year at Colby College, in the fall of 1967, I was invited to dinner by my art history professor, William B. Miller, to meet Peter Myers. Bill and Peter had known each other at Harvard in the 1930s, and Peter was visiting Maine to do research for the Maine Catalogue of the Historic American Building Survey. From that first meeting until Peter completed the text of "The Historic Architecture of Maine" for the catalogue published seven years later, I shared information with him, and we became close friends in the process.

For a college student entering the field of art and architectural history, Peter Myers was a wonderful mentor to have. Born in 1916, Peter developed an interest in history and the arts at an early age on walks through Boston and Cambridge with his father. Of the same name, his father was a newspaper reporter who had served as a staff member of the World Peace Foundation and worked as a State Department official during World War II. While studying at Harvard with Kenneth John Conant, the younger Myers developed a lifelong passion for the Greek Revival in 1938, when he wrote and photographed for a paper on buildings in that style in Cambridge. While still in college, he helped found the Society of Architectural Historians.

After graduating in 1940 (John F. Kennedy was a classmate), Peter managed exhibitions at the New York Public Library until 1943, when he entered the U.S. Army. His art history degree earned him a place in the Monuments, Fine Arts, and Archives division, where he served until 1946. He saw duty in England, France, and Germany, where he worked to recover art stolen by the Nazis. Two highlights of his service were his roles in saving Tiepolo's ceiling in the Residenz at Würzburg and in preventing the theft of tapestries by an American officer.

In 1948 Peter earned a master's degree at Columbia under Talbot Hamlin, remembered today for his highly influential *Greek Revival Architecture in America* (1944). Between 1947 and 1966 Peter divided his time directing five museums and teaching at three colleges. In 1966 he began his twenty-year service with the National Park Service as the principal architectural historian for the Historic American Buildings Survey. This position gave him the opportunity to apply his wide knowledge of American architectural history on a national scale and to influence the recordation of many of the country's most significant buildings.

During his first museum directorship at Zanesville, Ohio, between 1947 and 1955, Peter learned of the Midwestern work of Isaiah Rogers and embarked on a lifelong search for information about this major antebellum American architect. In 1949 he learned from Rogers's granddaughter in Cincinnati that the architect's surviving papers and drawings had been destroyed in a garage fire the previous year, but his diary had survived. With her permission, Peter deposited the diary at the Avery Architectural and Fine Arts Library of Columbia University, ensuring the preservation of one of the most significant documents in American architectural history.

In his long and active life, Peter presented lectures and published scholarship, including articles and book introductions on American architecture and related topics. He considered his Maine Catalogue the most significant of his writings. Unfortunately, his more than fifty-year quest for Isaiah Rogers did not result in the monograph to which he aspired. During my last visit with Peter and his wife, Anne, in Alexandria, Virginia, he showed me his research and impressed upon me that when he died, I was to take possession of his files and see that a proper biography was published. Our last communications, by letter and phone in September 2003, were to celebrate the recent discovery at the Maine Historical Society of architectural drawings from Rogers's office for the Middle Dutch Reformed Church in New York. Peter died the next month at the age of eighty-seven.

My promise to my friend is now being fulfilled with the publication of this excellent biography by James F. O'Gorman, one of this country's leading scholars in architectural history. With a background himself as a practicing architect, and a specialist in nineteenth-century American architecture, he has published studies of Charles Bulfinch, Henry Austin, Gervase Wheeler, Hammatt Billings, H. H. Richardson, Frank Furness, Louis Sullivan, and Frank Lloyd Wright. He is especially qualified to transform Peter's research as well as his own into a book that provides significant insights into the architect's life and work while addressing the broader issue of the evolution of American architectural practice before the Civil War. Those who care about the U.S. cultural history are indebted to James O'Gorman for giving us this masterful portrait of Isaiah Rogers and his contributions to the American scene.

Earle G. Shettleworth Jr.
Maine State Historian

PREFACE

Rather than architecture, per se, this book describes the architectural practice of one pre–Civil War American, based largely on his own words. It is not so much about the work of Isaiah Rogers as about the way that work was accomplished—what Rogers did to get buildings built (or not built). It differs from other monographs I have written on the buildings of nineteenth-century architects because the primary source is different from the sources available for those studies. Unfortunately, the bulk of Rogers's major works, and most minor ones, too, has vanished, and little survives in the visual record to document the effort he put into many of his unexecuted projects.

This book is drawn chiefly from an extraordinary set of pocket-size daybooks (hereafter called his "diary") that he kept during his long career. In them, day-to-day architectural chores appear within the flow of his life, and so they appear here as well. Although some journals of his contemporaries have been preserved, I know of none quite as extensive. Its existence permits a more three-dimensional portrait of one architect's working life than most monographs can achieve. It does not cover his entire career—the first twenty or so years are missing, and they, as well as other significant gaps, must be filled from other sources. But what we do have is a rare, highly detailed account of a practicing architect's method in the early years of the profession in the United States, as well as his work as overseer of construction before the rise of the general contractor. This identification as both designer and builder led to confusion among his contemporaries about the role of the architect in the building process as it was perceived at that time. Rogers's diary is a slice of the history of architecture that is seldom so complete for this period, and it is the point of view from which the following narrative is presented.

Like many of his contemporaries—men such as Alexander Parris, T. U. Walter, John Haviland, or Robert Mills—Rogers not only designed buildings but also directed their execution. The process was time-consuming, detailed, tedious, and often frustrating and ill-rewarded. This book, which covers the steps necessary to achieve a building, tries to capture something of the breadth, the fatigue, the frustration, and the hurly-burly of that process. Because it is a study of Rogers's career as a whole, his unrealized projects—over which he labored sometimes for months and, a few times, even years—are treated in nearly as much detail as his completed works. So, too, are projects he undertook without commissions, when he was simply following a restless urge to practice his vocation at all times. My aim has been to produce a broadly horizontal coverage of his career, as opposed to studying in-depth a few built or projected works.

Rogers began working as a teenage apprentice about 1818, but his diary, forty small notebooks in all, begins in January 1838 and runs, with a few gaps, into February 1856. (For Book 2 [1839], Rogers used a printed calendar for 1838 and changed the dates of some days of the month, which can lead to confusion.) Parts of 1861 and 1867 are also preserved. All are housed at the Avery Architectural and Fine Arts Library at Columbia University but were transcribed under the direction of their collector, the late Denys Peter Myers, in a typescript encompassing some twelve hundred pages. Myers published his findings, and the path that led to them, in an article titled "The Recently Discovered Diaries of Isaiah Rogers," which appeared in *Columbia Library Columns* in November 1966. (My own preliminary research can be found in the Winter 2009 issue of *Nineteenth Century*, "Gleanings from the Diary of Isaiah Rogers, Architect," a hurried piece with several errors.) The diary, as described by Myers, encompasses "small pocket books written in faded lead pencil in a miniscule and sometime illegible hand." Most of the booklets are labeled "T. J. & J. Smith's Improved Patent Metallic Paper Memorandum Book with Metallic Pencil," with the writing instrument provided in a sleeve. They range in size from roughly 4 by 3 inches to 6.5 by 4 inches.

In them, Rogers wrote in a fairly clear hand that would be legible were it not so faint. His orthography "presents problems," wrote Myers, and it is in the spelling of personal names "that the real challenges arise." Such is true for all proper names. Myers's transcription, which I have used extensively, obviates some of these problems, but others remain, and one needs to compare the typescript with the originals (using a magnifying glass and a strong light), keeping in mind the people and situations around Rogers at the time. The identity of some people cannot be established, but with the help of other sources it is possible to decipher many of the actors in the accounts. This is also true of the fate of some projects. A few sketches are scattered throughout the booklets, some with measurements of buildings to be altered, a few partial plans, slight views of derricks, church pews, funereal monuments, and one view of a house he was to remodel. Most are unidentified or too schematic to be of much use to the scholar.

The diary is focused on the architect's work, with some notes about his family. Observations about the world are rare. Because Rogers wrote for himself, he usually included only partial information about people, places, or commissions. To flesh out a fuller picture, I consulted outside sources. One fundamental reference for the early years is William Wheilden's biography of Solomon Willard, Rogers's mentor and collaborator. A large gap in Rogers's own record omits 1862 to 1865, coinciding with his work at the Treasury department in Washington, D.C. Fortunately, those years have been well covered in larger studies by Antoinette J. Lee and Pamela Scott; also surviving is the diary of his nemesis A. B. Mullet. I have summarized those sources here. The letters of Horatio Greenough illuminate the episode of moving the statue of the seated George Washington from the U.S. Capitol. To help place other recorded people and events in context, we now have the wonder of the Internet, offering the resources of Wikipedia (for initial guidance) and such databases as American Historical Newspapers, the American Periodical Series, and Fultonhistory.com as well as the online archives of the *New York Times,* the *Boston Globe,* and smaller local papers. City directories provide further information. Because these sources are easily accessed online, I have limited the number of notes. Of course, where specific modern scholarship is available, I have made use of it. Elizabeth Jones's master's thesis on Henry Whitestone has been most helpful, for example; her forthcoming monograph on his career will complete the picture. Through the generosity of Earle G. Shettleworth Jr., I have had access to the useful research files left by Peter Myers. Those papers have been greatly augmented in the preparation of this book, with the entire collection deposited in the archive of Historic New England in Boston.

Even though much of Rogers's executed work is gone, many of his most important buildings stood in the center of cities (which spelled their doom when those cities were redeveloped in the next century; fire was also a common threat). The visual record of those places, left to us in illustrated publications and vintage prints and photographs, allows for some understanding of his accomplishments. Where possible, I have deliberately chosen early engraved or lithographed views over later photographs. They are more indicative of the buildings' origins. What must have been a huge output of drawings by his office over some forty-five years has been reduced to the relatively few sketches now known, and his letters, except those written as part of his duties while serving as Architect of the Treasury and now stored in the National Archives, seem mostly to have vanished. The same can be said of business papers generated by his firm over half a century.

Unlike his contemporaries, who worked mainly along the eastern and southern rim of the United States, Rogers designed and supervised the erection of buildings across the country as it existed during his lifetime. (The exceptions were William Strickland, who produced major structures in Nashville; James Gallier and James Dakin, who left New York for careers in the Deep South; and a few others who erected scattered buildings inland from the coast.) His reach extended from Maine to Alabama and Georgia, from Boston to Chicago and Milwaukee, from New York to Cincinnati to Louisville, Nashville, and New Orleans. Rogers designed, and often executed, nearly every building type known to the era. To put this far-ranging career into a coherent chronological package, I have contextualized the diary: I have rewritten, condensed, clarified, and augmented the information therein. It should be understood that his writings needed much interpretation—and at times imaginative leaps—to clarify shorthand references. Since my aim is a broad sweep of his production, I leave it to local historians to plunge into research on specific works listed in the Appendix. This book is neither a definitive monograph nor a catalogue raisonné, although I have mentioned each of the works for which I found useful information. It should also be noted that, although Peter Myers intended to produce the definitive study of Rogers's career, this is not the book he would have written.

I provide a chronological outline of the architect's practice to introduce in some detail an important career, to emphasize the richness and variety of the history of the developing architectural profession in America. However, many details of Rogers's life as designer and builder I could not include. Certainly, much important information about individual buildings is now long gone and can never be retrieved. Nonetheless, I think introductory monographs of this kind are valuable, however incomplete they might be. This book is intended to establish a basis from which further research can proceed. In more than one instance, I end the discussion with a question rather than an answer, when documentation was not at hand. I leave much to be mined by future researchers.

Many people unknown to me assisted Peter Myers over the long years he nurtured his investigation. I thank them but cannot name them. The reader's and my own primary debt is to him, but I must also recognize those who helped me during my research and writing, especially Jeanne Hablanian of the Art Library and Maggie DeVries of Visual Resources, Wellesley College; Michael J. Lewis of Williams College; Walter E. Langsam for Cincinnati works; Roger G. Reed of the National Park Service; Pamela Scott in Washington, D.C.; Earle G. Shettleworth Jr. of the Maine Historic Preservation Commission; and Carole Ann Fabian, director of the Avery Architectural and Fine Arts Library, Columbia University.

For a text covering a career that spanned so much geography, debts for specific help have piled up. Others who have contributed essential assistance include Erica Hirshler of the Museum of Fine Arts, Boston; Damie Stillman of the University of Delaware; Brooke E. Henderson of the Art Library, Susan M. Goodman of the Clapp Library, and students Delanie N. Goerig and Naureen Mazundar of Wellesley College; Carolyn Yerkes, Janet Parks, and Brooke Baldeschwiler of the Avery Library; Katherine Burger of the Kornhauser Health Sciences Library, University of Louisville; Antoinette J. Lee of Washington, D.C.; William R. Black Jr., formerly of Ray Black & Son, Inc., General Contractors of Paducah, Kentucky; George E. Thomas of Civicvisions, Philadelphia; Dale Stinchcomb, Harvard Theatre Collection; Lorna Condon, librarian and archivist of Historic New England; Susan Maycock and Charles M. Sullivan of the Cambridge Historical Commission; Robert Gamble of the Alabama Historical Commission; Jean Dunbar of Historic Design, Inc.; the antiquarian bookseller Charles B. Wood

III; Elizabeth Jacks of the Thomas Cole National Historic Site; Lauren B. Hewes, Georgia Barnhill, Andrew Bourque, and Christine Graham-Ward of the American Antiquarian Society; Alan Aimone, reference librarian at West Point; Mary Beth Betts of the New York City Landmarks Preservation Committee; Phil Nuxhall of the Spring Grove Heritage Foundation, Cincinnati; Patrick Snadon of the University of Cincinnati; Betty Ann Smiddy of Cincinnati; Erick D. Montgomery of Historic Augusta, Inc.; Bert Lippincott of the Newport Historical Society; John Hapgood at the National Gallery of Art; Sarah Jane Poindexter at the Filson Historical Society; Arlene Schwind of the Victoria Mansion in Portland, Maine; Elizabeth Roscio of the Bostonian Society; Jhennifer Amundson of Judson University; Karl Kabelac of Rochester, New York; Lori Chien of the Jervis Public Library; Russ Hatter of the Frankfort Historical Society, Kentucky; William Blair Scott Jr. of Lexington; Roy Lambert of Aurora, Indiana; Pia Oliver of Randall House Rare Books; Suzanne Ullrich, Sue Hurst, and Cindy Schuette of Hillforest; Robin McElheny of Harvard University Archives; Kevin Rose of the Turner Foundation; Kara M. Jackman of the Theological Library, Boston University; Robert Wojtowicz of Old Dominion University; Bruce Laverty at the Athenaeum of Philadelphia; Dani Fazio and Sofia Yalouris of the Maine Historical Society; and Dennis De Witt of Boston. The inevitable errors and omissions are all, of course, my own. I am sure they will be erased or filled by students who follow.

Last but most important, I am very happy to acknowledge a faculty research grant from Wellesley College as well as a generous subvention for illustrations from the McNeil Fund of the Art Department at the college, facilitated by Alice T. Friedman, and a Franklin Research Grant from the American Philosophical Society.

ISAIAH ROGERS

Introduction

THOSE WHO would search for lasting fame should think twice about the practice of architecture. There are, of course, the superstars—Michelangelo, Christopher Wren, (perhaps) Frank Lloyd Wright—and any number of only slightly less familiar names that have survived the years, but outnumbering them are the dozens of other architects who, despite having given usefulness, stability, and grace to the constructed environment, found no such recognition. Many were leaders in their own day, but that day no longer engages us. Such is the case of Isaiah Rogers, who is mentioned for one or two lost works in books about nineteenth-century American architectural history, but whose important career has remained unexamined and unsung. Only among a few local historians—namely, in the Midwest, where the Cincinnati chapter of the Society of Architectural Historians is named in his honor—does his memory, if not his buildings, survive.

Rogers deserves better. During his remarkably full career, from 1822 to 1868, he loomed large in American architectural history. While most of his peers practiced locally, Rogers built a national practice and was among the first to do so at such a scale. He produced or projected significant buildings for Mobile, Alabama; Augusta, Georgia; Bangor, Maine; Boston, Brookline, Lowell, Cambridge, Milton, Worcester, and Swampscott, among other Massachusetts locations; New York City and West Point; Richmond, Virginia; Newport, Rhode Island; Cincinnati, Dayton, Toledo, Springfield, and Columbus, Ohio; Frankfort, Louisville, and Paducah, Kentucky; Nashville and Memphis, Tennessee; Chicago, Illinois; Milwaukee, Wisconsin; and many places in between. He moved his office from Boston to New York to Cincinnati (with a branch in Louisville), following the westward march of the country's urban population. His clients both east and west represented the leaders of society. He was patronized in Boston by the Eliots, Lawrences, Shaws, Lymans, Forbeses, and Perkinses; in New York by John Jacob Astor; in Cincinnati by the Longworths, Taylors, Probascos, and so on.

Nor did he produce only minor buildings. Early on, Rogers created what is often called the first luxury or "grand" hotel in the United States. He followed with many works of architectural and engineering distinction, such as the Merchants' Exchange in Boston, realized with the help of associates such as Solomon Willard.

He was granted three patents for bridge design and another for a burglar-proof vault, and he eventually held the title of architect of the Treasury department, a federal office, under Abraham Lincoln. But time has not been kind to Rogers's memory. The majority of his buildings have been much altered, destroyed by fire, or otherwise removed from America's ever-changing cities. Few of his drawings or letters survive, and so far none of his many models have been found. Yet, it remains possible to trace more than just the outlines of his life and work.

Rogers entered the history of American architecture at the introduction of Grecian forms, which were to dominate the field into midcentury. And he entered that history in Boston, where the Grecian style was given a powerful local expression through the use of granite building blocks, some huge, extracted from the newly opened quarries at Quincy. In Boston and New York, he used that style and material to build monumental structures that established his reputation. He also quickly adopted ferrous structures and details and was among the earliest users of terra-cotta in this country. When he moved west, he favored Italianate or early Romanesque forms while occasionally engaging in the Gothic, keeping up with changing fashion. He continued to erect urban landmarks, predominantly hotels, exchanges, banks, theaters, public buildings, and churches, but among the other architectural types that rose from his drawings were houses, at least one observatory, commercial spaces, tombs, and a hospital. Another product of his roving mind was a design for a steam-powered gunboat for the Mississippi River, which he sketched in June 1861. He entered into some of the most prestigious competitions of his day, with intermittent success, and counted many friends, plus an enemy or two, among his competitors.

Rogers's diary records the life of a busy architect through the mid-nineteenth century, reporting from the inside, as it were, on the career of an antebellum architect and builder. It covers the myriad activities of an early practitioner in the era before the founding of the American Institute of Architects, ever present as he designed structures and then, in that era before the rise of the general contractor, sought out the materials and workmen to build them under his constant supervision. He often acted as paymaster as well. Like his fellow architects, Rogers struggled to have his services recognized and remunerated. As is evident in the chapters that follow, the architect in this period was a different man (no American women were practicing) from the architect of today.

The diary entries range from the professional to the personal, depicting a man imbued with the religious fervor well known in the era of the Second Great Awakening. Like so many countrymen of English heritage, Rogers observed the Sabbath as a day for churchgoing and relaxation with family, finding fault with those (mostly recent arrivals) who played games on that day. He avidly read the "Good Book" and the lives of prominent preachers. He was a Universalist, one who sought common principles through most religions; when on the road, he often attended services of other denominations (except Roman Catholic, but for once when he admitted he "stopped a short time" in a Cincinnati church to listen to the chant) because, as he said, believers will all be equal in heaven. He could be skeptical of what he heard from the pulpit, however. At a Congregationalist church in Milwaukee in September 1854, he found "an old fashioned sermon about hell and the old devil . . . a piece of contradiction from beginning to end."

In his twenties, Rogers joined the Masons, the Massachusetts Charitable Mechanic Association, and, later, the Independent Order of Odd Fellows and was active in all of them. He became an early member of the Boston Artists' Association, founded in 1841.[1] He was a Whig, the party of "internal improvements," and worked for many likeminded clients. Despite being an admirer of Martin Van Buren, he voted for William Henry Harrison, the Whig candidate, in 1840. Rogers was in Richmond when news came of the president's death after just one month in office. He reported that it "cast a gloom over the people"; he returned to his lodgings and did not go out again that day. He later voted for Lincoln. Other than these details, Rogers never mentions the major historical and political events of his day, including the Mexican War of the 1840s and the Civil War of the 1860s (other than a reference to work at Camp Dennison), even though he lived and worked near the fault line between North and South.

Although of limited formal education, Rogers had a large capacity for learning. He read broadly for both entertainment and instruction, avidly attended theater, sat through lectures on a wide spectrum of topics, visited panoramas, showed his works at mechanics' fairs, served as judge for exhibits, and gazed at spectacles, including a giraffe on display in New York. He once paid fifty cents to view Thomas Cole's painting *The Voyage of Life*, finding it "very good," and spent a like amount to hear Charles Dickens speak in Boston in 1842. When Jenny Lind performed in Cincinnati, he took his entire family to hear her sing. At least once he visited a phrenologist. He had several daguerreotypes made of himself and some of his buildings. He liked an occasional glass of lager or wine (and sometimes made his own), happily received gifts of brandy, at least once bought a demijohn of whiskey (perhaps for workmen), and on occasion enjoyed a good "segar." When he found time to revisit the homestead in his native Marshfield, Massachusetts, he walked the woods and shore, sailed, fished, hunted, and picked wild fruits and the produce of his garden. He was gregarious, a characteristic that stood him in good stead on his many travels. He was usually a considerate man, often helping less fortunate citizens and, on one notable occasion, treating kindly the architect who replaced him on a job. He was somewhat too trustful in financial matters, a trait that almost cost him dearly. He could be sarcastic, too, as when noting in 1850 that "some wise ones" thought his entrance design for a Cincinnati hotel "would not look right." Of false modesty he had none. Among the projects submitted for the Hamilton County courthouse competition, he stated flatly that his was "the best plan."

The diary shows him to have been a man of much intellectual and sufficient physical energy, indefatigable despite a less than robust body that was increasingly afflicted by poor hearing, a weak heart, and sundry other ailments. He does not dwell on these until late in life. His recording is laconic and matter-of-fact, contains little reflection or retrospection, offers minimum criticism, and says nothing about architectural theory. It is often tediously detailed with work and itemized expenditures of even a few cents. Rogers was no saint, but one discerns a warm human being, a usually fair employer, a man who relished both leisure and toil, a caring father and husband. Rogers and his wife, Emily, had eight children, four of whom reached adulthood. The loss of the other four to smallpox occurred in New York during a two-week period at the end of 1838. Among all the facts and rare bursts of passion is this one heart-stopping outcry: "The year ends with sorrow and affliction of the severest kind."

Rogers's remarks about fellow architects allow us a rare look into professional interactions in the antebellum period. They reveal not only a level of competition we might expect but also a friendlier intercourse than we might imagine. Rogers met, consulted with, befriended, and occasionally scowled at many of the most prominent practitioners of his day. With them he exchanged ideas, studied drawings, conversed about products and fees, and visited their buildings, whether in their company or not. Some of this exchange occurred before he joined the attempt to found an American Institution of Architects in 1836 and his discussions with David Henry Arnot about a similar effort in 1846. (Oddly, he was not among the founders when the American Institute of Architects was finally established in 1857; a gap occurs in the diary for that year, which might have told us why.)

Rogers's relationship to Alexander Parris was mixed. He thought a communication by Parris in the *Boston Courier* in December 1837 was "good on heating and ventilating." But the next year, when Parris sought Rogers's support for his design in the competition for the Boston Custom House, Rogers ignored his request, probably because Rogers's friend Ammi B. Young, the eventual architect of the building, was also in the picture. Rogers did show Parris around his New York Merchant's Exchange while it was under construction, and in March the two visited the Capitol in Washington, D.C.

Young was Rogers's exact contemporary and perhaps his closest connection among peers. No rivalry seems to have existed between the two. Young appears in the diary from 1838 (the year the surviving diary begins) to 1861, with the earliest entry referring to his work at the customhouse. According to the account, Young conferred with Rogers from the design's inception, when the latter was superintending his great Merchants' Exchange in New York, and continued to do so during the long construction. The two architects even visited Quincy together to look at stones being prepared for their projects. Enough evidence suggests that Rogers may be thought of as a collaborator, or at least a consultant, on that major monument. (Also of note: as Architect of the Treasury during the war, Rogers did plan exterior repairs to the building.) In 1840 Rogers called the rising customhouse "a splendid piece of construction in all its parts," and seven years later he stood in the rain to witness its illumination when it was finished.

The two friends dined and spent time together, loaned each other money (Rogers seems to have borrowed from everyone—colleagues, workmen, and clients alike), shared draftsmen and tools, and examined their respective projects from the planning stages to completion. In 1838 Young showed Rogers the model of his entry for the Ohio statehouse, a competition for which Rogers was preparing his own proposal; he thought Young's looked "very well." (Neither man won, although Rogers eventually had a hand in finishing the building.) In March 1845 Rogers guided Young through the interior of his Female Orphans' Asylum in Boston, and while in Washington in 1853, he looked at Young's drawings for federal customhouses and suggested improvements in floor construction "and cast iron laths for ceiling and walls," an element of Rogers's continued search for fire-resistant buildings. In 1862 he replaced Young as Architect of the Treasury, apparently without the mutual acrimony that occurred when A. B. Mullett replaced Rogers in 1865.

Solomon Willard, who was early on Rogers's mentor and eventually his collaborator, appears frequently in the first part of the diary and, hence, in this book. It was Willard who gave him his start and supplied the great blocks of Quincy granite that went into Rogers's major works in the eastern United States. On occasion, Rogers encountered William Strickland, and the two men talked about architecture. They remained friends, although Rogers disliked the proportions of Strickland's Tennessee state capitol. He knew James Dakin in New Orleans and, in 1851, supported his work on the local customhouse; he wrote a report for the commissioners favoring Dakin's project. Also appearing occasionally in the diary pages is Gridley J. F. Bryant. In 1851 Rogers and Bryant went to look at the Charles Street prison in Boston. He thought it very good work but did not like Bryant's radial plan as well as his own contemporary T-shaped layout for the jail in Cincinnati.

Rogers was out of step there—the hub-and-spoke model took over prison design—as he was in rejecting the suspension system for bridges, several of which he inspected firsthand. He met Adolphus Heiman in Nashville after the opening of the latter's suspension bridge across the Cumberland River. John A. Roebling never appears in the diaries, nor does Charles Ellet Jr., but Rogers's own work on iron arched bridges implicitly criticizes their suspension system, especially the first such structure to carry a train, the 825-foot span across the Niagara River. At the falls in September 1854, with work on the structure nearing completion, Rogers "found the workmanship very good, but . . . [did] not like the suspension principle," although he admitted that, seen from below, he found it "a most sublime sight." This was one of Rogers's rare statements of aesthetic effect. He later unsuccessfully proposed to cross the Ohio River at Cincinnati with an iron arch bridge of his own design, at the very spot where Roebling's dramatic suspension span still carries traffic north and south.

During the 1840s and 1850s, Rogers encountered John Notman of Philadelphia from time to time and was always glad to see him. He ran into John Haviland in Washington in January 1847, while both awaited the decision on the Smithsonian Institution competition. He knew Robert Mills in the 1840s but thought, as have many since, that the interior of his Monumental Church in Richmond was very bad. James Renwick Jr.'s name appears in the diary in connection with the Smithsonian competition, and at other times as well, but nothing suggests that the two were friends; Rogers lost the competition to Renwick and thought little of the completed building. He appears to have been friendly with Martin E. Thompson in New York, and several times he lost work to or took over work begun by Calvin Pollard. After a brief partnership with the Bostonian Richard Bond, the two had a falling out. Occasionally, a little-known or never-discussed architect appears, men such as Levi Mann of Boston, George W. Mygatt of Milwaukee, Thomas J. Sparrow of Portland, Maine, Owen G. Warren of New York, and J. B. Young of Detroit or Dayton. The names Thomas Thomas and Thomas Thomas Jr. of New York appear without comment on a flyleaf of the diary for 1853. Rogers does not mention, however, that the latter had published *The Working-man's Cottage Architecture* in 1848.

Rogers met Minard Lafever in Boston in 1845 and later, in Brooklyn, looked at what seems to have been Lafever's just-finished Holy Trinity church. "Some things I liked," he wrote, "more than the Trinity which I went to this morning" (presumably Richard Upjohn's church on Broadway, finished in 1846; he mentions Upjohn a few times when he loses a commission to him). In the fall of 1844 Rogers attended talks on architecture at the Lowell Institute by the enfant terrible of Boston architects, the liberally educated and well-traveled Arthur D. Gilman, who championed learned international design over the products of self-taught locals like Rogers. Gilman was hard on Rogers's works, and Rogers was in general not impressed with Gilman's lectures. He saw Thomas Ustick Walter over the years, with Walter at least once borrowing money and, on other occasions, showing him around Girard College in Philadelphia (Rogers placed third in the competition for the school layout) and the additions to the U.S. Capitol. While at the college, Rogers saw three of the columns for the main building raised in place "to good effect." He thought the new work on the Capitol "very elaborate and expensive." Walter was later to compliment Rogers as a reliable builder.

From the diary we also learn that, despite his spotty education, Rogers grew into an inquisitive, omnivorous reader, not only of practical reference works but of a broad variety of subjects. In the absence of accessible public collections of books on architectural technology, history, theory, and style, Rogers, like his peers, gathered his own library and worked his way through much general literature as well. He often mentions buying, trading for, or consulting works, without giving the titles; these include publications on theaters, bridge construction, and cottage design. If he did not own Stuart and Revett's bible of the Grecian Revival, *Antiquities of Athens,* he certainly knew of and used it early on. Although the title does not appear in his diary, because either the surviving record begins late in the day or the publication was a multivolume and expensive work, he did crib from it the details of the Choragic Monument of Lysicrates and ancient works to be found at the Tremont House and other early buildings.

Among his architectural books identified or identifiable, two other standards appear: Vitruvius, in the James Newton edition of 1791, which he purchased at auction in Boston in February 1838; and Jean-Nicolas-Louis Durand's richly illustrated *Recueil et parallèle des édifices* of about 1800, a title he acquired in April 1842 in a swap of a book on Arabian antiquities with the New York–New Haven architect Ithiel Town. As Henry-Russell Hitchcock pointed out in his magisterial history of nineteenth-century architecture, Durand's doctrine of pure classical revivalism had a formative impact early in the century in America.[2] Durand's book was certainly of more use to Rogers than a work on Near Eastern history (how or why he had it would be instructive to know, although the question remains hardly possible to answer). In October 1848 Rogers bought what must have been Henry Bernard's much-used *School Architecture* in the edition of that year. It might have proved useful later when he laid out a schoolhouse for Ironton, Ohio.

For residential design, which increasingly landed on his drafting boards, he acquired parts of A. J. Davis's *Rural Residences* from that architect in November 1839 and October 1844; what looks like the early volumes of Joseph Nash's *Mansions of England,* purchased in December 1841; and in January and April 1849, parts of David Henry Arnot's *Gothic Architecture Applied to Modern Residences.* For technical help, he added Morrill Wyman's 1846 *Treatise on Ventilation* in February of that year and, in March 1849, Thomas Ewbank's *Description and Historical Account of Hydraulic and Other Machines for Raising Water,* available in many editions including those of 1842 and 1846. This was certainly a desirable work for a man who spent great spans of time devising water systems for large public buildings.

In the fall of 1851 Rogers was reading John Ruskin's newly published *Stones of Venice,* the only historical-critical work on architecture he mentions. That he does not note the earlier *Seven Lamps of Architecture* may mean that as a practical man he had little real interest in theory. In addition, he owned books of history and travel, in which buildings were often illustrated and discussed, including a "large volume on Egypt" he wanted to consult during his brief period toying with that exotic style; James Ingram's *Memorials of Oxford* of 1837; volume one of John Lloyd Stephens's *Incidents of Travel in Central America, Chiapas, and Yucatan,* which he was reading in August 1841; a set of Erasmo Pistolesi's *Antiquities of Herculaneum and Pompeii,* for which he paid $36 in 1842; and one of Austen Layard's works on Nineveh, which he was reading in 1853.

It is indicative of Roger's inquisitive mind that when he moved to Cincinnati, he recorded reading books on Native culture that seem to have been rare in period inventories of libraries owned by American architects. In fact, his interest stemmed from earlier: in late 1839 he bought (and read in three days) John Delafield's *Antiquities of America.* He later owned Thomas McKenney and James Hall's *History of the Indian Tribes of North America,* a three-volume series of colored lithographs after paintings by Charles Bird King (whom he visited in Washington). That handsome work was published in Philadelphia in 1836–38, purchased by Rogers in September 1842, and custom-bound for him in September 1852. In Cincinnati he borrowed "new works on Indian antiquities" in October 1848 and read Squier and Davis's Smithsonian publication *Ancient Monuments of the Mississippi Valley* that same month. In January 1849 he visited the "ancient mounds at Portsmouth, Ohio, and took a hickory stick "as a memento of the place"; on another occasion, he picked up pieces of flint he thought were Indian arrowheads. In March he "finished reading Antiquities of Ohio."

Compared with the architectural libraries of his contemporaries, especially the collection of T. U. Walter, these direct references seem meager. But they cannot be a complete list of his collection, for more than once he recorded pulling off the shelf an unnamed book for inspiration on a project or to generate a discussion with a prospective client, a common practice among his peers. The surviving diary begins nearly two decades after he began practice, a time when he would have started acquiring books to learn his vocation. He also records the need to send his books to auction in 1846 after becoming the victim of the defalcation of a client whom he trusted, although he does not mention it again. If he did lose his books at that time, he quickly replaced them. We get an inkling of the importance of his library as it existed in Cincinnati in August 1854, when he insured his house for $500, his furniture for the same amount, and his book collection for $1,000.

That collection contained more than books on architecture—it seems also to have been representative of the popular taste of the period. As was common practice, Rogers kept domestic animals and had treatises on horses and cows. His general reading included the Bible, books on history, religion, biography, geology, science, agriculture, and popular literature. His recreational reading—and he had much time to read during his many travels to distant building sites and material suppliers—formed an eclectic mix. History titles he mentions cover Oxford, Egypt, Greece, and Mexico; he also read about Lynn, Massachusetts, where he designed two houses, at least one of which was built. His biographies recount the lives of John Trumbull, Benjamin Franklin, Hosea Ballou (who presided at his marriage, in 1823), A. C. Thomas, Reverend H. B. Soule, and Horace Greeley. Popular literature included Washington Irving's *Knickerbocker's History of New*

York, Harriet Beecher Stowe's two-volume *Uncle Tom's Cabin* (followed by attendance at a "Tom show"), James Fenimore Cooper's *The Spy,* Walter Scott's *The Lady of the Lake,* Henry Ward Beecher's *The Star Papers,* and something by the novelist Frances Trollope, perhaps because of her Cincinnati connection. He mentions forgotten tales more popular with the general public than with the literary critics, such as Emerson Bennett's *Kate Claredon; or, the Necromancy of the Wilderness,* George James's *The Old Oak Chest,* John Frederick Smith's *Ashton; or, the Will and the Way,* Eugene Sue's *Mysteries of the Heath,* and Julia Kavanagh's *Grace Lee.* All that despite the admonishment he received from the pulpit about the "folly and injury of novel reading." For headier fare, he acquired Alexander Humboldt on the cosmos, Robert Owen on reforming society, and Charles Lyell's pioneering *Principles of Geology.* In the religious vein, he read Universalist tracts and works exposing the horrors of Roman Catholicism. The last book Rogers mentions is an unnamed title by John Billings, the popular humorist.

But above all, we learn from Rogers's diary much about his architectural practice, which covered the critical years when he and his peers struggled to gain recognition as professionals before the founding of the American Institute of Architects and the appearance of the general contractor after midcentury. His time spent drawing pales in comparison to the time he spent managing logistics: supervising construction, contracting for materials and skilled and unskilled laborers, arguing with supervisors, and paying bills. Not to mention the hours frittered away with lawyers and in courts defending a decision or trying to get paid. We learn much about the difficulties of pre–Civil War architects in defining their role in the building process, and much, too, about myriad construction details. Rogers's dual responsibilities as designer and builder reflected the period's confusion about the role of the architect. Many times architects struggled for control over their work, wrangling with building committees, owners, suppliers, and workmen. Some jobs went smoothly; others did not. In February 1840, for example, Rogers went to court to demand "pay for services rendered in making plans and superintending" a bank building. That he won the case was somewhat unusual, and his financial award was niggling. In April 1842 he notes that the building committee of the Merchants' Exchange in Boston intended to use his services "and then pay me what they pleased without consulting me.... I do not agree to this," he harrumphed.

Rogers was ready and willing to defend his fees. For each project, he estimated the cost of building, sometimes asking the advice of builders. Although common today, in the early 1800s payment as a percentage of a building's overall cost was a rarity. In mid-February 1838 Rogers declined a commission to design a "sugar house" because the client was "not willing to pay two and one-half per cent for plans and overseeing." (When asked later, however, he did inspect the foundations.) If he did earn a percentage, no standard existed to set the amount. In

March 1851 he agreed to plan and superintend the Hamilton County courthouse in Cincinnati for 2 percent, and in July he proposed to design and supervise construction of a synagogue for 5 percent. Four years later, in the same city, he contracted to superintend his planned alterations to a hotel for 5 percent on cost, tasked with employing all the workmen and managing the entire business end of the job. He often worked for a flat fee, especially when only drawings were wanted, and even then he at times had to fight to collect. Money owed for work in the late 1840s remained unrecovered into the 1860s. None of these problems were unique to his practice. Indeed, not until the founding of the American Institute of Architects in 1857 were efforts made to set national standards governing architectural practice, and even with that organization's influence, it took a while for those standards to be general recognized.

Much less of Rogers's time was taken with designing than with supervising, yet without the former activity there would not have been the later work. It is a measure of the simplicity of the drawing-board side of the business that his office frequently changed addresses and rarely had more than a few assistants, unless he was *en charrette* for an important job like the Merchants' Exchange in Boston or the competition for the Smithsonian Institution in Washington. Theodore Voelckers worked for him in the early 1840s, often taking charge of presentation perspective renderings; he eventually moved on to his own practice. Theodore Washburn passed through and left under a dark cloud. William Henry Bayless, nephew of the artist Thomas Cole, helped for a while. Solomon Willard at least once—during the Smithsonian competition rush—came up to give a hand with drawings. Other short-time draftsmen seem to have drifted in and out of Rogers's office until his son Willard became a regular member in 1843. He was joined by Irish-born Henry Whitestone in 1852 and A. B. Mullett in 1857. All of the latter three would eventually become Rogers's partners. When the others left and Rogers died, Willard carried on the Cincinnati firm.

All of his assistants could draw, but Rogers took the lead on all projects. He was trained in draftsmanship in Boston, probably by the housewright Jesse Shaw and, surely, by Willard. Although few of Rogers's drawings are known, at least one contemporary—Dakin, the New Orleans architect—recommended him as a "good draftsman." Through much of his career Rogers, whose days were filled with travel and supervision, often drew at home at night, probably squinting by the light of whale oil, candle, or gas. He was known to draft on the fly, as in Kentucky in January 1853, when he set about making drawings on the spot for the rebuilding the recently burned Louisville Hotel.

He must have occasionally traveled with drawing instruments, and in fact he mentions buying a pocket set of such tools in February 1839. Paper and other supplies he could buy on the road. The traditional term "on the boards," referring to an architect's design work, was literal. Again and again, Rogers ordered boards from carpenters for specific projects, presumably to be placed on a table and used one at a time for separate drawings. (On one day in 1855 he reported laying paper on twenty-two of them!) The board would be covered first with cloth, usually muslin, and then with wove paper (often the ubiquitous J. Whatman brand), which was held in place with adhesive. Rogers once noted the purchase of "gum [Arabic] and brush for pasting paper." He bought cloth, paper, and glue as needed, along with pencils, India rubber, and India ink, but writes little about his specific drafting instruments.

Rogers usually proceeded to "plan" a project, using the word to mean any of the basic drawings—plans, elevations, sections, details—in the design process; he rarely used these specific terms, and then only later in his career. He almost never wrote that he was "drawing" or "designing" a building. Projects were first "sketched" in pencil, then "outlined" in ink, "figured" (dimensioned) or lettered, and, lastly, colored or shaded. These would usually become contract documents signed by architect, client, and builder to be augmented by detailed construction drawings as building progressed. The copying of such documents is mentioned but rarely. The diary seems to indicate that Rogers laid out most of the basic and working drawings in pencil, but others finished them in ink and usually produced the more presentable color graphics, especially the perspective views. For a competition in Cincinnati in early 1850, for example, Rogers was a bit miffed that he was showing his own "sketch" while the designs of others were "drawn and highly colored." (He won anyway, but the decision looks to have been rigged.) There is no naming of individual draftsmen on surviving drawings; where the few are signed, the signature is Rogers's own since these were contractual documents.

In the early nineteenth century, perspective views of prospective buildings were new to the American scene. Benjamin Henry Latrobe introduced the practice in the Mid-Atlantic states about 1800, but in New England such projections did not become common until a generation later. One surviving example from Rogers's office is the 1837 unsigned view of the Middle Reformed Dutch Church in New York. This type of drawing might be lithographed, as was B. W. Thayer's 1842 print after the well-known view of Rogers's Merchants' Exchange in Boston. Such views were not meant only for the client. They spread proof of the architect's talents before and after a building was realized, and they were distributed for that reason. Rogers used them as advertising. He had a view of his famous Burnet House in Cincinnati lithographed on stone about 1850, and in 1851 he ordered twenty prints of his (unrealized) design for the Hamilton County courthouse in Cincinnati. Original drawings could be bound into a book for presentation to a client, and both originals and copies were framed for exhibition at mechanics' fairs and elsewhere. To extend the impact of his advertising in the 1850s, Rogers arranged to have "cuts" (wood engravings) of drawings produced for publication in local newspapers.

Rogers and his peers extensively used models of entire buildings, and smaller versions of structural and decorative details such as trusses and column capitals, which were usually commissioned from professional makers. He learned of their use from Willard, a much sought-after model maker in his own right. The models were made for show at exhibitions and to direct stonecutters and other workmen. Those for Rogers's several bridge designs were sent to the Patent Office, as was customary. At this writing, none of the many models mentioned in his diary are known, but they clearly formed an important part of his operation.

Rogers's career began in the aftermath of the War of 1812 and ended in the aftermath of the Civil War. As with any long span of time, society during this period was marked by great change. By the time of his death, the architectural profession had evolved dramatically from the days of his Boston apprenticeship. Its leaders in his youth, men like Benjamin Henry Latrobe and Charles Bulfinch, had been born in the enlightened eighteenth century; those who emerged after his death, such as Frank Furness and Richard Morris Hunt, came of age in the industrialized nineteenth. Specialization took command. Where Rogers usually spent his days directing the erection of buildings or hunting for materials and workmen, drawing when he could find the time, the new architects—many trained in schools abroad—largely spent their time sitting in offices directing the graphic production of a host of assistants. General contractors such as Norcross Brothers took over direction not only of site work but of drawing the construction details as well.

In 1829 Rogers's Tremont House in Boston represented the cutting edge of American architectural development; in 1869 his Lagonda House in Springfield, Ohio, followed a shopworn formula. During the years between, though, he drew and built some of the most socially, artistically, and technologically important buildings in the United States. One of his obituaries stated that he was probably better known than any other architect in the country. Today he is largely forgotten, certainly beyond a few dedicated scholars.

This book seeks to begin the restoration of his memory to its rightful place in the history of American culture by outlining his projects on the basis of his own testimony, verified against independent sources. Here, for the first time, Rogers's career may be seen as something approaching a whole. What follows is history in real time, the quotidian life and practice of a pre–Civil War American architect and builder as seen through his own eyes.

CHAPTER

1

Marshfield and Boston
1800–1834

By 1800 Marshfield, Massachusetts, had enjoyed a long and quiet history as a farming and shipbuilding town. Edward Winslow was the first Englishman to arrive, in 1632. The settlement sat, as the town still does, on the Atlantic coast between Duxbury and Scituate, some twenty-five miles south of Boston, and it is perhaps best recognized outside the state, if at all, as the later home of Daniel Webster. Certainly one never had reason to suspect that Marshfield would give birth to an architect described in his obituary sixty-nine years later, with only slight hyperbole, as "in his profession . . . perhaps better known than any other person in the country."

The early centuries in this Pilgrim town were filled with industrious pursuits until the Revolution, when the strong Tory leanings of many inhabitants led to a moment of disquietude that, with the characteristic long memory of the Yankee, is still recalled locally. The *Resolves of the Town of Marshfield* of 1774, although carried by just one vote, affirmed allegiance to George III. Despite a brief occupation by the Queen's Guard, the town nonetheless ranked among the first to declare independence from Britain. When peace returned, the Rogers family, established locally since at least 1690 and building ships since the mid-1700s, set up new works in East Marshfield on Gravelly Beach and the North River. Those yards thrived from 1790 to 1829 led by skilled ship-carpenters, according to the historian of the industry.[1] Peleg Rogers Jr.'s yard stood near Little's Bridge, across the river. Among his many offspring was Isaac, farmer and presumably shipbuilder, who lived in a house on Main Street near the yard, the house that his son Isaiah would be born in and later remodel. Throughout his career, Isaiah

13

Rogers continued to refer to the town as "home," a place where he found rest and relaxation fishing off the bridge, and he continued to contribute to its life even as he moved farther away.

Baby Isaiah arrived near the middle period of this marine industry, on August 17, 1800, the son of Isaac and Hannah Ford Rogers.[2] The extended family was large, as were most in those years, and Isaac and Hannah added their share to the population—ten children in all. Isaiah's siblings appear from time to time in his dairy. His brother Jotham seems to have worked with or for him for a while early on. We know little of the future architect's first years, although no evidence indicates they were different from those of any boy in his time and place. He must have had some formal "common" schooling, but his diary suggests it was not heavy on grammar. He probably learned the use of carpenter's tools from his father and uncles, and we do know that he helped on the family farm. In 1852, while working in Cincinnati and having acquired a spread outside that city, he noted that he had not held a plow in thirty-five years, and it pretty well tired him out.

At some point, however, he distinguished himself from other Marshfield lads hopping clods behind the plow. He later credited a neighbor and relative by marriage, a future one-term congressman and customs officer at nearby Plymouth named Edward Preble Little, with giving him a push away from his hometown. An 1840 diary entry describes Little as the one who gave him "the first impulse" and calls him his "old friend and protector in my young days" to whom Rogers owed "not a little for my progress through the world so far." Lucky is the person who finds a relative, friend, or teacher astute enough to recognize a diamond in the rough. Although just nine years older than his friend, Little already knew something of the world beyond the North River. In 1800 he had joined his father, Captain George Little, as a midshipman commissioned by John Adams aboard the frigate *Boston*. We are to understand, then, that under Little's urging, at about age seventeen or eighteen (some thirty-five years before he held a plow again), Isaiah walked away from the farm, but not forever. He would return often to visit family and friends, including Little. The twenty-five-mile hike to Boston carried Rogers from rustic hinterland to rapidly developing urban center and on to an apprenticeship—we do not know by what connection—with Jesse Shaw, a carpenter and builder.[3]

Boston was rapidly expanding when Rogers arrived, but in those early years of the nineteenth century, Bostonians knew little of and barely understood what we now think of as the profession of architecture. Rogers arrived around the time that Charles Bulfinch, among the earliest in town to be called an architect and whose daytime job was as an urban administrator, left to supervise the ongoing construction of the U.S. Capitol. Only then might Bulfinch be considered an architectural professional, although he also functioned as a clerk of the works, in modern terms. Bulfinch was a well-read, Harvard-educated gentleman who had made the European grand tour, but many of the men who laid out Boston's buildings in this period came from the construction trades. They were carpenters, joiners, masons, glazers, and such, who taught themselves to outline simple diagrams of their work and to understand the rudiments of the classical orders, gleaned largely from books.

Few of these men considered themselves architects in the years before Rogers walked into town. Jesse Shaw seems never to have done so, and the handful who did tacked the term onto their trade as builders. By 1806 Peter Banner, a British immigrant, listed himself as "Architect and Builder," and the American-born Asher Benjamin called himself "Architect and Carpenter." Alexander Parris's practice in the 1820s and 1830s has been called the "first professional office in the city," and many future architects trained there. But the division of participation in the building process, as represented by the contrast between designer and builder, did not happen overnight. Benjamin, in his *Practical House Carpenter* of 1830, could proclaim that "mechanics were dependent upon the architect's instructions," and early on Rogers billed himself as an architect. But in fact the bulk of his working time, then and in his maturity, was consumed in procuring men and materials for building and in superintending construction. Like Bulfinch, he did much of his drawing after dark, when the building site was closed.[4]

Books on architecture were available in Boston, at least after 1809 for members of the Architectural Library,[5] and potential clients probably possessed a selection of standard works. For this reason, many of the buildings erected in these early years should be viewed as collaborations between gentleman/client and builder/architect. Caleb Snow's *History of Boston* of 1825, for example, praises the commissioning committee "who designed and erected St. Paul's and the architect [Parris] and artists who superintended the construction." Something of the same collaboration must have taken place at Tremont House, Rogers's career-making hotel of 1828. During his time with Shaw, Rogers surely focused on learning how to build, although to do so in this period of Roman- and, later, Greek-based neoclassicism, he needed to have at least perused such works as Asher Benjamin's *Country Builder's Assistant* of 1797 and subsequent editions. Shaw later taught drawing to apprentices, so Rogers may have had his first encounter with the drafting board under his guidance, but he would have finished that training under Solomon Willard, his next mentor. When Rogers arrived in town, Shaw was busy on Beacon Hill. The newcomer learned from the housewright to build, we suppose, in wood and brick, the primary materials of that residential development. Granite was just beginning to be introduced as an important material for details as well as large constructions. The growing cities of the new century needed monumental architecture in place of the small-scale wood and brick buildings inherited from the colonial and Federal eras. For Boston, with the coming of Grecian-based design, that meant buildings of monumental granite construction.[6]

The Boston area may have had an overabundance of carpenter-builders around 1820, for some of them began to drift southward looking for work. It was easy to get away via one of the schooners that regularly carried cargo and passengers from Long Wharf or T-Wharf straight to cities in the Gulf region. Freed by force from Spain in 1813 as a by-product of "Mr. Madison's War" with the English, Mobile became part of the new state of Alabama in 1819, and the cotton boom made it thrive. Shaw continued to work as a Boston housewright, but Rogers must have ended his apprenticeship by about 1820 or 1821 and then caught the wind on a ship headed for the Gulf. Although no known document records his move, while in Mobile in the early 1850s working on his design of the Battle House hotel, he wrote in his diary that he had run into an old "Negro" man who remembered him from his earlier stay. Talbot Hamlin and others have credited Rogers with the construction of a theater in Mobile, a building that has held a place in Rogers's biography because it is presumed to be his earliest known executed work. The only record of the theater's appearance occurs in the bottom-right margin of the Goodwin and Haire map of Mobile dated 1824.[7] It burned in November 1838, a common fate for hastily erected wooden buildings and other construction types, especially playhouses lit by candle or whale oil and, eventually, gas.

How the young Rogers acquired the skill to design even a simple theater remains unexplained, but his eagerness for knowledge is emphasized in the *Biographical Encyclopaedia of Ohio,* published just seven years after his death. This earliest account of his life, although written in the vagueness of the short memoir and the fullness of expression characteristic of the age, is generally accurate. It states that "by close and careful study in afterlife he acquired a valuable fund of information on a vast variety of subjects and an acutely intelligent appreciation of the utilities and beauties of science." Guides to theater design did exist and may have aided him in laying out the theater in Mobile. One such English publication—Benjamin Wyatt's *Observations on the Design for the Theatre Royal, Drury Lane . . . Accompanied by Plans, Elevations, & Sections, of the Same* (1813)—was perhaps too recent, but it explained the architect's reasoning. The biographical entry adds that Rogers "early displayed an admirable taste and sound judgment in all matters relating to the architectural profession, and devoted the whole of his leisure time to the requisition of an extended knowledge of its rules and principles." He studied the plans of others when he could and "copied [them] with zealous and scrupulous care" while reviewing "all the works of architecture that he could procure."[8]

The city of Mobile paid $25 for a set of plans for a theater that would accommodate an audience of one thousand and be located on the corner of Royal and Theatre Streets. A meeting of subscribers occurred on December 20, 1822, and the cornerstone was laid in early April 1823. Rogers seems to have left Mobile aboard a northbound schooner in 1822, so if he did design the building, presumably as an enticement to support for the project before the December meeting, he did not erect it or supervise its construction. The building was in use by 1824. A contemporary description lists the standard pit, boxes, and gallery in the interior; an engraved exterior view shows a gabled boxlike building with stepped parapets on the narrow side and a triple arcaded entrance in the center of an octastyle row of what were probably pilasters or pilaster strips, rather than engaged columns. Robert Gamble, senior historian at the Alabama Historical Commission, doubts that the building was "any great shakes architecturally—just a barn-like wooden structure providing space for performances in a boisterous seaport . . . newly come under the Americans."[9] In 1828 one local newspaper described the theater as a "dull, huge, misshapen pile that would defy the architect to designate to what order it belonged," although another called it "an ornament and credit to the City."[10]

To what order, or style, a building "belonged" was a concern in this period. Grecian neoclassicism had by then reached the Eastern Seaboard, carried on the wings of English immigrants such as Benjamin Henry Latrobe in the Mid-Atlantic as well as from books, ranging from Edmund Aikin's basic *Essay on the Doric Order of Architecture* (1810) to the multivolume *Antiquities of Athens* (1762–1830) of James Stuart and Nicholas Revett. As the sculptor Horatio Greenough later wrote, this period "sought to bring the Parthenon" into the streets and "to make the Temple of Theseus work" in the towns.[11] In Boston, Parris's St. Paul's Episcopal Cathedral of 1819–20, with its temple-form portico of Doric columns and tall pediment, was quickly followed by a building he designed with a similar portico for Bulfinch's Massachusetts General Hospital, both having proportions more Roman than Grecian. Willard's U.S. Branch Bank of 1824 and Parris's templar ends at the 1824–26 Quincy Market edged closer to the Grecian ideal. Fundamental, not just stylistic, changes in the local architecture were reflected in these works, with the church's drum-stacked sandstone columns and the hospital portico's granite drums for its columns quickly superseded by monolithic granite supports at the bank and the market. The local Grecian episode and Rogers's early works in the city were to be marked by large—and in some cases huge—units of granite construction.

Rogers began his career as Boston grew into a city, rapidly expanding its landmass as well as its population, from 43,000 in 1820 to 61,000 in 1830. He entered the local architectural scene at a recognizably transitional stage, just as Grecian neoclassicism became the rage and granite assumed its place as the material of choice for monumental public and commercial buildings.[12]

He might have remained just a builder and minor designer, like Jesse Shaw, rather than becoming a major architect who was also an innovative builder had not a second skilled mentor appeared. Solomon Willard was an extraordinary individual; he was truly what is too often by a stretch called a Renaissance man.[13] His background was similar to Rogers's. Raised in western Massachusetts, the inquisitive son of a farmer who taught him carpentry and joinery, he appeared in Boston in 1804, built a spiral staircase at Asher Benjamin's Exchange Coffee House of 1806–9, and then gained such a reputation as a fine woodcarver and model maker that he eventually worked his way through Providence and Baltimore to Washington, D.C. There, he built a model of Bulfinch's U.S. Capitol. Back in Boston about 1820, Willard joined Alexander Parris in introducing Grecian neoclassicism to the city's streets. Early on he had acquired books on architecture and the geometrical construction of perspective drawings, and in 1809 he and others founded the Boston Architectural Library. In those years, according to his biographer, his time was occupied by "architectural drawing, carving in wood, [and] various studies in chemistry and geology." By the early 1820s Willard not only practiced architecture, he also "received pupils in his studio near St. Paul's Church," in what is now Tremont Street, "and gave lessons in architecture and drawing." Best known as the designer of the Bunker Hill Monument of 1824–42 (for which he also supplied the granite), Willard designed and saw erected the U.S. Branch Bank, in the Grecian Doric style, and the Norfolk County Courthouse of 1824–26. His biographer quotes testimony by a person who claimed to have known all the Boston artists and mechanics of the period, and not one possessed "greater original powers of mind, combined with uncommon practical skill of execution." During the early 1820s, Rogers came under Willard's wing, and without doubt he received the best training in Grecian architecture and granite construction available in the city. It was the beginning of a long association that was fruitful for both men and for the history of American architecture. It was further solidified by Rogers, who named his first-born son (and future partner) Solomon Willard Rogers.

Rogers was back in Boston by 1822, the year the town became a city, to begin what might be called something of a post-apprenticeship or junior partnership with Willard. The team would turn out some of the most impressive works of the so-called Boston Granite Style, and not just in the city proper. Rogers worked at his drafting board and supervised construction while Willard developed the quarries in Quincy, which he began to operate in 1824, and oversaw construction of the Bunker Hill Monument. Their close association has at times led to confusion about the authorship of some buildings and monuments. Under Willard's instruction, Rogers not only acquired a postgraduate education in Grecian architecture and massive stone construction, learning from a master how to draw and use models, he also became skilled in executing ornamental carvings. A bill dated May 1826 from Rogers charged $260.38 for "Carving Capitals for Church in Cambridge at 5 Shillings per inch Measuring acrost the neck of Collum," including twenty-four "Caps" for large and small columns and pilasters.[14] This bill must relate to the campaign for Christ Church in Cambridge. Regular services at the Episcopal church, housed in Peter Harrison's handsome building of 1759, were all but abandoned in the early 1820s, and the structure had fallen into disrepair;

fund-raising allowed extensive work to be undertaken on both the exterior and interior.[15] Rogers's contribution has presumably been swept away by later changes.

During this period, Rogers also took a wife. On October 15, 1823, he married Emily Wesley Tobey of Portland, Maine, with the famed Universalist minister and noted theologian Hosea Ballou, pastor of the Second Church in School Street, presiding. Rogers would often listen to Ballou's sermons (and those of others in Boston and elsewhere, for he gave all but Roman Catholics a hearing), and he acquired a copy of Maturin Ballou's biography of his distinguished father when it came out in 1854. That year, according to his dairy, Rogers sketched, probably on his own initiative, an unrealized monument of unknown design for the deceased cleric, presumably for Mount Auburn Cemetery in Cambridge. (Ballou's grave there has been marked since 1859 by an over-life-size standing figure of the preacher by Edward A. Brackett.)

While Willard was busy with the bank and courthouse, he was also beginning to plot the construction of the Bunker Hill Monument and may have directed over to Rogers some lesser commissions, including private and probably speculative residential jobs in a city whose population had grown rapidly in recent years. Among Rogers's first documented Boston buildings, some were of the sort he must have worked on for Jesse Shaw. Neither early nor later did he escape what one of his contemporaries, the New York/New Orleans architect James Gallier, called the "horse-in-the-mill routine of grinding out drawings for the builders."[16] As for T. U. Walter and others, monumental buildings made Rogers's reputation in his day and ours, but early on his bread and butter depended on a lot of drafting jobs for small compensation.

The Suffolk County Registry of Deeds for 1824 and succeeding years records detailed specifications for several urban houses and stores to be erected according to Rogers's plans, thus making these documents part of the legal process.[17] No drawings or buildings seem to survive. Rogers is named the designer of some eleven brick houses in 1824, including an adjoining three on Purchase Street for the merchants Hall J. and James How (or Howe) that were probably intended for resale. At two-and-a-half stories, these were common Boston middle-class town houses of the period. The upper facades were to be of brick "laid close and handsome," with the ground stories in front of "Stone neatly tooled with stone caps and cills to Windows & Doors as shown on the plans." The "parlours [were] to be finished with double Architrave" and "given with a large and handsome chimney Mantletree [and] Free Stone hearths and jambs." In each house was to be "a handsome flight of Stairs in every way equal to" those found in another set of three houses on Pleasant Street, "which is to be our model." Rogers had simultaneously designed a pair of houses on Pleasant Street, and perhaps this note is a reference to them or the drawings for them, since they could not have yet been erected. Workmanship must be done "to the satisfaction of Mr. Rogers who drew the plans, and is to superintend the building." An 1828 contract for a pair of houses notes they were to be built according to his design, except for changes to the front doors and that they could sit higher if the owner wanted. These references suggest that Rogers and his employers, like modern developers, worked from standard plans for middle-class housing that could be modified at the client's will, but only before the contract was signed.

In 1825, when he first listed himself as an "Architect" in the *Boston Directory*, Rogers designed a large brick building for Ebenezer Smith. The latter required five sheets of drawings, all signed by the contracting parties. The structure was intended for a parcel at Merrimack, Portland, and Market Streets, on what must have been an awkwardly shaped lot at the edge of Bulfinch's 1808 Mill Pond landfill. It was to be set on the lot lines "& circulated round the two extreme ends as shown on the plans." This sounds like a foreshadowing of the rounded ends of the Tremont House facade three years later, which was intended to mask an irregular site, although curved front corners were also common for houses sited on regular lots. In 1826 Rogers added to the urban streetscape some eight "bricks," including two with ground-floor stores at State Street and Merchants Row, a particularly desirable location. Such residential/commercial combinations were common in Boston from the 1820s to the 1840s, as seen in a drawing by Charles Roath, Rogers's contemporary, now in the collection of Historic New England.[18] Rogers's work in this field did not end with these commissions. Records indicate his hand in seven houses in 1827, two houses and three stores in 1828, and at least one house in 1829. After a period in New York, Rogers returned to Boston in the mid-1840s and added many more domestic works to the city. It is doubtful that any survive.

Rogers's rise was swift following the deluge of repetitive urban residences, which appears to have tapered off, at least for a while, after 1827. He was out on his own by 1825, although his first major work did not reach the drafting board until two years later. With the completion of his winning design for the Tremont Theatre of 1827–28, the twenty-six-year-old beginner added his own neoclassical temple facade to his adopted city, albeit in the form of a nearly flat wall, rather than a columnar portico, and of somewhat mixed stylistic heritage.[19]

Disgusted with the management and offerings of the proprietors of Bulfinch's Federal Street Theatre, a group led by the lessee, the Boston-born actor William Pelby, had advertised a $50 prize for "the best Plan of a building with a granite front." (In such statements, as in Rogers's diary, "plan" meant "design," not just a drawing showing the horizontal layout of rooms, as it most commonly denotes today.) Rogers took the prize with his large ink-and-wash drawing of the facade, his oldest known graphic and one that no doubt bears witness to Willard's teaching. The drawing is inscribed on the reverse, along with the imprimatur of Gilbert

1. Tremont Theatre, Boston, Massachusetts, 1827. Front elevation. Graphite, ink, and wash on Whatman paper, approx. 19 x 27 in (48 x 69 cm). Courtesy Winterthur Museum.

Stuart. (Fig. 1) Presumably serving as advisor to the nine-man building committee, also named on the reverse, the distinguished portrait painter wrote on May 9 that he did not see "that the Front of the building, limited as it is [he probably meant by its site], admits of a better distribution," and then he signed his name. To the announced premium, the committee later added a $200 payment, probably for supervising the construction.[20] Rogers's career was off to a flying start. While praising the facade as "the most perfect piece of architecture in Boston," Henry R. Cleveland nonetheless found fault with the steepness of the roof. It was "too great for classical elegance."[21] Rogers's entry was seen as preferable to one other known submission: Martin E. Thompson and Ithiel Town's "Front Elevation of the New Boston Theatre," which "flirted with a choice of Corinthian or Gothic."[22] Rogers would later get to know both Thompson and Town, and he would often find himself in competition with many of his peers.

The character of this his first significant work, and thus of Rogers's talent at the beginning of his career, can be demonstrated only by scrutiny of the drawing. It serves us much better than the Mobile theater that is only attributed to him. The low-relief frontispiece that Rogers drew consists of a five-bay wall, of which the center three bays project slightly to form a thin salient topped by a tall pediment. At ground level, deeply drafted rustication (a lingering echo of the Italian Renaissance palazzo) surrounds three segmental-arched doorways. The flanking walls at this level show dressed ashlar. Four Grecian Ionic pilasters set between Doric antae, or corner pilasters, articulate the second-story wall, for which no stone is indicated. A vertical oval window surrounded by a garland is centered within the pediment, whose material is also not indicated. Trabeated windows set into shallow recesses topped by segmental arches flank the main entrances. Above are three tall trabeated windows surmounted by short cornices resting on consoles, or curved brackets. Above them, indented rectangular panels occupy the spaces between the central pilasters; these are flanked by round-arched niches intended for statues, which are also topped by square recessed panels. Iron gates to either side of the front would allow access to alleys for deliveries to the rear of the building, which was eventually erected in brick. Rogers's task was to design what used to be called a "Queen Anne front to a Mary Jane back," a chore he would continue to encounter.

The cavity of the theater's cornerstone, laid on the July 4, 1827, contained a silver plate measuring roughly seven by five inches that was engraved by the artist Abel Bowen with the names of the trustees, officers, the building committee for the company, all leading businessmen of the city, the lessee, President John Quincy Adams, Governor Levi Lincoln, Mayor Josiah Quincy, and the young architect, who must have been proud indeed to appear in such distinguished company.[23] Although Gilbert Stuart could not imagine a better solution for the design of the frontispiece, it was altered a bit in execution. Among Alexander Jackson Davis's contemporary views of Boston, one from 1828 shows the facade as first erected,[24] as does Philip Harry's later view of Tremont Street (see Fig. 8). The shape of the ground-floor windows were changed, fanlights appeared above the three entrances (an alteration that had been sketched in on the original drawing, perhaps by Rogers, and decidedly not derived from Grecian antiquity), and the niches remained empty (by about 1840, representations of the muses Melpomene and Thalia were installed in them). The pediment lacks the garland-surrounded oculus shown in the drawing. Davis's lithograph also shows that the facade was constructed of three different shades of granite: the basement was gray Quincy stone and the second-story wall was dressed ashlars of blue granite. The four Ionic pilasters, each constructed of three dressed slabs, were of white Eastern granite, making them stand out from the plane of the wall and the antae, which continued the ashlar of that wall. Dressed Quincy ashlar reappeared in the pediment, with cornices composed of Eastern granite.

The whole produced a contrast of parts unlike the overall gray of most local contemporary neoclassical buildings, but it also added to the disjointed assembly of bits and hues, including that quotation from the Italian Renaissance on the ground level, which prevented Rogers's first attempt at a templar front from achieving a unitary statement. It showed the faults of a beginner and could have been thought (almost) perfect only because there was little in town to compare it to. In fact, as a planar facade (there apparently being no room for a portico on the site) it was a step back from the achievements in granite Grecian works of Parris and Willard.

The design of a temple front hardly needed much justification at the time, but laying out a theater's interior likely required some study. By 1827 Rogers might have had access not only to existing theaters in Boston but also to such publications as Benjamin Wyatt's 1813 monograph on London's Drury Lane Theatre. Although that building looked nothing like the Tremont Theatre, Rogers would have found much useful information in the fifty-five-page treatise on the arrangement of such a special building. Whether he had access to Wyatt's work is unknown, but we have seen that his first biographer emphasized Rogers's capacity for learning, and this is not the last time the book will be mentioned in this chapter, as its format might have inspired that of Eliot's *Description of Tremont House*.

The theater's three arched openings at ground level gave access to a large hall flanked by offices, each lit by one of the lateral windows. Curved staircases ascended to a lobby behind the dress circle. A "saloon" lit by the three tall windows had retiring rooms for ladies and gentlemen at each end. Box holders could find relief in the water closets leased to a concessionaire, a convenience for which Rogers's Tremont House of the next year would be particularly remembered. The plan of the theater proper was a broad half ellipse, which brought the back row of seats toward the stage. Early on Rogers began to create innovative designs, not always with success. Three tiers of boxes had floors that raked thirty-six degrees, for uninterrupted sight lines, but the design proved so unpopular that they were almost immediately rebuilt. The auditorium, which could normally seat about fifteen hundred, was richly decorated in blue and gold. Cut-glass chandeliers holding purified wax candles hung from the second and third tiers; these lit the space until replaced by gas chandeliers in 1832. A bust of Shakespeare flanked by emblems of Comedy and Tragedy presided over the proscenium, and Apollo and his chariot appeared below.

No views of the interior have survived; indeed, it barely existed before being redesigned by Rogers. Besides reflooring the boxes, he widened the pit, enlarged the orchestra, and redecorated the proscenium with motifs found on the Choragic Monument of Lysicrates at Athens, a classical source known from Stuart and Revett's *Antiquities* and much copied during the Grecian rage in America. His need to rework the interior shows that he remained a novice theater designer even after two tries (if we include Mobile). He would come closer to perfection in later work. Rogers may have been gifted, but his gifts took time to mature. Nonetheless, his achievement here would soon garner him a more important commission for a building across the street.

The Tremont Theatre went on to have a short and checkered history. Competition from other newly constructed theaters, the popularity of Lyceum lectures (for which Rogers projected a building of unknown design for Mayor Martin Brimmer in 1843), and a wave of religious reform (theater had always been morally suspect in New England) drained it of audiences. Richard Stoddard reported that by April 1843 the Baptists had bought the building for use as a church. In fact, on December 21, 1842, Rogers noted that he was making plans to alter the fifteen-year-old building for religious services. (That entry might strike a sad note were it not known that architects like new business, even it if tramples on their own work.) He reported making "another sketch for a church on the site of the old Theatre . . . using old materials making a new front"; the next day he estimated the cost of the changes. His entries end there (the diary has a long gap after mid-March 1843), but the Baptists did go on to have the building altered, reordering the interior for religious services and commercial offices and adding shops along the building's Tremont Street face.[25] The highly opinionated Arthur D. Gilman excoriated the resulting facade of what was then called the Tremont Temple as "Vandalic spoliation."[26] He was not an admirer of Rogers's work and must have been reacting to the architect's own changes. Fire destroyed the building in 1852, as it did in 1879 to its successor, designed by William Washburn, as well as the third temple in 1893. Washburn's second replacement still stands.

In July 1827, just a few months after winning the competition, Rogers responded to an advertisement and won another competitive premium, this time $100, "for the best plan of the intended Masonic Hall" in Augusta, Georgia. As at the Tremont Theatre, the clients were looking for a showy facade. Rogers triumphed over ten other "front elevations . . . submitted to the board, several of which were elegant and appropriate, and did great credit to the draftsmen."[27] For a young architect, even one who might have already had another southern work to his credit, a building in Georgia would seem far afield, but the cotton trade linked New England to several cities in the South. In addition, Rogers had been admitted to the Columbian Lodge of Masons in Boston in 1825. As such organizations are created to do, his membership brought connections that would profit him in the coming years. This commission well beyond Boston anticipated the direction of his expanding career.

Augusta's Masonic Hall rose on Broad Street in 1828, financed thanks to money raised by lottery. On a plate deposited in the cornerstone, a pair of local builders, John Crane and William Thompson, was credited with the design, although Rogers later listed it as his work. The terms quoted above make clear that, as winner of the competition, he was required to develop only the facade, whereas Crane and Thompson apparently organized the rest of the building and supervised its construction. We know Rogers's facade from hazy vintage photographs;[28] a better view is a wood engraving after a drawing by Walter Goater that appeared in *Frank Leslie's Illustrated Weekly Newspaper* on August 14, 1880, at the time the building was demolished. (Fig. 2) The front was a taller (by one story) and more

2. Masonic temple, Augusta, Georgia, 1827. Broad Street facade. Wood engraving after a sketch by Walter Goater published in *Frank Leslie's Illustrated Weekly Newspaper,* August 14, 1880. Courtesy Augusta Museum of History.

extensively glazed reflection of the parti at the Tremont Theatre and, on the whole, seemingly more cohesive than its Boston forebear. An ashlar ground level, perhaps intended for shops (anticipating what would happen when the Tremont Theatre was redesigned as a church) "supported" a two-story tetrastyle temple front of superimposed engaged fluted columns that were squat Doric at the second level and taller Ionic above. These stood between closed end bays embracing niches topped by half-round arches. Large trabeated multipaned windows filled the intercolumniations. A tall pediment that loomed over its adjacent commercial neighbors capped the templar facade.

The next two years found Rogers creating temple-form churches in Boston for the Trinitarians and the Methodists, which suggests (and his later diary confirms) that, unlike his narrow-minded contemporary Richard Upjohn, he was happy to create spaces for congregations other than his own Universalists. On June 20, 1827, the Trinitarians laid the cornerstone of their Pine Street church. It was intended to be one of two buildings planned for the denomination, with the other destined for the southern part of the city.[29] The cornerstone listed Rogers as architect, along with the members of the building committee composed of the merchants William Ropes, Charles Tappan, Hiram Bosworth, Hardy Ropes, and Isaiah Waterman.[30] The Reverend Lyman Beecher, patriarch of the celebrated Beecher family who had championed the congregation as a foil to the surging Unitarians within Congregationalism, addressed the crowd on the occasion.

The buildings went up quickly—dedication of the church took place just six months after the laying of the cornerstone. The structure is known from a couple nineteenth-century views that, alas, are not in complete agreement. Abel Bowen's 1838 *Picture of Boston* tells us that its hexastyle Doric portico above a series of steps was "taken from the Temple of Theseus at Athens," which, as we know from Horatio Greenough, was a popular source of inspiration available in Stuart and Revett's *Antiquities*. The low pediment, at least in Bowen's view (the earliest we have), supports a peristyle tholos, or round columnar tower, and a thin spire, but his rendering of the portico columns gives them more Roman than Grecian proportions. (Fig. 3) The picture in the *Boston Almanac* of 1843 probably better captures the proportions of the portico but lacks the tholos, perhaps by then removed or a reflection that it had never been built and that Bowen's view was based on Rogers's drawings or a model. The design of the four windows of the side walls abandoned Grecian precedent altogether and harkened back to eighteenth-century half-round arches. The interior was said by Bowen to be finished "in a plain neat style." Like the Tremont Theatre, the building suffered changes early on. The interior was remodeled in 1843, and by 1860 the portico had given way to an Italianate facade. Even in that eclectic condition, however, the Pine Street church no longer stands.

The Methodists plotted their own church contemporary with that of the Trinitarians' on Pine Street. In 1796 they had erected their first Boston building, a wooden structure of four walls and a gable roof, on what became Methodist Alley. A committee report dated April 3, 1827, preserves a proposal for financing the erection of two new churches, one at the north and one at the south of the city (as with the Pine Street congregation), both with "rooms underneath to let."[31] Although the southern church seems never to have materialized, at least from Rogers's drafting board, he did design for a site in North Bennet Street a "handsome brick edifice combining simplicity and neatness with the requisite grandeur and ornament," according to Abel Bowen. The author has little to say about the architecture because, despite that "grandeur and ornament," there was little to say. An illustration in *Sketches of Boston, Past and Present* (1851), published a year after the building had been sold to the Free Will Baptists, shows it as a masonry near copy of the wooden Methodist Alley building: a plain neoclassical design with astylar front (without columnar articulation) and a gable outlined as a pediment by horizontal and raking cornices. In the center of the front, above high steps, the architect grouped three trabeated doors topped with short cornices on consoles. With the exception of a half-circular window in the pediment, the consoles were the only ornament. Even lacking Pine Street's columnar portico, the Methodist

3. Pine Street Church, Boston, Massachusetts, 1827. From Abel Bowen, *Bowen's Picture of Boston* (Boston: Otis, Broaders & Co., 1838). Courtesy Historic New England.

church evoked a templar image to Timothy Ashley, whose poem, read at the dedication in September 1828, hoped God would "on this temple smile" and "streams of universal love/Their courses to this temple make."

As at the Tremont Theatre, a silver plaque placed in the cornerstone of the new church named Rogers as the architect. The laying of that stone occurred in April and the dedication less than six months later, the simplicity of treatment expediting another speedy job despite an unhappy interruption. The most memorable event associated with the building happened at the earlier date. Bowen gives a full account of the hair-raising and bone-breaking "awful occurrence" at the cornerstone ceremony. Construction having by then reached the underflooring of the sanctuary, and the speaker having reached the point in his sermon to the crowd gathered on that flooring where he alludes to a time when "the material walls of the edifice should have crumbled into dust," the floor gave way and nearly two hundred people were thrown to the leasable depths eleven feet below. "It was like one of the terrible scenes of war or earthquake," wrote Bowen. A "confused, horrible and bloody dream" ensued, as shattered timbers crushed flesh and bone "like tender herbs of the field." Despite Ashley's subsequent prayer, God forgot to smile on the half-finished temple that day. Although no immediate fatalities occurred, three congregants eventually died of injuries. There is no available record of the architect's whereabouts at the time, or of his reactions to the calamity, but apparently neither he nor the builder caught any blame.

By 1828 Rogers had to his credit a small number of public buildings, of which at least three—the theater and the two churches—were visible accomplishments to potential Boston clients. He also had at home the evidence of other creative efforts. January saw the birth of his third child and first son, named Solomon Willard Rogers, who was to join his father's office in the 1840s and become his partner in the 1850s. Not being easily satisfied, Rogers went on to produce more children with Emily, eventually eight in all. The year would also bring the commission that remains his most lasting monument long after its destruction: the famed Tremont House hotel.

In his early practice, the young man from Marshfield had rubbed elbows with major figures in Boston and proven himself capable of accomplished design within the confines of the templar form. With the Tremont House—by consensus the country's first world-class luxury hotel and the model for and namesake of others in cities east of the Mississippi and beyond—he would break out of that formal mold to create an original variation on the Grecian theme, proving himself an innovator at planning and building large, technically advanced complexes and gaining a national reputation in the process. As Molly Berger wrote, "The Tremont tied concepts of civic importance to architectural design, function, and technological innovation, and its legacy influenced an entire century of hotel construction."[32] Rogers's clients, the proprietorship of the hostelry, represented a group of interrelated leading merchant families led by William H. and Samuel A. Eliot, Thomas Handasyd and James Perkins, and Andrew Eliot Belknap. In the next decade, Samuel A. Eliot would become mayor of Boston and then treasurer of Harvard College; in both offices he would request projects from Rogers. Thomas Handasyd Perkins was the city's "Merchant Prince" and a leader in its lucrative China Trade; he and Andrew Eliot Belknap would commission more works from Rogers. William H. Eliot, a Whig lawyer and one of the largest stockholders, would publish anonymously in 1830, the year before he died, a landmark architectural description of the building. In 1840 Rogers recalled him as the "best friend I ever had, the memory of which I shall ever cherish. . . . He by his aid in my circumstances was the main spring to all my after success. He gave me not silver and gold, but . . . good precept and confidence to pursue my course, and . . . a good name and reputation." He was, in short, the successor to Edward Little and Solomon Willard in recognizing real talent in the young architect and furthering his career.

Even with such august backers, there existed no assurance of success when the project began. The Tremont's predecessor, Asher Benjamin's huge Exchange Coffee House, had failed at enormous monetary loss to its proprietors even before it was reduced to rubble in a fire in November 1818.[33] The need for its replacement was keenly felt in the city by 1822 as interurban, national, and even international commerce began to grow, with new means of transportation creating a demand for comfortable and secure temporary accommodations. Two years later the state legislature incorporated a company for the purpose of "constructing a building or buildings to be used as a Public Hotel," but three more years went by before funds accumulated and a project materialized.[34] The site of the new building was away from the commercial center and diagonally across from Rogers's theater on what was by then called Tremont Street. It lay between the Old Burying Ground and the corner of Beacon Street. As often happened in the center of Boston, the lot was irregular. When a model of the building, then briefly called the City Hotel, was exhibited in the "saloon" of the theater across the street, the *Boston Weekly Messenger* had to apologize for first naming Solomon Willard as the designer and then correctly credited Rogers, "a young architect, whose talents bid fair to recommend him to more notice and patronage."[35] And young he was—still twenty-seven in June 1828—for such a risky, complex, and important undertaking. The leap from carving wooden capitals at Christ Church in 1826 to designing and supervising the erection of an unprecedented 170-room luxury hotel with monumental granite portico in 1828–29 emphasizes Rogers's extraordinarily rapid early advancement.

No evidence indicates that Rogers had to endure a competition for the hotel commission. His only real local rival for the job would have been Alexander Parris, who was then at work on the Unitarian Church ("Stone Temple") in Quincy and the ongoing Quincy Market in Boston; but of course Parris was associated with the failed Exchange Coffee House. Bulfinch was in Washington, and Willard was preoccupied with the Bunker Hill Monument. The mention of Willard's name in the *Messenger* in connection to the building may suggest that he was approached first, that it was assumed he would get the job as a man of much experience, and that he turned the project over to Rogers, his former and future associate, knowing him capable of the challenge. Whether that scenario is true, once again someone—that is, William Eliot—recognized qualities that set Rogers apart. The proprietors broke ground in June 1828 and laid the cornerstone on the Fourth of July, a favorite day for such undertakings at the time. In that stone was deposited, as usual, a silver plate naming the governor, the mayor, the proprietors, and Isaiah Rogers as architect. The building opened just fifteen months later with a lavish banquet, in October 1829.

We know that Rogers, following Willard's example, used models extensively throughout his career, both of whole buildings and for details of structural and decorative parts. The diary is full of references to them, but none is known to survive. As noted, a model of the hotel could be seen locally, and George Harvey's watercolor perspective of about 1830 may have been based on it.[36] No original architectural graphics for the building survive, but drawings of it appeared in *A Description of Tremont House, with Architectural Illustrations,* a slim, eleven-by-fourteen-inch folio published in 1830. Within the thirty-five pages of text are thirty-one plates of drawings lithographed by the Pendleton brothers. The plates attest to Rogers's study with both Jesse Shaw and Solomon Willard. For the decorative capitals, he relied on the draftsmanship of their maker, the carver Levi L. Cushing.

A Description of Tremont House was a unique American publication. It followed English precedent, of course, but it was most strikingly different from the domestic works on architecture, such as those of Asher Benjamin, Owen Biddle, Minard Lafever, and Edward Shaw, that also appeared in the early nineteenth century. Beginning with a frontispiece of a perspective view by James Kidder, engraved by Annin & Smith and probably based on Rogers's model, the book contained plans, elevations, and sections, as well as construction details of stonework and joinery and a detailed guide through the building in an unsigned text by William Eliot. The book not only spread Rogers's reputation far and wide, leading to many later commissions for urban hotels, it was also unprecedented in the evolution of the practice of architecture in America. Several eighteenth-century English publications reproduced design drawings of specific buildings, at least one of which, Charles Middleton's *Plans, Elevations, and Sections of the House of Correction for the County of Middlesex* (1788), is listed in the 1809 catalogue of the Architectural Library of Boston. But a more likely inspiration for Eliot's work is Benjamin Wyatt's 1813 *Observations on the Design for the Theatre Royal, Drury*

Lane . . . Accompanied by Plans, Elevations, & Sections, of the Same, mentioned earlier in connection with the Tremont Theatre. With its frontispiece perspective view of the theater, its lengthy text, and eighteen engraved plates with descriptions, Wyatt's was surely the kind of monograph Eliot must have known.[37] The *Description* differs in one important aspect from such English models, however. They were produced by the architect, whereas the *Description* is the work of the (unnamed) client, and that suggests the different status of the architect in England and America in the 1820s.

Nothing exactly like Eliot's publication existed in the United States. *A Description of Haviland's Design for the New Penitentiary,* a twelve-page pamphlet that included a bird's-eye view of Eastern State Penitentiary in Philadelphia, appeared in 1824 but was written by the architect, the English-born John Haviland, to accompany his proposal for the prison. It was part of the process of "selling" the design and preceded construction. In Eliot's independent, post-facto description of the finished hotel, the principal workers are listed but it is the demonstrated skill of the architect that is celebrated by his client. The general effect of the building's exterior, wrote Eliot, "is imposing from its magnitude and its just proportions; and the selection and execution of the decorated parts of the façade exhibit the classical taste of the Architect, and his judicious adherence to the established principles of Grecian Architecture." In this early period in the development of architectural practice, when the nature and value of the architect's services were little understood or appreciated, Eliot's *Description* emphasized the role of the designer in the achievement of the building. Rogers's name does not appear on the title page, nor does Eliot's. It does appear, however, in the quotation of the cornerstone text. Eliot's commemorative publication is as much a landmark in the architectural history of this country as it was a monument to the designing architect, his extraordinary creation, and the society it was erected to serve. In Molly Berger's words, "Eliot's focus on the building's architectural detail firmly linked the hotel [designed by a Whig architect] to a Whig vision of the nation's future."[38]

The hotel's 205-foot-wide Tremont Street facade rose three stories above a ground floor. (Fig. 4) At the corners were colossal antae "resting" on a belt course at the top of the ground floor; these enclosed the regular march of eleven trabeated windows at every level, each containing double-hung, six-over-six pane sash, those of the principal story covered with architraves and those above cut cleanly through the ashlar. The antae "supported" a Doric entablature decorated with a fillet and guttae. This was *ex libris* historicism: Eliot footnoted many references to specific examples from Stuart and Revett's *Antiquities of Athens,* a luxury publication that more likely would have been in his or another proprietor's library and made accessible to Rogers, rather than being in possession of the young architect. As the *Description* says, the principal parts of the ornamental work "either as precise copies or general imitations, were derived from books not easy to be obtained, and have not before been executed in this country," the latter part of the statement a more than slight exaggeration.

Dressed Quincy granite formed the exterior walls of the front, the ashlars hammered by convicts at the local prison (such a practice would be frowned on now but was common in Rogers's lifetime). The receding wings, with lockable private rooms off a double-loaded corridor, were built of brick. Their exteriors could have been designed by any housewright in the city, hence Eliot's focus on the dramatic Tremont Street facade. The fluted granite columns of the Doric portico, itself adjusted for the site from a plate in Stuart and Revett, were monoliths six diameters (twenty-six feet) in height that weighed fourteen tons each. It required seventeen yoke of oxen and a pair of horses to bring just one of the gigantic columns to the building site from the schooner that had floated it from the dock at the quarry in Quincy.[39] And yet this was child's play compared to what would follow at later buildings from Rogers's drawing board and Willard's stone yard. The "belvedere,"

4. Tremont House, Boston, 1828–29. The rooftop tholos was never erected. Engraving by Annin & Smith of James Kidder's view of the Tremont Street facade, as published in [William H. Eliot], *A Description of Tremont House, with Architectural Illustrations* (Boston, 1830). Courtesy Historic New England.

or peripteral tholos, that appears on the roof of the hotel in both James Kidder's view published in the *Description* and George Harvey's view, both surely based on the model, probably never materialized.[40] It was a variation without pedestal of the one Abel Bowen showed atop Rogers's Pine Street church.

The center of the hotel's Tremont Street facade was marked by an entrance portico. From there one passed through sixteen-foot-high paneled oak doors that swung on bronze hinges to reach a series of convex steps that climbed to a rotunda beneath a domed stained-glass skylight. This covered the first hotel lobby and reception area (in earlier inns, the visitor checked in at the bar). (Figs. 5–6) This was the public area. The office accessed a residential wing on the left, a courtyard (which Rogers called a "piazza") ahead, and a grand dining room on the right. The courtyard floor was at street level; a gallery surrounded it at the main-floor level. To the left and right of the entrance hall stretched a corridor leading past gas-lit public rooms, which overlooked the street below; it led to a curving staircase at each end. Because Beacon Street met Tremont at a seventy-degree angle, and the left lot line was parallel to Beacon, a deviation in the plan's axis was effectively masked on the exterior by segmental convex walls at either end of the facade, although it must have been noticeable on the interior because of the tilted axis of the hallway from lobby to courtyard. (The lobby of the building now occupying the site and currently housing part of Suffolk University clearly shows this deviation in the canted row of elevator doors seen from just inside the Tremont Street entrance.) Rogers would eventually gain something of a reputation for cleverly masking such irregularities. In 1839 he used the same device of rounded bays to hide the irregularity of the plan for the Exchange Hotel in Richmond.

The Boston hotel encompassed 170 rooms, including private apartments for families, all heated by fireplaces and supplied with running water. Eight bathing facilities were located in the basement. The dining room, seventy-three feet long and fifteen feet high, had two rows of freestanding Ionic columns based on those of the Propylaea of Eleusis in Stuart and Revett; it received heat from two fireplaces and hot air sent from the kitchen below. (Fig. 7) The room's design showed that Rogers still had much to learn about hotels. A visitor in the early 1830s criticized it as defective in taste and proportion, with its ceiling too low, a fact borne out by the section in Eliot's *Description*.[41] The columns reduced the useable space, and a view in *Gleason's Pictorial* for February 1852 shows that they had been removed, perhaps when Rogers did more work in the building in the 1840s.

The services we take for granted today were in their infancy at the Tremont, but they were ingenious. The kitchen rested above a deep well projected to supply an "inexhaustible" flow of water. At the time, the city had no common source of pure water, and would not until 1848.[42] The rooms and the row of eight privies at the rear of the courtyard received water pumped up to reservoirs and cisterns located in the south wing and on the roof. These could also supply water in an

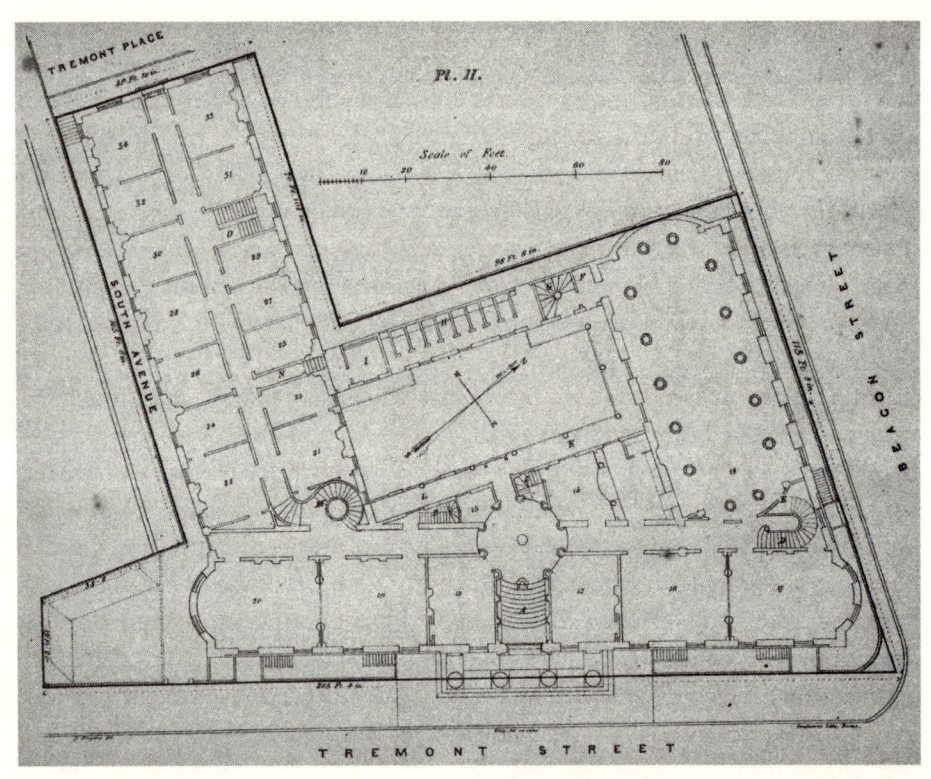

5. Tremont House, Boston, Massachusetts, 1828–29. First-floor plan. From [William H. Eliot], *A Description of Tremont House* (Boston, 1830). Courtesy Historic New England.

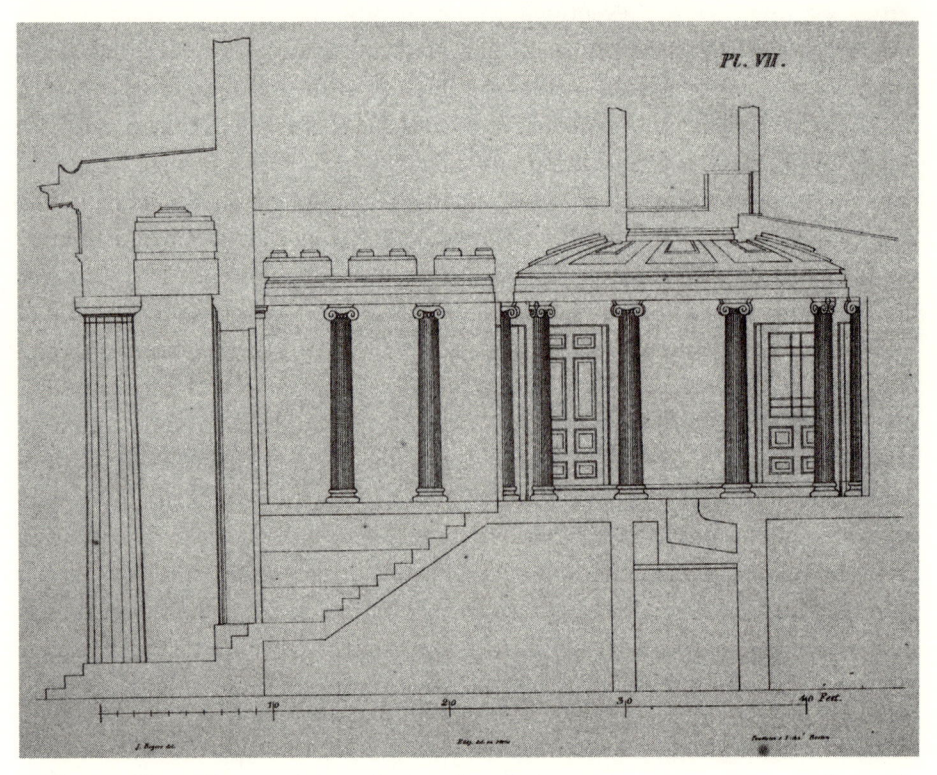

6. Tremont House, Boston, 1828–29. Section through the portico, entrance steps, and rotunda. Drawn on stone by Isaac Eddy and printed by Pendelton. [William H. Eliot], *A Description of Tremont House* (Boston, 1830), plate 7. Courtesy Historic New England.

emergency. Remembering the fate of the Exchange Coffee House just ten years earlier, the architect adopted many details of the design and fabrication thought to ensure protection from the spread of fire, such as installing plaster fire stops in floors and walls. Building against fire was a concern of architects in this period, especially Robert Mills and Rogers, who over the years gave great attention to the problem. At the Tremont, wastewater descended to cesspools in the cellar, then to the common sewer, and finally, no doubt, into the harbor. Eight privies for nearly two hundred rooms sounds extremely inadequate, but along with those in the theater across the street, they must have been among the earliest of such conveniences in the United States. The hostelry also provided a newly invented "annunciator," a system of bells for communicating between individual rooms and the office, installed by Seth Fuller and detailed in Eliot's book. Whether Rogers conceived of all or any of these innovations, he needed to organize his hotel to accommodate them.

"First class" hostelries had already been erected in America at this time, but the Tremont was the first so-called luxury establishment, featuring design, technology, and service amenities unknown in those earlier buildings.[43] In 1811 New York's City Hotel (also called the City Tavern) had established the precedent for large urban hotels, with its 137 rooms distributed over five floors of two adjoining houses. In Boston, Asher Benjamin's Exchange Coffee House rose seven stories around a dome-covered galleried court intended to serve as a merchants' exchange. There were shops, a ballroom, and a Masonic lodge, too, but the whole production was as gauche architecturally as it was unstable financially. The National Hotel in Washington, D.C., encompassed six converted row houses. David Barnum's Baltimore City Hotel of 1825–27, designed by William F. Small, came closest to the Tremont. It was a four-story-plus basement brick building enclosing 172 rooms, including a dining room for five hundred, bathing rooms, a barbershop, and a post office. Rogers would stay there on his later trips up and down the coast. The Boston papers were not impressed with it, as compared to the Tremont.

In its own time, the Tremont set a new standard in luxury hotel design and services. This feat was repeated, with or without variations, across the eastern half of the United States in the coming years, often by Rogers. In Maine, for example, he flipped the Tremont plan for reuse at Bangor House of 1833–34, a building that reflected its provincial location by its brick walls and wooden portico painted to imitate stone. That hostelry contained 115 rooms, including suites "consisting of a sitting room elegantly furnished, with one and sometimes two sleeping rooms attached." Public areas had Brussels carpets underfoot, marble mantels, mahogany chairs, sofas, tables, and hanging lamps, all warmed by Pierpont grates and Nott stoves.[44] Rogers's later hotels would not imitate the look of his Tremont so closely. Gallier and Dakin's St. Charles Hotel in New Orleans of 1835–37 modified the Tremont plan, used Rogers's device of a curved side bay to mask an awkward street corner, and added a gilded dome (after a fire in 1851, Rogers con-

7. Tremont House, Boston, Massachusetts, 1828–29. Plan and section of dining room. Drawn on stone by Isaac Eddy and printed by Pendelton. [William H. Eliot], *A Description of Tremont House* (Boston, 1830), plate 14. Courtesy Historic New England.

tributed significantly to the building's resurrection). The Tremont plan reappeared in Boston at the United States Hotel of 1842. And where the architecture was not strictly followed, the hotel's name was; Chicago and Philadelphia, to name just two, had their own "Tremont" hotels (Rogers would stop at the Chicago one in 1854). The influence of Rogers's planning (although not his facade) in time reached as far as John Gile's 1864–66 Langham Hotel in London.

The Tremont House was erected by the local elite for the traveling elite. Over the years it hosted a long list of important visitors, from Davy Crockett to Charles Dickens in 1842. (The Englishman probably did not know it, but Rogers attended a lecture by him on January 24.) Thackeray, the Irish actor Tyrone Power, Fanny Kemble the actress, Alexis de Tocqueville, and Abraham Lincoln all enjoyed its comforts, as did many other then-notables who have since slipped out of memory. The famed Saturday Club, which included Ralph Waldo Emerson, Henry Wadsworth Longfellow, and Oliver Wendell Holmes, met there until William Washburn's Parker House opened in the 1850s. The architectural critic

Montgomery Schuyler stayed several times. Rogers often housed himself in his hotel, or dined there with friends, or bathed there when he visited from New York or farther afield. Boston's famed historian Samuel Eliot Morison, who lived on Beacon Hill as a boy, recalled that when they were young, his grandmother and her siblings took weekly baths there.

With the completion of Rogers's hotel opposite his theater, and his later addition of fence, corner posts, and gateway to the Old Granary Burying Ground, the block of Tremont Street between Beacon and Park Streets could have been called Rogers's Row until the destruction of the theater in 1852 and the demolition of the hotel forty-three years later. Philip Harry captured that streetscape in his view of about 1842, looking north from near the cemetery gate. (Fig. 8) This is one of

8. Philip Harry, *Tremont Street, Boston*, ca. 1842. Oil on panel. At left are the corner pier of Rogers's Old Granary Burying Ground fence and his Tremont House; Peter Harrison's King's Chapel and Rogers's Tremont Theatre are at right. Museum of Fine Arts, Boston; Gift of Maxim Karolik for the M. and M. Karolik Collection of American Paintings, 1815–1865.

the purest urban vignettes we have—another is the restored Faneuil Hall Market Place, happily still with us, if somewhat altered—of the granite Grecian transformation of Boston in its early years as a city. In that transformation, Rogers had, in a few short years, become a leader.

The architect's early string of winning competition entries came to a halt in the late 1820s and early 1830s, although he would enter his share of later contests. In June 1829, with the end of the Tremont House construction in sight, Rogers entered the competition for City Hall in Albany, New York.[45] Other entrants included the firm of Ithiel Town and Alexander Jackson Davis of New York; Minard Lafever, also of New York; Edward Shaw, Peter Banner, and John Kutts, all of Boston; and Philip Hooker of Albany. Although Rogers made the "first cut," he might have been relieved that he did not move on—the building committee voted for a pastiche of Hooker's elevation topped by Kutts's cupola, and it split the $100 premium between the two. In fact, this occurrence was common, as was the lack of payment for all entries, until the American Institute of Architects began trying to assert some control over such matters later in the century. After much discussion in the press, the building became largely Hooker's (locals always had an advantage in competitions). Although Rogers requested the return of his drawings the next year, they have never been found.

He fared better but still did not win the competition for the design of Girard College in Philadelphia, a complex that eventually cost nearly $2 million.[46] On his death in 1831, the banker and philanthropist Stephen Girard left a fortune to found a school for orphan boys, tightly defining its architectural manifestation, at least in terms of utility and materials. In February 1833 the results of a competition that had been announced in June of 1832 found Thomas U. Walter of Philadelphia the winner, William Strickland of Philadelphia second, and Rogers third. As with the Albany contest and many others, local architects seem to have had an inside track. For his efforts, Rogers presumably gained the $150 third-place premium, with Walter claiming the $500 first prize. The still-recognizable names among the many who did not place or show are Edward Shaw and John Kutts of Boston, John Haviland of Philadelphia, and Town, Davis & Dakin of New York. The competition drawings still exist, as do Walter's buildings.

For his entry, Rogers used a rectangular grid to organize a series of dormitories and dining halls around the central block of classrooms. (Fig. 9) Where Walter's classroom building is a hugely expensive Corinthian peripteral temple, hardly in keeping with Girard's frugal wishes (well-presented entries often win competitions even when they ignore budget and program), Rogers eschewed columns on the main building but added porticos to the outbuildings. In contrast to the delicacy of Walter's colonnade, Rogers chose the masculine Doric order as appropriate for the school, one more easily worked in the granite he would have undoubtedly specified. In a recent critical discussion of the entries, Michael J. Lewis wrote

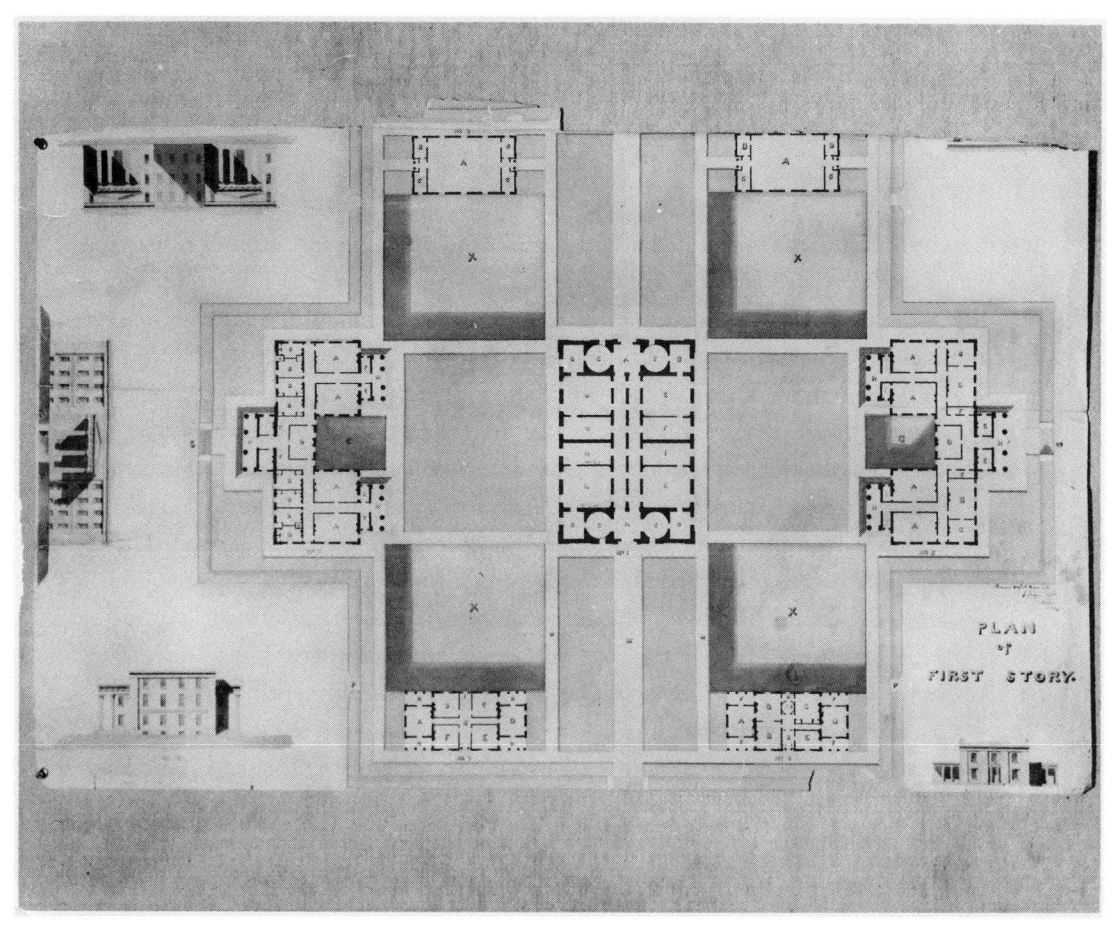

9. Competitive design for Girard College, Philadelphia, Pennsylvania, 1832. First-floor plan. Ink, wash, and watercolor, 27 x 43 in. (69 x 109 cm). Historical Society of Pennsylvania, Stephen Girard Collection.

that Rogers's project "was as fiercely original as anything he ever did" and that his buildings in general "were stamped by a highly individual sense of character." Rogers later visited the college with Walter and, unusual for him, liked what he saw in the work of a competitor. Much later, Walter would endorse Rogers's employment at the Ohio statehouse.

During these early years, Rogers developed into the full-service architect he would be until his death. Town houses, a theater, churches, a large urban hotel, and a town hall[47] all came from his drafting board and were realized in the late 1820s, but this activity did not mean he eschewed smaller, out-of-town commissions. Nor were templar fronts left entirely behind. Standing as witness is the wooden tetrastyle portico he drew apparently in 1830 or 1831 for a modest late Federal-style house in Lancaster, Massachusetts. For inspiration, he again cast his line into a copy of Stuart and Revett to fish out the order of the Nike temple on the Acropolis at Athens. The client was Joseph Andrews, a copper and wood engraver and publisher. In late April 1835 the *Columbian Centinel* carried a notice of sale for the house "recently in the possession of Mr. Joseph Andrews" and went on to say that the "front in the Grecian Ionic style of architecture [is] from a plan drawn by Rogers." The beautifully executed fluted wooden order, another of Rogers's fronts, supports a rather tall pediment, once the site of a semicircular window. Not to be overlooked is the wooden parlor fireplace frame copied from the one in Plate 28 of Eliot's *Description of Tremont House*. In the sweep of Rogers's life and work this home is minor but worth noticing nonetheless, for so much of the architect's achievement has been leveled by time, fire, or man.

Rogers's success at the Tremont House at the age of twenty-nine made him the go-to architect over the next four decades for large urban hotels east of the Mississippi (James Dakin was his distant rival). Meanwhile, local commissions for other building types continued to appear as well. After some five years of discussion, in 1830 the Masonic Grand Lodge of Massachusetts appointed a building committee that consisted of Grand Master Joseph Jenkins, the architect of the Hanover Street Church of 1825 but largely forgotten today, as well as Elijah Morse, Asa Eaton, Charles Wells, and Benjamin Smith.[48] Lodge records credit Jenkins with the selection of the lot adjacent to St. Paul's Cathedral, on the corner of Tremont Street and Temple Place. Some confusion exists about the designer of the building, but these same records make clear that, although Jenkins superintended the work, he was not the designer, for he "procured plans & models" for the building at the cost of $191.19. That Jenkins picked Rogers over himself attests to the latter's growing reputation. We might think that Rogers, a Mason, would have preferred to supervise construction too, earning more money and more control, but Jenkins's presence might have worked against that idea in the minds of the clients. With much ceremony, Jenkins laid the cornerstone on October 14 after a grand procession that left Faneuil Hall, marched through Merchants' Row and State and Court Streets, and ended at the building site, all despite the fact that Masonry at this point "was bending beneath the violent and unmerited attacks of public opinion." The order of procession included the principal architect carrying the emblems of the medieval builder—square, level, and plumb—and that architect's name is given as "Mr. Rogers." The Masons dedicated their new hall on May 30, 1832 (or 5832, by their reckoning).

The animated lithographic view of the crossing of Tremont Street and Temple Place drawn by B. F. Nutting and published by Annin & Smith in 1832 shows the original exterior of the new Masonic Hall.[49] It reveals an approach dramatically different from the one Rogers had taken just three years earlier at the Masonic Temple in Georgia. (Fig. 10) The building rose next to St. Paul's as a rectangular block of rubble granite contrasted with a dressed stone base and trim; the whole was topped by a gable roof that showed between the towers as a series of raking crenellations. The walls were opened by a variety of pronounced shapes scattered across their surfaces: quatrefoil, trefoil, rectangular, tall with pointed arches, all

10. Masonic Temple, Boston, Massachusetts, 1830. Drawn by B. F. Nutting and lithographed by Annin & Smith, 1832. American Antiquarian Society.

thickly outlined in dressed stone. Only the three-story lancet above the entrance on Tremont Street enclosed bar tracery. The four-story stair towers were tightly confined by continuous, pronounced, dressed-stone corners terminating against the sky in squat pinnacles. Gothic linear lightness gave way here to massive solidity. The Masons' hall and a drawing room occupied the top, or attic, floor set beneath six skylights; the floors below housed smaller halls and schoolrooms, where Bronson Alcott held his famous (or infamous) experimental school for children from 1834 to 1838, and a chapel could be found in the basement. The Masons, needing more space, sold the building to the federal government in 1858 for use as a courthouse. In 1880 it was jacked up, two stories were inserted at ground level, and its profile and fenestration were changed for the use of the R. H. Stearns department store. In 1908 the company replaced that building.

Past hesitancy to affirm Rogers's hand in the design of Masonic Hall probably stemmed from the awkwardness of the result. Henry R. Cleveland wrote of the "small spires that stick up like asses' ears at the front corners." He went on to condemn the building as "barbarous enough" but concluded that "criticism is wasted on such a building; the whole is bad."[50] The architect would endure harsh censure from other critics during his career, but he rarely remarks about them in his diary.

Although Rogers had mastered the possibilities of Grecian composition, here he or his clients chose what we, with great generosity, might call Gothic. Even the *Boston Globe* in 1902, long after the building's alteration, could still complain about the unfortunate exterior in which "no true or pure order of architecture has been preserved." In the 1830s the Gothic Revival was still in its "Gothick" phase, in which medieval forms were used decoratively and without an understanding of the totality of the Gothic system. Few books on the style existed, and none from American sources, and local buildings were equally rare. Bulfinch had shown an interest in Gothic as early as the 1790s, and for his Federal Street church of 1809 he tacked Gothick details onto an otherwise Federal-style meeting house. In 1832–34 Rogers (perhaps in partnership with Richard Bond, although an official report dated 1851 mentions only him) added to this body of work with his Unitarian First Parish Meeting House in Cambridge.[51] The clients were both the parish and Harvard College in the person of its president, Josiah Quincy III. In September 1836 Eliza Susan Quincy painted a fine view of the original exterior front and spire, appropriately juxtaposed with Harvard College. After rejecting a design by Asher Benjamin, the committee accepted Rogers's third plan, with slight changes. Because of the cost of the rough stone first proposed, and with brick also being rejected, the meetinghouse was built of wood. The original contract called for erecting Rogers's design without a steeple and with clapboard siding for not less than $11,000. Partly funded from Josiah Quincy's own pocket, the steeple was erected and the exterior sheathed rather than clapboarded. Quincy later contributed to the vane at the top of the steeple, over Rogers's objections. Dedication took place in December 1833.

Rogers Gothicized what is basically an eighteenth-century meetinghouse—the exterior walls covered with sanded paint and with the tower-belfry-spire set on the axis of a gabled "preaching box"—by adding cut-out pointed arches, staggered buttresses, and tall pinnacles. (Fig. 11) Pointed arches were found in the interior also, but the room was covered by the hint of a dome on pendentives, much as Bulfinch had used in his New South Church of 1814. That interior succumbed to the English colonial revival craze of the early twentieth century, and much of the exterior medieval trim vanished in later hurricanes. Other architects in the 1830s attempted to produce more typical Gothic churches, but not until Richard Upjohn gave the area a learned example of the style at St. Paul's in Brooklyn (1848–52) did ecclesiastical Gothic achieve local respectability. Rogers would use details of the style sparingly in future work.[52]

The architect may have felt on safer ground when he next designed a non-denominational "Summer Church" in Nahant, Massachusetts.[53] In July 1831 a subscription for funds to build the structure, led by William H. Eliot, Rogers's former chief client at the Tremont House, drew early members of the Brahmin elite: Thomas Handasyd Perkins (also a member of the Tremont committee), William Prescott, William Appleton, Samuel Atkins Eliot (another Tremont client), David Sears (a would-be client), Peter Chardon Brooks, Elbridge Gerry, Theodore Lyman (for whom Rogers would project an unbuilt house in Brookline), Robert Gould Shaw (later associated with the Boston Merchants' Exchange), the Lawrences (for whom he would work), an Amory, and a Lowell. These names controlled the financial and social tone of the city and formed a list of Rogers's powerful patrons. He provided them with an austere tetrastyle Tuscan temple whose order was Roman rather than Greek. A half-circular window in the pediment rested on the architrave, and the cornices were pronounced. Services began in the summer of 1832; according to his diary, Rogers enlarged the building in 1845–46. Damaged by storm in the next decade, it was replaced in 1868 by the existing Nahant Village Church, designed by Ware and Van Brunt of Boston.

The commission for Boston's Commercial Wharf building came to Rogers in 1832.[54] On July 18 the building committee studied his drawings, which showed the southerly front and two end elevations and a basement, and voted unanimously "that the said plan of elevation be . . . approved." Once again it seems that Rogers's contribution was in the design of the exterior. The contract for stone was signed two weeks later, and a year after that the building was in use. According to John Bryan, Rogers rough-hammered exterior stonework was important both economically, because it was cheaper than the smoothly hammered surfaces of recent buildings, and visually, for the play of light and shade over walls that were otherwise left plain. Also noteworthy was the use of monolithic granite-slab construction at street level. With this building began the intensive mid-nineteenth-century development of the Boston waterfront. The nearby Custom House Block of 1837 has also been attributed to Rogers.[55] Both buildings survive as altered.

11. First Parish Church, Cambridge, Massachusetts, 1832–34. Courtesy Historic New England.

In February of the same year, the Worcester architect Elias Carter agreed in writing to erect a group of four houses in that city's Lincoln Square for Stephen Salisbury II, using drawings provided by Rogers.[56] The facade of each was three bays wide and three and a half stories tall. Entrances were deeply recessed; windows with six-over-six light sash were flanked by louvered shutters; brick denticulated cornices formed the only decorative touches. Fronts were guarded by cast-iron fences upheld by granite posts. In short, they were much like the numerous domestic "bricks" Rogers had designed for Boston in the preceding years, but he was soon to be presented with more of a challenge.

In 1833 Captain Robert Bennet Forbes, a China Trade merchant like his uncle Thomas Handasyd Perkins, decided to build a country house in Milton, Massachusetts.[57] Given the architect's stellar social connections, there was no question he would design it. The house began to rise on the crest of Milton Hill in June of that year, and Forbes moved in during May of the next. For planning the house, which cost just over $21,000 to build, Forbes paid Rogers $52.50 and called that low fee "unnecessary" in his tabulation of expenses. Timber for the house was cut and fashioned in Maine, a feat impossible without those "unnecessary" drawings, and then brought up the Milton River in a schooner and carted up the hill by oxen.

The original appearance of the front is known from a daguerreotype, a new way of recordation that Rogers was early to embrace for his own portraits and views of his some of his buildings, although this one must have been taken several years after the completion of the house. (Fig. 12) Before its later alteration, the house rose two and a half stories above a granite basement. The fifty-four-foot front is divided by four extraordinarily broad pilaster strips of horizontal flush boards that "support" an entablature bedecked with portholes surrounded by wreaths, as depicted on the Monument of Thrasyllus in Stuart and Revett. On the four-bay exterior flanks of the house, the pilaster strips are narrower and interrupted by the roofs of piazzas that extended right and left from the main block. The slight hipped copper roof was concealed by a low parapet, beyond which rose a large, low octagonal cupola lighting the central staircase. The Ionic distyle-in-antis entrance, its location marked at the skyline by a broad flat pediment, gives access to a central hall dividing four square corner rooms and leading to a circular stair. From the entrance, the tight spiral of the staircase and its handrail form an eye-catching twirl. (Fig. 13) It is the kind of entrance vista that Rogers would use often in large domestic plans. The house exists as altered by Peabody and Stearns of Boston in 1872–73 and is now open restrictively as the Forbes House Museum, dedicated to the history of the China Trade. What appears to be a barn designed by Rogers survives on the property.

The Forbes house was among, or perhaps the first of, a series of like residences in the Boston area that took the form of a squarish low-roofed block with Grecian

12. Captain Robert Bennett Forbes house, Milton, Massachusetts, 1833–34. Original Adams Street front. From a daguerreotype. Historic American Buildings Survey, Library of Congress.

details, central hall, and spiral staircase, often beneath a low cupola. The exteriors of these houses were marked by flush siding and wide pilasters dividing bays. Perhaps Rogers initiated the type. The Salisbury House of 1836–38 in Worcester is close enough to the Forbes house to have been designed by Rogers, although it was built and perhaps cribbed from him by Elias Carter.[58] The Jared Sparks House in Cambridge of 1838 is a stripped version of the same parti.

Among Rogers's early churches is one that fits neatly into local ecclesiastical tradition. In 1828 a little-remembered architect named George Watson Brimmer laid out Trinity Church in Boston in a heavy, blocky, sparsely ornamented lithic style with Gothick embellishments. Two years later Solomon Willard, it is said, designed a similar church for the Reverend Lyman Beecher that is still standing on Bowdoin Street at the back of Beacon Hill. These are two variations of what Abel Bowen called "*primitive Gothic*" (his emphasis), in which the basic building material trumped medieval style.[59] They are in fact an expression of Boston's love of powerful granite architecture in these years: ashlar stone masses of undressed parallelepipeds rising on Bowdoin Street to single-stone merlons and forming battlements at the skyline. Openings are pointed or quatrefoil, with rudimentary tracery.

Three years later, when he designed St. Peter's Episcopal in Salem, Massachusetts, Rogers created his own version of the church as a "mighty fortress."[60] (Although the phrase was Martin Luther's, paraphrased from Psalm 46, it seems to be ecumenically applied.) He produced it with a sharp eye on Bowdoin Street. His church in Salem sits on a corner, whereas the one in Boston is hemmed in by adjacent structures, but the schemas are the same. (Fig. 14) In fact, Rogers lifted the arrangement and features from Willard's earlier church but elongated the proportions. Thus the openings in the tower, consisting of a broad Tudor entry, tall pointed lancet with tracery, and a quatrefoil beneath battlements, occur in both, although Rogers's tower is taller and more slender, and the quatrefoil is something of his own devising. He did not, however, repeat the Bowdoin Street church's neat ashlar, for his building has rough, irregular rubble-granite walls. It survives somewhat altered, most importantly by the 1845–46 addition of an apsidal chancel with details by Richard Upjohn, a necessity of Anglican worship neglected in the

13. Captain Robert Bennett Forbes house, Milton, Massachusetts, 1833–34. Hall stairway. Photo by George M. Cushing for the Historic American Buildings Survey, Library of Congress.

original plan. Rogers may have used this same ecclesiastical parti a few years later at the Church of the Messiah in New York.

For Suffolk Bank on State Street, from 1833–34, Rogers returned to the classical formula for a commercial facade, one that he would use again at the Merchants' Exchange in New York, one of his most important buildings.[61] For a confined city lot overlooking the State Street site of the Boston Massacre, in front of the Old State House, his task was once again to create a striking front, as he had at the Tremont Theatre. This time, however, he produced a coherent three-dimensional construct. After considerable membership skirmishes and design changes, the Board of Directors voted on May 7, 1833, not to have a plain front to its new building, by which they seem to have meant an astylar one; rather, "having examined and compared the respective merits of the second designs . . . as drawn by Mr. Rogers, the architect, [and finding that the cost differential was not too great] . . . do approve and adopt the design for a front having Ionic Columns, leaving the [Building] Committee to adopt such plans for the ground floors as they shall see fit." That is, the committee was interested in external show, not internal convenience. Three months later the board instructed the committee to "finish the Directors Room according to the plan drawn by Mr. Benjamin [presumably Asher]." From these far-from-sufficient data it would seem that Rogers was in some circles thought of as a man who designed facades, with others brought in to lay out interiors.

The Suffolk Bank front elevation is long gone but well known from a photograph and a wood engraving published in the August 1, 1836, edition of the *American Magazine of Useful and Entertaining Knowledge*.[62] (Fig. 15) In a five-bay, visually two-story schema, the ground floor consisted of stout granite piers framing multipaned windows and a central entry, while a colossal fluted Ionic order embraced the two upper stories. The tetrastyle, or four freestanding columns and the antae that embraced them, supported an architrave punctuated with Thrasyllus wreaths, one of Rogers's favorite decorative devices at this period; the recessed wall behind was opened by large trabeated windows, and at the feet of the columns a balustrade, probably of wrought iron, closed off the resulting shallow terrace. A low rudimentary pediment embracing the four columns sat above the architrave, and an axial anthemion rose against the sky to crown the whole. The parti here was effective but not innovative. Predecessors and progeny abound. One predecessor, more delicately detailed, is La Grange Terrace (or Colonnade Row) in New York of 1831–33; one progeny was Rogers's own Merchants' Exchange in New York. The Suffolk Bank front came down about 1900.

Although most of Rogers's early work, like the Suffolk Bank, is credited to him alone, the *Boston Directory* for the years 1833 and 1834 lists him as the partner of Richard Bond, a former housewright and contractor about whose background little is known. Given these dates, Bond may have had a hand in the design of

14. St. Peter's Episcopal Church, Salem, Massachusetts, 1833–34. Watercolor by George Augustus Perkins, 1833. Photo by Robert Merrill. Courtesy Peabody Essex Museum.

15. Suffolk Bank, Boston, Massachusetts, 1833. State Street facade. From Walter Percival, *The Pictorial Library of Useful Information and Family Encyclopaedia* . . . (Boston: Phillips, Sampson, 1851). Author collection.

the Forbes house in Milton, the church in Cambridge, or both, although payment for each went to Rogers alone. Why he thought he needed Bond's support is unknown. By 1826 Bond had designed the Green Street Church, for which he gave Abel Bowen a detailed description of a brick gabled building with cupola, a building on which he scattered, inside and out, bits and pieces based on Grecian sources, such as the Choragic Monument of Thrasyllus and the Parthenon.

Early in 1833 the partners, in answer to an advertisement the previous year from the Treasury department, produced "with considerable labour and expense" a set of drawings and specifications for a custom house "contemplated to be built by the Government" in New York.[63] The notice offered "a high premium to the successful candidate, whose plan should be accepted." These drawings were destroyed in the conflagration that swept the Treasury office the last day of March that year, so the partners and other entrants petitioned the Senate and House for "a suitable compensation for the loss sustained . . . as you may in your wisdom see fit to allow them." As late as February 1842, congressional committees were still kicking around the petition. Whether the architects ever received recompense remains unknown. Such a struggle for government payment was to occur often in Rogers's career. What is known is that the partners did not win the competition. The design of the customhouse erected on Wall Street (now called the Federal Hall National Memorial; 1834–42) came from the firm of Town and Davis, and this building would eventually become a neighbor of Rogers's Merchants' Exchange. It was not the last disappointment Rogers would have when contending for federal commissions.

Bond's name has from time to time arisen in conjunction with the First Parish Church in Cambridge, and his 1835–36 Unitarian church in Andover, Massachusetts, is a recognizable variation of that earlier work. But New England boasts many similar Gothick churches. (The contemporary Congregational church in Uxbridge, by an unknown architect, more closely follows the Cambridge example.) The partnership seems not to have ended amicably for reasons only hinted at when Rogers departed for New York. For the Merchants' Exchange commission in Boston in 1840, Bond lost to Rogers, and in February of the next year he refused to shake hands with him. "This from one I had assisted to his present place in standing as an architect, I thought rather cool," a resentful Rogers wrote in his diary. However, the entry goes on to say that he presumed it was "all on account of my not giving up my interest to his on what he thought might be his." This statement remains enigmatic but points to some dispute involving credit for work done jointly. It might be a reference to the merchants' exchanges for New York City and Portland, Maine, that the two men were designing at the time. In late 1845 Rogers was asked to criticize an unidentified design by Bond "to decide on the fitness of it." He declined and "gave his reasons, not being on good terms" with the man. Would that we knew those reasons. Such a rupture would not be unique in Rogers's career, for in the 1860s he was to end a relationship with A. B. Mullet under similar disgruntled conditions (by contrast, his association in the 1850s with Henry Whitestone seems to have ended amicably). Bond went on to become an important architect in Boston, designing Gothic Gore Hall, the library for Harvard College, in 1838, among other local works, and planning Oberlin College in Ohio.

In ten years of youthful work in Boston, Rogers had set himself off from other local architects and garnered a fine reputation far beyond the city's limits. He had designed town houses, country houses, churches, at least one theater, a Masonic temple, a bank, a precedent-establishing hostelry, and probably other works whose authorship is lost to history. The Tremont House was to generate other commissions throughout the country, first of all in New York.

CHAPTER

2

New York and Boston
1834–1841

ABOUT 1830 the famously wealthy John Jacob Astor, former fur trader, merchant, investor, and real estate tycoon, decided to build a luxury hotel in the fashionable section of lower Broadway in New York City. Trade from the Midwest through the Port of New York had greatly increased with the completion of the Erie Canal in 1825, and the city's population blossomed to nearly 250,000, although settlement above Fourteenth Street was sparse. Astor was astute enough to see that the world would come calling at his door in ever greater numbers. Despite what has recently been called his "get-and-keep policy about money," Astor was prepared to spend lavishly on his monument.[1] Such a man would want the best, and the best hotel architect in the country was in Boston. But not for long. On July 4, 1834, a "goodly number of citizens assembled to witness the ceremony of the laying of the corner stone of Mr. Astor's Hotel," at that point called the Park for its proximity to the City Hall grounds.[2] Among other mementos deposited in a cavity within the stone were the latest issue of *Mechanics' Magazine,* complete with a full-length portrait of General Lafayette, and a silver plate inscribed with the names of Astor, the builders, the superintendents, and Isaiah Rogers, who was also named among the superintendents. The architect had shifted focus, and would eventually shift headquarters, to Manhattan.[3]

Despite his well-earned position as premier hotel designer, Rogers was not the only person the wily Astor engaged. In 1830 he offered a prize "for the best plan and elevation of a contemplated Hotel, to be erected on Broadway, opposite the Park," and that award went to Calvin Pollard, then a partner in Farnham & Pollard, House Carpenters, who only a decade later began to call himself an architect.[4] Although a large collection of Pollard's drawings survives at the New-York Historical Society, none dates from earlier than 1834. In addition, a perspective of a project for the hotel by A. J. Davis has been dated 1830–32. A characteristically severe box composed of encompassing colossal free-standing Doric piers rising to a plain entablature and surmounted by a large glazed penthouse, it was the kind of thing that later made Davis the darling of historians of the midcentury modern movement in the 1950s.[5] The lack of articulation (other than the entrance in the form of an aedicule) and of fenestration makes the scale of Davis's project difficult to read; indeed, it was probably an ideal conception. The plan of that building has not survived, if it were ever drawn, but the Royal Institute of British Architects in London has in its collection a lithograph of a less idealized plan and perspective for the hotel, signed by Town and Davis and dated 1832. The square plan imposes symmetry on Rogers's layout of the Tremont House, with a central entry leading to a lateral cross corridor that extends past public rooms and a pair of matching courtyards to reach a rotunda that is lined with columns and surmounted by a dome and tholos. The perspective shows a stone block with monumental temple-form portico and corner towers rising to secondary tholoi.[6] Despite such competition, however, Rogers's reputation carried the day.

First meetings between architect and client came too early to be recorded in the diary, as did the process of the design, which must have taken place in both Boston and New York. Certainly, it was the success of the Tremont House that got Rogers the job. What was soon called Astor House—with the owner engaged in every detail—was in fact the Tremont scheme redux for what a local paper called "the first commercial city on these shores." In October 1832 the public learned that the building "was expected to exceed in magnificence any thing of the kind in this country—even the far-famed Boston Tremont House."[7] In terms of lateral dimensions, that was hardly the case, although Astor House would be a story taller than the Tremont. By the date of that notice, perhaps, Rogers had written the unsigned and undated specifications for the masons and carpenters, a copy of which exists. This document—twenty-four printed pages with handwritten additions in ink—must be among the earliest surviving examples of printed specifications in the United States.[8] It mentions Rogers's Boston hotel as the standard several times and cites the Erechtheion in Athens as the source for the eight marble columns of the entrance hall, which was also to have a paneled ceiling in the Grecian style, "the plans for which *will be* drawn in full" (italics added); it refers to other executed as well as forthcoming drawings. The modern practice of having all drawings finished, specifications written, and contracts signed before the start of construction was not part of the process during Rogers's career. The specifications also state that all materials for and work on the building were subject to the approval of the superintendent or superintendents, whereas the owner reserved "to himself the privilege of making such alterations during the progress of the work as may be found expedient, and the value of same . . . to be ascertained . . . [by] disinterested parties."

A description of the hotel published at the time the cornerstone was laid reads like a new Tremont Hotel.[9] From this and other sources we learn that Astor House was to be (as it became) an austere parallelepiped that stretched some 200 feet along Broadway, from Vesey to Barclay, and nearly 150 feet along both those side streets. (Fig. 16) Rogers specified the exterior to be blue Quincy granite ashlar "of perfect even color," a material that would produce a large coherent block of a building reticently ornamented. The main facade, four floors between shops and attic, was framed by colossal corner antae supporting an attic in the form of an entablature. According to the architectural critic Montgomery Schuyler's 1911 description, the attic windows were round and wreathed with carved granite, Rogers's then-favorite motif for that location.[10] They were subsequently enlarged into rectangles. The New York *Mirror* complained during construction that the exterior was not sufficiently ornate, a criticism that would be applied to many of Rogers's subsequent hotels, which were sometimes labeled chaste. A central entrance on Broadway and private entrances for ladies on the other two sides (a feature Rogers had not incorporated into the Tremont plan) interrupted the row of shops that lined the streets. These ground-floor commercial spaces had no precedent in the Boston hostelry, which had been purposely located away from the press of retail business, but would find their descendants in Rogers's later hotels. The window openings of the floor above the shops, the *piano nobile* of this Grecian palazzo, showed pilasters and pediments; those above cut directly through the ashlar.

The inset entrance porch seems to have been among Rogers's first monumental distyle-in-antis compositions. Two monolithic fluted Grecian Doric columns set between enclosing piers supported a frieze of triglyphs and blank metopes as well as a low pediment adorned with an anthemion crest at the apex and, according to the specifications, "acroteria at the angles," all of blue Quincy stone. This feature showed New Yorkers what the Boston Granite Style had by then accomplished in monumentality and use of precedent. The porch led to "clear blue Philadelphia marble" steps (again quoting the specifications), through the main entry and up to an entrance hall embellished with those marble Erechtheion-derived Ionic columns. A corridor ran the length of the rooms behind the Broadway facade; those in the corners were public, one for ladies and one for gentlemen. Off the ends of this corridor, the two principal staircases led floor by floor to the top of the building. Along the Barclay Street side sat the dining room, one hundred feet long, forty broad, lighted by windows on both sides and seating three hundred at once. The dining room columns were white pine and of the Corinthian order. (Fig. 17) An originally tree-bedecked courtyard over one hundred feet wide occupied the center of the plan. At first open to the sky, it was covered in 1852 by

16. Astor House, New York City, 1832–36. Engraving published in Herrmann J. Meyer, *Meyer's Universum* (New York, ca. 1852). Author collection.

17. Astor House, New York City, 1832–36. Dining room. New York Historical Society.

James Bogardus with an elliptical, suspended cast-iron and glass roof to create a rotunda for use as a barroom and lunch counter called "The Exchange."[11]

Rogers stayed at the Astor on trips to the city but characteristically, if surprisingly, makes no mention of the change. The upper floors housed more than 320 (the numbers varies in the sources) lockable apartments, each with a fireplace, an arrangement that created a row of chimneys above the cornice along the side streets. According to the specifications, Astor was to supply marble mantelpieces. A visitor to the hotel just after it opened added other details.[12] It was lighted by gas, he noted, and water closets were located off corridors near to each suit. Seventeen bathing rooms and two shower baths could be found on the Barclay side. Water was pumped by steam from a well to the top of the building. There were also four cisterns.

Simeon and Frederick Boyden originally ran the establishment, and as one poetaster described it: "When Boyden's portals wide were thrown / They came from south, and east, and west; / The marks of travel to the bone / they bore, and sought their place of rest."[13] The luxury hotel as urban destination was born at the Tremont and established at the Astor. The opulence was unprecedented, even in Boston. As Justin Kaplan notes, Astor House gave "evidence of what money could accomplish when joined with vision, energy, mechanical ingenuity, running water, indoor plumbing, and Medician magnificence."[14] In Molly Berger's phrase, the place became a "bastion of Whig gatherings."[15] Among the hotel's long list of famous guests over the years were many politicians, including Henry Clay and Jefferson Davis, and celebrities such as Jenny Lind and Charles Dickens (lately a guest of the Tremont). William James was born at the Astor. Daniel Webster announced his retirement there: "I go to Marshfield," he told the crowd. Abraham Lincoln slept there, and he spoke to a gathering from the top of the main entrance portico, as depicted on the cover of *Harper's Weekly* for March 2, 1861. The building survived into the early twentieth century, until John Jacob's descendants had it demolished by stages, in 1913 and 1920.

During these years Astor called on Rogers for other projects, few of which came to fruition. In some cases, it seems that Astor, characterized by Kaplan as a "predatory, stone-hearted, parsimonious monster of greed,"[16] was using Rogers as a kind of unpaid or poorly paid legman. He certainly gave the architect the runaround, which Rogers characteristically records without editorial comment. If we can believe his diary—and Rogers seems not to have been the kind of man who would lie to himself—in what he called "jobbing," the architect planned additions to Astor's brownstone in Broadway, including fireplaces and a furnace, and the two men talked at Hellgate about a stable for Astor's country house on the East River. Later, Astor ordered another plan of the addition to his Broadway house because the first one was lost. He liked the design and asked Rogers to get an estimate of cost, but the architect writes nothing more of the project. In March 1840 the two went together to select the site where Astor intended to build his library. (Two years earlier he had begun to think of endowing a public library in the city, under the urging of the educator Joseph Cogswell.) "He wished me," wrote Rogers, "to make a sketch of the building for the lot I recommended" on the corner of Lafayette and Astor Places. Overnight the architect had worked up plans and an $85,000 estimate. The next day he delivered his sketch, but Astor told him to leave it, he did not need it, for he already had one that he had forgotten to mention the day before. Deliberations about the library extended for several years, until Astor's death in 1848, when Alexander Saeltzer designed the *Rundbogenstil* building on Lafayette Place, completed in 1853.[17]

According to Montgomery Schuyler, within five years of his arrival Rogers had done much to Hellenize the architecture of New York. Having made his entrance with a most impressive accomplishment, he was immediately given a second local commission that would prove to be even more challenging and more dramatic. The Merchants' Exchange Company of the City of New York needed a new building in which to conduct business. The company had incorporated in the early 1820s, and in 1827 Martin E. Thompson designed its first building and supervised construction of "one of the most substantial and conveniently arranged public edifices in the United States," according to the *New York Tribune*.[18] Thompson's structure, which occupied a site half as large as the one eventually given to Rogers, stood as a nine-bay, three-story block centered on a recessed tetrastyle Ionic portico and topped by a tall, octagonal, domed clock tower. The building is known from A. J. Davis's view of the front elevation, reproduced by Imbert's Lithography, but it burned to the ground in mid-December 1835, part of more than $17 million in damage caused by a conflagration in that part of the city. Its blazing demise was portrayed in a lithograph by Nathaniel Currier. As with Astor House, Rogers was not a shoo-in for the job of designing the new building because something of a competition existed here, too. A newspaper report from early May 1836 notified its readers that John Haviland of Philadelphia had received first premium for his plan.[19] Why Haviland did not execute his entry is unknown, but he was just then occupied with his 1835 Egyptian design for the Halls of Justice, otherwise known as "The Tombs," a commission he won in a competition that Rogers had also entered.

Rogers must have designed his exchange building sometime between the December fire and the spring of 1836, when work began, although as usual he continued to draft details as construction proceeded. In October 1838 a Mr. F. Basham exhibited a "beautiful plaster" model of the new building at the Fair of the American Institute that must have been based on Rogers's drawings, for the structure was then far from complete.[20] Basham showed his model again at the Mechanics' Institute's fair in September 1839, by which time Rogers had bought it for the Merchants' Exchange Company for $100.

Because the profession of general contracting was as yet unformed, Rogers sought bids for work as they became necessary, drawing details for various suppliers and craftsmen as he went along. Work did not proceed unhindered, and

Rogers ran into the kinds of problems frequent in the early days of architectural practice in the United States. He groused about the chairman of the building committee for assuming "more than he knows how to direct for the advantage of the progress of building." He complained about his fee, and he thought his clients not very kind when they refused the use of one of their rooms "for my pupil [probably William Henry Bayless] to finish some plans in by himself for a few days." Quarrels with and among workmen had to be arbitrated. He sometimes needed work to be redone or materials returned when they did not meet his expectations. At one point Rogers told the head of the masons that he ought to resign because he was interfered with by management. In April 1840 it seemed to him that he had "but a little to say about the work without giving offense." Despite such hitches, the building progressed apace.

C. H. (Hammatt) Billings, formerly of Ammi B. Young's office, drew the view of the exchange building that was engraved by John Archer and published by Samuel Walker about 1843. It shows the Bostonian's "stupendous building"[21] standing on its roughly rectangular site bounded by Wall, Hanover, and William Streets, with a main front of some two hundred feet on Wall Street. (Fig. 18) In Billings's view, the narrow street becomes a broad piazza alive with passersby: men

18. Merchants' Exchange, New York City, 1836–42. Wall Street front. Drawn by C. H. [Hammatt] Billings, engraved by J. Archer, published by S. Walker, Boston. Author collection.

and women in pairs or groups, on horses, on foot, in a carriage, pushing a barrow or pulling a cart, with dogs running and barking among them. It is the image of a busy metropolitan agora, with Rogers's monumental facade as backdrop. In the composition of that facade, the architect recalled his recently completed Suffolk Bank on State Street in Boston, but, as he did with Astor House in relation to the Tremont, he enlarged it to fit its new ambience.

When construction began on the exchange, just up Wall Street work was under way on Town and Davis's temple form for the U.S. Custom House, a commission Rogers had lost in competition. There, a Doric colonnade fronts a circular domed hall that is surrounded by monolithic Corinthian columns and extended laterally by four recesses, a juxtaposition found again at the New York exchange. Some scholars have noted similarities between Rogers's exchange and Karl Friedrich Schinkel's Altes Museum of 1824-30 in Berlin, although the resemblance could be no more than the same combination of a colonnaded facade, a second range of columns at the entrance, and a dome-covered interior rotunda. Rogers handled these elements differently from and, it must be said, less dramatically than the German architect. A reduced version of Rogers's parti would appear in Portland, Maine, when Richard Bond's 1835-36 design for that city's merchants' exchange was finished in 1840.[22] Or was Rogers's design an enlarged version of Bond's? And was that somehow the cause of their quarrel?

The facade of the splendid building shown in Billings's view survives in a sadly altered state. The structure served as a customhouse until 1907, when National City Bank took it over and commissioned McKim, Mead & White to double it vertically (and redo the interior). That firm stacked a second row of columns on top of Rogers's and completely redid the spaces beyond. It now houses condominiums called Cipriani Club Residences, its original majestic presence reduced by the crush of later Wall Street architecture, to say nothing of current security methods in the financial district.[23]

Blue Quincy granite ashlar forms the original exterior of the exchange, as it did at Astor House.[24] Rogers's Wall Street front is a parade of twelve freestanding fluted Grecian Ionic columns set between doubled antae; these stand above a high basement of deeply drafted blocks and support an entablature and stepped parapet. The original colossal columns are monoliths in the Boston fashion, with those in New York the largest to date at nearly thirty-three feet tall and weighing thirty-three tons each. Six other columns stand in the entrance recess. Rogers could not have seen this major work become a reality without his former mentor's help. The Exchange Company purchased Willard's Wigwam Quarry in Quincy and hired him and his crew to split out the stones and dress them. The dressed blocks were moved to the wharf at Quincy Point by specially designed carriages (Fig. 19), themselves each weighing between eight and nine tons, and drawn by seventy oxen.[25] The granite was then floated to Manhattan on schooners and again

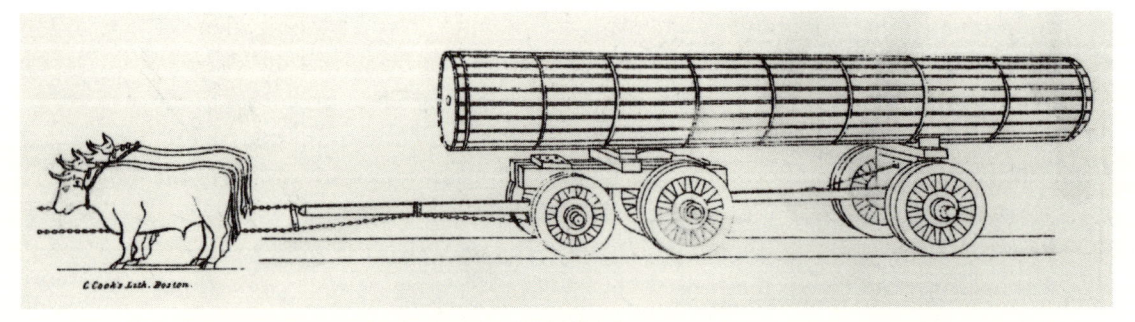

19. "Hauling Columns." Printed by C. Cook's Lithography, Boston. S. Willard, *Plans and Sections of the Obelisk on Bunker's Hill* (Boston, 1843), plate 14.

trucked to the site, where they were hoisted into place by huge wooden derricks. The method of large-scale construction echoed those of classical antiquity.

During this work, a correspondent of the *Public Ledger* in Philadelphia, who waggishly signed his piece "Scagliola" (a process of painting stucco to imitate marble), visited the quarries in Quincy and interviewed Willard, who "may be ranked amongst the first engineers of the day."[26] He watched as the men cut out two blocks, each measuring eighty-two feet long by eight feet square (if wanted, he wrote, a block as large as sixteen feet square could have been freed). The quarriers handled them "with as much ease as a stick of cord wood." It took two years to produce the finished columns. These the reporter compared to the stones found at ancient Baalbek, which he claimed measured a mere seventy-two feet long and eight feet square, and to the columns of Young's federal customhouse in Boston, then under construction. According to the article, the latter were larger than the ones for the New York exchange, although in fact the twenty-two Doric columns in Boston—pulled to the site by twelve teams of horses and sixty-five yokes of oxen—are roughly the same in length but heavier, weighing forty-two tons. Rogers was conversing with Young during the design and construction of the customhouse, beginning at least as early as January 1838 (the first surviving diary entries), when erection of the Merchants' Exchange was under way. Schuyler, the critic, went so far as to call Rogers a collaborator on Young's Boston building.[27] As Willard's biographer wrote about the exchange, in a succinct statement of landmark architecture as collective effort: "the splendid edifice, wrought out of the rocky ledges of Quincy . . . stone by stone, stood in symmetrical beauty . . . in the great commercial metropolis of the nation . . . [and demonstrated] the taste and genius of the architect as well as the skill of the superintendent of the quarry and the industry of the men."[28]

The internal structure of the exchange was made up of brick arches with floors of hydraulic cement quarried at Kingston, New York. This method of so-called fireproof construction had been introduced by Robert Mills earlier in the century. With the fate of Thompson's earlier building in mind, no wood was used in the construction, which was thus considered entirely resistant to fire. The building was not finished until 1842, but by the end of 1841 reports already noted that many of the 164 rooms had been let to banks, insurance companies, engravers, stationers, brokers, and the like. For a period, Rogers rented one for his office. According to the *New York Tribune,* the shape of the site was somewhat irregular, but "the architect has so skillfully arranged the building, that there is but little if any appearance of irregularity in the apartments into which it is divided." It was another example of Rogers's clever sleight-of-hand planning.

In the center of the interior stood the exchange proper, a rotunda eighty feet in diameter, with four large recesses, and ninety feet high to the base of the dome. (Fig. 20) It was coffered, modeled on the Pantheon in Rome, and reported to be

20. Merchants' Exchange, New York City, 1836–42. Interior of the rotunda. *American Architect and Building News,* 1910–11.

the largest in the country at the time. The space was illuminated by a skylight 110 feet in circumference. Pairs of Italian marble Corinthian pilasters forty-one feet tall framed two fluted columns standing in front of each of the recesses. Model makers working from Rogers's drawings produced patterns for such decorative details as column capitals. How much more sophisticated they were than those he had carved for Christ Church in Cambridge just fifteen years earlier. The final cost of the building was well over a million dollars.

Not everyone thought the expenditure worthwhile. Indeed the high cost led to the early demise of the Exchange Company, which resulted in the reuse of the building as a custom house. The unidentified author of an article in *Putnam's Monthly* was vitriolic in his response to both structure and designer. "Whether we look at the unimposing character of the structure itself, the immense amount of money actually thrown away, the absurd arrangements of the interior, and the utter want of design, resulting from an entire lack of knowledge and taste in the architect, which are the chief characteristics of the building, and which make the dreariest, least inviting, and most expensive place of business in the city; we are at a loss for a comparison.... We wish the unfortunate architect, Isaiah Rogers, no more punishment than to have his name carved ... on the pediment; there to survive the blows of Fate and shocks of Time, with his offspring, which we prophesy ... will outlast the pyramids, and remain as food for inextinguishable laughter to generations ... yet unborn."[29]

After such a negative attack, not the last Rogers would suffer, Solomon Willard seems to have thought he could say little more than "so far as regards the architectural taste of the building and its execution, I never doubted that they would be considered respectable."[30] The building was more than that, of course. As the distinguished historian Talbot Hamlin observes, nowhere in the country had "such a monumental structure been so grandly conceived, so simply and directly planned, and so beautifully detailed."[31] It was, he states, "one of the great architectural triumphs of that period," a building "welded inextricably into one powerful organic conception that shows Rogers as a great architect in the fullest sense of the word." The New York Merchants' Exchange gained early international fame. It was one of four American buildings illustrated in Part 7 ("Geschichte der Baukunst") of the *Bilder-Atlas zum Conversations-Lexikon,* published in Leipzig in 1849.[32]

Just as at a later time the steps in front of the Lincoln Memorial became a national stage, so did the broad stairs of the exchange become the setting for important gatherings before the Civil War. Daniel Webster delivered a famous speech on the American fisheries from the spot, the Hungarian politician Lajos Kossuth made his first public appeal for American aid against Austria, and Stephen A. Douglas railed against the extension of slavery after the Mexican War.[33] But great architecture is no guaranty against alteration or destruction or the demise of the institutions it contains. The Merchants' Exchange Company, certainly to the satisfaction of the *Putnam's* reviewer, had failed by midcentury. It was not the first time, nor would it be the last, that an overambitious budget would lead to the demise of the institution for which a building was erected.

The New York exchange building occupied much of Rogers's attention in these years, but he did find time to visit Astor House on December 6, 1836. He was attending the founding meeting of the American Institution of Architects, called by T. U. Walter, William Strickland, and A. J. Davis. This event marked the first (short-lived) attempt to form a professional association. Besides the three conveners and Rogers, also present were John Haviland, Ammi B. Young, Ithiel Town, Minard Lafever, Asher Benjamin, Alexander Parris, and several more architects of lesser reputation. Rogers's erstwhile and soon-to-be estranged partner, Richard Bond, also attended. Rogers likely endorsed the high-minded mission to instruct the public "for the proper appreciation of this noble art," but one can imagine his more personal satisfaction in showing this distinguished group of peers the wonders of his newest hotel. According to a brief mention in the diary a decade later, at the time of the controversial competition for the Smithsonian Institution, he and David Henry Arnot, an architect from New York, discussed the creation of an architectural society, so it is strange that Rogers was not among those who met in 1857 to form the American Institute of Architects, the still-vital organ of architectural professionalism. Perhaps he viewed it as a largely New York organization, whereas by then he was fully ensconced in Ohio and Kentucky.

While work on the Merchants' Exchange in New York progressed, Rogers entered the competition to design the Ohio statehouse in Columbus, drafting his project in June and July of 1838. In his office then was a nineteen-year-old assistant named William Henry Bayless, the nephew and former ward of Thomas Cole. According to the artist, despite working on Rogers's drawings for the competition, Bayless also joined his uncle in submitting another design, which took third prize.[34] In a letter dated October 31, 1838, Cole viciously attacked Rogers's project as a "heap of absurdities . . . [with] porticos and Gables thrown into a Great heap without harmony of parts."[35] Of the more than fifty proffered designs for the statehouse, most are now lost, including Rogers's. Cole's entry and two others were awarded a prize, and A. J. Davis made a Grecian Doric composite of the three for the building begun in 1839. This result was not uncommon for such competitions, as seen in the contest to design Albany city hall. The long history of the construction of the Ohio statehouse ended with Rogers wearily supervising the final stages early in the 1860s.

Contemporary with his work on the New York Merchants' Exchange, Rogers began receiving commissions for other buildings in Manhattan and elsewhere. For New York he produced the most important of his fully realized ecclesiastical works, the Middle Reformed Dutch Church on Lafayette Place and Fourth Street, near La Grange Terrace. According to Schuyler, the church provided a place of worship for "one of the oldest and richest" congregations in the city. The contrast is enormous between this brick and stone building and Rogers's wooden First Parish Meeting House in Cambridge of 1832, although their interiors might have resembled each other somewhat. The laying of the cornerstone took place in November 1836, but the work continued to preoccupy Rogers even after dedication on May 9, 1839, for this commission ended in a lawsuit (a frequent occurrence in his career). In the dispute between the church and the builder, Daniel Haselton, over "deficiencies and extras," the architect supported the builder.

Despite the date the cornerstone was laid, the church's plan (now at the Maine Historical Society in Portland) bears the date September 5, 1837. It is signed by Isaiah Rogers as architect, William Mandeville for the building committee, and Haselton the builder. This contract document was made after construction had begun, a process often described in the diary. Since original drawings from Rogers's office are rare, we should examine this survival closely. A sketch in pencil by Rogers would have typically preceded this layout, which was drawn on a 40-by-24.5-inch sheet. It is back-lined in ink (a method of varying the width of certain lines to enliven the drawing) and colored with washes. Shown is a rectangular building measuring seventy-five by ninety-eight feet (not counting the western extension, for the robing and other rooms) fronted by an octastyle portico whose center intercolumniation is slightly wider than those to the left and right. Also indicated are a tetrastyle second row of columns between antae before the entrance, and another, smaller tetrastyle colonnade, intended to support the organ loft beyond the portal and carry some of the weight of the steeple. Superimposed in pencil on the plan of the ground floor is the outline of the octagonal belfry with circling columns. The color-coded walls indicate a stone exterior with brick backing, a common construction technique. Pilasters embrace the exterior corners of the block, a detail Rogers used frequently on various building types. An iron fence is suggested, enclosing the flagstone pavement on the two street fronts. Within the building, center and side aisles between pews lead to the reading desk, which is set on a semicircular dais. Rows of tiny circles indicate slender (probably iron) columns, intended to uphold the side galleries. A small pencil sketch indicates the side elevation of a pew, and a note signed "J. S." says that the arrangement of seating near the reading desk could be changed.[36]

The sheet on which the church plan appears is marked for a geometrically constructed perspective view (also in the collection of the Maine Historical Society). It is large, indicating that Rogers must have had a sizable drafting table in his New York office. (Fig. 21) Although the architect signed the official plan, the perspective is unsigned, so it could be the work of Theodore Voelckers, who executed other views of Rogers's New York works. (Architectural drawings of this period exhibit little individuality.) The view predicts what was erected, including the Ionic order at ground level and the Corinthian of the belfry, the line of acroteria along the

21. Middle Reformed Dutch Church, New York City, 1836–39. Presentation perspective. Pencil, ink, and watercolor, 50 x 29 in (127 x 74 cm). Courtesy Maine Historical Society, Portland.

lateral skyline, and the crown molding of the pediment. It also shows the tholos-belfry and slender octagonal steeple that recurs in the engraved view of the 1850s by Whitney, Jocelyn & Annin (perhaps based on this perspective). Rogers seems to have designed the terminal with one eye on John Nash's similar feature at All Souls Church in Langham Place, London, of 1822–24. Erected with some difficulty from Rogers's second design, it was reinforced with iron bracings in April and May 1839, with the vane and ball being added to the pinnacle in February of the next year.

According to Montgomery Schuyler, the tholos was a wooden homage to the Choragic Monument of Lysicrates, although larger, and church authorities insisted on putting the spire atop it. A detailed description of the church published in 1856 notes that the steeple, "placed upon a building of Grecian and Roman design, presents an incongruity not reconcilable to correct principles of taste; yet custom renders such an appendage so necessary a feature in Christian architecture, that its omission . . . would hardly be tolerated."[37] Rogers at one point was consulted by the church committee about leaving it off; it was soon taken down and is missing in the photograph of the then-demolished church that appeared in an article by Schuyler published in the May 3, 1911, issue of *American Architect* magazine. His description notes the church's massive granite presence. Not only did it exhibit an "octastyle portico of monolithic Ionic columns of impressive magnitude," but, the portico being pseudodipteral (two columns deep), it included "a second range of four more of these costly monsters, each of which was dragged to its site by twenty yokes of oxen." Cost seems not to have bothered the congregation, for in place of Rogers's usual tin or galvanized iron roof, the building was covered with copper.

The roof was a single span of heavy timber construction unsupported by interior columns. The room below seated about fifteen hundred worshipers, with five hundred more accommodated in the galleries that extended around three sides and were supported by the delicate columns indicated in the plan. Three aisles separated the seating into four areas, the outer two intended for Sunday school children. In 1855 the church interior was remodeled, with the cumbersome columns flanking the pulpit and those sustaining the organ gallery and steeple replaced by iron supports to enlarge the capacity of the house. A "chaste" pulpit, composed of pure white statuary marble, stood between columns; above it was a skylight glazed with stained glass "of subdued, unpretending colors." A full entablature with dentil cornice carried around the interior. From it sprang a slightly elevated dome divided into panels and finished with enriched moldings and ornamented work "so arranged with openings disguised by the panelings, as to give sufficient ventilation to the entire interior." The church was lit by gas and heated by stoves. There is no indication in the diary that Rogers, then living in Cincinnati, directed the later changes.

The grand house of worship fell to the wreckers in 1887, about a decade and a half after Walt Whitman lamented the American spirit of "pull-down-and-build-all-over-again" in his *Democratic Vistas*. As the architectural critic Ada Louise Huxtable wrote more recently, the American city is never finished. Fire did take many of Rogers's buildings, but it is this ever-churning urban energy that also accounts for the poor survival rate of his works. Together with Tremont House, Boston's Merchants' Exchange of 1840, and the 1848 Burnet House in Cincinnati, his three New York buildings—Astor House, New York Merchants' Exchange, and Middle Reformed Dutch Church—constitute the crest of Rogers's early career. Even though they have been demolished or, in the case of the exchange, radically altered, they should be better known. For these works alone he ranks with the greatest antebellum architects.

Among other commissions on Rogers's agenda in 1835–36 was the second building housing the Bank of America on Wall Street, in the shadow of the exchange, for which Theodore Voelckers drew a perspective in early 1841. (Given the late date, rather than an anticipatory view, it must have been intended as a logo for the establishment or, perhaps, for the portfolio of his work that Rogers mentions in connection with his 1838 bridge over the Harlem River.) A local newspaper reported looking at "the powerful foundation of the new building of the Bank of America, at the corner of Wall and William" and "examining the immense iron safe constructing [*sic*] to hold the notes and specie" in mid-August 1835. Another paper marked the opening of the building in mid-September 1836. "Its external appearance," it reported, "is very chaste and elegant; and the interior well answers to the outward show of neatness, good taste and convenience. . . . [It] is an ornament to Wall-street."[38] The recessed front showed the public a distyle-in-antis Quincy granite arrangement some fifty feet wide. It consisted of two fluted Corinthian columns standing at the top of broad steps and set between ashlar piers, surmounted by a high architrave, block parapet, and anthemion. (Fig. 22) A row of windows, arranged beneath recessed square panels along the right flank, lit the banking room until its demolition in 1889. For Merchants' Bank, located two doors down from the Bank of America, in 1838 Rogers more or less reproduced the design of that Quincy granite portico, even reusing the proto-Corinthian order of the Tower of the Winds. Voelckers drew a perspective of that building, too. Compared to the limestone front of James Dakin's contemporary and more imaginative Bank of Louisville—it, too, a distyle-in-antis composition—Rogers's bank facades seem orthodox but sturdy.

In 1840 Rogers again created a near copy of the parti for the Bank of America at the Exchange Bank in Richmond, Virginia, although he topped that structure with a pediment. By June the building committee had on hand "several plans," presumably designs from a selection of architects, but members agreed not to consider them until Rogers, in town on other work, had a chance to draft his own concept. They obviously gave him leeway as the out-of-town expert. By the end of June he had submitted his design, which he modified in July and again later, and

22. The Bank of America, New York City, 1835–36. Wall Street front. Collection of Denys Peter Myers.

23. Exchange Bank, Richmond, Virginia, 1840. Photograph taken after the Civil War. Prints and Photographs Division, Library of Congress.

work commenced shortly thereafter. By the end of August the building committee accepted his "estimate of erection according to the last arrangement" of about $157,000. As for the two earlier New York banks, the granite was extracted from Willard's Quincy quarry, but the bricks for the arches came from Philadelphia and the carpenters from New York. Six marble mantels and glass were shipped from New York at the end of September, and the building was finished around the new year. The result drew the admiration of the Richmond *Compiler,* which noted on July 7, 1841, that the "chaste edifice deserves more than a passing notice. . . . Mr. Isaiah Rogers, the talented Architect whose genius is so finely displayed in the design of the [nearby] Exchange Hotel, is also the Architect of this pretty Bank building." The structure suffered much damage in the bombardment of Richmond in 1865 (Fig. 23), after which Rogers's portico was reused for the Union

Bank & Federal Trust Company. Such distyle-in-antis templar fronts can still be seen in many a small-town bank throughout the United States.

Rogers next turned to another Wall Street bank and office building that he identifies as the "United States Bank in New York"; its representative was George Griswold, late of the Bank of America. The August 11, 1838, edition of the *Commercial Advertiser* announced the association between Griswold of New York and Richard Alsop of Philadelphia to transact business under the name "The United States Bank of New York." Griswold immediately engaged Rogers to design a building containing a bank and offices, and the architect went to work in his scant free time while superintending both the Merchants' Exchange and the Dutch Reform Church, running all over New England looking for proper stone or taking on other chores. The outcome was not pleasant. By the end of the month Griswold had purchased a building at 34 Wall Street, intending to demolish it and erect his new banking house on the site. "We have no doubt that the new building will be an ornament to the city," said the *Connecticut Courant* on August 25. It seems that Griswold, who disliked parting with money unnecessarily, did not want to pay for such an urban amenity. In September, Rogers gave him "another plan of the plainest kind," then sent a drawing of the front of the bank to stonecutters for an estimate. Building must have begun soon after, with consultations and changes to details accompanying the work, for in October Rogers wrote that all progressed well. At the beginning of December 1838 the *Daily National Intelligencer* announced the bank was "rapidly putting up" its building, with an expectation of occupancy by May of the next year. In an entry dated November 12, 1838, however, Rogers noted that he had declined "serving" Griswold any longer, "as he makes so many alteration[s] and sets aside all my instruction[s]." Nevertheless, the diary contains later entries about the roof and stone steps, and one dated December 11 notes that two stories of the front had been erected. On January 12, 1839, the architect wrote that the last stone had been set that day.

The story of Rogers's business with Griswold did not end there, however. Seven months later, after a long discussion, the client declined to pay his bill—a familiar story in the early history of the architectural profession. In February 1840 Rogers took the man to court, suing for "pay for services rendered in making plans and superintending [the] bank building in Wall Street." His most important witnesses were afraid to testify and were released, which, Rogers complains, "went to my injury very much. A rich man can control the feelings of too many men to the injury of their fellows when he undertakes to do so." He eventually won a $300 judgment in his favor, or $150 less than his bill, netting $87.84 for the job, after expenses. Such were the lives of architects before they banded together to demand professional status and lobby for the value of their services.[39]

Amid the onrushing recitation of all this work attempted and done, an arresting and tragic personal episode occurs in late 1838. It begins with a mid-December notice that his wife, Emily, was very sick, as were two of their six children. The youngsters were diagnosed with smallpox. Soon three were down, then all six, "some severe, and some comfortable." Isaiah Augustus Rogers died on December 24, with his father suffering "severe loss and affliction." Two days later three others were extremely ill, two dangerously so. Cecelia died on the twenty-ninth, Phoebe Mann on the thirty-first, and Frederick was of grave concern. This necrology is interrupted by what, given Rogers's taciturnity, constituted a *cri de coeur:* "Wife very low in health and spirits from her great affliction which she has been called upon to bear. This year ends with sorrow and affliction of the severest kind. May the God of all goodness grant us health and prosperity for the future, as is consistent with His Holy will and pleasure. Amen." But "sorrow and affliction" were not at an end: Frederick died on January 2. Four of six children dead within two weeks! By January 7 Rogers was back burying himself in work, but repercussion from the episode was still to come. Richard K. Frost, a doctor who had recently been found guilty of fourth-degree manslaughter in the death of a man he treated with herbs in the Thomsonian manner (an alternate medical system discredited at the time), was falsely implicated in the children's deaths and had to implore Rogers to endorse a public statement saying that he had not treated them. Thus the family's private grief rubbed against larger societal issues.[40]

During this crisis, Rogers's output slowed considerably but did not cease altogether. His speculative design for a bridge for the Croton Aqueduct, a massive construction project begun in 1837, is a well-documented example of his working on problems that interested him whether or not he had a commission. A combination of diary entries and a rare preserved letter, dated June 1, 1838, tells the story. In mid-April of that year he had begun a series of entries concerning a proposed "aqueduct across [the] Harlem River," recording a conversation he had in New York with (Gridley?) Bryant. Meanwhile, he went out to examine the stone at the place in New York where the bridge was to cross the river. By May 1 he was planning an eight-arch bridge, which he quickly changed to five arches for the reason given in a letter he sent on June 1 to Joseph Barnes, apparently an assistant to John B. Jervis, chief engineer of the aqueduct.[41] (He had already given Barnes some plans on June 7.) "By your particular request," he wrote, "I send you a plan of a Bridge designed to cross the Harlem River for the purpose of conveying the water of the Croton River to the City." He included a list of specifications and cost estimates, which he had "submitted . . . to two practical men . . . in the business of Quarrying Dressing and Building with Granite the last fifteen years"—perhaps Solomon Willard and James Savage—and they had agreed with his estimate of $822,000. "I presume," he continues, "it will be considered by many in offering this estimate and remarks that I have meddled with a subject which did not concern me but a little. When I first commenced the sketch it was merely to see if a Bridge could not be constructed with 5 arches and save some of the expenses of the Coffer dams of so many of the Piers shown in the report of the Commissioners." (Jervis's erected design consisted of fifteen arches.) Rogers goes on to say that he little expected anyone on the project to ever see his proposal. "Had you not called on me with one of your friends [Gridley Bryant?] it probably would have passed to my Portfolio with many other of my sketches without having been seen by anyone. If it will be of any use to you it is at your service to do with it as you think best." Would that such a portfolio had survived! Discussion in the diary stops for a while, but Rogers pursued this project off and on throughout the next two years. As far as we know, the work here began his life-long interest in bridging long and short spans.

Nearly two years later Rogers returned to the problem. In late April 1840 he had given up thinking of an arched stone structure and instead drew a sketch "for an iron bridge to cross the Harlem River for the aqueduct." A few days after that he designed another, "without any piers in the river making a span of 620 feet." In this he anticipated by three-quarters of a century the altering of the original Jervis-designed, fifteen-arch High Bridge, whose middle arches were replaced with a steel span of about 450 feet. Rogers's entries also indicate that his generosity with his ideas could be matched by caution. He did not hesitate to show this project to his friend Ammi B. Young, who appeared to like it, but when an unnamed visitor called to talk about the bridge, Rogers "rather suspected that he wanted to draw my plan from me to profit by himself" and refused to let him see it. This new proposal must have been created for his own amusement because, at the time, the Jervis High Bridge was under construction. By May 17, when he visited the site, he found it "under good way, piles for one of the piers down." Still, Rogers must have been held in some respect by Jervis. His last entry occurred on September 3, 1840, when he went to visit the Harlem River site "by invitation of the Commission" and found the work on the piers for the stone arches very good. With some time on his hands in 1846, he again visited the nearly completed Croton system and found it a marvel of the age.

Commissioned work in this period included frequent drafts for houses; such requests were characteristic of his career, and he could turn them out quickly to earn $2, $5, or eventually more if he did not supervise construction. He sketched a house for Havana, for example, and among the identifiable New York projects in 1838 and 1839, he worked briefly for the Red Hook Company, which had been organized to construct several houses and a hotel for that section of Brooklyn. Apparently, financing failed and nothing came of the scheme. In April 1838 Rogers designed a house for George A. Jarvis, a wholesale grocer and philanthropist, for which he received immediate payment of $5. Whether that job resulted in the residence Jarvis built in Brooklyn in 1844 remains unanswered.[42] In May 1839 he drafted houses and a store in Lafayette Place for a Mr. Brandegee, almost certainly Jacob Brandegee, who lived a 3 LeRoy Place, Bleecker Street, in 1842, another client who led him to silent frustration. That site nudged the development of fashionable addresses along the street, which had been begun a decade earlier by Isaac Pierson. In August, Rogers "set some men to work" for Brandegee, but the client dismissed them before noon. That is the last entry about the project until February 1845, when the *New York Herald* listed Brandegee among the city's wealthiest residents. Rogers then designed a store for him "as per letter received" and bargained for stone for the building. In April he tried to get a check for services from Brandegee's wife but had no success—and there the references end. He also drew houses for the New Brighton section of Staten Island, apparently for a Mr. Davis and a Mr. Gibson, otherwise unidentified, and "made [an] estimate for Capt. Glover's house of rough stone in Broadway" in July 1839. This was perhaps Andrew B. Glover, listed at 310 E. Broadway in 1842. Further details about these projects are wanting.[43]

Early in 1838 the architect worked on the design of an unnamed Unitarian church. By February 19 he was already drawing a section "of a church for Mr. Pierson to be located on Broadway" and by February 28 he had nearly completed a perspective view; by March 3 he had finished drawings, and four days later he was seeking an estimate of cost. The entries end there. The only building that fits these particulars seems to be the Church of the Messiah, dedicated in May 1839 at 728–30 Broadway, in Waverly Place, and which survived until 1865. (Fig. 24) The pastor was the Reverend Orville Dewey, late of Massachusetts, a man who would presumably favor Rogers as the architect. A Mr. Pierson, who worked in some important capacity at the Merchants' Exchange, then under construction, appears often in the diary in these months. Pierson might have been a leading member of the congregation and supervised the erection of the church.

What gives this attribution some weight is the structure itself: it was a refined version of the type of Boston granite Gothic that Rogers had followed at St. Peter's Episcopal Church in Salem just a few years earlier (see Fig. 14). The tall blocky central tower was opened by the stacking of portal, pointed lancet, and (here, round) window, while merlons ranged across the skyline. What places it in New York rather than Boston is the dressed stone moldings of the openings, ornamental carved belt courses, and worked jambs and label profiles of the main doorway. These kinds of refinements, largely unknown in Massachusetts churches of this type, suggest that the stone was not granite, for Bostonians usually—although not always—avoided trying to carve such tough material. This detail suggests that Rogers did not supervise the construction, if it was indeed his design, because during those days he was piling up massive granite blocks at the Middle Reformed Dutch Church, not to mention the Merchants' Exchange. The local papers called the church a "model of fine architecture" with a "spacious and most beautiful interior" at its dedication in early May 1839, but in September 1853 an anonymous (and sour) critic for *Putnam's Monthly* admitted that he did not know the name of the architect of the Church of the Messiah but trusted "that he has repented of his deed." It was perhaps the same critic who, eight months earlier, had savaged the Merchants' Exchange in the pages of that magazine. Reticent even in private, Rogers never recorded his reactions to abuse of his work.

In late September 1839, Samuel F. B. Morse and John W. Draper introduced the daguerreotype to New York by taking a picture of the new Unitarian Church of the Messiah. It is said that they viewed the building on Broadway from Morse's

24. Here attributed to Isaiah Rogers, Church of the Messiah, New York City, 1838–39. Broadway front. *Putnam's Monthly* 9 (September 1853). Picture Collection, New York Public Library, Astor, Lenox and Tilden Foundations.

studio on the third floor of the University of New York, on Washington Square.[44] Rogers clearly became interested in the new visual and technical phenomenon, paying for a chance to view the process three months later, in December 1839, and ordering a daguerreotype of his exchange building in May 1840, for which he paid $5. We know other daguerreotypes were taken of his work—of the Forbes house (see Fig. 13) and the hotel in Madison, Indiana, for example—as well as of himself. He was surely among the first American architects to record his work with this new technology.

Rogers had other ecclesiastical projects on the boards at this time, although some remain difficult to trace, either because they appear in fleeting references to tasks that probably went nowhere or because his information is scant. These included a church for Elizabeth Street in the city, one (alteration) in the Bowery, and another for Troy, New York, the plans for which he sent off on May 6, 1839. Just over a year later he received $200 for those drawings.[45] He studied other projects as well. In addition to the Ohio statehouse competition, he worked on drawings for a theater. On September 27, 1839, the National Theater, newly redecorated and housing a company under the direction of the Anglo-American actor James Wallack, fell victim to an arsonist, taking with it three churches and several other buildings. Proposals were soon afoot to erect its replacement at Leonard and Church Streets, an "edifice to be . . . on a style of greater extent and pretensions than any other attempted."[46] For some reason Rogers took a defeatist attitude toward this project, perhaps because it was not an official commission, for he admitted to himself that his "prospects for making plans [were] not much." Nonetheless, on October 5 he began to draw a new theater, which he located on nearby Broadway at Chambers, and had worked evenings on it for nearly two weeks when Wallack visited his office and, in the architect's absence, "took minutes" of the plans. Wallack was involved early on in the rebuilding of the National, so Rogers must have gotten the location wrong. Drawing continued through the end of the month, when he learned that the committee "had engaged Mr. [Calvin] Pollard to make plans for them." (The New-York Historical Society owns Pollard's album of nine signed contract drawings entitled "Plans and Elevations of the New National Theatre," dated April 21–28, 1840.) Undeterred even by his own pessimism—when he smelled a potential commission, Rogers did not give up easily—he continued to work his proposal and called on a member of the committee in early November. At that point diary references to the project cease. The sequence of events suggests that either Rogers had executed his design "on spec" or he was unaware that he was in competition with Pollard. The building erected from Pollard's design opened in October 1840 and succumbed to arson seven months later.[47]

Rogers also worked on a hotel for "Pearce" (Pierce) Butler of Philadelphia and the South. Butler was one of the richest men in the country through inheritance, one of its largest slaveholders, and, since 1834, husband to the actress Fanny

Kemble in a famously fraught union whose troubles began over Butler's treatment of the slaves at his Georgia plantations just as Rogers received the commission.[48] He worked on the drawings through the fall of 1838, visited Butler at his mansion in Philadelphia in November, and sent him the drawings in June 1839. He heard that Butler thought of proceeding and received $359.60 from him four months later. But apparently nothing ever came of Rogers's design.

There was other than original work, too. Although frequently rivals, Rogers and Calvin Pollard joined forces at least once. In October 1838 the two examined the roof structure of old Trinity Church in Broadway. They found it spreading, causing an inclination of the interior columns, and recommended bolting four strong iron ties tight across the building. That measure was accomplished, but it was unable to save the venerable ecclesiastical structure. A statement appeared in the *Commercial Advertiser* on September 2, 1839, describing the repairs and reassuring the congregation, but the church was soon pulled down and replaced by Richard Upjohn's canonical neo-Gothic design, dedicated in 1846.

Even in this period, not all of Rogers's work was local. As the architectural historian Mary Woods reminds us, in those days "every major architect in New York, Philadelphia, Boston, and Washington, D.C. travelled afield to find work": Town, Davis, Walter, Upjohn, Strickland, Mills, and so on.[49] Rogers had been to Alabama early on and would go again. He was now to supply Virginia with examples of his work, and he would eventually find himself building in Indiana, Illinois, Ohio, Tennessee, and Kentucky as well as Louisiana and, perhaps, Wisconsin. The Richmond bank was far from his only commission in the South before the Civil War. On August 28, 1840, the *Richmond Whig* declared that city "in a prosperous condition, and rapidly advancing in improvements. . . . Despite the adversity of the times [the Panic of 1837 and its aftermath] she has made many advances during the last twelve months." Such progress was reflected in a growing population. Among the improvements were not only Rogers's Exchange Bank but also, more important, drawings for the Exchange Hotel and its "sister," the Merchants' Exchange, which also came from his hand.

The *Whig* had reported in early July 1839 that subscriptions for stock in the hotel were enough to guarantee its success, although a year later funds were still short, and they never did reach enough to support a prosperous operation by the original owners. The paper announced that "beautiful drawings . . . may be seen at Messrs. Fry's Counting Room [eventually Hugh W. Fry & Sons, commission merchants], where subscriptions will no doubt be received," and the subscription books soon closed.[50] That same month, Rogers noted his engagement to draw a plan for the hotel, and, true to form, it was on the boards within twenty-four hours. By the end of the first week of August, his drawings were on their way south, but as usual many design revisions and details, as well as specifications and estimates, would need to be written. March 1840 found him in Richmond explaining the plans, and November saw him complaining that the committee had altered his arrangement. In March 1841 he examined the work that had already been accomplished on the foundations, considered it badly done, and recommended it be rebuilt. In general he considered the quality of Southern labor—and, in fact, Southern society—not up to Northern standards. When he came across a dilapidated mausoleum, "as all things appear in southern places," on an estate near Norfolk, Rogers wrote that "no mark of energy or character as is presented by northern people" appears in the South. While engaged on buildings in Virginia, he sent workmen down from New York when he could, engaging McLellan and Ambrose of Manhattan as builders for the Richmond hotel.

By combining descriptions published in the December 1840 *Whig* and the July 1841 *Compiler*, we obtain a good sense of the hotel, or what the latter called "an Architectural pile that will become the boast of the South and that constitutes a noble ornament of our city." The building was a rough quadrangle with a hollow square center. The main front stretched 130 feet, the wing on the left 170 feet and the one on the right 160 feet. Among the notable features of the interior was a vestibule with vaulted ceiling supported by columns of variegated marble (perhaps *scagliola*), between which were statues emblematic of the seasons. "In this vestibule . . . [is] a beautiful device to conceal the angular defect of the front line, and such is the success of the plan without and within, that the stranger would hardly discover but that the building was a perfect square." Unfortunately the "device" is not explained. Where Rogers had hidden the angle of the sides of the Tremont House by external means, here he seems to have worked the same magic on the interior. A spacious entrance hall followed the vestibule, with its double range of columns, tessellated floor, and registry office. From there, passages led to each wing, a bar and large public dining room, and several ample drawing rooms and parlors. Upstairs were more parlors and some 140 rooms. The *Compiler*'s reporter found the ladies' drawing room a "picture of Eastern magnificence," the walls figured "in the chaste style of Watto." The exchange building to the south of the hotel embraced a spacious reading room as well as a ninety-by-forty-foot hall for public meetings, lectures, and other gatherings.

The Alexandria *Gazette* explained the origin of the brilliant lights used in the hotel.[51] They were produced by the patented "chemical oil" of Benjamin Franklin Greenough of Boston, a product he announced in 1840 that was examined and endorsed by the Franklin Institute of Philadelphia in 1841. It would seem that either Rogers or his clients were up-to-date in hotel appointments. The oil was "not oleaginous or greasy," explained the newspaper, "does not injure furniture or clothing upon which it is spilled, unless on fire, when the burning would be similar to common alcohol." Greenough, a chemist by profession, went on to other incendiary inventions, including an improved flamethrower used in the Civil War.

It was not just for the interior of the Exchange Hotel that Rogers created a variation on the Tremont. On the stuccoed granite ashlar exterior, he took the curved bays he had used in Boston to hide the awkward angle between front and side elevations and moved them to the front, where they were again meant, even in this location, "to conceal the variation from the right angle in the building," according to the *Complier*. He embraced them with square corners that were framed by pilasters, and stretched a tetrastyle range of colossal fluted Grecian Ionic columns between them. (Fig. 25) These were monoliths. Rogers's entries for April 30 and May 1, 1841, tell us that the men were "at work all day drawing up from the wharf to street one of the columns," which was hauled "with a puncheon and horses." There were twenty-six horses, he wrote, "not a very heavy load for them." In the end everyone involved was "very much fatigued, having encountered much dust and wind." When all the columns were raised, "there was great excitement . . . [and] several hundred lookers-on." Standing on the high basement, the columns reached past three floors to support an entablature that was the twin to the Tremont's. With the supports in place, the architect paused long enough to write, in a rare statement of self-satisfaction, that "the work so far looks very well, and everyone speaks of it with great praise." He added, "I too think it will look well."

Above the hotel's entablature was a blocky pediment and Rogers's favorite crowning device, a belvedere in the form of an Ionic peripertal tholos over thirty feet high. It would appear that this time the rooftop feature was erected, for the paper reported that "the view from this is one of the most lovely and picturesque that 'ever solicited the pencil of the New Panoramist.'" George Endicott of New York produced the lithographic view of the completed hotel. In mid-January 1842 Rogers mentions writing to Frederick Boyden, the hotel's original manager, late of the Tremont and Astor House, about having such a view drawn.[52] It shows the usual street theater around the building, with a dray, a cart, barrows, horsemen, dogs, strollers, and African American figures carrying loaded baskets on their heads. Despite the well-marked private entrance usually reserved for ladies on the side, a man and woman emerge from the main entrance, presumably to climb aboard the waiting carriage.

Writing of the dedicatory dinner at the hotel on July 1, 1841, an event that Rogers attended, the *Whig* doubted "whether a company of gentlemen ever sat down to a repast so beautiful in its arrangement on the table, or arose from one inspired with such feelings of hilarity and good wishes for the swimming prosperity of the host."[53] Alas, despite protestations of recovery and the good cheer at that banquet, a lack of adequate funding led to the early acquisition of the establishment by John P. Ballard, whose own Italianate hotel of 1855–56 stood across Franklin Street. He joined the two structures at the second story with a neo-Gothic pedestrian bridge. Richmond's Exchange Hotel closed in 1895, and Rogers's building was demolished in 1900.

25. Exchange Hotel, Richmond, Virginia, 1839–41. F Street front. George Endicott lithography, New York. Valentine Richmond History Center, Virginia.

But Rogers had still other work on the boards. In November 1838 Major Richard Delafield of the Corps of Engineers, the energetic, newly named superintendent of the U.S. Military Academy at West Point, called on him "to get a plan of buildings" in New York, and the architect traveled upriver to visit the site and was "very kindly received" at the major's house. Delafield had been appointed to revive a drifting institution, and among his solutions was architectural renovation, beginning with the barracks. That November he named a board to write a program for new buildings, and by mid-December Rogers had finished the outline of a design. What happened next is not entirely clear, but we know that in January 1839 Delafield sent a request for the plans to the architect, asked for a revision, and early the next month wrote a memo sharply criticizing them.[54] "They are in *no manner* suited to our wants, or the discipline of the Corps," he wrote, "and would cost 1/2 a million." He would not submit them to the board, being as they were "in principle worse than the existing buildings altho *very* elegant." There is no indication that Rogers ever saw this memo. According to his diary, and drawings now in the National Archives, he continued to work on the project through the first half of 1839. Several surviving plans and elevations for the barracks exist from his hand, including a classical scheme dated April 1839 and a castellated scheme dated June of the same year; these stylistic options were increasingly offered by architects to clients in this period.

Rogers's classical design proposed a pair of symmetrical two-story ranges of rooms centered on an Ionic octastyle pedimented portico facing outward and an Ionic tetrastyle portico facing inward. (Fig. 26) The castellated design shows one range (perhaps two) of two stories divided by a central Tudor archway and towers. A two-story pointed arcade ranges down the rear of the row facing the parade. (Fig. 27) If these were Rogers's attempt to hang on to the commission, they did not (and could not) help. Delafield had already appointed the English-born architect Frederick Driaper to replace Rogers. Driaper's own Tudor Gothic submission impressed Delafield, but not so much that the superintendent did not substitute his own design for the buildings in a version of that medieval style. His drawing for Tudor Gothic barracks is also at the National Archives, and construction began in 1845. Delafield seems to have been using architects to feed him ideas for his own designs, a relationship made possible by the wobbly status of the profession in this period.

In mid-February 1839, about the same time he was dismissing Rogers from one commission, Delafield again traveled to New York to request plans for an "observatory for West Point." Rogers dutifully sat down to produce drawings later that month and early the next. The old chapel, which housed the observatory and library at the military academy, had burned in February 1838. Rogers designed a new observatory to be part of the rebuilt chapel, often attributed to him, but Delafield ultimately designed and supervised its erection in 1839–41.[55] It was built of granite and red sandstone in the castellated style (the first such design at West Point). Of the three towers, the central one rose in a high-profile dome twenty-seven feet in diameter; it was built by Henry Fitz of New York. It housed the equatorial telescope, which rested on six twenty-four-pound cannon balls rolling in cast-iron grooves.[56]

To what extent Rogers may be credited with some West Point installation remains in doubt, but in July 1839 he returned to the academy, examined the work in progress with Delafield, and received $325 for his "plans of Public Buildings at West Point." That relatively hefty sum must reflect a substantial contribution. About this time, the architect also drew "Plans and elevations for Barracks and public buildings for the Military Academy." (This sheet is filed with others in the National Archives.) The similarities between Rogers's four-part plan for a multipurpose building, as shown on the right side of this layout, and the plan of the library Delafield built are suggestive of the former's influence. Although Rogers's drafted plan rises to neoclassical elevations, unlike the castellated style that was built, the organization of that plan seems to resemble what was erected by Delafield. Rogers's layout consisted of four separate square rooms, one of which was a library equipped with two tiers of bookcases, and another was a lecture

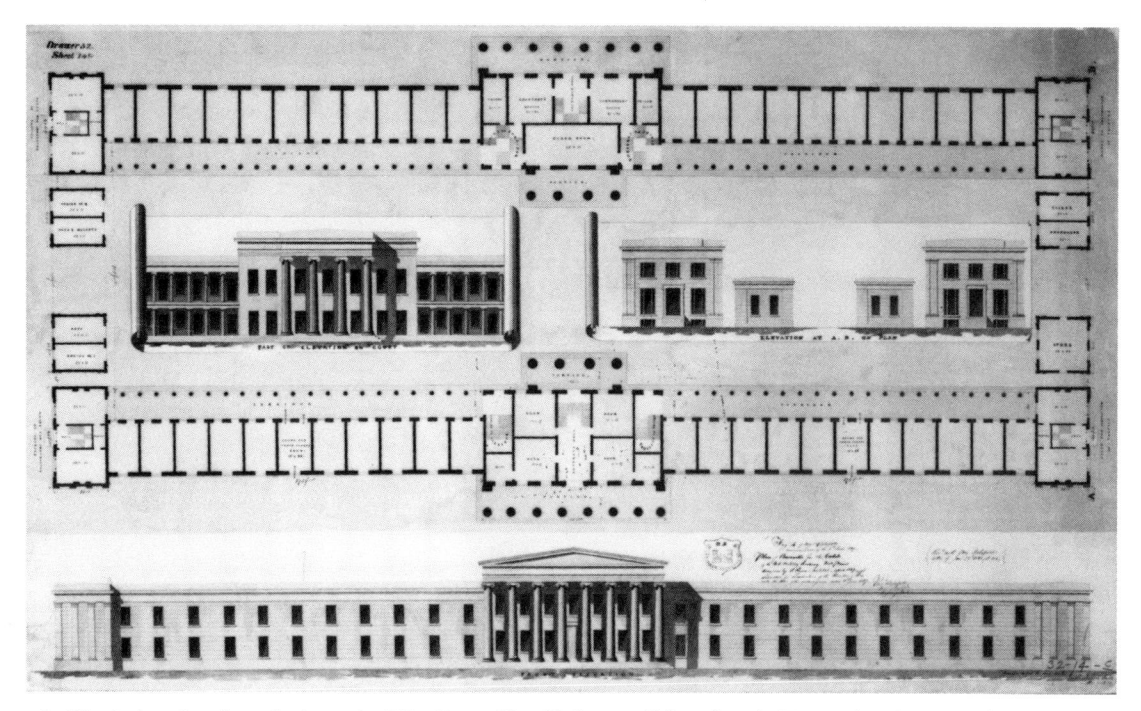

26. Classical project for cadet barracks, West Point, New York, 1839. Ink and wash. National Archives, Washington, D.C.

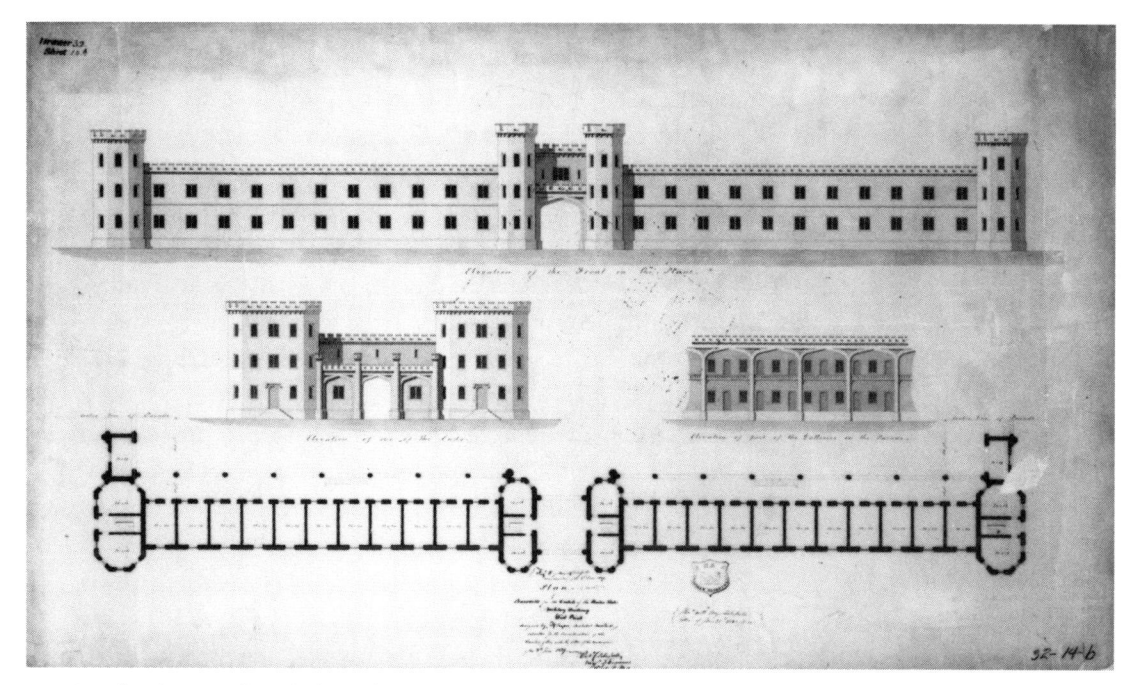

27. Castellated project for cadet barracks, West Point, New York, 1839. Ink and wash. National Archives, Washington, D.C.

room. Delafield's was "originally designed for four purposes," a library with two tiers of bookcases, administrative offices, a lecture hall, and the astronomical observatory. Again, the suspicion arises that Delafield was using Rogers. In early November 1840, he requested the architect's West Point drawings, which, always accommodating, Rogers dug out of storage and sent upriver. Then all is silence. Still, there is some truth in mentioning Rogers's name in connection to work at West Point during these years. Perhaps a future scholar will define his role more precisely.

Such frustrated labor as Rogers experienced at West Point was and remains the common lot of architects. Only the most fortunate will have more projects built than unbuilt. In April 1837 the Boston Common Council had solicited cost estimates for a new city hall, and a year later a call went out for proposals. On the evening of February 5, 1839, while still in New York, Rogers took pencil in hand and commenced to plan the building, continuing work on the project over several nights. Back in Boston on March 11, he called on Samuel A. Eliot, his former client at Tremont House and now mayor of the city, and showed him the drawings. Eliot said they looked expensive and asked for a cost estimate. (At West Point, as here and elsewhere, Rogers seems to have overdesigned the project, knowing it would be scaled back, rather than risk that a more suitable scheme would be reduced—a process often said to be a time-honored architect's trick.) Rogers again worked on the project when back in New York, and in April he returned to Boston, where Eliot appeared to like his design very much. In June the building committee recommended that it be accepted,[57] but in September the mayor asked for still another plan, which Rogers worked up in drawings and sent to Eliot's office on November 25. The project then vanishes from the diary just as a new mayor, Jonathan Chapman, took office in December, promising to reduce the city's debt. Although land had been purchased for the building, no money would be forthcoming for a new city hall. That would have to wait until 1860, when Gridley J. F. Bryant and Arthur Gilman designed the Second Empire building on School Street that is now called Old City Hall. Meanwhile, the city converted the former Suffolk County courthouse into its administrative headquarters and moved there in 1841.

While engaged in these projects, Rogers received a commission for a fence to be built at the Old Granary Burying Ground in Boston, between Peter Banner's Park Street Church and Rogers's own Tremont House. It was a small project that seems to have taken a great deal of time. We first hear of a plan on May 3, 1839, and Rogers, always prompt, sent the drawings to Andrew E. Belknap in Boston eleven days later. In August, Belknap asked for another design, followed by an estimate in October. Rogers signed the contract in Boston on November 11; two weeks later he explained his design to Solomon Willard, and two days after that he went with a stoneworker to measure the site. The next month he was still drawing or redrawing the fence. In April of the next year, Belknap introduced him to Chapman, the new mayor, and he struck an agreement "to pay some money on account of stonework" on the fence, funds that quickly went to Willard in Quincy. Rogers was back at the quarry in June to discuss the fence with Willard, and in July he examined work at the site and saw a model for either the piers or the gateway. By September 11, he could record that the "cornice" of the gateway was to be finished in ten days. But Rogers had begun to plan his monumental Merchants' Exchange for State Street in Boston and his interest in the fence must have noticeably diminished, for we hear no more about it. The *Boston Morning Post* for October 13, 1840, reported the project completed.

The Old Granary's iron fence, its corner piers, and its gateway still exist, perhaps the only remaining evidence we have, excepting the altered Commercial Wharf and part of the attributed Custom House Block, of Rogers's contribution to the urban fabric of early nineteenth-century Boston (see Fig. 8). The fence is of cast iron and rests on a retaining wall composed of large slabs of granite, including one some thirty-three feet long. For the stonework piers and gateway, he chose Egyptian forms as appropriate to funereal architecture. In that choice, he followed the lead of other examples of the Egyptian Revival style that flourished in the United States from the 1820s through the 1840s, given impetus by Napoleon's 1789 march up the Nile and the many publications that emerged from this event after 1809.[58] The stonework is carved with appropriate Egyptian devices, which the *Morning Post* thought "in excellent keeping" and appropriate for a graveyard, although the paper criticized the entrance gate as out of proportion to the rest. The blocky corner piers bear high-relief images of *Tempus Fugit,* the winged hourglass, while the main gate, made of two granite piers holding up an architrave with cavetto cornice, displays upside-down torches on its flanks and the winged orb above. Preliminary drawings show that the architect originally thought of paired obelisks flanking the gate and a winged eye of Horus on the architrave. (Fig. 28) Indeed, Rogers had displayed a ten-foot obelisk cut from the Graniteville Quarry on Staten Island (an operation in which he had invested) at the Twelfth Annual Fair of the American Institute, held at Niblo's Garden in New York in October 1839.[59] The preliminary granary drawings also show an iron fence ornamented with decidedly classical anthemia instead of the inverted torches that ultimately appeared.

About a year after finishing the Old Granary enclosure, Rogers again turned a small amount of his divided attention to the same sort of assignment in Newport, Rhode Island, for the Jewish cemetery there. Funding for the work came from Judah Touro, a Newport-born New Orleans philanthropist. Once more, Egypt provided the forms. On February 15, 1840, and for days afterward, an advertisement appeared in the *Newport Mercury* requesting proposals for itemized cut granite and mason's work for the fence posts as well as separate proposals for cut granite for an Egyptian portal, or gateway, including pedestals, thirteen-foot-long

28. Old Granary Burying Ground, Boston, Massachusetts. Preliminary design for entrance gateway and fence, 1839. Ink and wash. Boston Public Works Department.

tapered piers, and lintel, all dimensions minutely specified. Also sought were separate proposals for two "Thebian obelisks" with tapered shafts fifteen and a half feet tall.[60] To view the working plan and elevation, surely from Rogers's hand, as were the published specifications, responders were directed to the store of Isaac Gould & Son, a prominent tailor on Thames Street. In Boston on September 1, 1841, Rogers "made a bargain" with Touro's representative to build the fence from his design for $11,290. In the days following, he reworked drawings and drafted the contract, but near the end of December he was still figuring the plans. On May 19, 1842, the *Herald of the Times* of Newport could report that work had just commenced, that Rogers had prepared the materials (meaning, presumably, he had the granite blocks extracted by Willard at Quincy and dressed there) during the winter, and that the fence would be complete in about two months. (Fig. 29)

Rogers did supervise at the Newport site, but he also had Isaac Gould and his son Nathan to keep an eye on the work. Descendants of Daniel Gould, early settler of the town and a Quaker radical, the Goulds served as caretakers of Touro Cemetery. In 1854 Nathan Hammett Gould was named in Judah Touro's will as the heir of his deceased friend Isaac Gould, who died in 1853; he was given a handsome legacy and told that he "should continue to oversee the improvements in said Cemetery and direct the same."[61] The will was not read until Judah Touro's death

29. Jewish Cemetery gate, Providence, Rhode Island, 1840–42. Author photo, 2013.

in 1854, but the instructions merely formalized a longstanding arrangement—it is clear that Nathan was to step into his late father's position.

The Goulds and Rogerses likely first met over this commission. At the beginning of construction in May 1842, Rogers visited a Friends Meeting in Newport with the Goulds and spent an evening at their house, and the next day he had Isaac measure him for a coat. In June Rogers borrowed $50 from the tailor. As work unfolded, Rogers's visits to Newport, sometimes accompanied by his wife, Emily, drew the two families together. During 1843 and 1844 Nathan and Rogers's daughter Emily Jane exchanged visits between Newport and Boston or Marshfield. Rogers sketched a design for the front of the Goulds' shop in January 1845, and later that year Nathan and Emily Jane were married.

The Newport cemetery's gateway is a near copy of the one in Boston, with its winged orb above the opening and upside-down torches on its piers, but minor differences (in the carved torches and elsewhere) render the Newport gate slightly more elegant. The iron fence is a variation of the one in Boston, but its granite posts take the form of the obelisk. As in Boston, the Theban obelisks never materialized near the gateway. Rogers paid Voelckers $6 in early August 1842 for "perspectives of tombs and monuments for the Touro Family," then hired a man to build an iron fence around them. Rogers designed the obelisk for Judah Touro in 1855.

With work at the Jewish cemetery winding down and the enclosure of the family area under way, Rogers could concentrate on a fence for the synagogue down the street, also a gift of Judah Touro. Because the building is a fine example of Georgian classicism, Rogers took his cue for the gateway not from Egypt but from Peter Harrison's round-arched pedimented portico. His semicircular archway is set within piers capped by an inscribed lintel and pediment, but it is inert and lacks the ineffable presence of the cemetery gate. Rather than obelisks for the posts holding up the spear-shaped ironwork of the fence, Rogers drew simple tapered square ones with flared caps. By September 1842 his men were pulling away the old fence, and by November he could declare the work nearly complete. By November 10 he had received $2,114.41 for the project "in full of all demands."

Other than the gateways in Boston and Newport, Rogers attempted at least two other Egyptian-style projects during his New York period. In 1831 Mount Auburn Cemetery in Cambridge, under the direction of its founder, Dr. Jacob Bigelow, had erected a large wooden Egyptian-style gatehouse from Bigelow's design, and rebuilt it in granite in 1842. In August of that year Rogers obtained a plan of the structure from Willard, who supplied the granite for the rebuilding, with the thought of making a design "of the same proportion." The project occupied that month, with a trip to Cambridge to see the gate, a sketch and a developed design by Rogers, drawings by Voelckers, and an "estimate of cost of gateway at Mount Auburn as per plan $10,500." Yet it is unclear whether he was working for the cemetery or himself. Rogers was a man full of energy, and at times, it seems, he labored at his drafting boards on projects that were not commissions. The Mount Auburn project occurred during a slow period in his practice and may have been just an exercise in the use of Egyptian forms for a building larger than the two cemetery gates. Still, like Richard Delafield at West Point, Bigelow, an amateur architect, was not above requesting drawings for buildings at Mount Auburn and then ignoring them in favor of his own designs. He seems to have done just that two years later with the competition for the cemetery chapel. Rogers went so far as to estimate the cost of his design, so he must have had a concrete reason for doing so. As seems to have happened with John Jacob Astor's library and at West Point, perhaps he was being used.

Rogers's other Egyptian project in Boston came in early February 1843, when he drew an Egyptian front for the Lowell lecture room he designed for Mayor Martin Brimmer, although he quickly changed to a Grecian elevation (the project was unrealized). Although no further mention of such exotic work appears in the diaries, Rogers did continue to show interest in the style. In February 1838 he had attended lectures on the monuments of ancient Egypt given by James Silk Buckingham at the Chatham Street Chapel in New York[62] and went to see Frederick Catherwood's *Panorama of Thebes* in April of the next year. It was also during this time that he wanted to consult a "large volume on Egypt" in his library, which could have been any number of books on the architecture of the Nile. He also paid for two courses of lectures on Egyptian architecture and hieroglyphics, given by George Robins Gliddon from October into December 1844, and found them very good;[63] in Cincinnati in fall of 1851 he was reading a book on the pyramids.

One of Rogers's last New York projects of these years began on October 25, 1841, when he was summoned by Henry C. Murphy, the mayor of Brooklyn. Murphy was contemplating a new city hall using "old materials of the building commenced some years ago," and the next day he lent the architect "old plans to copy." The old materials could only have been the foundation of the building designed by Calvin Pollard in 1835, and the old plans by Pollard as well, for it had never reached much aboveground. Throughout the next month, Rogers worked on his design. In the new year, he spent money for cotton cloth for his drawings and for a picture frame to show off his elevation, but on January 11, 1842, he learned that "they had about made up their minds to take Upjohn's plan," and he dropped the matter. In the end, Richard Upjohn's project, like Pollard's, was not built. Pollard revised his earlier scheme in late January, and what is now the Brooklyn Borough Hall, a marble Grecian building with a hexastyle Ionic portico, was erected under the supervision of Gamaliel King between 1845 and 1848.[64]

Business occupied the bulk of Rogers's time in New York, as elsewhere during his busy life, but he did occasionally take time to relax. He visited the *Great Western*, I. K. Brunel's paddle-wheel steamship designed to cross the Atlantic in record speed, when it arrived from its maiden voyage in April 1838. Despite the ship having caught fire coming over, injuring Brunel, Rogers was much pleased. "Beautiful work and a very fine vessel," he wrote. In April 1840 he went to see Monsieur Bihin, the Belgian Giant, who at eight feet six inches was the well-proportioned tallest and strongest man in the world, finding him "a very pleasant appearing gentleman." In July he paid six cents "for looking at a shark." He does not say where. He attended theatricals, including a performance by the Irish comedic actor Tyrone Power in November. One day in Philadelphia he looked at Girard College, the Fairmount Waterworks, and the fair of the Franklin Institute; he also went to the theater and ended with a "splendid collation" back at the institute, furnished by the fair's committee. On trips to Richmond, he caught George Frederick Cooke in "Richard the Third" and Edwin Forrest's "Richelieu; or, the Conspiracy!" and "Metamora; or, the Last of the Wampanoags." In July 1841 he had his head examined by a phrenologist, who found it "for the most part very correct."

In the 1830s Rogers moved his office to New York, where he produced some of the canonical monuments of the Grecian Revival in America: Astor House, the Merchants' Exchange, and the Middle Reformed Dutch Church. From that office he also designed major buildings in the South, and he continued to produce impressive designs for New England. Already in this era, such conspicuous success brought with it commercial endorsements—for Peel's Protractors, Hoffman's Cement, Patent Beam Derricks, American Crown Window Glass, Sumner & Stevens's Galvanized Tinned Iron Plates, and so on. Boston was to reclaim Rogers, intermittently at first and then more completely after seven years in Manhattan, recalling him to create the city's own Merchants' Exchange. Then, after a few more years and a brief stop back in New York, the West came calling.

CHAPTER

3

Boston and New York
1841–1848

IN THE LATE 1830s and early 1840s, and probably earlier, Rogers employed a few assistants in his office, including William Henry Bayless, who appears in diary entries from mid-April 1838 to mid-January 1841. His uncle was the artist Thomas Cole, who called on Rogers at the early date because he "wished more compensation" for his nephew. In late May, Cole noted in a letter that Bayless had studied with Ithiel Town and was "now with Mr. Rogers who is erecting our great exchange."[1] Thereafter Bayless received sporadic payments from Rogers, as if he were called in when the drafting schedule became tight. He worked on the drawings for the New York Merchants' Exchange and the Ohio statehouse, for example, and on January 20, 1840, Bayless and another draftsman, a "Mr. Schmidt," worked on framing plans for the Richmond Hotel in Virginia. On January 22, 1841, Bayless received $100, the "balance due him for services rendered as per agreement," and then disappears from the diary. He remained in New York and held the position of professor of perspective at the National Academy of Design from 1844 to about 1852 while also practicing architecture in Cincinnati from 1849 to 1856.[2] According to the *Daily Ohio Statesman* for February 9, 1850, he entered the competition for the Hamilton County courthouse, made it to the final round of judging, and lost the commission to Rogers. Few of his buildings are known.

Schmidt is probably Frederick Schmidt, a New York architect who for a time shared a street address with Rogers. He was engaged on January 15, 1839, to work for $20 a week for one year. He drafted on various jobs until November 1841, but he too seems to have opted not to follow Rogers to Boston when the latter returned to supervise construction of the exchange building there. Schmidt's final payment came early in July 1842. In June 1841 Rogers contacted a third man, Mr. Shelden, who is also not further identified but was perhaps Richard A. Shelden, a New York architect listed in city directories from 1847 to 1851. Rogers proposed that he "work on plans of my bridge for lithographing to be put in a pamphlet giving description [of it] . . . in all its details. Agreed to give . . . [him] $500 per year and 10% of all money received for plans which I should have to draw. He agreed to think of it." Whether that happened we do not know, although Shelden may have produced the drawings for Rogers's patent for a cylindrical lattice bridge that was granted on November 10, 1841. Rogers did pay him $100 on June 15, "on account of drawing," and he was still with the firm in early 1842 but received payment "in full" in April.

The two most important assistants, men who spanned the years of work in New York and Boston, were Theodore Voelckers and Theodore Washburn. Rogers hired the twenty-five-year-old German-born Voelckers in November 1840 at $14 week, "as long as I should like him and have anything for him to do." By January, Voelckers had agreed to work for a reduced $10 a week and was soon producing perspective renderings. He appeared among the architects listed in the Boston directory and is named as a witness on Rogers's 1841 bridge patent. That year and the next he worked on drawings for the Boston Merchants' Exchange and joined in the celebration on the laying of the first stone. He regularly appears in the diary as draftsman on various projects: finished plans for Theodore Lyman, a perspective of the Touro family tombs in Newport, and so on. (Rogers seems to have rarely drawn his own perspectives.) Personally, Voelckers was leading a life of woe. Rogers signed bail bonds for him in April 1841 and August 1842, and in that year both his young daughter and his wife died. Rogers last mentions him on March 16, 1843. A gap in the diary prohibits us from knowing under what circumstances Voelckers left the office, but he went on to produce notable buildings around Massachusetts until his death in 1879.[3]

With Bayless, Voelckers, Schmidt, and Shelden busy drafting in the office at various dates in the early 1840s, Washburn seems to have been more of an all-around general helper to Rogers in the construction of the Boston Merchants' Exchange: a drafter of contracts, stand-in superintendent, handler of accounts, and legman. The brother of the housewright Jeremiah and the architect William, Theodore was the Whig boss of Boston's sixth ward.[4] He first appears in the diary as simply "Mr. Washburn" in the fall of 1840. In December of that year Rogers entered into an agreement with him "to do the work of the building of the Exchange together, Mr. Washburn to receive for his part of the proceeds 2/5, and I to receive 3/5, Mr. Washburn to give all the attention which is required." In describing the "New Exchange" on its completion, an August 26, 1842, article in the *Liberator* gave great credit to "Mr. Rogers, the architect, for his chaste designs, classic and elegant taste; and to Mr. Theodore Washington, the associate of the architect, for the manner in which he has forwarded the work."[5]

The two men visited various ward rooms together in November 1840 "to hear the speaking," as Rogers wrote in his only mention of an interest in local politics, and they socialized much together over the next couple years. Washburn vacationed with the Rogers family at Hampton Beach in the summer of 1842. It must have been particularly hurtful, then, when Rogers tried to talk to him that fall about "his balance [of Exchange accounts] which he had overdrawn . . . [and] used to his own affairs," but "he could or would not give anything like satisfaction." On the advice of Andrew Eliot Belknap and others, Rogers decided to "commence a suit against him to recover the money . . . or to make him give me security for the balance." In December, Rogers noted that Washburn had left, and thereafter he spent days checking the exchange documents, had copies made of his dealings with his assistant, and found Washburn's account "a curiosity, indeed absurd in the extreme." The same gap in the diary that leaves us in the dark about Voelckers's departure has us wondering about Washburn's as well, just as he, Rogers, and financial referees were dancing around one another. A legal notice in the *Boston Daily Atlas* of February 5, 1844, named him as a deceased member of the firm of J. Washburn & Brothers. Although his brother William seems never to have worked directly for Rogers, he too went on to become an important local hotel designer.

While work progressed on the Merchants' Exchange in New York, Rogers received the commission to design a building of the same type in Boston and began bouncing back and forth between the two cities, even as he continued with the Exchange Hotel and a bank in Richmond as well as lesser commissions along the Eastern Seaboard. His range of movement in this period stretched from Maine to Virginia, just as later in his career it would extend from Chicago to New Orleans. How he kept it all straight is a wonder, although of course the diary entries helped. He not only drew but also supervised the construction of these huge buildings, which entailed frequent trips to inspect worksites and the quarries at Quincy, where he conferred with Solomon Willard about the immense stones extracted from the ledge. It is inaccurate to say that Rogers left Willard behind when he struck out on his own in 1825, for the latter's importance to the success of Rogers's early triumphs equaled his own, something that Willard's biographer expressed rather gently. In addition to Rogers's many trips to Quincy, the biographer wrote, Willard made seven or eight visits to New York during construction of the exchange there "and no doubt gave Mr. Rogers much valuable assistance in his plans."[6]

In a way, Rogers's career anticipated those of twentieth-century American architects such as Charles Moore, who spent their lives flitting among distant jobs via airplane, although his mode of travel was wagon, horseback, carriage, omnibus, gig, stagecoach, buggy, skiff, and, later, the new "train of cars" and the steamboat. As an indication of the crowded peripatetic life Rogers led in his most active years, the diary records seventeen trips from New York to Boston, including Quincy, and eight from New York to Richmond in a single year, from the beginning of drawings for the Boston Merchant's Exchange and the laying of its cornerstone. In addition, he had on the boards or was concerned about, discussing, sketching, or supervising miscellaneous projects, including work at John Jacob Astor's houses; selection of the site for a library for Astor and sketching a design for it; the Old Granary Burying Ground fence in Boston and those for the Touro Cemetery and the synagogue in Newport; a design for the Harlem aqueduct; finishing the Bunker Hill Monument; plans for a bridge to span the Mississippi; a grave marker for a Mr. Lee, intended for Mount Auburn Cemetery; a model of a cylindrical bridge for exhibition at Niblo's Garden in New York (for which he received a patent); the erection of a full-size version of that bridge between Faneuil Hall and Quincy Market in Boston; a house for a Mr. Duval in Virginia; a monument to John Thornton Kirkland, former president of Harvard, that took the form of a cenotaph inscribed with a Tudor arch, set atop Harvard Hill at Mount Auburn;[7] drawings of a depot for the Western Railway in Boston, a building erected in 1841, perhaps after his design; houses for Horace L. Kent and a Mr. Dudley in Richmond; a design for an orphan asylum for girls, also in Richmond; and a project for a house in Brookline for Theodore Lyman. Not all came to fruition, but each took up Rogers's time and energy. Those that count most or can be identified—built or not—will be discussed in this chapter.

To focus more closely on Rogers's itinerant existence, we can specify his travels during a period of little more than one month in 1840. His career counted less draining stretches, but it had busier ones as well. On August 1, Rogers returned to New York from Massachusetts. On the tenth he went back to Boston by steamer. On the thirteenth he was again in New York. On the twenty-second he again traveled to Boston and then to Quincy by horse and gig the next day. On the twenty-fifth he stopped briefly in New York, left the next day via sleeper car for Philadelphia and then Baltimore, took a steamer to Washington, a stagecoach to Fredericksburg, and on to Richmond, having survived a major train wreck on the last leg. Not only was rail travel "on the cars" of the period uncomfortable and sooty, it was frequently dangerous as well. A timber left on the track by careless workmen caused the accident, which, according to the diary, derailed the engine, tender, and baggage car.[8] The presence of a high bank on either side of the tracks prevented the passenger cars from falling over, thus avoiding injury for most travelers. After three days in Virginia, Rogers repeated the trip back to Philadelphia. September 1 saw him again in New York, where he found his home stripped of all furniture except the beds, because of a mistaken sheriff's order. This incident occasioned one of the few sustained outbursts of anger in the otherwise even-tempered diary, so heartfelt that his usually serviceable (if not always perfect) grammar became fractured: "This is human nature," he wrote, "treacherous and villainous in the extreme, when coming as it does from those who use soft and friendly words at your face and behind you conduct [themselves] so as to wound the most hardened heart. I would have charity for all, but trials like this is calculated to cheat her [Charity, presumably] of her due, and harden the kindest feeling of man from their natural course and lead the mind to doubt the good to be derived from those heavenly feelings." Negotiations quickly corrected the error, but when returned, the furniture showed signs of rough handling.

Rogers battled other problems occasioned by life on the road. In January 1841 he encountered a form of corporate highway robbery. According to a notice published in the *Baltimore Sun* (but unmentioned in the diary), while aboard a stagecoach en route from Fredericksburg to Washington, a distance of some thirty-five miles over a passable road, he and his fellow travelers were "compelled to remain over night, in a small tavern, with barely half the accommodation required," despite that only twenty-five miles remained. To continue that night, they were told they would each have to pay $1, in addition to the fare, bringing the cost of the sixty-mile trip to $7. Thirteen gentlemen, including Rogers, signed and published a complaint of the "delay and imposition" to their journey caused by the management of the Stockton, Falls & Co.'s Line.[9] Given the conditions of the inns of the time along such a route, one can imagine the men piled into two, at most three, beds, trying to rest after a long day on the road. And Rogers having created luxury hotels! Strangers sharing beds on the road was common, but on another occasion in September 1842, Rogers declined to do so, stating that it was against his principles.

Rogers did occasionally find time to relax and, very occasionally, reflect. He often went to theater wherever he worked, and he sometimes attended balls. In New York on New Year's Day 1841, he went to see Mrs. W. G. Jones, a celebrated actress, in the role of Pauline in Bulwer-Lytton's popular five-act melodrama "The Lady of Lyons." At the end of March he dined at Barnum's Hotel in Baltimore and then climbed to the top of that city's Washington Monument, the design of Robert Mills, and "had a fine view," attending theater later in the evening.[10] Back in Boston he went to his Masonic Temple to hear George Vandenhoff read from the different poets as part of his series of lectures on elocution, then caught Vandenhoff's wife's version of Pauline in "The Lady of Lyons," and finally saw the two of them in "King John" and the last act of "The Merchant of Venice." He took Emily and daughter Cornelia to see the celebrated German ballerina Fanny Elssler, returning alone to see "Fanny" twice more during her whirlwind tour of the United States that year. In December in Boston he took in Dion Boucicault's jolly five-act romp "London Assurance," first produced abroad just six months earlier. One August day in 1842 he went bathing with friends at Coney Island. And at the end of that year he again saw Vandenhoff act and caught a performance by Madame Céline Céleste, the celebrated French dancer.

All this activity was squeezed into the otherwise busy practice of architect and builder. Record of Rogers's work on a project for the Boston Merchants' Exchange entered the diary on August 4, 1840. The need for an exchange had long been recognized, a charter from the state secured, stock issued, and a suitable site on State Street, in the heart of the financial district, had become available with the removal of the State Bank. According to the *Boston Evening Post* for October 31, the program called for, in addition to the stock exchange, "a variety of offices for Banking, Insurance, Railroad, and other institutions, together with numerous lodging rooms, and a large Restaurateur . . . where permanent and transient residents can enjoy comfortable board, at reasonable rates, in the very centre of business." It was to be the commercial equivalent of the more social Tremont House of just over a decade earlier and, like it, express the Whig program of "internal improvements," here represented by the railroads. Moreover, it was said, at an anticipated return of eight percent on investment based on the record of the New York exchange, one had "every reason to suppose" it "would prove . . . profitable to its stockholders."

A week after Rogers recorded the existence of the Boston exchange commission, he traveled there to present drawings and an estimate to the broker Samuel Henshaw, representing the building committee. Ten days later, he was called back to Boston from New York and given instructions to alter the scheme. He noted that a Boston paper had published a description of the plans and an estimate of $165,000. Indeed, the *Post* article announcing the project named the architect but cited the estimate, with land, as $310,000. Rogers's building, it reported, would create "ample and convenient rooms for half a dozen insurance offices, for three banks, for the Chamber of Commerce, for several railroad companies, and numerous offices for business men—together with a spacious saloon for an eating house, drawings rooms, and many sleeping apartments and lastly a grand area for an Exchange." The plans had not yet been finalized, however. Discussions continued through November between the architect and the committee, which included Andrew Eliot Belknap, whom Rogers knew well from the Tremont House and other Boston ventures. Redraft followed redraft. At a meeting early in December, Robert G. Shaw, president of the Exchange Company and chairman of the directors, suggested that Rogers "dispense [with] the pedestals [piers?] and make the front lower." This the architect did that evening "by cutting the plans and shifting the door up and dispensing with the pedestals," which, he thought, "makes a material improvement in appearance." The diaries are salted with disagreements with clients, builders, workmen, and so on, but this note suggests that Rogers was humble enough to recognize an improvement wherever it originated.

At this point, December 9, it became apparent that Rogers had competition for the commission from none other than his estranged partner, Richard Bond. Although Bond received two votes from committee members, Rogers's project carried the day. The pro-Bond board members—"crooked minds," Rogers called them—continued to cause trouble for the architect, but he thought "they will be made straight before the building is complete." An agreement to erect the approved design was signed on December 12, although the contract came only in March 1841.

Work on the preliminary drawings for the building continued in New York through December 1840 and into January 1841. Rogers declared them complete on February 2 and took them to Boston, where they were approved by the committee, although as usual he records making further alterations over the next several months. At one meeting, for example, the committee voted "to vault all the stories of the front section . . . on State Street," a change that certainly required new drawings. Rogers proceeded to discuss stone and stonework with Willard and others, seeking estimates, and continued to discuss the drawings and arrangements for materials with committee members, adjusting details slightly as needed. Rogers then tried to lay down the law about who was to give instructions to the workmen, stating that the company's building committee needed to work through him and not directly with the workers, but, he concluded, "it has been otherwise to a great extent and I have had to suffer by their mistakes." An architect's control over a building site had not been fully established by 1840. At noon on April 17, 1841, workmen "laid the first stone in the center of the front trench on State Street . . . after which [Rogers] took a bottle of champagne wine" with his assistants. Thomas Handasyd Perkins, another merchant of great importance in Rogers's early career, spoke at the laying of the cornerstone on August 2.[11] The building opened on May 1, 1843. According to Robert G. Shaw, the speaker at that event, the architect "with exemplary fidelity and dispatch . . . delivered . . . the building finished according to contract and to our entire satisfaction."[12]

Simultaneously under construction in Boston was the federal customhouse, the design of Ammi B. Young, with whom Rogers was well acquainted. Young offered the services of his local drafting staff in preparing the working drawings for the Merchants' Exchange, a gesture that Rogers thought "friendly and generous." Rogers was never to head a big office, and he took advantage of the offer, paying Hammatt Billings, who was then near the end of his stay in Young's office, for twenty-four days' "service copying plans" of the exchange. Billings had drawn the perspective view of Rogers's New York exchange, but it was Voelckers who produced the impressive image of Rogers's Boston building within its environment, a view lithographed by B. W. Thayer & Co. in 1842. (Fig. 30) It shows, rather erroneously, State Street looking like an urban square commanded by the building. As Billings had in his New York view, Voelckers enhanced the dimensions of the narrow street and enlivened it with popular activity: a newsboy selling papers, a person with a copy of the *Transcript* under one arm, an African American chimney sweep who peers out at the viewer, many conversing businessmen, a yapping dog, two or three escorted women, a one-horse shay, and, in the center, a Harden &

Co. dray piled with goods on which rides a box labeled "LRogers Archit," another "I.R./Bost," a third "T.V.," and a fourth "Henshaw/Boston." Voelckers swept the street clean of horse droppings, but a fellow smack in the center appears to be urinating. In Voelckers's view as well as in vintage photographs, Rogers's majestic building acted as backdrop to all this urban animation, what Jane Jacobs later called the "ballet of the street." The fictive templar facades of the ambient buildings, shown on the side street to the right, rival in severity some of the projects signed by A. J. Davis.

Although the Boston exchange boasted an impressive interior (for a while Rogers would occupy a fourth-floor office), including an imposing main hall, once again the architect's major civic effort was to be found in the seventy-one-foot-wide temple front, the grandest on the south side of State Street along the stretch from the Old State House toward the wharves.[13] (see Frontispiece) Rogers gave the schema a fresh interpretation. He planned a tetrastyle facade of fluted colossal piers—rather than the usual columns—standing between antae, with the central intercolumniation, that of the entrance, slightly wider than those on the flanks. The squared capitals of an anthemion set within volutes were a variation of the canonical Corinthian order. The antae were articulated into paired, slender pilasters. An architrave and a low pediment, both unornamented, topped the

30. Merchants' Exchange, Boston, 1840–43. View on State Street. Drawn by Theodore Voelckers; lithography by B. W. Thayer & Company, 1842. Boston Athenaeum.

four-story facade. Over the two-story central entrance was a high-relief emblem of commerce and navigation, appropriate for a mercantile center in an international seaport; it featured a globe topped by an eagle, resting on crossed cornucopias and surrounded by cargo packages, Neptune's trident, Mercury's caduceus, and other suggestive devices. Who designed this work of art is not remembered. It was a rather loosely tossed together composition and did not please the dyspeptic Arthur D. Gilman, whose scathing 1844 review dismantled the building piece by piece, including the relief. The architect, he wrote, "must, in sooth, be a superstitious mortal, who could put his faith in such an uncouth enormity."[14] But as a fellow critic said, Gilman "thinks a lofty, sarcastic tone may ride him safely over all. He has, no doubt, learned to believe ridicule his *forte*."[15]

Gilman failed to mention, but it was the magnitude of the piers and antae that truly amazed. They formed the crowning glory of the Boston Granite Style. At nearly forty-two feet tall and weighing fifty-five tons, the monoliths exceeded not only those for the Merchants' Exchange in New York but also, it was popularly said, the ones quarried when the pharaohs ruled Egypt. (For a comparative example from antiquity, look to the Pantheon in Rome, whose portico columns are granite monoliths that soar forty-five feet.) Stones for the Boston exchange were split from the ledge in Quincy during the spring and summer of 1841. On July 28 Rogers made a trip to inspect the dressing of three piers and the stone for the other three, "one to be split out this week." There was much discussion with Willard and others about quarrying, costs, and shipping the stones to Boston. Their arrival by wagon and oxen from the schooners starting in mid-September excited "a good deal of notice," including the vandalism of the riggers' ropes by "some villain, no doubt from jealousy." After lengthy onsite preparation, the colossi were hoisted into place one by one using a derrick that Rogers said he devised after studying the one used by Young at the customhouse.[16] Despite such basic leverage, the work went up with surprising speed. The first of the piers took its upright place on September 23. "Had a hard day's work but all things safe," Rogers wrote. With the last of the piers standing on October 16, he dined at the Tremont House with Andrew Belknap and other friends. His matter-of-fact description of the realization of his design for the building's front belies enormous effort by many people. Although squeezed tightly by its neighbors, the facade dominated its block of State Street. It formed the crowning example of what Douglass Shand-Tucci characterized as the local "disinclination to separate design from construction, this insistence on the unity of the two," the result of "the slight differentiation made between the architect and the engineer."[17]

Rogers was indeed as much engineer as architect, as his designs for bridges attest. Many of his contemporaries, especially those in the Mid-Atlantic who descended from Benjamin Latrobe, were also gifted engineers, but Tucci put his finger on the difference between the Grecian works of fellow architects and the mature work of Rogers. Their designs usually proceeded from style learned in books, whereas, after his first few works, Rogers's designs essentially stemmed from what Frank Lloyd Wright called the "nature of materials." Even in the home of the "Granite Style," no other architect achieved the celebration of monumental granite architecture that Rogers realized in the facades of the New York and Boston exchanges. They were the culmination of his eastern work. When he shifted to the west, he continued to derive architecture from his own expressive use of materials, but those materials were altogether different.

The Merchants' Exchange in Boston stretched from State Street through to Lindall, all but its facade buried in adjacent structures. A description based on Voelckers's perspective, written before the building was finished, says that it was "crowned with an [octagonal two-stage] observatory, from which rises the staff of Mr. Parker's telegraph."[18] Rogers recorded sketching the "observatory and telegraph" on November 22, 1841, just two years after Samuel F. B. Morse and Alfred Vail patented the first practical telegraph based on electromagnets, and he finished the plan of the "cupola for [the] telegraph" three months later. That suspicion remained about the telegraph's reliability is suggested in Voelckers's view by the gentleman with spyglass perched precariously on the roof, as well as the traditional signal flags that flutter from atop the mast. They bear such labels as NEW YORK LAND MAIL, EASTERN MAIL, and so on. Although Rogers mentions the beginning of work on the cupola in June 1842, later images of the exchange fail to show this skyline feature.[19]

For the interior, Rogers specified a cast-iron structure and stone and iron staircases under a roof framed in wrought iron and covered with galvanized sheets, materials he now frequently used. (In this era of frequent and devastating fires, Rogers and others spent much time studying fireproof methods of building. Iron construction was considered the safest, and it took several urban conflagrations to show that, although iron did not burn, it would melt at high temperatures and lose structural strength.) A post office occupied part of the ground floor, which was vaulted throughout. Banking, insurance, brokerage, and business offices filled the front of the main floor above, and a hotel occupied the rear. The basement contained baths, and a telegraph office was nestled beneath the gable. The main indoor space, the eighty-foot-long Merchants' Exchange and Subscribers' Reading Room, sported eighteen twenty-foot Corinthian columns coated with *scagliola* imitating Sienese marble. Its central dome was lighted by a stained-glass skylight. A view that is said to be of the hall raises more questions than it answers, including the identity of the statue shown at the rear, perhaps of some Whig politician but unmentioned in available descriptions.[20] Once again a grumpy Gilman came down hard, writing that the room, "with its flat dome, its bright scagliola columns, its composed [plaster] capitals, its staring white walls, and its profusion of plaster ornaments, now cracked in every direction, presents a tawdry and miserable failure. Such things as these are not architecture, but frippery." Obviously he did not approve of *scagliola*. The next generation of the Boston Board of Trade must have agreed with him, for it remodeled, "and to some extent rebuilt," the interior in the early 1870s.[21]

The public viewed Rogers's building more favorably. The 1849 edition of John Hayward's *Gazetteer of Massachusetts* gave "great credit . . . to Mr. Rogers, the architect and contractor, for his chaste designs, classic and elegant taste, and for the manner in which he forwarded the work." In assessing Rogers's career, it is worth repeating that the fully conceived professional architect, a person largely separate from the physical process of building, was not yet the norm in the United States. Many times, Rogers ran what we might call a design-build office, rather than operating as a disinterested third party representing the client in dealings with a builder, which is the role of the modern architect as eventually defined by the American Institute of Architects. The "contractor" designation in Hayward's description should also be noted by those who seek the origins of general contracting in this country.

Arthur Gilman's printed attacks did not go unanswered, if only in the privacy of Rogers's diary. Six months after Gilman's article appeared, in October 1844, Rogers attended a couple lectures by the architect and critic that he found to be "about the same old story on architecture finding fault with everything and suggesting nothing which can remedy the evil." He also wrote that he "did not like his views on architecture," that the lectures were "very dry, only giving the history as he read it." That is about as critical as Rogers ever got, and he continued to attend Gilman's lectures the following month. He also worked on improvements to the Boston exchange in 1854, while living in Cincinnati.

Rogers seems to have added one more building to State Street during this period (and drafted another at State and Congress Streets in 1845). He has been credited by several authors from various periods with the stringent bowed front of the nearby Brazer's Building of 1842, located at the southwest corner of State and Devonshire Streets. (Fig. 31) The diary contains no mention of a building by this name, but it does record the existence of a "schedule of stone for a building" on this corner that was left by Mr. Lawrence, the man in charge of the stone-dressing operation at the state prison in Charlestown, where so many of the pieces of granite-style Boston were hammered by the inmates. The facade was monumental and impressive, a convex grid of heavy trabeated granite piers and spandrels infilled with windows and devoid of ornament—Rogers's most stripped-down work—but the building behind it was forgettable. Like some of the projects by A. J. Davis, this stark elevation captured the admiration of historians of the modern movement, such as Winston Weisman and Henry-Russell Hitchcock.[22] Ironically, this most austere of Boston Granite statements was replaced in 1894–97 by a richly ornamented, eleven-story tower from the office of Cass Gilbert. It was his first skyscraper.

31. Brazer's Building, Boston, Massachusetts, 1842. State Street front. *Boston Almanac,* 1856. Courtesy Historic New England.

As usual, Rogers's time was not completely taken by supervising the construction of the Boston Merchants' Exchange.[23] Other local work that overlapped this primary task included a house for the Brookline estate of Theodore Lyman, the philanthropist, politician, author, and mayor of Boston in 1834–35. He proved to be a client difficult to satisfy, and the process was ultimately futile. The architect was called to Brookline in mid-August 1841 to receive instructions about planning a house, although real work on the drawings seems not to have begun until the following November. On August 26 Lyman called on Rogers, wanting a "new sketch of a house such as would be plain and convenient." Drawings took up Rogers's evenings until mid-December, when he finished the plans "and cut them out of board," perhaps meaning that he removed them from his drawing board or made a cardboard model. In mid-January 1842 he had another "finished" drawing, an "outline of elevation of principle front with a tower." By the end of the month, Lyman ordered working drawings. On February 8 the client arrived at the office, looked over the drawings, and approved them. He returned ten days later and approved them again. On February 26 Rogers paid Voelckers for finishing the plans (again), and there the project stopped. No more is heard of Lyman in Rogers's office, apparently because the client had switched architects to Richard Upjohn. Although Upjohn had moved to New York in 1839, sometime in 1842 or 1843 he sent Lyman a bill for the house: "2 Elevations 3 Ground Plans Plan of roof and a

Perspective view framed $35." His well-documented Italianate villa for Lyman no longer exists.[24]

The design and construction of architectural projects did not occupy all of Rogers's working hours. We know that by at least 1838 he had turned his active mind to the problem of designing bridges, and wherever he traveled he stopped to study the construction of new spans. The diary records his work on March 19 of that year on the design for a bridge to be used "for a railroad or common way," and the next day he finished a pencil sketch "for a cylinder bridge to be constructed either of iron or wood." This seems hardly suitable for a railroad or for long spans (although some of Ithiel Town's contemporary lattice bridges did serve trains and crossed respectable distances). In November 1840 Rogers wrote that he "made [the] first sketch for a bridge intended for the site laid out for a bridge at Grand Tower [a natural stone formation near Cape Girardeau, Missouri, once planned for a bridge support but never used] on the Mississippi River, it being 1,750 feet wide, designed after the plan of my cylinder bridge," but as far as we know the bridges he built to this design were much shorter and destined for foot traffic. In late February 1841 Rogers was called upon by "a gentleman from the West" who wanted to talk about a railroad bridge across the Mississippi, which he thought would be built with European financing. All this activity appears to have been part of the general discussion that began in 1839 about leaping that barrier to westward expansion (Charles Ellet Jr. proposed a suspension bridge at St. Louis also at this time), a desire fully realized after the Civil War by the erection of the existing steel arch bridge at St. Louis that is named after its innovative designer, James B. Eads. It also suggests that by the late 1830s, Rogers had a reputation as a man who studied the engineering of bridges with considerable spans. This too set him apart from his leading architectural colleagues, few of whom branched into purely technological problems. It did not profit him much, however. Whereas Town lived handsomely on revenue from his patented truss bridges, Rogers seems to have gained nothing from his three patents for truss and arch designs, and he saw the erection of only a few small examples of his cylindrical design.

Rogers never realized a trans-Mississippi bridge, but he did achieve smaller spans. By March 28, 1840, he had begun work on a model of his cylindrical scheme, and in October he showed it at the fair of the American Institute at Niblo's Garden in New York City. He walked away with a gold medal. The next year, for the triennial fair of the Massachusetts Charitable Mechanic Association held at Faneuil Hall and Quincy Market in Boston, Rogers, an association member, erected a full-size version to connect the two buildings. (It had been the fair's custom since 1837 to erect a temporary bridge at the second level to facilitate pedestrian traffic.[25]) In April Theodore (presumably) Washburn measured the seventy-six foot four inches to be spanned, and Rogers designed a bridge for the site and then fabricated the elements locally. The structure was built on the ground and hoisted into place, probably by derricks. When the fair opened in October, the bridge, "or more properly it might be called a tunnel," was described as a great curiosity.[26] "It is of a cylindrical form, ninety feet in length and ten feet in diameter. It is composed of narrow strips of board, crossing each other angularly, like lattice work, and resembling open basket work. These are riveted together, and the bridge . . . will easily sustain the weight of any number of persons. . . . It is one of the most ingenious pieces of mechanisms at the present exhibition." Surprisingly, no image of this marvel has come to light, but we can assume that it was a version of the "Spiral Cylinder Bridge" for wood or iron construction for which Rogers was granted U.S. Patent No. 2,347 on November 10, 1841. The designs on file at the Patent Office show a Grecian distyle-in-antis entrance pavilion at either end of the span, with fluted Doric columns flanking the foot- or carriageway. (Figs. 32–33) A footway with level flooring is set within the latticework cylinder, "the lattices formed by spiral braces" surrounding the core.[27]

The word *lattice* in his descriptions makes one wonder if Rogers had in mind improvements to Ithiel Town's famed lattice truss bridge, patented in 1820 and again, improved, in 1835. Like Town's, Rogers's design used standard-size simple connections, repeated over and over.[28] Frederick Spencer's 1839 portrait of Town now at Center Church, New Haven, shows him displaying a view of his bridge with Doric distyle-in-antis portals more elaborate than, but very similar to, what Rogers drew for his patent. If that image circulated, Rogers might have seen it. He had certainly met Town in these years: he mentions a "Mr. Town" in August 1840 (although it is unclear if it was Ithiel), bought six books from the architect/engineer in April 1841, and swapped books with him a few months later. What got Rogers thinking in this direction is unknown. He does not discuss the virtues of his design in his diary—why would he?—nor does he in the patent, but he might have thought that curving Town's lattice would stiffen it. In March 1841 Rogers sent plans and specifications, presumably for his cylindrical bridge, to Marseille, France. The purpose remains to be discovered, although it may have been related to the European financing for the railroad bridge across the Mississippi. In early 1844 Rogers was again planning a bridge for that year's triennial fair of the Mechanics Association, and in late March he gave an iron fabricator its dimensions. However, the bridge erected that year was designed by Thomas Willis Pratt and his father, Caleb.[29] Although best known for the Pratt Truss of the same year, for the fair they erected a suspension bridge (probably to Rogers's double disappointment in view of his declared dislike for that structural system).

In late December 1841 and January 1842 Rogers planned improvements to the Tremont House; these included a bridge to span the courtyard and was certainly another version of his patented design. He wrote on March 17 that the bridge was raised into position, and he found it "ample in strength and fitted well." By the next year, Lewis Dunbar Brodie, an eminent British civil engineer and former student of the famed I. K. Brunel, learned that "for some years" the Tremont had a bridge made up of "an elliptic tube of lattice or trellis work," seven to eight feet high and four and a half feet wide, "with a span of about 120 feet." He noted that "stiffening was provided by an iron bar along the spine and by the timber floor."[30] An English visitor to the hotel might have conveyed this information, but certainly the dimensions are incorrect. The plan published in William Eliot's

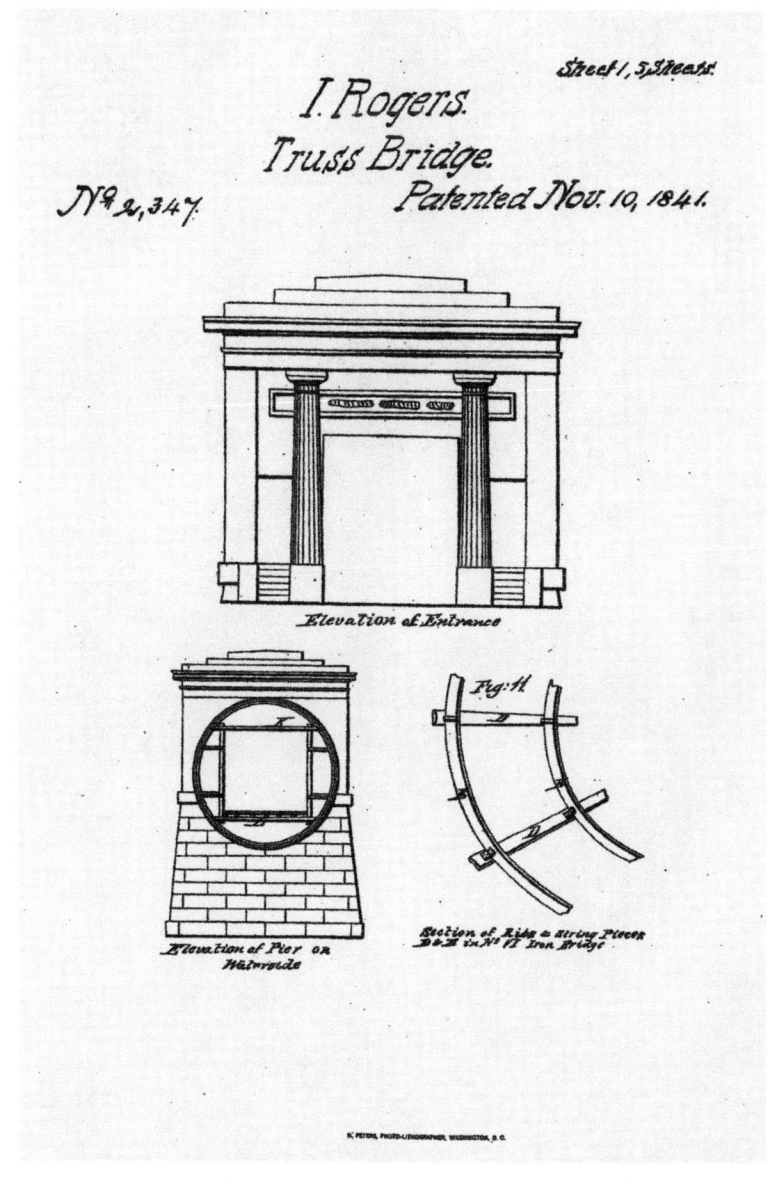

32. Cylindrical lattice truss bridge, 1838–41. Elevation, section, and detail of assemblage. Lithograph after drawing, from U.S. Patent No. 2,347, granted November 10, 1841.

104   CHAPTER 3

Description of Tremont House shows no such length possible in the courtyard. No coeval documentation reveals where the bridge was located, and the local press seems, surprisingly, not to have noticed it.[31] The only reasonable location would have been as a connection from the corridor off the rotunda to the privies, for the original plan shows a tortuous approach to the latter, around corners and up stairs. Although a bridge would seem to call too much attention to privies, such was the location of the bridge of the same design that Rogers installed at the Burnet

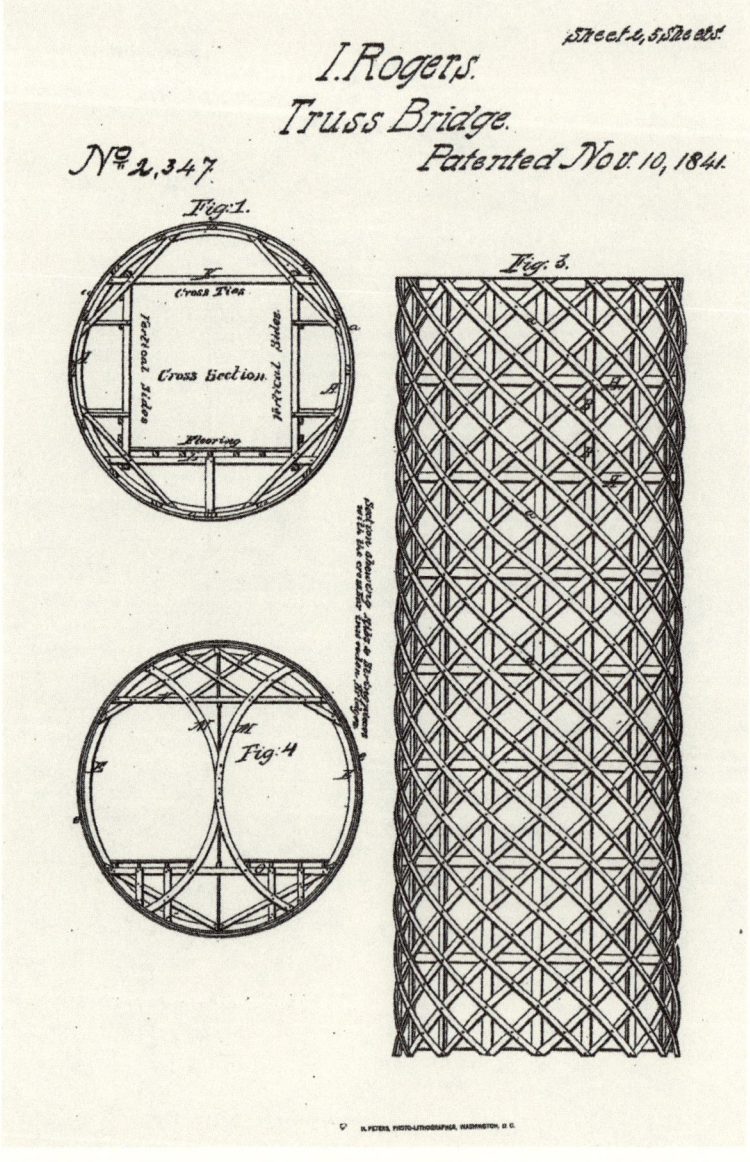

33. Cylindrical lattice truss bridge, 1838–41. Elevation and sections of lattice cylinder. Lithograph after drawing, from U.S. Patent No. 2,347, granted November 10, 1841.

House in Cincinnati later in the decade, as well as at other hotels that came from his drafting board. The Burnet iron and canvas bridge did lead to outhouses on the edge of the courtyard, but again, no views of it are known. During the 1844–45 remodeling of the Tremont House, Rogers apparently adjusted the bridge, without noting where it was.

It was during this period that Rogers shared with many others a concern for the fate of the Bunker Hill Monument. Although there was confusion at first whether the pillar had been designed by Robert Mills or Solomon Willard, it was the latter's creation and he supervised its erection.[32] The long process began in 1823, but according to Willard's own testimony, the final design was not determined until early July 1825. Plans and models were exhibited for the men in the granite business, but no proposals were forthcoming, so the Bunker Hill Monument Association acquired its own quarry in Quincy, and work commenced under Willard's direction in 1827. The supply of money quickly ran out, however, and beginning in 1829 activity ceased for several years. In 1840, when only a stump stood at the site, and with many convinced that the monument would never be finished, a group of wealthy civic-minded men, including Boston's Amos Lawrence and New Orleans's Judah Touro, came forward with funds and work recommenced. During the next few years, the monument is very much in evidence in the pages of Rogers's diary.

On September 10, 1840, the architect attended the Whig convention held on Bunker Hill, and there beheld "the grandest sight" he had ever seen: "People by the acre . . . and all of them exhibiting the most enthusiastic good feeling toward each other, and not an angry word" did he hear. But standing at the foot of the truncated monument, he and others in the crowd must have longed for its completion. In Quincy the next day to inspect stone for the Merchants' Exchange, Rogers talked to Willard and found him discouraged, "inclined not to do anymore about the finishing of it." Rogers "tried to persuade him to go on, offered to contract for it and let him go on and finish it in his own way, if he would not give it up. Willard [seemed] rather favorably inclined to the proposition" and gave encouragement that he would do so if Rogers could sign a contract for the stonework. Later that month Rogers received a letter in New York from James S. Savage, a Boston builder who early on had worked on the monument as well as the New York Merchants' Exchange, asking him to return to Boston "and endeavor to induce Mr. Willard to take hold of the work and complete it." Although Savage and Rogers then proposed to contract with Willard, in the next month the three men were still discussing "the best mode of conducting the completion of the Monument." With Willard and Rogers preoccupied with other projects, to say nothing of Rogers's roaming between Massachusetts, New York, and Virginia during the next months, nothing more is heard of Bunker Hill in the diary until early February 1841, when architect and builder talked about its progress. In early November of the previous year, Savage alone had been awarded a stonework contract for $43,800 to complete the obelisk, and construction resumed when weather permitted. At another conversation in mid-March, Savage asked Rogers "to name the sum [of money] I thought I should have," and Rogers replied that he wished Savage "to fix it in his own way" and that he "would be content." Such was not to be the case.

In late May, Rogers twice visited Bunker Hill and found Savage "progressing very well." We hear nothing more about the project until July 23, 1842, when Rogers and many others went to watch the last stone raised. Six weeks later, he and Willard rode up the steam car used to hoist stones to the upper reaches of the 221-foot monument,[33] landing at the window near the top. Rogers's characteristically laconic entry gives no sense of the excitement they must have felt looking over harbor and city from such an unprecedented vantage point. Savage had earned good money on the contract, and on March 15, 1843, Rogers called on him and talked "about a share of profits in the job of Bunker Hill Monument. He made me an offer of $500. I told him that 10% was what I thought of. He thought it too much. Left the subject there." Rogers no doubt wished he had made a firmer deal with the builder when he had the chance. Ten percent of Savage's contract would have amounted to $4,380, a handsome reward at half that figure, so Rogers thought his participation more important than Savage did. The architect's side of the story ends at the long gap in the diary in 1843, during which the monument was dedicated. It seems clear, however, from Rogers's private testimony that, although his name appear neither in William Whieldon's account of the monument's history in his biography of Willard nor in Willard's own description of the obelisk, Rogers played a significant part in restarting the project. Savage obviously recognized that fact, however stingy his offer, and Willard and Rogers continued to work in unison.[34]

Monumental stone architecture occupied much of Rogers's time in the East, but smaller chores were always there to fill the gaps. The source of one such task was Enoch Redington Mudge. A native of Lynn, Massachusetts, Mudge was general director of Astor House in New York in 1839 and the next year opened the St. Charles Hotel in New Orleans, a building Rogers would get to know later. In November 1839, during Rogers's New York days, Mudge engaged him to lay out a hotel to be built in Washington, D.C. The architect worked on the drawings through the rest of the year and was paid $200 in February 1841, but nothing seems to have come of the project. Returning to New England after a few years, Mudge eventually became a noted textile manufacturer, a Massachusetts state senator, trustee of the Museum of Fine Arts, Boston, and donor of Ware & Van Brunt's St. Stephen' s Episcopal (Mudge Memorial) Church in his hometown.

In 1843, still in New Orleans, and still a young man, he commissioned a summer residence from Rogers to be built on his 130-acre estate in Swampscott,

Massachusetts (then part of Lynn but after 1852 a separate town). Although a gap occurs in the diaries from the end of 1843 to early 1844, presumably when Rogers would have recorded this contact and his plans, by February 1844 the house was on its way. In early June, visiting the structure now well along, both Mudge and his wife reported themselves "well pleased," and handed over $996.21 on account. Later that month Rogers paid for "Gothic ornaments from New York," and in July the client ordered the rooms painted in "fresco" (probably *fresco secco*). Henry Dieffenbach, a now little-known itinerant decorative painter, executed that work. By early August the house was nearly completed to the client's satisfaction. That satisfaction was proved when Mudge asked Rogers to design a cottage for an unrecorded location (Rogers charged him $3) and other work, including a boarding house for his mill workers, in 1846, and a hotel for New Orleans after the architect had moved to Cincinnati. In late September, Rogers sent an assistant to Lynn "to put up the pinnacle" on the house; this was certainly the prominent feature on the peak of the front gable. As work reached its end, Rogers borrowed $3,000 from Mudge on a three-year note with semiannual interest (the reason will be explained below).

Mudge's "Elmwood" was inspired either by the fashionable Gothic cottages published by A. J. Davis in his *Rural Residences,* which we know Rogers owned by 1839, or by those published by A. J. Downing in 1841 and 1842. (Fig. 34) In fact, Davis's Henry Sheldon 1838–40 house in Tarrytown, New York, as it appeared in Downing's *Treatise on the Theory and Practice of Landscape Gardening* (1841), is a dead ringer for Elmwood except for a rear extension of the plan that produced a second lateral gable. The Sheldon house is depicted with vertical board-and-batten siding, whereas Elmwood was built of an unusual brick-backed granite veneer laid in vertical lozenges. Who thought of this detail we do not know, but Rogers apparently never used it again. The carved ornamental barge boards of the main gables were de rigueur for the style, as were the prominent clustered chimney stacks. The trabeated windows were inset with Gothic arches; battlements crowned flat roofs to either side of the center. Beneath the main gable, a four-posted porch with balcony above gave access to the house through an ogee archway. Inside, the layout was familiar in Rogers's domestic planning: a central hall led to a staircase, in this case a design with paired branches reversing directions from the landing. To one side lay double parlors; another room and the dining room were to the left. The house was pulled down in 1954.

In early March 1843, Rogers was in Marshfield pruning trees when Jarvis Braman arrived from Boston to request a plan for a bathhouse in New York. Braman's Baths had been a fixture in Boston since 1835, when that neoclassical box around a pool rose on pilings in the Charles River at the foot of Beacon Street. With distyle-in-antis columns standing before a recessed center between broad side bays, the facade could well have been designed by Rogers, although to date no evidence of his authorship has appeared. Braman stayed the night at Rogers's homestead while the architect set to work on the drawings. By midmonth he had completed pencil outlines and specifications. Diary entries covering the rest of the year are missing, but it appears that nothing came of the proposal, perhaps because Braman was unwell; he died after a long illness in July 1850.

In 1842 Rogers had remodeled his Marshfield homestead, adding a front portico, among other things. In these years (as in most others) he received many commissions for domestic design, not all of which were realized. As early as July 1841, while in Richmond, he had sketched a dwelling house for Horace L. Kent, a local dry-goods merchant, and let him look over the drawing "and suggest, if he could, any improvement." Back in New York he worked on the finished drawings and specifications, which Kent picked up on one of his frequent trips north. After a long silence, in March of 1844 Rogers, again in Richmond, became disgruntled when he had difficulty collecting the fee for his design of an orphan asylum that he had sketched in February. The clients were disposed to pay nothing because they had not used his drawings. This refusal got Rogers's dander up. He called

34. "Elmwood," the Enoch Redington Mudge house, Swampscott, Massachusetts, 1843–44. Courtesy Swampscott Public Library.

the orphanage bunch "low, base, too mean to have the trust of anything in my view," but he finally received $50 and the return of the plans. (He was probably unaware that in March, Calvin Pollard also worked up plans for an orphan asylum in Richmond, likely the same project. Apparently it too went nowhere.[35]) Rogers's ill humor carried over to Horace Kent. "There," he wrote, "I encountered another specimen of Virginia honor. To settle the claim [presumably for his earlier set of drawings] without resorting to law, I concluded to take half of what was my reasonable due. Thus is added to the many dear bought lessons of instruction that I have had to pay roundly for in the course of my life. . . . let them take advantage of me again, if they can." Despite such bravado, Rogers did not remain sour. In July of the same year, he showed Kent Mudge's Elmwood and, after two more tries, produced new drawings for the house in Richmond. Kent then paid him $10 and returned home with finished plans.

The Kent house was built without Rogers's supervision, and it still stands at First and Franklin Streets as the Kent-Valentine House. Significantly elaborated in 1904, it now serves as headquarters for the Garden Club of Virginia and is open to the public. Post–Civil War photographs show it to have been a three-bay brick and stucco box containing three stories plus a basement, with two flanking wings of two stories plus basement, all capped with a wooden bracketed cornice and punctuated by trabeated windows.[36] (Apparently Kent had not been impressed by the Davisian Gothic of the Mudge residence.) One scholar has noted the influence of New York domestic architecture, especially evident in the cast-iron veranda that swept around the front and sides of the ground floor on the main block; the ironwork was likely shipped from Manhattan.[37] (Fig. 35) As was usual in Rogers's domestic plans, a center hall extends straight back from the entrance between parlors, reaching a staircase that doubles back as it ascends. The house retains its original twin Gothic parlors, presumably designed by Rogers, with their clustered columnar door frames, doors and jambs of paneled (vaguely Islamic) pointed arches, and marble fireplace surrounds with inset Tudor arches (Fig. 36) of the kind Rogers also used in the Henshaw sarcophagus at Mount Auburn and elsewhere.

During 1844 Rogers worked on other houses as well as cottages and domestic alterations at the rate of at least one a month. He received $5 for sketching changes to a Mr. Armstrong's house in Beacon Street in Boston, produced a cottage and outbuildings for a Dr. Walker in Cambridge, and remodeled Samuel Henshaw's house on Chestnut Street, among similar undertakings. In August he agreed to plan a $7,000 house in Watertown for a Mrs. Heard, and he again turned out several speculative town houses in Boston, as he had in the early 1820s. On July 19 he noted beginning the plans for houses in Washington Street for a Mr. Kimball. This was a row of sixteen "bricks," four with three and a half stories and the remaining twelve of two and a half stories, which Dudley G. Adams, housewright,

35. Horace L. Kent house, Richmond, Virginia, 1844. Photograph before 1904 additions. Cook Collection, Valentine Richmond History Center.

and Benjamin W. Kimball, provision dealer, contracted at the end of the month to build for Thomas J. Lobell. Separate contracts with Robert Titcomb for building stairs named Gridley J. F. Bryant as the writer of specifications. For Lawrence Richards, a stone cutter from Quincy, Rogers designed a two-and-a-half-story house on Washington Street, in South Boston, which Loring Pickering, a carpenter, contracted to build in August.[38] From late August until early December 1844, when he was paid off, Rogers worked steadily on a cottage in Newport for D. (presumably David) Sears, and then came another period of silence. Once again he lost a commission to the competition, in this case George Minot Dexter of Boston, who designed "Red Cross," Sears's Gothic summer cottage that is still standing on Oakwood Terrace in Newport. In August Rogers drew alterations for the Shawmut House on Hanover Street, but it remains unclear whether anything came of that effort. A Captain Comstock sent him to his drafting board to design a hotel in Newport that eventually became the Ocean House; erected without his supervision, it burned in 1845.

Also at this time, Rogers embarked on another episode in a long and ultimately unsatisfactory series of dealings with the federal government, especially the Department of the Treasury. These experiences were to prove thoroughly wearing. Reminiscent of his petition (with partner Richard Bond) to be paid for the 1833 New York customhouse design for the Treasury, the fraught history of Horatio Greenough's twelve-ton marble figure of a seated, toga-draped George Washington was to prove even more frustrating, and would last for an even longer time. The statue arrived from Italy in 1841 and was placed in the Rotunda of the U.S.

36. Horace L. Kent house, Richmond, Virginia, 1844. Gothic parlor. Historic American Buildings Survey, Library of Congress.

Capitol. In March 1842 the architect received a letter about a "pedestal for the Statue of Washington," and the next day in Boston he discussed the subject with a Greenough, apparently not Horatio but John James, his cousin and agent. In late October, Rogers was introduced to the sculptor in New York City, and the two had a long conversation "on the several arts and their perfection in the execution." In 1843 the controversial statue was moved from the Rotunda to the East Lawn, where it was enclosed in a temporary building.[39] In March, Horatio wrote that he was "very anxious to know whether Solomon Willard will come on to move the statue. I shall make a drawing for the pedestal." Willard was presumably too busy to leave Quincy, for in early July, Horatio wrote to John C. Spencer, secretary of the Treasury, that he had "called upon Mr. Isaiah Rogers Architect and engineer to . . . [erect] the pedestal and . . . [place] the statue thereon." He added that the "scientific attainments and the great experience of Mr. Rogers in moving large masses of wrought stone have decided my selection. . . . I have full confidence in his care and ability." In a second letter to the secretary at nearly the same time, Horatio informed him that with the "Pedestal for the Statue . . . having been finished and set up . . . agreeably to the contract entered into between Mr. Isaiah Rogers and myself," $1,700 should be made available "to meet the lawful demands of the said Rogers."

Getting ready to leave for England, the sculptor next wrote to his agent, John James, that Rogers was entitled to $1,900 "when the pedestal is placed in the building ready to receive the statue," plus a $5 per diem and his expenses, for overseeing the moving of the statue and its placement on the pedestal.[40] But then trouble began. Payment for the services of both J. J. Greenough and Rogers was suspended by the federal government until 1851, including $435 owed to the latter.[41] On visits to Washington from 1844 to 1847, and probably beyond (a gap occurs in the diary), the architect sought payment but was continually denied. On one related occasion in October 1845, he ended up in a D.C. police court and was fined $50. It is unclear why. J. J. Greenough received satisfaction in 1851, but Rogers did not. Frustrated with his failure to extract recompense from the U.S. government, he approached the Horatio Greenough estate in Boston. In March 1853 he spoke to the administrator regarding his participation in moving the statue. Doing so only added to his woe, for the estate wanted him to pay bills that did not belong to him, prompting him to seek legal help. In December, while in New York, he received from J. J. Greenough "a certificate of work done on removing [the] statue of Washington" a decade earlier. He then applied to the Suffolk Savings Bank for settlement of his account but was again denied because, he wrote, the estate had received an invoice from Italy that, if valid, would render it insolvent. Rogers could add this entry to his growing list of long-delayed or under- and never-paid accounts.

That Rogers had not lost his touch with monumental granite composition in the Grecian manner, and was not above reusing his own good ideas, is proved by his 1844 design for the town hall in Quincy. Construction was superintended by Willard, who was a member of the building committee and supplied the stone; for that reason he has at times been credited as designer, but Rogers's diary reveals something more like collaboration. Local newspapers report that on February 2, 1844, a town meeting considered whether "the Town will build a Town House"; eight days later the decision was affirmative, and a committee was chosen that included Willard. On February 17, according to the diary, Rogers was asked "to make a plan for a Town Hall at Quincy," and within a week he and an assistant he calls merely James had finished the drawings. On April 10, however, Willard requested new drawings. The decision had been made, not surprisingly, to build in stone rather than wood. Three days later, Rogers reports, Willard "came in . . . and took the plans of the Hall." By May 11, notices to constructors were published, with plans and specifications available in Willard's office. Diary entries thereafter concern Willard's excavating the stone and supervising the construction.

On October 19 the *Quincy Patriot* could crow that the town hall, whose facade "will be similar in appearance to the front of the Merchants' Exchange, Boston," will be "one of the most elegant edifices in New England."[42] (Fig. 37) The architect received $50 on February 14, 1845, for making plans. The payment does not completely rule out Willard's role in the design, for he received $280 for plans and supervision, but it is apparent that in this era Rogers and Willard frequently operated as a team. The front is certainly Rogers's own design, after the Boston exchange. As in that earlier building, four fluted Ionic piers between antae, all nearly twenty-seven feet tall, divide the facade into five bays, with the central entrance a bit wider than those flanking it. But the pediment of the smaller Quincy building is much taller, the doorway much lower, and the count of stories reduced from four to two plus a row of recessed panels beneath the architrave. Under the windows of the first and second floors is a frieze of low-relief anthemia, another detail found in the same location on the facade of the Boston exchange. The dressed granite ashlar flanks with incised windows, and the rough ashlar rear wall with half-circular opening under the gable, as well as the interior, were probably left to Willard. The forty-six-by-sixty-foot hall occupied the upper level. It is a pleasure to report that the facade exists in a relatively unaltered state.

Notices in the diary for these years also record work for Harvard College. In 1843 Josiah Quincy III, former mayor of Boston and Rogers's client at the First Parish Meeting House, asked him to design a president's house for the school. The signed drawings (now in the Harvard Archives) are matched by specifications dated December 8 of that year, but the house remained unbuilt. In December 1845 Rogers's old patron from the Tremont House, Samuel Atkins Eliot, then treasurer of Harvard, requested a new design for a house for Quincy. Rogers worked on the drawings over several weeks and then showed the results to Eliot, who "liked them very well" but suggested changes. A competing design from this

37. Town hall, Quincy, Massachusetts, 1844. Hancock Street front. Courtesy Historic New England.

year exists among the drawings of George Minot Dexter (in the collection of the Boston Athenaeum). Of Dexter's project, Eliot wrote to Edward Everett, Quincy's replacement as Harvard president from 1846 to 1849, that it "embraces most of the objects desired by you, which possibly may be a little less costly than that of Rogers."[43] This led to Everett's request for more alterations to Rogers's design. Drawings, specifications, and an estimate were delivered on February 14, 1846, and Rogers received $122.50, presumably for the second scheme. Then the project disappears from the diary, and the college had to wait until 1860 for a president's house, designed by E. C. Cabot.

The two sets of drawings for Harvard produced the same basic overall from, but the internal arrangements were significantly improved in the second plan. As the elevations show, the three-dimensional results would have been different as well.[44] In each, a squarish main house was connected by a corridor and conservatory to a free-standing library. In both, unlike many of Rogers's other domestic plans, the main staircase is off to one side of the central hallway, and thus out of sight from the entrance. The earlier design was awkwardly planned, however. (Fig. 38) One had to cross the drawing room to reach the rear of the house from the entrance hall, although the library beyond had its own entrance; to reach the dining room from the kitchen underneath it in the basement, food would have to pass through the main entrance hall. In the later arrangement, the service stair rises into a back hall behind the main staircase, from which a servant could reach the dining room unseen (see Fig. 40). The later scheme split the plan in half, with a hallway leading from entry to library, which had no separate entrance.

The proposed three-dimensional development of these plans demonstrates even greater differences. The earlier south elevation, thinly drafted in ink outlines devoid of shadows, shows a two-story plus low basement main house with fluted Corinthian entrance portico and side veranda defined by delicate arches and open strigil-motif balusters. (Fig. 39) Paired delicate pilasters embrace the corners of the block, a detail found in many of Rogers's buildings. The hip roof rests on deep eaves supported by slender brackets. A low corridor with trabeated glazing leads to the temple-form library, which is articulated with broad pilasters of a kind Rogers used at the 1833 Forbes house in Milton. The result is Grecian in detail, planar in composition, and a bit ordinary. The second design, dated just two years later, was for a larger house. It depicts a much more impressive project in a bolder graphic presentation that uses washes to capture the shadowed plasticity of the front elevation. The main block is now three stories plus low basement, including a three-story semicircular front projection rising above an arcaded porte cochere. The roof now rises from deep eaves supported by a bracketed cornice. Construction is heavier, with double-width brick and stone exterior walls, and the Italianate details are more plastic. (Fig. 41) The shift—from a domestic to an almost institutional scale—hints at the direction Rogers's work would take in the later 1840s.

Between the dates of these two residential projects, Rogers worked on an addition to Harvard's Dana Hall, the 1832 Grecian law school, between the end of April and early June 1844, when planning came to a halt.[45] During these same years he received a much more important commission from the college, the design of its new observatory, when President Quincy persuaded William C. Bond to become Harvard's astronomical observer. The project began sometime in 1843.[46] By late February of the next year, Rogers told Samuel Eliot that he needed to go to Washington to inspect the U.S. Naval Observatory, apparently to study the problem of building a revolving dome. On March 9 he was given "many hints about the fixtures of the dome" while in the capital, but thirteen months later, in April 1845, Eliot wanted him to again visit Washington and West Point as well. He then heard from Lieutenant Matthew Fontaine Maury, superintendent of the federal observatory, who shared "his views on his mode of fixing the dome." Rogers eventually used cannon balls as bearings, then a common method begun at West Point a few years earlier, either from his design or that of Major Richard Delafield, then superintendent of the U.S. Military Academy. He worked intermittently on

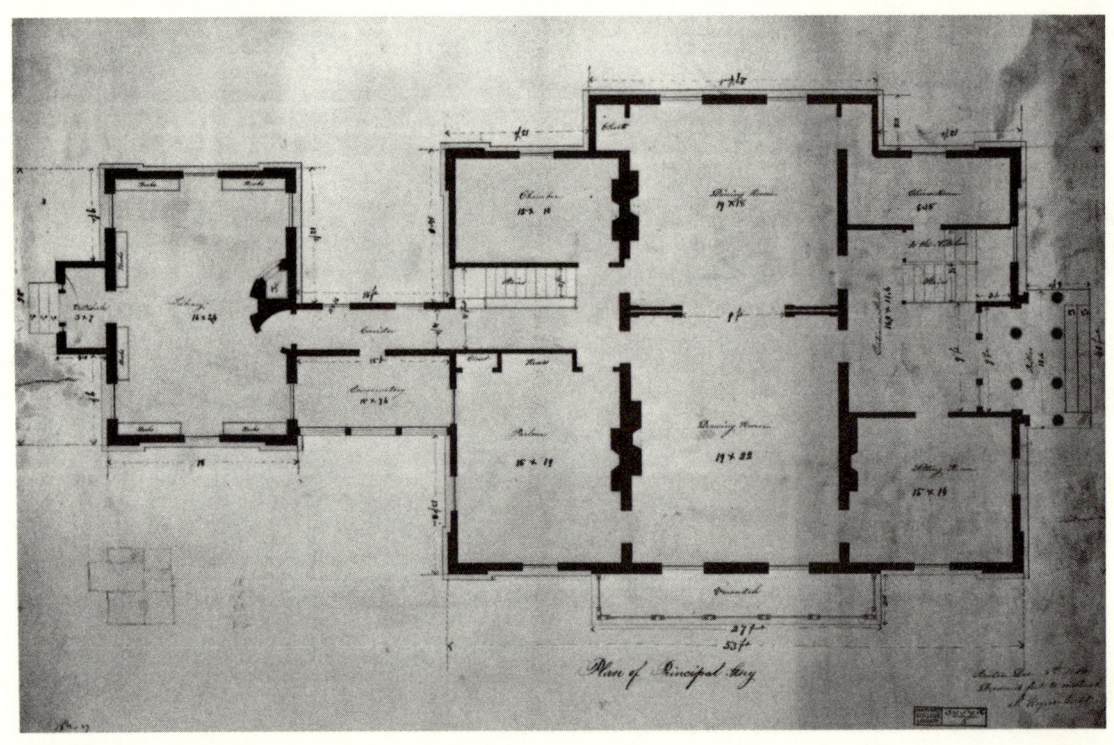

38. Project for the president's house, Harvard College, Cambridge, Massachusetts, 1843. First-floor plan. Pencil and ink. Harvard University Archives.

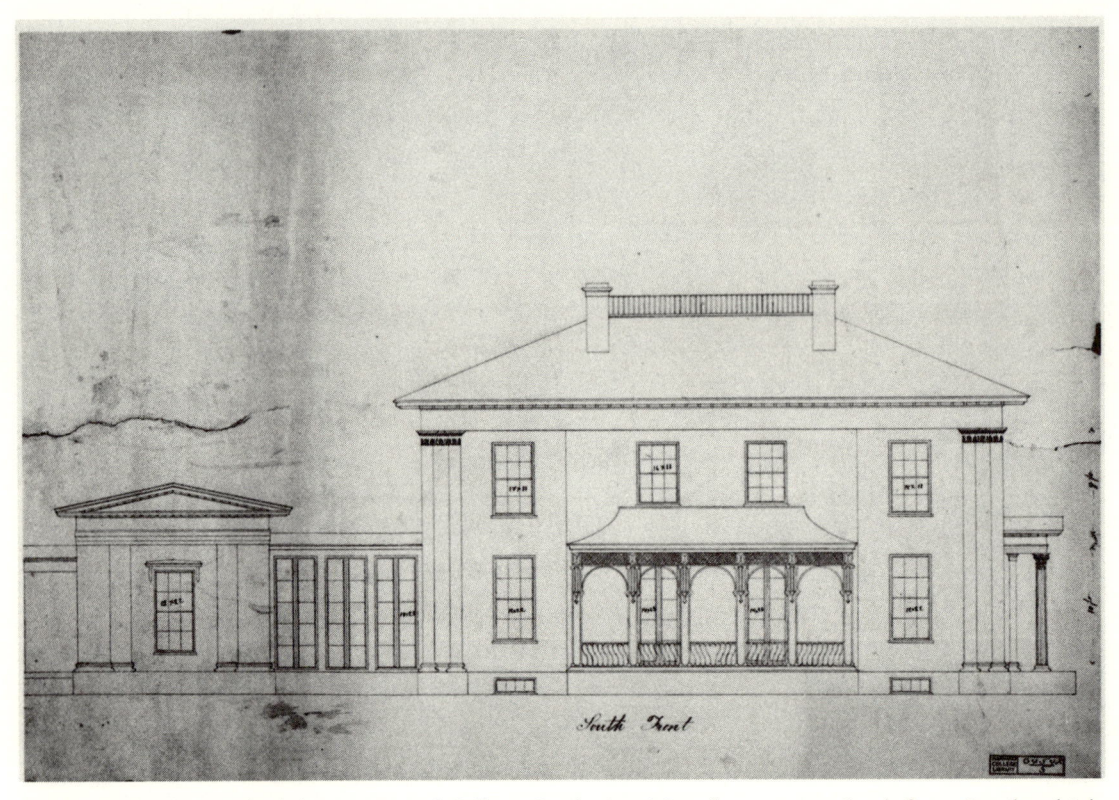

39. Project for the president's house, Harvard College, Cambridge, Massachusetts, 1843. South front. Pencil and ink. Harvard University Archives.

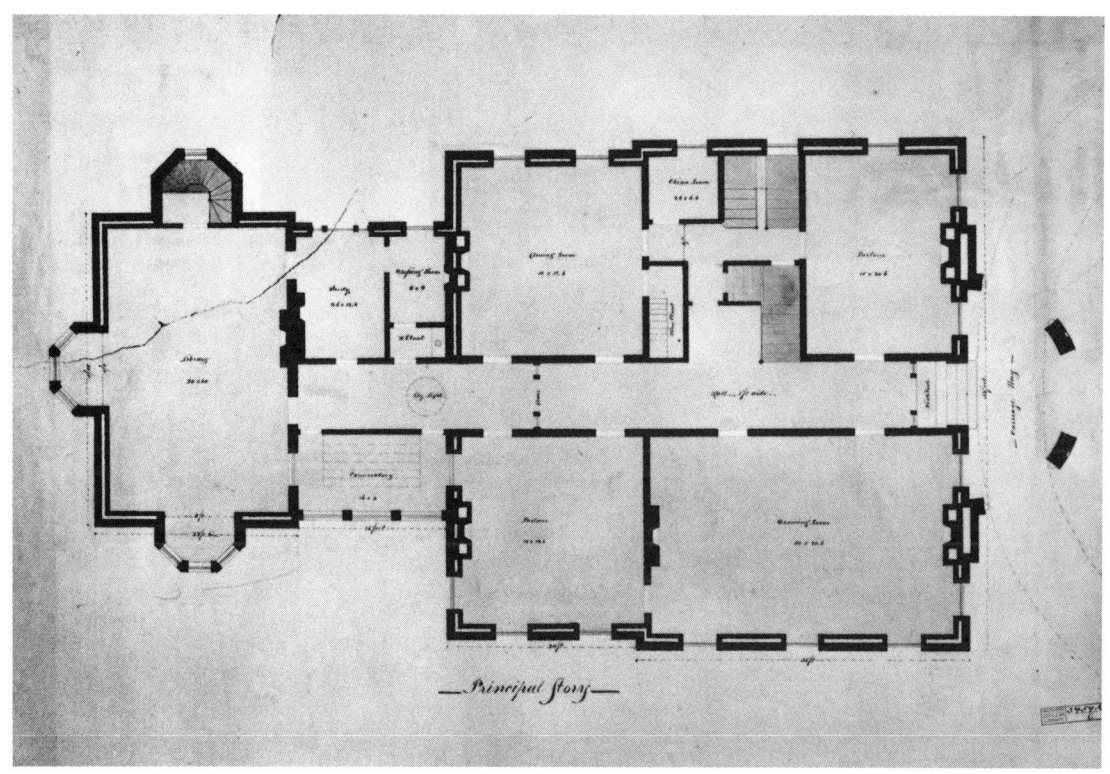

40. Project for the president's house, Harvard College, Cambridge, Massachusetts, 1845. First-floor plan. Pencil and ink. Harvard University Archives.

41. Project for the president's house, Harvard College, Cambridge, Massachusetts, 1845. Front elevation. Pencil, ink, and wash. Harvard University Archives.

drawings for the Harvard observatory as other projects allowed. By early June he could give Willard the model "of the stone for the telescope to stand on," and later that month he noted that William Bond "had got up a plan for sliding the shutter of the opening of the dome." Early in July, Bond "took the model to contrive the covering of the opening for the dome." Rogers was not one to discount the contributions of experts, although he did not suffer fools.

His own contribution to the observatory continued the honored Palladian villa tradition of a five-part, or quincunx, organization of volumes, with a central pedimented block (here domed) flanked by lower pedimented pavilions connected by even lower wings, or "hyphens." (Fig. 42) In one way or another, this Palladian scheme carried through his career to the very end. Work proceeded through 1845. When finished, the exterior walls met the sky in pronounced classical cornices. The dome, which rested on a low attic above a brick room fronted by an entrance pavilion, clearly expressed the presence of an observatory, the building's main purpose. The wooden east wing contained Bond's residence, while its twin, not erected until 1851, housed classrooms and a library. As Bainbridge Bunting and Margaret Henderson Floyd wrote in their standard work on Harvard's architecture, vintage photographs suggest that, "located at the crest of Observatory Hill . . . the building with its three pediments . . . must have originally presented a striking visual composition."[47] They also note the removal of the wings to erect later additions that have nearly swallowed what is left of Rogers's organization.

Rogers's work at Harvard, ranging as it did from domestic to institutional programs, was a microcosm of his career. If he was not asked to design "anything a man wants from a cathedral to a chicken coop," as H. H. Richardson, his more colorful successor, once said about his own abilities, he was willing and highly able to provide solutions to a wide range of society's needs. So we find that the *Boston Daily Atlas* for April 23, 1844, mentioned among its "Notices of Intention to Build" a project by "Isaiah Rogers, agent for the Female [Orphan] Asylum, on Washington Street." As early as July 1841 Rogers had begun to think about this type of institution when he was asked to plan "an orphan asylum for girls" in Richmond, Virginia, a project he worked on until March 1842. Apparently it never materialized. In February 1844 he turned his attention to the Boston institution, which had been founded early in the century and was well supported by the gentry, among them Amos Lawrence. We find him then looking over his "plans and books to find an idea for elevation of orphan asylum." Although he wrote that he found nothing, he nonetheless continued to work on the problem and "got out [an] elevation." After more evenings at the boards considering variations of the scheme, late in the month the ladies' building committee adopted his design and agreed "to raise such money as they could by subscription before starting the job." The result was a $25,000 building fund. The laying of the cornerstone at Washington and Asylum Streets took place in late June, when Lawrence "liked the

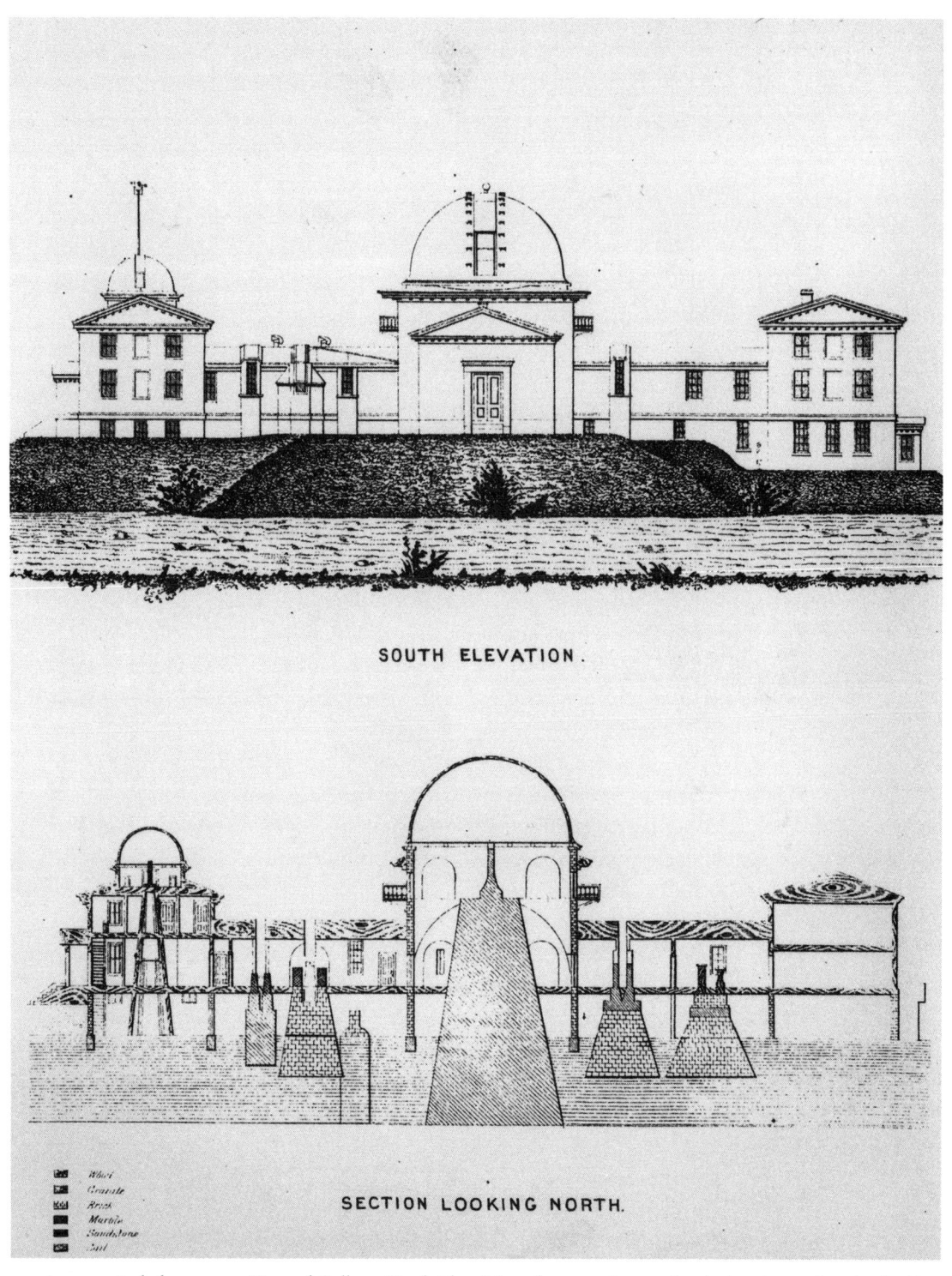

42. Astronomical observatory, Harvard College, Cambridge, Massachusetts, 1843–45. South elevation and section looking north. From F. O. Vaille and H. A. Clark, *The Harvard Book,* vol. 1 (Cambridge, Mass., 1875).

plan and work very well." It inaugurated a building "not aiming at elegance, but perfectly safe, commodious and respectable. Having from without not so much the appearance of a public building as to lose its domestic character; and yet easily recognized as designed for a larger [number of inhabitants] than any private family."[48] The orphans occupied their new home in late January of the next year.

The asylum rose as a three-story, five-bay brick block, with slight three-bay salient front capped by a classical pediment; it was entered through a granite aedicule. Although Rogers received instructions to design a cupola, images do not show any such crowning feature. His chief concern in the design of the no-frills building was protection from fire as it was then understood. Exterior woodwork did not connect to wood on the interior; all partitions were of plastered brick; the stairs were wrought and cast iron; the double floors were fire-stopped with plaster; and the place was well-ventilated by flues within the double-thick walls. All these features were more or less standard procedure for Rogers. The asylum could accommodate about sixty girls. The basement held bathing areas, a laundry, and storerooms; the first floor contained a matron's room, meeting room, schoolroom, kitchen, and dining room; and the upper floors housed dormitories, a recreation room, and a hospital with water closets and a bathing room. Rogers recorded the first occupation of the building in late January 1845, and two days later he "went to the Asylum and found all the little folks all right." In February 1846 he picked up Morrill Wyman's new treatise on ventilation[49] and immediately examined his arrangement. He found nothing to worry about except the privies, which he ordered rebuilt.

The next year, 1845, was typical of many others in Rogers's life: he worked on a constant stream of projects—some large, some small, some important, others not, some built, many remaining only drawings or perhaps a model. As usual, he worked on designs for new houses and cottages and alterations, including projects for a Mr. Nichols, a Mr. Hooper on Pinckney Street in Boston, a Mr. Sturgis in Roxbury, a Mr. Eldredge, and a Mr. Waterman, as well as shops, hotels, banks, a theater, tombs, a museum, and other building types. Some were from scratch; others were remodeling jobs. He sometimes provided sketches and billed accordingly. For many of the structures that were erected, not only did he draft a scheme and supervise construction, but he also bargained with suppliers, inspected their materials, arranged for shipments to building sites, kept the accounts, and paid the bills. In addition, he made frequent trips to Washington and spent weekends in Marshfield.

With the departure of Voelckers and Washburn, most of the time the Boston office probably consisted of Rogers and his son Willard, who started his architectural career in January; another assistant, James, is the only other staff member named regularly. In the first weeks of 1845, Rogers and James laid out drawings for stores on Court Street for Dr. George C. Shattuck. In early March he received

$76 "in full for making plans." Excavations at the corner of Sudbury Street began in October, apparently without Rogers's supervision;[50] the stores were swept away in the development of the current Government Center in the 1960s. Work also continued on the Harvard College Observatory. Among the houses Rogers designed (other than those noted above) was a summer cottage in Brookline for Mrs. William H. Eliot, the widow of his old friend and client from Tremont House days. He drew the house after showing her a "book . . . to look over sketches." The cottage was erected by 1845, and many times remodeled and augmented beyond recognition.

A design for Boston's Mechanics' Hall occupied many an evening as well. In January the *Salem Register* reported that the Massachusetts Charitable Mechanic Association had purchased the old Boott estate on Bowdoin Square for the purpose of erecting a hall. On January 8, Rogers began to draw, and in March he noted that the building committee had asked for a model of his design. In April he took his drawings to Quincy so that Willard could make it. In October the *Courier* saw the prospect of erecting such a hall as "now brighter, and many years *cannot* pass away" before it "shall be the admiration of our fellow-citizens." In the same month, the papers were discussing the many improvements in the city, although "the long-talked of Mechanics' Hall advances but slowly. Four of the plans offered by architects for competition have been modeled." It was generally understood that the committee could not decide which one to adopt.[51] Not until 1857 did a Mechanics' Hall rise on the site from the drawings of Hammatt Billings, Gridley J. F. Byrant, and N. J. Bradlee. The design and supervision of an addition to the Merchants' Bank also kept Rogers busy; this was, in part, a rebuilding of Willard's 1824 U.S. Branch Bank and later additions that stretched between State and Exchange Streets. The result was a granite facade with Grecian pilasters and entablature facing the exchange.[52] It was replaced in a later rebuilding by George Snell.

In February 1845 Rogers and James worked on drawings for a hotel in New York and sent them to George E. Watriss, formerly of the St. Charles Hotel in New Orleans and Astor House. In 1848 Watriss opened his own St. Charles on Broadway in a remodeled building formerly known as the Athenaeum; whether he used drawings by Rogers or another architect remains unanswered. Similar work followed: there was discussion about a hotel for Staten Island; he studied a design for one at Niagara Falls; and he received a request to design another for Nantasket Beach near Boston, which he did, although whether it was erected remains a question. Rogers also consulted with a group about a hotel in Montreal. When New York's Waverly House burned in July (along with 302 other buildings), Rogers set about drafting its replacement in September, although nothing seems to have come of that initiative. How many such projects resulted in buildings or alterations remains to be studied by local historians. A railroad depot for the

Mill Pond area in Boston entered the office in March and took time away from his proposal for the Washington Monument. Rogers also designed an athenaeum building in this period, probably intended for the 1845 competition for the Boston Athenaeum that was won by E. C. Cabot. For Samuel A. Eliot he drew an addition to the Nahant Church he had designed a few years earlier, and he made unspecified alterations to Eliot's cottage at Pine Bank, in Jamaica Plain.

The Canton trader M. H. Simpson numbers among Rogers's more exotic and frustrating clients in these years. With a large fortune gained from the China Trade and as co-owner of a famous collection of Chinese artifacts, Simpson and his partners, Joseph H. Weed and John R. Peters Jr., opened the Chinese Museum in September 1845 in the "entirely altered" former Marlboro' Chapel on Washington Street in Boston.[53] Thus began another tortured episode in Rogers's career. During that summer he had agreed to design and oversee the installation of exhibition cases for the museum. These were described by a New York reporter visiting Boston that month as "thirty eight large cases made of framed glass, varying in size from six or eight feet square up to the dimensions of a handsome apartment,"[54] which sound more like show or period rooms rather than display cases. From the beginning, the intention was to move the attraction to New York. On the day of the first recorded meeting between Rogers and Simpson, June 6, 1845, the Boston *Daily Atlas* (channeling the *New York Journal of Commerce*) reported that Simpson had purchased the old Grace Church on Broadway, a building that had become obsolete with the rise of the new Grace Church, James Renwick Jr.'s masterpiece of the early Gothic Revival. "We think it not improbable that the purchase has some reference to . . . [the] accommodation" of Simpson's collection, wrote the journalist. Apparently Simpson first thought of demolishing the church and replacing it with a new museum building, and indeed in early July he showed Rogers "a plan from New York drawn by Mr. [Calvin] Pollard." Rogers did not think much of it, and Pollard was seemingly dismissed. Simpson then sent Rogers to the city to halt the "taking off the roof [of the old church] if it was not already done." He had obviously rethought his decision to demolish and build something new; he now planned to remodel instead.

While the Chinese Museum in Boston drew crowds and journalistic praise, the New York plans began to founder. In early October the *Boston Evening Transcript* reported that the conversion of a church into a museum had been abandoned because of a misunderstanding among the partners. This claim was immediately denied in the same paper, which described the remodeled structure as being two stories, with the Chinese Hall on the upper floor. "The building will be one of the finest ornaments of the city. The front will present a splendid Chinese temple" designed by John R. Peters, an engineer. Nonetheless, in late July, Simpson had already asked Rogers to lay out a "good plan for a hotel" at the site, and in mid-October the architect again mentioned a hotel on Simpson's lot on Broadway. Rogers went to the drafting board, even though he learned that three other unnamed architects were also making plans. Meanwhile, he was overseeing the installation of the exhibitions for the Chinese Museum in the Marlboro Chapel. That show closed in February 1847, still with the intention of being transferred to New York, but accommodations were not yet prepared, so it became a wandering attraction. Rogers eventually visited the show in Philadelphia. In the same month, Simpson commissioned the addition of a cupola to his house in Boston's Somerset Place. It was finished by Christmas, the one visible achievement (other than the museum cases) to materialize from all of Rogers's work for the dithering Sinophile.

Among the funereal works that came from Rogers's drafting board over the years was a granite vault at Mount Auburn Cemetery for Samuel Henshaw, a member of the building committee for the Merchants' Exchange who had remained Rogers's friend. Founded in 1831, Mount Auburn was the first ornamental "Garden of Graves," a parklike area that replaced the grim burial grounds of colonial times. Here were ornamental tombs, landscaping, and plantings; it was thought of as anything but morbid, offering educational and uplifting collections of art, architecture, sculpture, landscape gardening, arboriculture, and botany. Architect and client visited Henshaw's cemetery plot on September 23, 1844, and three days later Rogers bought a "book on tombs" for $5.[55] Drawings began that fall. In early May 1845 Rogers went to Cambridge to lay out the work; on June 8 he "measured stone from Baltimore for Mr. Henshaw's tomb," and in July he traveled to Quincy to inspect the work. It was delivered to the site in November, when Rogers found a workman to set it. The design called for a boxy granite sarcophagus, ornamented with a low-relief blind Tudor arch, that was set atop a single-chamber vault nestled into the hillside on Narcissus Path, then overlooking Forest Pond (now gone). (Fig. 43) Henshaw's name, the date 1845 (of the tomb, not his demise), and the lot number (534) are the only inscriptions. This last piece of information appears on a 2½-inch-thick "tablet" of marble shaped like an escutcheon, which Rogers mentions in a note at the beginning of one of his diaries for that year. Among Henshaw's funerary neighbors is Arthur Gilman's Winchester mausoleum, a much more elaborately Gothic composition of about the same date.[56] The contrast between the two points up Rogers's chaste esthetic.

Given his hectic schedule, when did Rogers find time for relaxation? If not at his drafting board in the evenings or on charette for a competition entry, times that might require him to work until two in the morning, he often attended the theater or lectures (on mnemonics, astrology, animal magnetism), played whist or bowled (even once sketching a bowling alley design for New Bedford, Massachusetts), called on friends, or "walked out" into the city. He could often be found at the Lodge of Odd Fellows, the Columbia Lodge of Masons, or Mechanics' Hall. Weekends found him in Marshfield, where, if he had not carried work along, he would prune trees, fish, hunt, pick wild berries and grapes, and make port wine.

43. Samuel Henshaw Tomb, Mount Auburn Cemetery, Cambridge, Massachusetts, 1845. Author photo, 2012.

Sundays would find him spending the day in church, listening to sermons by Hosea Ballou and others. Because he traveled so much, he was often away from Emily, but on September 29, 1845, the whole family gathered in Boston for the wedding of his daughter Emily Jane and Nathan H. Gould of Newport, Rhode Island, which took place at Trinity Church on Summer Street. Gould went on to become a prominent local citizen, serving as a director of Redwood Library, master of the St. John Lodge of Free and Accepted Masons, secretary of the Newport Gas Company, treasurer of the Newport Historical Society, and guardian of the Jewish cemetery as heir of Judah Touro.[57]

The summer of 1845 saw a couple starts that eventually led to the building of Boston's famed Howard Athenaeum. In June a group led by the actor W. L. Ayling, later to be stage manager at the Howard, approached Rogers with the idea of creating a theater in Boylston Hall. Apparently nothing came of that idea, but in late November the distinguished American actor James Henry Hackett, famous for his portrayal of Falstaff and lately off the boards in London and living in New York, approached Rogers "about making plans for [a] theater" to be erected on Tremont Street. As usual, the architect wasted no time getting to the drawing board, working through the next day, evening, and day after, when he presented plans, elevations, and a section to Hackett. Happy with what he saw, the actor asked for an estimate of cost and a schedule of rent after the drawings were altered to accommodate a men's club. The project was shelved after a failed series of calls "on gentlemen to assist in getting up a theater on the Athenaeum lot in Tremont Street." The client and his architect "gave it up for the present." Had it been erected, it would have been Rogers's old Tremont Theatre redux. The failure to attract support for this venture probably owed much to the involvement of Rogers and Hackett in the production of the Howard Athenaeum.

When the wooden Millerite Tabernacle on Howard Street burned after William Miller's prediction of the horrific Second Coming failed to occur between March 21, 1843, and March 21, 1844, it was replaced by a theater named the Howard Athenaeum. That venture also failed, making the location available for a new opera house called the Howard Street Theatre, known more commonly by its former name, the Howard Athenaeum.[58] The commission entered Rogers's diary in mid-March 1845, and the cornerstone laid on the Fourth of July 1846 contained, among other memorabilia, a daguerreotype portrait of the architect taken on June 18.[59] (Fig. 44) Ten days earlier the owners, J. M. W. Boyd and Duke Beard, had signed the building contract with Lemuel M. Standish and Charles Woodbury.[60] During construction, Rogers rented an office across the street, where he continued drafting details of the building almost to the last minute, and whence he could conduct daily inspections of the site. He was also engaged in other projects and, as we shall learn, in the throes of a financial disaster.

According to James Henry Hackett's obituary in the *New York Times* on December 29, 1871, the Howard Athenaeum was built for him, and he managed it successfully until moving on to New York and Rogers's 1847 Astor Place Opera House. Although Richard Stoddard's dissertation on the Boston theaters does not mention him in connection with the Howard, Rogers's diary records Hackett's active presence during the planning process.[61] In early May 1846, for example, a conversation in New York with the lessee Thomas Ford discussed Hackett taking over management of the house. On May 15, Ford and Hackett went to Boston to look over the plans and suggested improvements, which Rogers thought "can be made." On May 20 in New York, Rogers had a long conversation with Hackett about the opera house, went with him to look at the Park Theater, and came away with "some valuable information." In July, carpenters were brought up from New York and advised him "on the manner of framing the stage floor." In mid-August Hackett inspected the work and expressed much satisfaction; a month later the two talked over the finishing of the house. The venue opened on October 5, less than four months after the laying of the cornerstone. The speed with which such buildings were built reflected the lack of complicated infrastructure, such as temperature-control systems, electricity, and so on, the installation of which now prolongs construction. In this case, it might also suggest that some of the former theater was reused. The active life of the house began with a performance of Sheridan's comedy "The Rival," featuring Mrs. Malaprop.

Tudor seems to have been Rogers's choice of style briefly in the mid-1840s. He used it for his funereal works, and the *Boston Evening Transcript* described the Howard Athenaeum as having a Tudor-style soda water manufactory in its enormous ground floor that was in fact a brewery run by the proprietors of the house, Messrs. Boyd and Beard. Beer and opera might now seem an unusual combination, but until the arrival in 1848 of pure water from Lake Cochituate, west of the city, the consumption of strong beverages was preferred over the generally putrid liquid available from city cisterns and wells. Pointed lancets with bar tracery opened the high-gabled, rubble-granite front of the building on Howard Street. (Fig. 45) The side walls were of brick, as was common. The use of Tudor Gothic for a theater was apparently unique in the history of the building type.

The theater's auditorium on the upper floors consisted of a parquet and three tiers of boxes. (Fig. 46) The floor sloped gradually toward the orchestra, "sufficient

44. Isaiah Rogers. From a daguerreotype taken in Boston, Massachusetts, June 18, 1845. Bostonian Society.

45. Howard Athenaeum, Boston, Massachusetts, 1845–46. Howard Street front. Harvard Theatre Collection.

to permit an uninterrupted view of the stage, which . . . can be seen as well from one seat as from another," a feature that had marked the former Howard Athenaeum, a theater Rogers knew well from attending plays there. During the design phase, Rogers (perhaps with Hackett) had gone to a theater in New York that had flat seating and expressed disappointment at being unable to see the performance. He paid particular attention to the acoustics; the horseshoe plan made it possible for the "most remote listener . . . [to] hear as well as those who are nearest the stage." The plan also contained some twenty dressing rooms and four "saloons." Over three hundred spring-cushioned cast-iron armchairs provided seating in the parquet. Although the *Transcript* omits this detail, the house sat sixteen hundred comfortably, two thousand in a pinch. The columns upholding the boxes, stairs, and other features were of cast iron. A domed ceiling covered the auditorium. Over time the house suffered redecorations and a shift in the character of its offerings. Long before it closed in 1953, it had become a burlesque house in Scollay Square, where the likes of Sally Rand and Ann Corio took (most) of it off for sailors and college boys. (The one time Rogers recorded attending a burlesque performance, he wrote that he was filled with disapproval.) An arsonist destroyed the empty relic on June 20, 1961, and a plaque at the site recalls only the Howard's later, grittier days and says nothing about its creators.

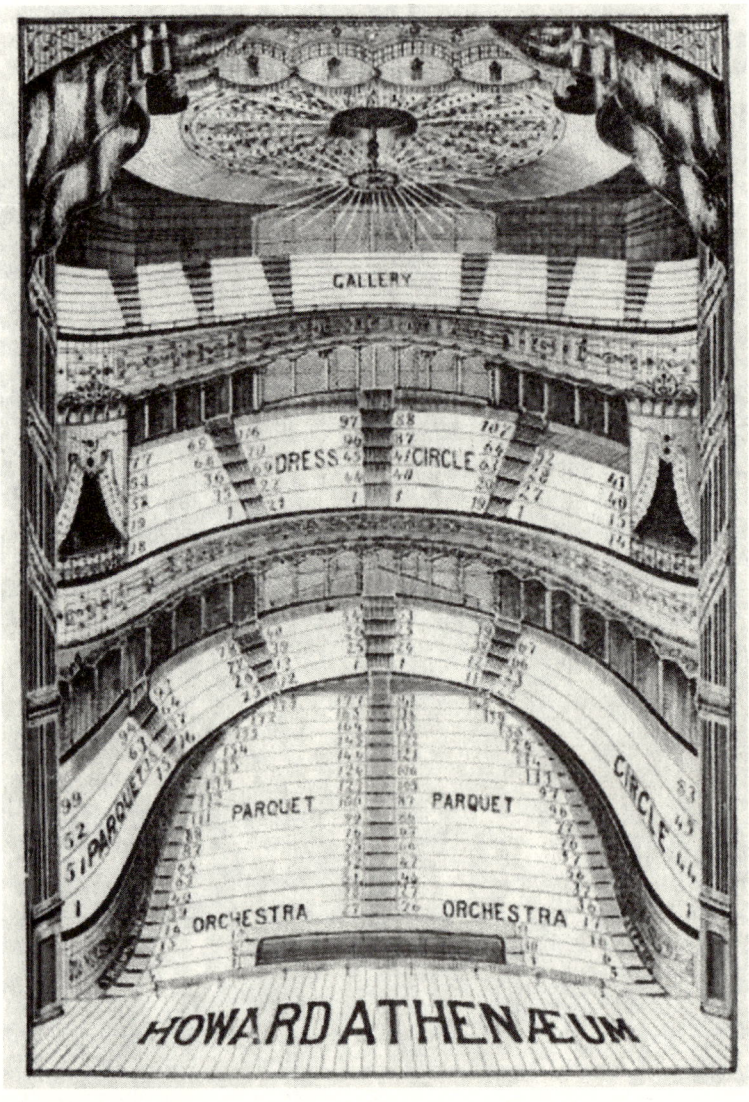

46. Howard Athenaeum, Boston, Massachusetts, 1845–46. Interior. From James Henry Stark, *Stranger's Illustrated Guide to Boston and Its Suburbs* (Boston, 1883).

In March 1844, while Rogers was in Washington, Enoch Pratt, chairman of the Congressional Committee on Public Buildings and Grounds, asked him to sketch a plan for the Washington Monument. Despite a competition for that monument in 1836, no winner had been selected.[62] The next month, Pratt published a report on the "National Monument" in which he championed and illustrated a design by William Strickland for a multistory circular temple.[63] In 1845 Robert Mills's design was chosen in the teeth of much criticism, but no construction began until 1848. If Rogers did produce a design in 1844, it was ignored by Pratt, but according to the diary he didn't get around to drawing his proposal until the following February. He worked on it into early March 1845, but does not mention it again.

In the files of Denys Peter Myers, a photocopy of an engraving seems to be the only surviving visual evidence for this project. It is a sectional view that is difficult to interpret fully but seems to involve a roughly 680-foot obelisk rising out of a stepped pyramid, with groups of sculpture at the corners. (Fig. 47) Within the hollow pyramid, Rogers proposed to cluster what looks like a forest of Grecian columns, stepped from Doric to Ionic to Corinthian, that supports the spike above (thus, he too intended to use the same mix of classical and Egyptian forms for which Mills's design of an obelisk rising out of a tholos had been much criticized). This seems to have been his variation on the Bunker Hill Monument, with which he had recently been much concerned. At the same time, the city of New York was seeking a design for its own monument to the first president, and on March 1, 1845, Rogers noted vaguely that he had "Paid for Washington Monument plan of New York, $1." His frequent competitor, Calvin Pollard, had been awarded the commission in June 1844, but public outcry generated alternate proposals during the next year.[64] Rogers may have been double-dipping, hoping to win one of the commissions. He got neither. Mills's monument stood only as a stump until long after the Civil War, and in 1855 Rogers again turned his attention to its design. No drawings intended for this second stab at the problem have yet come to light.

The Washington Monument was not the only unrealized project for the capital that Rogers worked on in the mid-1840s. Before and during the Howard Athenaeum campaign, he concentrated (when time permitted) on potential federal commissions. He left early during the opening performance of Sheridan's farce to work until midnight on a project for the Smithsonian Institution, and since February 1845 he had been lobbying for another project, an addition to the War and Navy offices. While in Washington, he was introduced to a member of the House of Representatives, probably Daniel P. King, a Whig from Massachusetts, who asked him to submit a project for the Navy. He may or may not have been aware of the history of that ill-fated commission, which began with specifications written by Colonel J. G. Totten, the chief of engineers, in early 1842. House Document 85, dated January 25, 1843, proposed an "Additional Building for War and Navy Departments." By then William Strickland had submitted a proposal, Robert

47. Proposed Washington Monument, 1844–45. Central vertical section. Reproduction from the collection of Denys Peter Myers.

Mills was soon to submit alternate designs, and another scheme was proposed by John Notman.[65] Both Strickland and Mills were supported by influential backers, including Robert Dale Owen, representative from Indiana, and President John Tyler for Mills. Back in Boston, Rogers began belatedly to work on a scheme. On February 17, 1845, he sent off plans and estimates. On his next trip to the capital in April, he tried to obtain information about his proposal for the building, but got no satisfaction. In September, friends advised him to procure endorsements from distinguished men in Boston and New York. Again in Washington, D.C., on September 25, 1845, he called on William L. Marcy, the secretary of war, and was informed that "the subject of the public buildings was settled in the previous April and was given to Mr. Strickland of Philadelphia." However, this (erroneous) news did not stop him from continuing to promote his own plan.

Strickland had been working on his project for the building since 1842. When it looked like the push to build was losing steam, or that the projects in hand were not what was wanted, apparently there were those in the government who hoped the submission of a new design might reinvigorate the process. The next month, Rogers located the drawings for his proposal after a bit of a search among various committees and made copies of them. It seems that he may have misunderstood the situation, since he mentions nothing about a competition. He persisted in lobbying for his design, and, whether known to him or not, so did Mills. By late October, Rogers was working on new plans, and by early November these had advanced far enough for Levi L. Cushing to begin a model; by the end of that month Rogers, had sent his drawings off to Washington.

His self-promotion carried into the new year. On January 1, 1846, Rogers turned his attention to flogging his new design on the ground. He had the model moved to the office of George Bancroft, the distinguished historian and then secretary of the Navy, where the chairman of the committee looked at it and "seemed well pleased." He then took people to the War Office to study the model. Colonel Totten said he would "do all in his power to aid . . . in procuring the job." He received encouragement from Robert Owen, who apparently felt that backing Mills would no longer do any good. Rogers had his model moved again, this time to the Capitol, where a great many people saw it. He reports that Secretary Marcy "promised to send me word in time for me to explain my . . . plans to the committee." Finally, Rogers went to see the new president, James K. Polk. But the timing was off; all his energy wasted. The declaration of war with Mexico in May ended the process—the housing needs of War and Navy would have to await A. B. Mullett's huge 1870s Second Empire building, located across from the White House. The tale of this ill-fated endeavor—added to his ongoing struggle to be paid for his efforts moving Greenough's statue of Washington—should have discouraged Rogers from trying to do business in Washington, but it did not. One fatiguing failure immediately followed; another, even more disillusioning, was to meet him in the 1860s when he took a full-time job with the U.S. government.

Still fighting for his War and Navy project, Rogers talked to Representative Robert Dale Owen about plans for a competition for a building to house the newly endowed Smithsonian Institution. A bill for the building's erection submitted by Owen had passed Congress in August 1846, and a committee was formed in early September.[66] By then a suggestive design and detailed program had been laid out by David Owen, Robert's brother; it was critiqued by Robert Mills, who had sketched out his own project as early as 1841, just a few years after James Smithson had made his extraordinary donation and long before the building was authorized. The program nonetheless remained in flux. On his return to Boston, Rogers threw himself into the design and supervision of the Howard Athenaeum. As that wound down, he began to study the Smithsonian program in September 1846, undaunted by his recent unhappy experiences in the U.S. capital. It was to prove another exercise in frustration.

On September 2, 1846, Rogers heard through intermediaries that Robert Owen wanted him to go to Washington and "look after" the Smithsonian building. Once there he called on Owen and Rufus P. Choate of Massachusetts, "who goes for a very large library," on September 7. Rogers traced David Owens's suggestive plans in order to study them back home and returned them later in the month. He also inspected the proposed site on the Mall in the company of several dignitaries, including the president. He was instructed to "make a sketch of a plan . . . differing from the plan [of David Owen, presumably] as I might think for the best." Back in Boston, he began to study his proposal when he found time. Members of the building committee, which included Colonel Totten, Robert Owen, and William Jervis Hough, the Democratic congressman and one of the regents of the Smithsonian, visited Boston that month as part of a multicity tour to interview potential architects, including Ammi B. Young. They checked into the Tremont House, took a tour with Rogers of Faneuil Hall, the customhouse, and other sites, and had a long talk with him about the project.

Rogers worked on his Smithsonian design off and on, often late into the night and even on weekends while in Marshfield, until the middle of December. The submission deadline was Christmas Day. As time ran short, Solomon Willard came up from Quincy to help with drafting the entry. His twenty-three-year-old son Willard and James, Rogers's assistant, also pitched in. By December 16 he had "all the plans finished and fixed on cloth" and estimated the cost of the project; three days later, drawings, specifications, and estimates were packed and shipped by Adams Express to Washington. Only three of Rogers's drawings for the Smithsonian survive in that institution's archive: two floor plans and the east elevation. (Fig. 48) We do not have his specifications or estimate. Without more information, it is difficult to judge his proposal, but one is left wondering what he did during all the time he spent on the plans. Since he closely followed David Owen's

48. Project for the Smithsonian Institution, 1846. East elevation. Smithsonian Institution Archives.

schema and the rules of the competition, his problem mainly involved the exterior envelope. His drawing, despite all the hours spent on it and assistance received, is weak. The rules permitted only line drawings without color or shading, and his back-lining and faint washes hardly broke the rule. There is evidence of haste or inattention: on one sheet an explanatory note referring to the support of arches is assigned a number that does not appear on the plan. His east elevation would have risen as an incoherent mash-up of rather unruly forms, battlemented towers, and crenellations galore. The exterior wall of the semicircular lecture room to the south is opened with a stack of half-circular, then Tudor, then Gothic arches. The effort was far from his best, a combination of unfamiliar styles favored by the building committee. No perspective of the proposal survives in the archives, and there too he seems to have adhered to the rules even if other entrants did not.

Rogers followed his drawings to Washington, called on Owen on Christmas Eve, and then went to the Capitol to look at the competition entries. "There were a number of plans offered," he wrote, "very handsomely drawn and perspective plans colored up and shaded very pretty to look at." The building committee's announced preference for the style was Norman, or Early Gothic, or a combination of the two. This was no blind competition: the drawings were all signed. John Notman, Owen G. Warren, Wells and Arnot submitted Gothic entries; John Haviland sent in a Norman proposal; James Renwick Jr. offered plans in both styles; Howard Daniels chose Italianate.[67] Rogers's, as noted, was an eclectic mix. Over the next few days, he visited various offices to pitch his proposal and distribute letters of endorsement from various politicians. Although Marcy had given him the impression that the winner was already "in view," he was assured by Colonel Totten on January 1 "that no plans had been adopted and that all confidence was placed in my ability and experience." That same day, he called on Owen and heard to the contrary "that they had selected Mr. Renwick's plan and that he was going to set about revising . . . [it] and reducing the thing to the sum [that is, budget] proposed."

Undeterred by Owen's news, Rogers continued to lobby vigorously for his design to influential people and revisited the exhibition of the entries. He realized that his did not stand up well by comparison, so he took his drawings and stretched them on frames "so they could be seen to better advantage." Meanwhile, the rumor mill was in full operation. While Rogers twiddled his thumbs in the city awaiting official word of the results of his labor, during which time he took another look at the entries and called on the artist Charles Bird King, a Washington correspondent for the *Boston Recorder* reported on January 14, 1847, that he had been selected by the regents; even a newspaper as far away as Portland, Maine, got wind that he "will probably" be the architect.[68] On January 20 the regents agreed to let the architects explain their plans, but they adjourned before Rogers was called. After they received a letter from Andrew Eliot Belknap, one of his Boston supporters, refuting charges related to the "professional character of Josiah [Isaiah] Rogers," he was allowed to explain his project and distribute his "testimonials." Rufus Choate told him he favored his appointment, but perhaps reflecting their state of mind, he joined Arnot and Haviland in a tour of the Congressional Cemetery.[69] That was on January 22. The next day, Rogers reported that the regents had made no decision, but there existed "a strong look at adoption of Renwick's plan after all that has been said and wrote on the subject"; he admitted to being "rather low spirited about any success." On January 25 he was still having Choate draw up "resolutions . . . to offer to the Regents . . . in relation to appointing an architect." Three days later he learned they had "adopted Mr. Renwick's plan, but had decided on no plan to build by. *No architect appointed*" (his emphasis). But of course there had been, and in fact the whole process had been a charade.

Then began what has been called by one scholar a "tempest" among architects, and by another a "rebellion." Rogers's "impression" that the winner had been already been selected, which he received from Robert Owen on Christmas Eve, before the closing of the competition, was correct. In fact, three weeks earlier, before all entries had been received, the building committee announced to the Board of Regents that it had decided the prize should go to James Renwick Jr. Since Renwick's project needed to be adjusted to meet new circumstances, his success was not announced until late January 1847, when he was hired as the supervising architect of the building at $1,800 a year. With some justice, the defeated entrants mounted an angry campaign criticizing the competition. William Elliot, a Washington architect, led the attack with a letter to the editor in which he reviewed the rules that had been violated: inter alia, only line drawings without color or shading were permitted. Nonetheless, he noted, some competitors had been allowed highly colored perspectives (Renwick even submitted a model). David Arnot, an entrant Rogers seems to have spent time with during and after the long wait to learn who had (already) won, likewise complained bitterly of the way things were handled in his *Animadversions on the Proceedings of the Regents of the Smithsonian Institution in the Choice of the Architect* of 1847. Their shouts fell on deaf ears: young Renwick's design (with later alterations) still stands impressively as the so-called Castle on the Mall. When Rogers saw it in December 1853, he thought it "very inferior and badly constructed."

Renwick's was certainly among the top entrants in the Smithsonian competition, and he was powerfully backed. Rogers was not helped by his weakly presented entry, for competitions are often won by those who ignore the rules and send in lavish displays. Those rules were especially friable before the late nineteenth century, an era when the relationship of the architect to the public or the client was ill defined. We see this situation demonstrated often in Rogers's diary, and we see it here. One of his supporters informed him that William Jervis Hough, the most important member of the Board of Regents, had said, probably with one eye on Rogers's drawings, that he "could not design a plan of a building, was only capable to erect it." Rogers's innovative planning for the Tremont House and other irregular sites, as well as many other designs, gainsay such a statement, but given what we know of the character of Rogers's entry, this conclusion seems reasonable.

Originally, Rogers was one of the three architects given special consideration. According to the minutes for the meeting of the Smithsonian Regents on February 20, 1847, when a discussion about payment for designs arose, the committee stated that early on it had written to Notman, Renwick, and Rogers "asking for their plans and promising remuneration of some sort to be wholly determined by the board. All other architects . . . submitted plans voluntarily and were not promised any remuneration. Thus . . . the three architects 'stand on different footing than all others.' "[70] Nonetheless, although other entrants received payment in January, Rogers was initially told that the regents "did not think I had any claim for all I had done," which he thought "very strange and unaccountable proceedings." After several petitions to Robert Owen and others, however, in March 1847 he received $250 for his trouble. Certainly he must have had his fill of the Washington quagmire; and yet he was to return to the capital fifteen years later, and with an even more bitter result.

During 1846, in the midst of all his efforts for the competition, Rogers continued to be busy with various projects. He was joined in the office by (Morris?)

Geschiedt, and he drew and frequently supervised the building of houses. These included a town house for Daniel P. Parker on Beacon Street and ten houses planned for the corner of Harrison Avenue and Indiana Street; houses for a Mr. Freeman in Roxbury, a Mr. Parker on Beacon Street, a Mr. Gray, and a Mr. Boles; outlying cottages such as the one for Mr. Sturgis, location not noted; "such alterations as I might think for his comfort" for William Lawrence's house on Tremont Street as well as other work; alterations to a house of Samuel Farrar in Bangor, Maine;[71] a house for a client in Providence; boarding houses for Enoch Mudge's mill; shops on Long Wharf in Boston; supervision of the Howard Athenaeum; and a tomb for an unnamed client in New Orleans. He also drafted alterations to the old Town House for use as the city hall of newly incorporated Roxbury, now part of Boston; the alterations there were to be confined to the interior.[72] It is unclear whether anything was ever built. At the same time, his trusting nature—or naiveté in matters of business—was leading him into a financial disaster.

The story begins early in 1846, when a broker named H. H. Dexter approached Rogers to design several houses at Harrison Avenue and Indiana Street in Boston, where building lots were advertised for sale into April. Dexter published notice of his intention to build and asked Rogers for drawings for four, then five, then six, and finally ten houses at this location, homes to cost between $2,200 and $2,690. On March 19 Rogers "agreed verbally to build them for him." After a series of alterations to the drawings requested by Dexter, including a "circular corner" for one, Rogers began to plot and oversee the driving of pilings. He then, oddly enough, "executed [a] mortgage deed for $1000 for one year," giving Dexter a "certificate of value of my place at Marshfield." It is indicative of Rogers's surprising lack of wariness in financial matters—at least in this case—that his notes about what happened next are hard to follow (although admittedly they were not intended to be read by outsiders). In early April he received $500 from Dexter "on account of contract for dwelling houses," $490 of which he immediately gave to the carpenter. That same day, he and Dexter signed the plans and specifications for building ten houses, but neither the mortgage nor the contract seems ever to have reached the Suffolk County Recorder of Deeds, contrary to what was customary.[73] Things started to go downhill when, two weeks later, Rogers could get no money from Dexter to pay the men. He "failed to pay his checks and kept out of the way" while Rogers had trouble placating unpaid suppliers and laborers. After a week of trying to hold things together, Rogers noted that Dexter had assigned "all his rights to his interest" to him "and also all his personal property." This would seem to have left Rogers accountable for the man's unpaid bills, and by May 9 the architect discussed seeking relief in chancery, or bankruptcy court, and tried to learn "what the law allows me to retain from being sold" to satisfy those debts. Somewhere along the line he had made a terrible mistake.

Things looked better on May 12, when Dexter promised to raise the money and give Rogers $1,000 on the mortgage, but the next day the architect learned that his associate "had cleared out and left me nothing." The news arrived that the broker had bought a bank draft worth 750 pounds using a check for $3,600 drawn on the Hamilton Bank, where he had no funds. "A Heavy and Successful Swindle" the *Evening Transcript* announced. Dexter returned to Boston from Portland the next day to refute the charge, apparently successfully, and a desperate Rogers accepted $150 in partial payment for the mortgage plus two notes for the balance of his debt, despite the unreliability of the man's paper. And that's all we hear from or about Dexter, who apparently vanished leaving Rogers holding the (empty) bag. It's also the last note about the Harrison Avenue dwellings, which seem not to have been built, although foundations had been prepared. In the aftermath of this sorry episode, Rogers put his library out to auction, made application at the direction of his lawyers "for [the] discharge of my debts by my giving up all my property," went the rounds asking for help from businessmen such as William Lawrence, and sought signatures from his assignees including Enoch Mudge, from whom he borrowed $3,000. He also bargained with the court for more time "to get money raised for [his] personal estate" and managed to do just that; he then lost and regained ownership of his Marshfield homestead, surviving the disaster only with the help of his many well-fixed friends. The architect had proven himself an accomplished designer and a gifted builder but an incautious businessman.

Rogers carried on with much other work through this defalcation, including his struggles in Washington, which his diary treats as just another line item in life. He designed a series of stores on Long Wharf for a Mr. Lamb that may never have materialized, worked on the president's house at Harvard, and supervised alterations to other buildings, including an "old medical college" that was to become a children's infirmary. A constant parade of residential work crossed his drawing board as well. Among the chores were alterations and additions to a house for a Mr. Ward that first appear in the diary in early April, while Rogers was struggling with the Dexter debacle. Plans were finished by the end of the month, and demolition began with the architect obtaining a sail to protect the work from weather. By mid-May the four-story brick addition had reached the second level, and roof trusses were being designed. To this point all had gone well, but then "Mr. Ward showed himself very nervous . . . and said some things I did not like." Rogers notes that he "explained to him the nature of the work," a speech he was often obligated to make. Again, things went smoothly for a while, with the architect making extended daily visits to the site, until Ward "agreed to let me off by my calling on him twice a day." It should be remembered that, in addition to dealing with the aftermath of the defalcation, in those days Rogers was supervising the erection of the Howard Athenaeum and knocking on doors in Washington, and soon he received a commission to remodel William Lawrence's house on Tremont Street. Nevertheless, near the end of the job, Rogers found Ward full of "dissatisfaction in my not spending my time all at his house." Two days later he received $301.15 "in full for services and plans," yet he agreed to continue "to render all assistance he may require in finishing the house."

Any architect then or now would say that residential projects, especially remodeling, are the most difficult, time-consuming, and frustrating work an architect can undertake. William Lawrence's domestic commission was equally tedious. The philanthropist was among the most name-worthy clients to enter the diary at this time, although nothing of lasting significance seems to have resulted from the association. The academy in Groton, Massachusetts, was renamed for the deep-pocketed and civic-minded William and his brother Amos, siblings of the even wealthier Abbott Lawrence, Whigs all of them, who furnished it with a library and scientific apparatus, enlarged its buildings, and ornamented its grounds.[74] In mid-December 1845, Rogers worked on drawings for William's house in Groton and for an addition to the academy. After suggested changes, he drew up an estimate for the latter on Christmas Eve. In August of the next year he had his assistant James draw a perspective for "Mr. Lawrence of Groton Academy" (present location unknown), and in October he worked on a fence for the school. Academy records show that William Lawrence donated $5,000 for an enlargement of the first school building planned by Rogers and erected in 1846–47. It burned down in 1868.

Other references to Lawrence focus on his plot at Mount Auburn Cemetery and his Boston house. Rogers's notes to himself in regard to Mount Auburn an addition to the Lawrence plot and a fence for it, which the architect laid out. They also discussed stained glass for his tomb, which Lawrence turned down as too expensive. That was in May 1846. William Lawrence died in Boston after a year-long paralysis, in October 1848.[75] Cemetery records show that he is interred in the Lawrence family plot across from Jacob Bigelow's cemetery chapel, but no stone marks his grave. The entire plot, however, is enclosed within a cast-iron fence ornamented with upright flaming torches that might be the same as what Rogers planned in 1846. Despite Lawrence's statement that he wanted the architect to design for his Tremont Street house something to make him comfortable, he proved to be a finicky client. A new interior stair and portico seem to have been the main changes to the front part of the house, but improvements in the rear were more extensive.[76] These included a kitchen and washroom begun in August. Daily site visits followed, as usual, and the project was finished by the end of the year.

A slow period ensued in which Rogers achieved little beyond some remodeling; work on drains, backyards, and bay windows; and projects for several hotels that never seemed to materialize. For one of these, in Washington, D.C., his office prepared a framed perspective. There were also several long stays in Marshfield—periods of rest after recent battles. This repose ended in April 1847, when Rogers received word in Boston that he was wanted immediately in New York "to see about making plans for the opera house at Astor Place." Eager as always when a commission rose on the horizon, he left for Manhattan at five p.m. that same day. The message had come from a Mr. Bragaldi, that is, Mario Bragaldi, the Milan-born artist, designer, and erstwhile architect who had decorated the Astor house dining room in 1843.[77] Rogers would consult with him during the design of the project. But the impetus for the building might have come from James Henry Hackett, for he was to leave the Howard Athenaeum and become lessee of the Astor opera when it was built. He is not mentioned in the diary in this connection, however.

The following day being Sunday, after talking over plans for the house with Bragaldi, Rogers went up to Harlem and looked at the nearly finished arcaded aqueduct of John Jervis's Croton water system. This was the project for which he had sketched unofficial proposals during 1838–40. What he now saw appealed to his developed sense of monumental lithic architecture: he called it a "stupendous construction" and "a noble structure of the age." On Monday he picked up a project for a hotel at Broadway and Chambers Street, then caught the steamer for Boston. On Tuesday he drafted plans for the hotel and the theater and then left for Marshfield. Back in Manhattan, he talked to a Mr. Brown "about commencing business in New York again," then went to see P. T. Barnum's General Tom Thumb, "a wonder of the ages." A talk with Bragaldi about setting up a New York office together "in making plans" came to no conclusion. They then discussed his layout for the opera house, and Rogers left for Boston after arranging that Bragaldi would notify him when anything was decided about the project.

The artist called him back in early May, expressing his agreement with the initiator of the project, the banker and real estate developer Matthew Morgan, to begin building the opera at $10 per day. Rogers rented quarters near the worksite, acquired bed linens from the Society of Employment for the Poor, borrowed an unnamed book on theater design, and started drawing fast to stay ahead of the construction already under way. Geschiedt and a Mr. Brandt assisted him, and his son Willard came to help. The drawings were a major production: at one point he worked simultaneously on "three sheets of elephant paper," a standard size at twenty-three by twenty-eight inches. A model of the roof trusses was in hand when the cornerstone was laid in July. The house opened in November 1847, seven months after Rogers first heard of the project, with one of the earliest performances of Verdi's "Ernani" in the United States.

The newspapers' judgments of the Astor Opera House interior ranged from beautiful to gorgeous.[78] (Fig. 49) It was arranged in a parquet, two tiers of boxes, and a gallery, not unlike the recently opened Howard Athenaeum. Also like that precedent, the room sat sixteen hundred comfortably, accommodating two thousand under pressure. Armchairs formed the seating in the parquet; the boxes had sofas. The railings in front of the boxes and gallery were of cast iron. The room was ventilated through an iron lattice that extended around the edge of the ceiling over the gallery. Again as in the Boston structure, the architect shaped the curve of the ceiling and the boxes "to give effect to the music." Bragaldi directed the painting of the scenery and decorated the boxes and the ceiling, which was made of wood "for the sake of acoustic advantages" and covered with canvas. The latter bore portraits of Mozart, Rossini, and Bellini. A large chandelier hung from its center.

As well designed as the interior seems to have been, based on contemporary expectations, the exterior was awkward—"of peculiar shape," according to the press. (Fig. 50) Here brick and brownstone replaced Rogers's beloved granite. One of its pediments, that above the entrance, rose in the same plane and at the end of a long two-story rectangular facade, producing a decidedly awkward unclassical unbalance. The ground floor was arcuated, and on it rested a colossal order. This consisted of Ionic engaged half columns of cut brick painted yellow, with brownstone capitals and bases, beneath the pediments.[79] On the elevation that extended away from the entrance pediment, however, the colossal order changed to Doric pilasters. The classical is a flexible system of design, as John Summerson

49. Astor Place Opera House, New York City, 1847. Ball of the New York Fire Department, n.d. Picture Collection, New York Public Library, Astor, Lenox, and Tilden Foundations.

50. Astor Place Opera House, New York City, 1847. Exterior. Picture Collection, New York Public Library, Astor, Lenox, and Tilden Foundations.

so cogently explained,[80] but this head-on collision was a solecism. The site at Lafayette, Eighth, and Astor Place was a difficult one, and Rogers had to adapt the building to it. But his solution, the result perhaps of the hurried history of the design, cannot be completely blamed on the location. It is possible to begrudge history for removing many of Rogers's buildings, but not the exterior of the Astor Place Opera House.

The proprietors had the house designed and erected to attract the cream of New York society, but it suffered a short downhill existence. The infamous Astor Place Riot of May 1849, in which 22 died, over 150 police and civilians were injured, and more than 100 were arrested, seems to have cursed the site. Although the dispute erupted between the followers of two egotistical actors, the American Edwin Forrest and the British William Charles Macready, they represented a more broadly based division between elite and popular culture. The opera-house dress code irked the populace. As a minstrel song from 1849 warned: "De Astor Opera is anoder nice place; / If you go thar, jest wash your face! / put on your 'kids,' and fix up neat, / For dis am de spot of de eliteet!"[81] The theater suffered the same fate as the Howard in Boston, but at an accelerated pace. American middle-brow consumers were a powerful force, then as now. From productions of grand opera, the offerings quickly evolved into popular plays, and the original scenery by Bragaldi was sold at a sheriff's sale at knocked-down prices. The company ceased to exist in 1853, and the building was sold to the Mercantile Library Association. Renamed Clinton Hall, it stood until 1890, when it was replaced by the ten-story block that still occupies the site.

In the interlude between work on the Astor Place Opera House and his arrival in Cincinnati, Rogers visited his hometown. There he designed the remodeling of the Second Meeting House, a liberal Unitarian congregation led by George Leonard since 1835, after estimating the cost difference of a new building versus repairing the old. He in effect clothed the eighteenth-century preaching box with a single central tower-belfry-spire. Its plan and roof section he measured and sketched in his diary in March 1847, with the same applied brittle Gothic details, pointed arches, faux piers, and crenellations he had used a decade and a half earlier at the First Parish in Cambridge. The building fell to the wreckers in 1977.[82]

Rogers's seven-year return to Boston, with its coda in New York, produced a diverse body of work, from grand successes like the majestic facade of the Merchants' Exchange and the composition of the Harvard College Observatory, through the peril of bankruptcy and frustratingly unrealized projects for the nation's capital, to the acclaimed Howard Athenaeum. By the end of this period he was pushing fifty years old, with more than a busy quarter century of laborious accomplishment behind him, and he might have considered slowing down. Instead, he charged ahead in an unfamiliar location. He anticipated John Soule's advice (often misattributed to Horace Greeley) and set his sights westward to "grow up with the country." His headquarters were now to be in Cincinnati, although his work also took him into Kentucky and the Deep South as well as Chicago, Milwaukee, and beyond. His peripatetic existence was far from over.

CHAPTER

4

Cincinnati
1848–1852

IN THE 1840s and 1850s Cincinnati, Longfellow's "Queen of the West," was a boomtown, the fastest-growing city in the country. Its population rose by mid-century to well over one hundred thousand. Its location was enviable. Situated on the Ohio River that flowed out of Pittsburgh and headed, via the Mississippi, to New Orleans, Cincinnati also connected outward on the Miami and Erie Canal. The railroad, which had arrived in 1836, soon linked it to Lake Erie and beyond, and for decades steamboats had been carrying passengers to Pittsburgh, New Orleans, and points in between. The urban vitality attracted travelers and immigrants, creating a diverse citizenry that included Germans by the 1830s—the artists Frank Duveneck and John Henry Twachtman grew up in that community—and Irish a few years later. It was an important place for dressmaking and furniture production, home of Procter and Gamble and the Singer Sewing Machine Company. Civic leaders such as Nicholas Longworth and Henry Probasco encouraged the arts, and it was a center of learning and letters. Frances Trollope and Harriet Beecher Stowe called Cincinnati home for a while, and on its Grecian campus, Lane Theological Seminary became a hotbed of religious and academic debate under Lyman Beecher, Caleb Stowe, and others. The city's position across the river from Kentucky led to much abolitionist—and anti-abolitionist—activity. (Remember Eliza's ice-hopping escape across the river in *Uncle Tom's Cabin* of 1852.) While Longfellow's 1854 poem "Catawba Wine" celebrated the area's vineyards,[1] its bustling meatpacking industry gave the city its more popular and unenviable name: Porkopolis.

In 1848 Rogers was called to this lively, up-and-coming metropolis by the proprietors of the Burnet House, a group of investors from the mercantile community that included Nicholas Longworth, whose vineyards Longfellow's poem celebrated, and Griffin Taylor, a wealthy businessman and civic leader. They wanted him to provide a design for and supervise the construction of a hostelry worthy of Cincinnati's aspiring stature.[2] It was to be named after Judge Jacob Burnet, who owned the land on which it would be built, and a joint stock company was to fund the enterprise. The hotel would be run by Abraham B. ("A. B.") Coleman, formerly of the Astor House in New York, who became the "principal agent in forwarding the enterprise." He and Rogers grew to be fast friends, working side by side on this and other projects.

Few men could call themselves architects in Cincinnati when Rogers arrived—only seven are listed in *Williams' Cincinnati Guide* for 1848–49. The most important were Seneca Palmer, designer of Lane Seminary and other Grecian works, the Irish-born William Tinsley, and Henry Walter, noted designer of several mostly Grecian churches, including St. Peter-in-Chains, the Roman Catholic cathedral. None could match Rogers's widespread reputation, especially his stature as the father of the modern hotel. The two most significant locally born architects during Rogers's tenure were James K. Wilson and his student James W. McLaughlin, but Wilson entered independent practice only in 1851 and then joined William Walter, Henry's son, in partnership that decade.[3] The diary mentions moments when Rogers crossed paths with these and other competitors in the city. The scarcity of architects with experience anywhere near his own certainly accounts for the early rush to commission him while he supervised the rising Burnet House.[4]

Whether Rogers thought of this move as permanent, he does not say. He relocated Emily, his daughter Cornelia (eventually to be Mrs. Samuel Hatch), and sons Willard and Isaiah Jr., rented a house on West Third Street opposite the site of the hotel, and soon joined a church. He and Emily (who can only be described as his long-suffering wife) seem rarely to have enjoyed a stable home life. They had lived in ever-changing rented quarters in various places, and in Cincinnati they moved many more times in coming years, even occasionally boarding at Rogers's grand hotel, until they established homes outside the city.

Rogers "came a stranger among us," said the local paper, "unacquainted with the material and workmen he must employ, and therefore . . . laboring under some disadvantages."[5] Drawings for the layout and digging foundations at the hotel began in spring 1848. The work progressed, with Rogers supervising daily at the site when he was not off examining materials, from stone to brick to timber to cast iron, bargaining with suppliers and tradesmen, recruiting fabricators, or working as paymaster for these myriad accounts. Rogers had help with the drawings from his son Willard, as well as from seemingly two other draftsmen who had worked for him in the east, one presumably (Frederick?) Schmidt. It was he who drew a "very good" perspective of the hotel in September–October 1848, but after a "little altercation" about his wages, Rogers paid him off and, one assumes, dismissed him, for he appears no more in the diary. In mid-June 1850 Rogers hired another unidentified draftsman who may have been a man named Titus, and he was drawing by November.

Rogers began writing specifications for the Burnet House in mid-August 1848, and the cornerstone was quietly laid on October 11 "with a few friends present." That lackluster event notwithstanding, local interest was such that he had to hire a guard to keep gawkers off the construction site. Work progressed with only a few hitches into early spring 1850. Rogers gave a description of the building to the *Chronicle and Atlas* on January 22 of that year, and on March 4, he wrote, members of the Ohio state legislature visited the site and reacted positively to the project. He took his first bath in the hotel on April 20, and the facility opened on May 3 with a grand celebration that was reported in newspapers countrywide. Rogers crows that two thousand people dined at the celebration (a number confirmed by other sources) and seemed much pleased with his creation. Attendees came from all over the region, from the "hard-handed laborer to the millionaire," according to the *Cincinnati Enquirer*. "Never have I seen a larger company so gratified and enjoyed themselves so much," noted Rogers in a rare if characteristically reserved expression of his feelings. One local reporter showed no such reserve when he called the event a "grand soiree, which . . . set the citizens of Porkopolis all agog."[6] Two days after the opening, the architect went over to the hotel, sat, smoked a "segar," and watched a great crowd of the idle curious. It was all very pleasant. Forgotten amid the popular success were the earlier grumbling about awarding the contract to him, apparently because he was an out-of-towner who brought along his own skilled workmen, as well as a report during construction that the building was ill founded and would collapse. Also cast aside was an undefined lawsuit whose beginning is perhaps lost in the gap of pages from July through December 1849. Although such suits seem to have been a way of life for Rogers in Cincinnati as elsewhere (and this one dragged on), his notes are usually too vague to allow detailed analysis without external information. Still, it did not take long for his office to receive other commissions. The shift in home base seems to have gone remarkably well.

In 1850 Rogers made arrangements with the local papers to reproduce "cuts" (wood engravings) after drawings of his building. The October 19 edition of the *Ohio Daily Statesman* headed its description of the Burnet House with an image that probably reflects Schmidt's perspective; about the same time, Adolphus A. Forbriger drew a view produced by Onken's lithography that may have been based on the same perspective. (Fig. 51) It shows the usual urban hustle and bustle of horses, coaches, and pedestrians milling around the corner of Third and Vine Streets, and rising above it all, the proud new Cincinnati hostelry ready to receive the world. The paper lauded Rogers, "to whose taste and judgment, the proprietors and public are deeply indebted" for "a monument which will hand his name

51. Burnet House, Cincinnati, Ohio, 1848–50. Lithograph by Adolphus A. Forbriger, published by Otto Onken, ca. 1850. Prints and Photographs Division, Library of Congress.

down to posterity as a master workman, and one who may with confidence be employed in the most intricate and responsible positions." The account added that the "style of architecture is entirely modern, and possesses many peculiarities that deservedly belong to Mr. Rogers." No wonder commissions soon rolled in.

Rogers proved adaptable to his new circumstances out west. His approach to design changed but remained founded on innovative planning, and it was still significantly materials-based. The Grecian era had mostly drawn to a close by midcentury, as did the early Gothic (except for ecclesiastical work), and Rogers's range of useful historical precedent changed quickly. The Italianate and early Romanesque took their place. But perhaps most important, the large-scale granite components that had made up his early buildings were no longer easily available (the rare exception was the granite for the front of A. B. Coleman's vault at Spring Grove Cemetery, shipped from Quincy in the 1850s). In Cincinnati, Louisville, and nearby cities, Rogers began to use different building components and lighter materials, such as stucco, and he joined the early adopters of terra-cotta ornament. He also increased the use of developing ferrous technology, not only for structural reasons but for aesthetic ones as well. The result was a less ponderous architecture than he had previously designed. But however his sources and materials changed, his acute sense of technical innovation stayed with him.

The Burnet House is long gone, but it was well described at its opening by a variety of newspapers. The architect's own detailed description, and observations "derived from the Plan Drawing" according to the *Chronicle,* gave a footprint of 212 by 209 feet, a height of six stories, and a count of 342 well-lighted and well-ventilated rooms. The paper, and so presumably the architect, stated that the style "may be called Bracketted Italian," which in its lightness and elegance "contrasts very well and strongly with the plain and heavy look of the Astor House." Rogers specified rough stone exterior walls backed with brick and plastered with "a solid composition." The Third Street front was molded into a five-part, or quincunx, composition of center and outlying wings joined by lower connectors; another paper may have been more accurate when it called the style the "Italian villa order."[7] Variations of this Palladian quincunx would mark many of Rogers's later hotels. The contrast in style with earlier works showed his ability to adapt to prevailing conditions. The axial main entrance, at the level of the *piano nobile* behind a hexastyle Grecian Ionic portico, was approached up a broad flight of stairs set between a divided forty-foot terrace over shops. The terrace, which commanded a wide view of the Ohio River and the blue hills of Kentucky beyond, could be reached only from inside the hotel. On the skyline above rose a 142-foot-high gilded dome forty-two feet in diameter that existed purely for external effect. Another version of his peripteral tholos, this one of the Corinthian order, and a flag (and telegraph?) staff rose above that. Eight shops, four each flanking the stairway, lined the front at ground level. Also at that level Rogers placed a seventy-six-foot-square barroom graced with thirty cast-iron columns, which was reached from inside by elegant iron stairways, as well as a courtyard, servants' rooms and storerooms, service areas, and rooms for bathing. The ones for ladies could be reached by inside stairs, the gentlemen's via an entrance on Vine Street.

It is clear from descriptions in the *Chronicle* and *Statesman* that the Burnet House plan, if not its elevations, was a slightly modified remake of those Rogers used for his hotels in Boston and New York. The main approach by stairway emptied into an entrance hall or lobby that measured forty by fifty-two feet; the space was embellished with eight iron Ionic columns and four antae, beyond which was the office. The entrance area led to corridors that ran parallel to Third Street and connected with smaller ladies' and larger gentlemen's dining rooms and parlors; there was also a children's dining room, said to be a new feature at the Burnet. The floors were paved in marble squares of different colors, a pattern Rogers seems to have favored. (Fig. 52) Using different geometrical shapes, he drew similar contrasting patterns for later buildings, such as the Ohio statehouse and Longview Asylum. The main corridor also led to broad flights of stairs that ascended to the rooms overhead; the well-ventilated kitchen was at the back of this floor. Water closets at the rear of the courtyard and outside the kitchen could be reached from the main hall across a "beautiful lattice-work bridge made of iron ... a new style of work, altogether—the invention of Mr. Rogers." A section through the bridge, which passed from front to rear of the courtyard, formed "an Ellipsis 8 feet high by 6 feet wide."[8] Rogers's diary tells us that he had drawn this feature by late October 1848; it was his patented bridge, first erected at Quincy Market in Boston and like the one he had added to the Tremont House earlier in the decade. It is amazing that such a distinct feature of these dramatic hotels seems never to have been captured by an artist or daguerreotypist.

The hotel's furnishings were lavish by existing standards. At least one newspaper credited the interiors to both architect and client, and Coleman did order furniture on trips to New York, according to Rogers. Since fire was a constant threat in hotels as in other public buildings, most of which were lighted by gas, Rogers made his characteristic fireproofing provisions, including a thick layer of cement beneath the finished flooring. When fires occurred in this building, and they did from time to time, they were easily contained and caused little damage. Rogers could quickly direct repairs, which the insurance company promptly paid. Upstairs rooms, all with bathing facilities and water closets, were accessible off double-loaded corridors, thus receiving light from either the exterior or the courtyard. Each had a marble fireplace. As at the Tremont and Astor, room ser-

52. Burnet House, Cincinnati, Ohio, 1848–50. Lobby. Collection of the Public Library of Cincinnati and Hamilton County, Ohio.

vice could be had using J. D. Jackson's "telegraph," the annunciator, "one of the most beautiful pieces of mechanism ever executed," according to one wide-eyed reporter. Under the management of Coleman, the hotel received high praise from most of its guests for the arrangement, architecture, and the murals by Francis Pedretti, an Italian-born decorator who arrived in Cincinnati in 1854 and worked in many of Rogers's buildings.

Over the years, the Burnet House was altered several times by James W. McLaughlin and others: the dome was removed, the entrance relocated around the corner, the original entry altered, and so on. It eventually became the next-door neighbor of H. H. Richardson's Chamber of Commerce Building. On his visits to the city while seeking that commission in 1885, Richardson chose to stay at the old-fashioned and much less architecturally distinguished St. Nicholas Hotel, a twenty-five-room gentleman's establishment.

Although the Burnet was an eye-opener in the West in terms of design sophistication and technical innovation, Blanche Linden reminds us that conditions were still relatively primitive in hotels of the period, judging by the standards of the next century. "Bituminous coal burnt in open furnaces and fireplaces provided both heat and pollution," she notes, and the untreated water supply originated in cisterns. Sewage was primitive; to use Ben Jonson's Elizabethan coinage, "merdurinus" discharge from the privies flowed directly into the Ohio River. Standards of cleanliness and hygiene were rudimentary; horse dung littered the wood block streets. Yet, the Burnet rose well above the average for those who could afford its luxuries. It became, again according to Linden, "a visible symbol of the city's prosperity, just as the proprietors had wished in commissioning it." Local papers understandably labeled it the greatest wonder of the West, and the *Illustrated London News* went further still, calling it the best hotel in the world.[9] This marked the second time Rogers's work had received rare international recognition, his Merchants' Exchange in New York having been the first.

In the first years after its opening, the Burnet House proved its value to proprietors and architect alike, becoming the center for local, regional, and national social activities, ceremonial celebrations, and political rallies: it hosted meetings of groups as varied as the Wool Growers Association, the Know-Nothings, the Ohio Agricultural Ball, and the Firemen's Ball. It temporarily housed such celebrities as Jenny Lind and her troupe; Amen Bey, Turkey's first envoy to the United States; Lajos Kossuth, the president of Hungary; Edward, Prince of Wales; General Winifield Scott; and the former U.S. president Millard Fillmore. Charles Dickens added it to the list of Rogers-designed hotels in which he lodged. Abraham Lincoln called for national unity from the hotel's front steps on his way to Washington in February 1861 (and would repeat the call at Astor House). But the grand hotel's most memorable place in America's history occurred one day in March 1864 when

Generals Grant and Sherman met there to plot the destruction of Georgia. The Sons of Union Veterans held meetings in that same room until 1926, when the hotel fell to the wrecker's ball.

For months after he began revising drawings for and supervising construction of the Burnet House, Rogers's diary has little to say about amusements because he had little time to enjoy them. Bit by bit, though, he and Emily, or more often he alone, began to enter Cincinnati popular life, to step out in the evening when he did not need to draw. The couple socialized with the Colemans and other friends. Rogers paid a dollar so that he and his wife could laugh at "Winchell's Drolleries," a performance by a roving single-name comedian called by the papers "inimitable" and "the funniest man in the United States." One evening they took advantage of living in Porkopolis and visited the market to see the "very fine" display of meats (rather like viewing the food halls at Harrods in London, although probably not as artistic). Rogers attended performances at the National Theater, including James Henry Hackett's popular portrayals of Falstaff and Rip Van Winkle, using complementary tickets from the actor (whom he knew from the Howard Athenaeum in Boston), sat in on lectures on biology and other sciences, and often went bowling with the fellows. He might smoke a "segar" in the evening, attend a meeting at Masonic Hall, or just gather with friends at his house or theirs. On the "cool and pleasant" Fourth of July in 1849 the Rogers family and another made an excursion to the Big Miami River. "All hands went to work," he reported, "some gathering wood and chips to make a fire, some after milk, some after water, and we soon had things moving toward . . . a fine dinner . . . on the grass."

At other times pleasure mixed with business. In February 1850 he had a "fine time" at a "Hebrew Ball," presumably with Emily, although she is not mentioned. Early the next November, Rogers got a "call to make a plan for a synagogue for Jews." He showed them a sketch, moved on to developed drawings, which he worked on nightly through the month, and finished the design by early December. In July 1851 at a meeting at Heidelbach, Seasongood and Company, a wholesale dry-goods supplier, he agreed to plan and supervise the synagogue for 5 percent of cost, but the project is not mentioned again.[10] He later declined a free ticket to a dance that might have been the Odd Fellows' Ball at the Burnet—he had "seen enough balls for the present"—but then he later attended the ball of the Ladies' Society of the Universalist Church, presumably with his wife.

As the Burnet House rose under the ever watchful eyes of Rogers and Coleman, the architect began to spend many evenings drafting other projects, from houses, hotels, churches (including one on Fourth Street), tombs, and shops (many with iron fronts) to a bank, market, restaurant, and fire watchtower. He also produced designs for the Hamilton County courthouse and jail (in a kind of competition) and, in early 1849, a public assembly room at Fourth and Vine Streets for a Mr. Bates. This was probably John Bates, proprietor of the National Theater on

Sycamore, between Third and Vine Streets, for whom he also sketched a theater for St. Louis. Other commissions included a building for Jenny Lind to sing in that was surely never erected (she appeared at the newly renovated National Theater during her visit to Cincinnati in 1851[11]) and stores for Griffin Taylor, also at Third and Vine. By the end of January 1850 Rogers was being sought after from downriver for a library in Louisville and alterations to the hotel there, among other work. He also consulted on several hotels in New Orleans and Mobile, Alabama. All this work flowed into his small office within a couple years after his arrival. Clearly the region's expanding population needed his services.

One of the first of these commissions—which were undertaken while Rogers supervised construction of the Burnet House—arrived in the early days of 1849 with a discussion about a building for the Commercial Bank to be erected on the east side of Main Street, between Third and Fourth. Revisions in the program, the result of meetings with Captain Jacob Stradler and James Hall, occasioned several versions of the design over the next month, and on February 6 Rogers made a bargain with the committee to superintend the erection of the bank for 10 percent of the cost. He then went back to the drawing board. First, an old structure had to be removed, materials procured, and workmen found. Rogers often gives detailed accounts of the building process, and his remarks on this project can stand for many other examples. They also give an idea of a design that no longer exists.

Work proceeded rapidly from later winter to early spring 1849. Digging of the cellar began in early February, and by the third week Rogers was laying out on paper the stonework for the front. By March 9 he was drawing a skylight, and a week later he received a proposal to handle the ironwork. By early April, "shears" were in place for hoisting columns and pilasters,[12] and by April 10 stone walls were ready for iron beams for the banking-room floor; some of the iron steps had also been installed. The banking-room floor beams were all in and "leveled up" by April 16, and within four days the second-story floor was placed. Five days later the workers "commenced to set the iron columns for rolling shutters." Next came iron columns for the first-floor front, and the roof was begun on April 28. By May 2 some jack rafters (suggesting perhaps a hip roof) were in place and the first section of pilasters installed; arched windows were set on the front, and part of the roof was tinned by May 9. Then plastering began, using cast-iron lathes, and skylights appeared by midmonth. Rogers was designing counters by early June; by midmonth, plastering was finished, the ceiling sash was readied for stained glass, and rolling shutters were put up. Flag floors were going in by mid-July. Surely all that iron was thought to make the building fire- and burglar-proof, and Rogers will later use the same methods and materials in other banks and stores. And here the schedule ends abruptly with a gap in the diary.

Meanwhile, by early May 1849 Rogers had begun to design a store on Main Street just down from the Commercial Bank, a commission that eventually became the four-bay, five-story wholesale hardware shop of Tyler Davidson & Company. Drawings must have occupied some of his unrecorded time, but it seems that the final design was not set, for in early January 1850 Davidson's brother-in-law and partner, Henry Probasco, discussed the possibility that Rogers might superintend Probasco's own design for the building, which apparently already existed. When Rogers told him he "did not approve [of] his plan," talks resumed the next day, with Rogers proving persuasive—a day later he recorded that "Mr. Probasco called and wished me to go on with their plans for the store and make the front to suit myself, that they would leave it to me." Rogers then began drawing a new front that was approved a few days later. This job sounds like a continuation of his frequent role as facade man; laying out a loft plan for a commercial building surely took little thought. In mid-February Rogers signed an agreement to direct the building of the store for a flat fee of $1,500. A separate payment for the design is not mentioned.

Thereafter, things moved along rather smoothly. In March, Rogers mentions drawings for the iron front and the need for conservation work on the adjacent store, caused by the removal of the old building on Davidson's lot. By July, men were setting iron columns in the ground-floor front and beginning to hoist stone for the upper floors, with the last stone in place by mid-August. On August 20 Rogers was writing a description of the building (now unlocated), and thereafter the shelving went in. The *Daily Gazette* for September 7 may have glanced at that description when it labeled the style "Domestic or Collegiate Gothic." Charles Cist's *Sketches and Statistics of Cincinnati in 1859* carried a wood-engraved facade of the store.[13] (Fig. 53) Rogers continued with the medieval forms he had occasionally used earlier in the decade. In Cincinnati he chose iron supports on the ground floor of urban fronts, as here and at the Commercial Bank, whereas he had used granite posts in Boston. The Davidson store's ground floor showed five Gothic clustered columns made of iron separating entrance and windows, a second floor of Gothic-arched windows surmounted by labels sitting on the first, and three more floors of continuous vertical piers, or "buttresses," as Rogers called them, rising to an ornamental cornice with corner finials. The buttresses of "fine blue limestone," according to the *Gazette,* stepped back at an angle at each floor but continued to describe vertical lines between the recessed pointed windows and labels of the upper floors. These continuous piers contributed to the emphasis on verticality, as did the narrow, attenuated proportions of the facade and the fact that the building rose higher than the neighboring haberdashery, also five stories tall. The effect was vaguely akin to those vertically articulated storefronts of the 1850s that gave such character to the area around Third and Chestnut Streets in Philadelphia, although it is difficult to imagine any connection.

The Davidson commission led to another, unrealized project for Henry Probasco. When he decided to build a mansion on his vast estate in Clifton, then a

53. Tyler Davidson & Co. Wholesale Hardware Store, Cincinnati, Ohio, 1849–50. Main Street front. From Charles Cist, *Sketches & Statistics of Cincinnati in 1859.*

suburb of Cincinnati, Probasco and his wife held a closed competition of sorts that included New York's A. J. Davis and the local architects John R. Hamilton, James W. McLaughlin, William Tinsley, and Rogers. Tinsley won with his Norman Revival design, "Oakwoods," which was begun in 1859 but finished only after the Civil War.[14] Rogers's design has not survived, but he would provide other homes in this affluent community.

The Episcopal congregation of Cincinnati, led by Reverend W. R. Nicholson, next engaged Rogers to design a church for the corner of Seventh and Plum Streets. Originally named St. John's, it later became St. Paul's Cathedral. Rogers received the order for the commission on June 30, 1849, and began drawing a few days later, but it was not until April 9 of the next year that he received official appointment as architect of the church. Then began another protracted and unhappy story, one indicative of the tenuous position of any American architect in the mid-nineteenth century. After Rogers worked on design changes to shorten the building to better fit its site and further developed the drawings, the congregation broke ground at the end of May 1850. Concrete foundations for the towers went in at the end of June, and work proceeded smoothly until the break in construction over the winter. When building resumed in the spring of 1851, Rogers upset the committee by revealing his estimate to complete the church. It became increasingly clear that funds were inadequate and more difficult to obtain. At the end of July came an order to stop all work but the plastering. When Rogers visited the inactive site early the next October, the watchman told him he had not been paid for a long time. The architect nonetheless continued to work, finishing a model of the roof at the end of the month.

A few days later came another altercation when the church committee tried to second guess Rogers's estimate. Always firm in the face of such doings, Rogers reported he was "determined that shall not be, if I can stop it." More negotiations followed and construction poked along, with Rogers trying with little success to raise money (even contributing some of his own) and sketching the arched main entrance portal. Discussion of cost and payments continued, including his proposal to relinquish his claims if the church were to be finished, but on December 8 he learned that the committee had employed other architects to complete it. Work then stopped permanently. The situation intensified two months later when Rogers was asked to divulge his accounts but answered that he would do so only if the committee paid him what was due. He then heard a rumor that he "had squandered the money on the church and abused their confidence," and he initiated a lawsuit to obtain his pay. His concern was so great that when he mislaid the drawings for the project, he worked himself into "a great excitement" thinking they had been stolen, but eventually he found them "tucked away very safely." He then made out bills for $450 and gave them to his agent to collect, but the rest of the

54. St John's Episcopal Church (later St. Paul's Cathedral), Cincinnati, Ohio, 1849–52 (unfinished). Exterior from Seventh and Plum Streets. Collection of the Public Library of Cincinnati and Hamilton County, Ohio.

story remains fuzzy as reported in the diary from time to time. In the early 1860s he was still holding a lien on the church and trying to collect his due.

For this Episcopal church commission, Rogers turned to a free handling of the round-arched Norman, or English Romanesque, style, but his struggles resulted in a crippled design that produced an awkward, ill-shapen, unfinished pile that must have irritated him for the rest of his life. (Fig. 54) Its stunted main towers capped by low shed roofs rose only to the ridge of the church. They were made of rough ashlar edged with quoins and stood at a forty-five-degree angle to the long axis of the nave, a most unusual arrangement. There seemed to be some reason for the tower facing the angle of the streets, but the one to the left of the portal must have looked extremely awkward next to the adjacent building. The rest of the exterior was stucco, perhaps as a cost-saving measure, and trimmed with stone. A well-wrought series of triple-dressed stone arches of diminishing radius framed the main portal, which was reached by a flight of convex steps. The dictates of A. W. N. Pugin and the Cambridge Camden Society about the appropriate style (Early English Gothic) and arrangement of an Episcopal church apparently had not reached Ohio at this early date, and the broad nave beneath a flat ceiling terminated in a shallow chancel beyond a wide arch. St. John's was, in fact, an old-fashioned Protestant meeting house. The church stood in its awkwardly interrupted state until demolished in 1937.

With the success of the Burnet House—not to mention the Tremont and Astor—it comes as no surprise that Rogers was immediately approached to design and erect other hotels in the Indiana-Ohio-Kentucky river district and, eventually, the Deep South. They came quickly and thickly to his attention. Already by August 1848 he had boarded the steamer *J. Q. Adams* bound for Madison, Indiana, down the Ohio halfway to Louisville. There the building committee for a new hotel gave him their views of what they wanted and showed him the site they had in mind, at the corner of Mulberry and Second Streets. He took the level of the grade at the location, where stood the old Fitzhugh's Hotel, and looked at some stone he did not like. Back in Cleveland he began to draw a first, and then a second, design with the help of his assistant Schmidt before that draftsman was sent packing in November. By mid-September the committee in Madison had studied Roger's proposal and liked it very much, but at this point the usual problem of financing seems to have arisen, for he was asked to estimate the cost of just half the front, and then for a new design to cost about $20,000. By mid-October the third design "pleased and satisfied" representatives of the proposed hotel, but in early November Rogers was asked to explain his design to an unnamed local architect, and he wrote to the committee "giving my reasons for declining." (The historian laments the loss of this statement of emerging professionalism.) The account of the hotel's opening in the *Daily Courier* for March 28 assigns the building to Francis Costigan, an "able and efficient" architect who "devoted his time and attention to the work," although Rogers received $160 for "making plans"; he also stayed at and attended the inaugural dinner of the hotel on March 28, 1850. It would seem that Costigan superintended the erection of Rogers's design. At the end of October 1848 Rogers spent a few evenings drafting a church or small chapel for Madison; whether it was built remains to be determined.

The *Daily Courier*'s account of the Madison House, "which ranks second only to the Burnet House in size, finish, and convenience," reported that it stretched nearly one hundred feet on Second Street and 136 feet on Mulberry, rising three stories above a low stone base. (Fig. 55) The painted brick exterior was organized in a shallow Palladian quincunx and capped with a bracketed cornice. One reached the main entrance "for gentlemen" up steps to a platform "made of the best limestone found in the West," upon which stood two "tower-of-the-wind columns" between antae surmounted by an entablature. A lingering bit of the Grecian Revival marked the otherwise Italianate building. From the entrance hall beyond that portal, one reached a crossing corridor leading to dining room, parlors, and stairs that ascended to about ninety rooms on the floors above. There was, of course, a central courtyard, although probably too small to require Rogers's lattice bridge. Gas manufactured on the premises lighted the building, and there was a telegraph, or annunciator, of J. D. Jackson's patent, precisely the same as the one in the Burnet House. The Madison House, the provincial progeny of the Tremont House, vanished long ago.

Rogers's subsequent hotel task was a remodeling. On the last day of January 1850 he "agreed to make another plan for [the] alteration of the mansion house" for John W. (rather than A. B.) Coleman. Here the meanings of *house* and *hotel* must be carefully watched. The Mansion House stood as a hotel on Main Street in Cincinnati; John W. Coleman's own dwelling house, alterations to which Rogers would plan later in the year, stood on Fourth Street. In mid-November, Rogers received pay ("Not enough") for work at both sites. He drafted a design to alter the existing Mansion House hotel during the evening of October 1 and showed it to Coleman the next day: "He was much pleased with elevations." Rogers worked on more drawings for the "mansion house" in mid-February, visiting the site and finding the work "getting along very well." On March 22 he detailed the cornice "for Mr. Coleman's house [hotel], Main Street," and the next week learned that the brickwork had reached the fourth floor; he gave "directions about the frontispiece to door" in early April but returned to see about it because "some of the wise ones thought it would not look right." He noted on April 12 the placement

55. Madison House, Madison, Indiana, 1848–50. Second Street front. Madison-Jefferson County Public Library, Ohio.

of the roof timbers for Coleman's "hotel" (the first time he used this word for the Main Street project), and on June 1 he "called up to Mr. Coleman's Waverly House," as the remodeled Mansion House had been renamed, and found it "nearly completed." On June 20 the *Cleveland Plain Dealer* published correspondence from Cincinnati about "another big Hotel" there, where "elegance, neatness and comfort are eminently combined." According to that paper, it was the just-opened Waverly House, built on the site of the Mansion House, on Main Street; the landlords were Elliot and Hendrickson. There is no mention of Rogers or John W. Coleman, who, although he sounds like the client in Rogers's diary, was also a mason-builder who had worked at the Burnet House. The remodeling of the Waverly Hotel (which no longer exists) should undoubtedly be added to the list of Rogers's Cincinnati works.

Immediately after the opening of the Madison House, Rogers received inquiries for two other outlying hotels, one for Dayton, Ohio, and the other for Niagara Falls. In July 1850 he rode in a buggy the sixty miles over to Dayton to breakfast with J. D. Phillips, for whom the hotel would be named, and listened to client expectations. Back in Cincinnati he worked on the design. At the end of the month he took a swing by rail and steamboat to Niagara Falls, passing through Dayton, Sandusky, and Buffalo (where another hotel was mentioned). The committee in Dayton liked the arrangement but suggested several minor changes. He also visited Woodland cemetery with J. D. Phillips but disapproved of its gateway. (He often disliked work of the kind he too had designed.)

By September 3 Rogers could begin to estimate the cost of the Dayton building. A member of the committee visited Cincinnati and found the estimate too high, prompting revisions to reduce the design; ground plans and a new estimate were sent off. While in Dayton overnight in mid-October, Rogers approved of the material and workmanship of the foundation and explained his plans. In late December he sent his new assistant, Mr. Titus, with revised drawings and instructions. In mid-May of the next year he responded to a call from the town to "show them how to proceed with the work." The 140-room Phillips House, at the corner of Third and Maine Streets, was in substance a larger reprise of the Madison House. (Fig. 56) Above a ground floor it rose to three stories of stark walls and regularly spaced rectangular windows. A faint five-bay central salient between bolder three-bay wings faintly recalled the quincunx organization favored by Rogers. Inaugurated with a lavish ball on October 14, 1852, the building was recorded in a daguerreotype by Dayton's A. (Albert) Bisbee (perhaps at Rogers's behest), which was exhibited that year at the third annual Ohio state fair.[15] The hotel came down in 1926.

From Dayton, Rogers went on to Niagara Falls. In March 1848 Hollis White and his partners received authorization from the New York state legislature to form a joint stock company to be called the Niagara Falls House Company for the

56. Phillips House, Dayton, Ohio, 1850–52. NCR Archive, Dayton History.

purpose of erecting a hotel there.[16] The company must have engaged an unknown architect sometime thereafter because in July 1849, more than a year later, White sent Rogers a set of drawings that immediately drove the architect to the drafting board to plan a better hotel, thus engaging him in a long, apparently fruitless endeavor to construct it. White, according to the *Albany Evening Journal,* was then the "well-known Host of the Eagle Hotel, at Niagara Falls, and a Whig of the earliest and truest stamp" as well as "a prince of good fellows." Rogers's identical political affiliation might have reinforced his acknowledged expertise in getting him this commission. And, although the history is anything but clear in the diary and not entirely clarified by other sources, he may ultimately have regretted it. After a year's delay, Rogers visited White in early August 1850, measured the site, saw the sights, and talked to a different man about another hotel; he began to draw later that month. By mid-September he could estimate the cost of his scheme in time for a visit from White to Cincinnati. The Albany paper reported on September 14 that White was about to erect a "splendid hotel" and wished him every success, both the plan and the location being admirable.

It is unclear whether that hotel ever materialized, but nearly four years later another letter from White sent Rogers back north to look over the subscription list and charter for what he now called the Niagara Falls Company Hotel. The architect then staked out the site himself and had it surveyed. Back in Cincinnati he set to drawing with the help of his son and Henry Whitestone, who had joined the office in 1852, having had two new drafting boards, one extra large, made for the project. By the July 4, 1854, Rogers, now back in New York, presented his plans for a hotel facing the falls; White was "very much pleased with them." Rogers then carried the drawings to Albany, where a Mr. Mitchell was contemplating building a hotel, and "tacked them up . . . for inspection by the people." In mid-August he began to draw a third scheme for the Niagara Falls hotel. After a fourth layout and a trip to Niagara in September, he produced a fifth, to cost no more than $100,000 but designed to be expandable. Not until March 1855 did Rogers write that Willard and Whitestone had "finished up" the plans. The architect and his help were busy with other projects during these years, so the fruitless interruptions of this hotel must have been frustrating, although Rogers never said so. There is no indication in the diary that a hotel from Rogers's design ever appeared at the falls, nor did a search of New York newspapers of this period alter that conclusion.

Rogers's practice continued to expand. By early 1850, at the latest, he had found Louisville, or Louisville had found him. Situated at the falls of the Ohio River some hundred miles downstream from Cincinnati, the city was then the tenth largest in the country and a thriving center for the slave trade and other commerce. What followed was a string of projects and realized commissions that would ultimately require the architect to open an office there. We first hear of a project for a library in February, when Rogers left a drawing for it with the "prominent capitalist" Lars Anderson, member of a distinguished Cincinnati family. He does not say why, and the project vanished. In mid-March he again visited the city to discuss the location of a proposed Masonic Hall, for which he sketched alternate solutions that convinced the committee to proceed with plans and an estimate; these he worked on through the rest of the month back in Cincinnati. Another meeting in Louisville on March 29 "sailed very well." Nonetheless, nearly a month later the committee returned his plans and asked for a new design. That one seems not to have satisfied, either, for nearly a month later, again back in Louisville, Rogers declined to present a bill for his unaccepted (and perhaps overpriced) work, telling the committee to "consider it a gift to the institution." His design seems not to have been built.

Within the year, however, a Masonic Temple began to rise in Louisville at Fourth and Jefferson Streets, the design of Elias E. Williams, a local architect.[17] Rogers seldom expresses frustration or anger in his dairy—what almost anyone else would have considered an unconscionable runaround (here as elsewhere during his career) almost never produces an outburst of wrath. Although no architect likes to lose a commission, Rogers may have been charitably inclined to give his time to a fraternal society of which he was a member. And in truth, in the spring of 1850 he was wholly occupied with Cincinnati buildings as well as drafting plans for an Exchange and Reading Room for Louisville and a design for alterations to the Louisville Hotel. The Davidson store construction, designs for the hotels in Dayton and Niagara Falls, some churches and houses, and other work, to say nothing of his judging the merits of drawings exhibited at the fair of the Ohio Mechanic Institute in October, delayed his return to the Louisville projects. Today's modern architectural office can simultaneously process diverse commissions with its large specialist staff, but in Rogers's time all design, procurement of labor and materials, and supervision for any project, large or small, fell on him, with the help of only a few hands.

When work permitted, Rogers recommenced drawing the exchange building for Louisville with the help of Mr. Titus; he estimated its cost and sent off the drawings. After another period, during which he began designing the synagogue for Cincinnati and other new work, he stopped at Louisville on his way downriver but does not mention any local projects. By the new year 1851, he was comfortably aboard the steamer *Brilliant,* enjoying the entertainment of minstrels while heading to New Orleans. On this trip and another, he would find his services useful in the Deep South. On his return upriver, he again stopped at Louisville and discussed the exchange building, including his charge for plans and superintendence of the work. On another trip south, he once more talked to people concerned with the exchange but says nothing more about it. After a second, long stay in New Orleans, he stopped briefly in Louisville, but again no building there is mentioned. In late March he was drafting plans for the Louisville Hotel and sent them off on April 9. But as more important work appeared, Rogers had to turn his attention to Cincinnati. All this long-range activity, successful or not, eventually convinced him to open a branch office in the Kentucky city.

The more important work in Cincinnati was the Hamilton County courthouse and jail. The old courthouse had burned in July 1849, and the project for its replacement appears in Rogers's diary on January 1, 1850, the date the architect showed Richard K. Cox, a county commissioner, his plans for the new buildings (note that there is a nearly six-month gap in the diary preceding that date). Apparently a competition for the new public complex had been ongoing, for two weeks later Rogers was told of some suspicion "that there was some foul play about plans." Nevertheless, the *Daily Ohio Statesman* announced on February 9 that of the designs sent in for the building, which apparently did not include one by Rogers, those of Howard Daniels, Joseph C. Sawyer, and William H. Bayless had made the cut.[18] Daniels had just finished the Grecian-style Montgomery County courthouse in Dayton; Bayless, Thomas Cole's nephew, had worked for Rogers in New York, as noted earlier; Sawyer remains obscure. Cox seems to have asked Rogers to submit a late proposal.

At the end of the month the architect recorded his doubts about exhibiting his sketches, which were probably in pencil, "with those drawn and highly colored" by other architects. He requested that his work be studied and then put aside, and if approved he would make a set that could be understood. In such a statement the man sounds either naive or mightily self-assured, and he was not naive in his work. He may have thought that his sketches fared poorly next to the finished work of other entrants, a recognition he must have taken away from the Smithsonian Institution competition. He then went to look at the exhibited plans, perhaps at Cox's bidding, found them "very indifferent," and turned with greater confidence to making new drawings during February, now at a larger scale, with the help of Willard. After silence for nearly a year, on January 30, 1851, Cox told him he could consider himself appointed as architect of the courthouse, and a few days later he offered to superintend construction for $3,000 a year. What the other competitors thought of this outcome is unknown. For Rogers it marked the beginning of yet another long, difficult building history.

Again there followed an extended delay. In June 1851 Rogers returned to work on large-scale drawings of the courthouse and "got eight boards full of details," showed them to a group of gentlemen, and worked on the specifications for it and the jail while a chain gang began digging the cellar. He then moved on to estimating the cost. The following month, in what may have been an early example of general contracting in this country, the county awarded a "responsible bidder," Milton H. Cook, the $468,732.55 contract to build the courthouse under the architect's supervision, and it directed Rogers to make all necessary preparations to proceed.[19] Cook, a forty-year-old well-known builder in Hamilton County, would work frequently with Rogers in coming years.

On July 1, the *Cincinnati Daily Gazette* welcomed Rogers's appointment, calling him a "prudent and careful builder" who had the drawings and specifications "nearly completed." It added that he employed a dozen persons in his office, although Rogers never mentions more than four at any one time during his entire career. The paper also advised that there should be "no unnecessary haste in completing these drawings and perfecting the plans and specifications" because experience proves that "thousands of dollars are lost by hastily adopting an unmature plan and changing it after the contract is made." That is to say, a badly thought-out building program will lead to change orders after construction begins and, hence, financial disaster. Indeed, Rogers and Titus continued drawing through the month. According to the diary, the architect was then to receive 2 percent of the entire cost of the buildings, considerably more than the sum he mentioned earlier.

With all contracts signed and drawings and specifications finished, Rogers and Cook went off to Dayton to look at stone. Work began on the foundations under Rogers's direction, but complaints were soon heard, and a new set of county commissioners, led by Jesse Timanus, ordered cessation of work in early November. Foreseeing a rough road ahead, Rogers "took plans of [the] court house and jail and put them in a safe place," probably in A. B. Coleman's strongbox at the Burnet House.[20] There they would lay until retrieved by him in 1855, four years later. By midmonth he had "nothing to do" and discharged his draftsman (presumably Titus) without mentioning any other employees. He and his son now made up the office. This season must have been a disappointing one, for in these days work had also stopped at St. John's Episcopal Church. Both projects would lead to long-lasting legal proceedings.

During its March 1852 term, the supreme court of Ohio ruled that the Hamilton County commissioners were within their rights to cease construction on the courthouse.[21] Sometime during the cessation, the county, led by Timanus, dismissed Rogers and appointed as architects the firm of Walter & Wilson; construction began using their significantly changed design. In July 1854 Timanus, by then superintending the building and obviously a Know-Nothing, signed a notice that appeared in the newspapers seeking 350 mechanics and laborers to work on the courthouse, preference given to "*American Protestants*" (his emphasis). He then issued a written order that all Roman Catholic mechanics be discharged.[22] The more enlightened county commissioners reacted immediately: they fired him. And none too soon, for in December it became known that he was under investigation as a defaulter to the county of between $17,000 and $18,000. It was alleged that he sold materials intended for the building and kept the proceeds, and his property was taken by the legal authorities while he was away on a bear hunt.[23] An investigation of the building's account books kept by Timanus, published in 1855, concluded that "to say the least, there has been gross ignorance and incapacity or wilful neglect" in accounting for the job.[24] Fraud on public works remains an ongoing problem.

Early in the same year, 1855, Rogers fetched his 1851 plan for the courthouse and had it engraved on wood for publication in the *Cincinnati Gazette,* accompanied by a brief description and specifications "in comparison with the present plans of the court house." It appeared on the front page on May 8 under a headline that called it the "plan . . . rejected by Jesse Timanus and for which the present plan was substituted" (probably meaning that of Walter & Wilson). The paper editorialized that Rogers's original design had been "summarily rejected and thrown aside, that the managing few [county commissioners] might embark in a reckless expenditure while professing economy." An exterior view of the courthouse had appeared in January 1855 in a lithographed perspective by Middleton, Wallace & Co., published in the first (and it seems only) issue of the *Western Art Journal.* The architect is not named. The view shows a solid four-square block then "in the progress of erection," a building rising from "a perfect square" occupying the entire site. It is an impressive Italianate design reaching up three stories, including the arcaded ground floor focused on a mighty hexastyle Corinthian portico and surmounted by a great dome on drum inspired by the Northern European Baroque. Minus the dome on drum, this is what was finally completed under Rogers's reinstated superintendence, but although it has been published as his creation,[25] it did not follow his intention. As erected, the courthouse was, in fact, largely the design of his replacement, the firm of Walter & Wilson.

Rogers's 1851 layout of the courthouse shows a design radically different from what was erected. It is a square-ended Greek cross, not a "perfect square," within which is another, smaller, round-ended cross turned at a forty-five-degree angle. (Fig. 57) The larger cross contains courtrooms, judges' chambers, clerks' offices, a library, grand jury room, and so on; the smaller cross holds the main stairs and meeting rooms. The crosses overlap in a central two-level rotunda fifty-five feet in diameter, which would have been surmounted by a dome on a well-lighted drum eighty feet in diameter. A gallery intended for public meetings or exhibitions was capable of accommodating 2,500 comfortably. The four open corners of the square site are occupied by courtyards enclosed at the sidewalk by iron fences. The

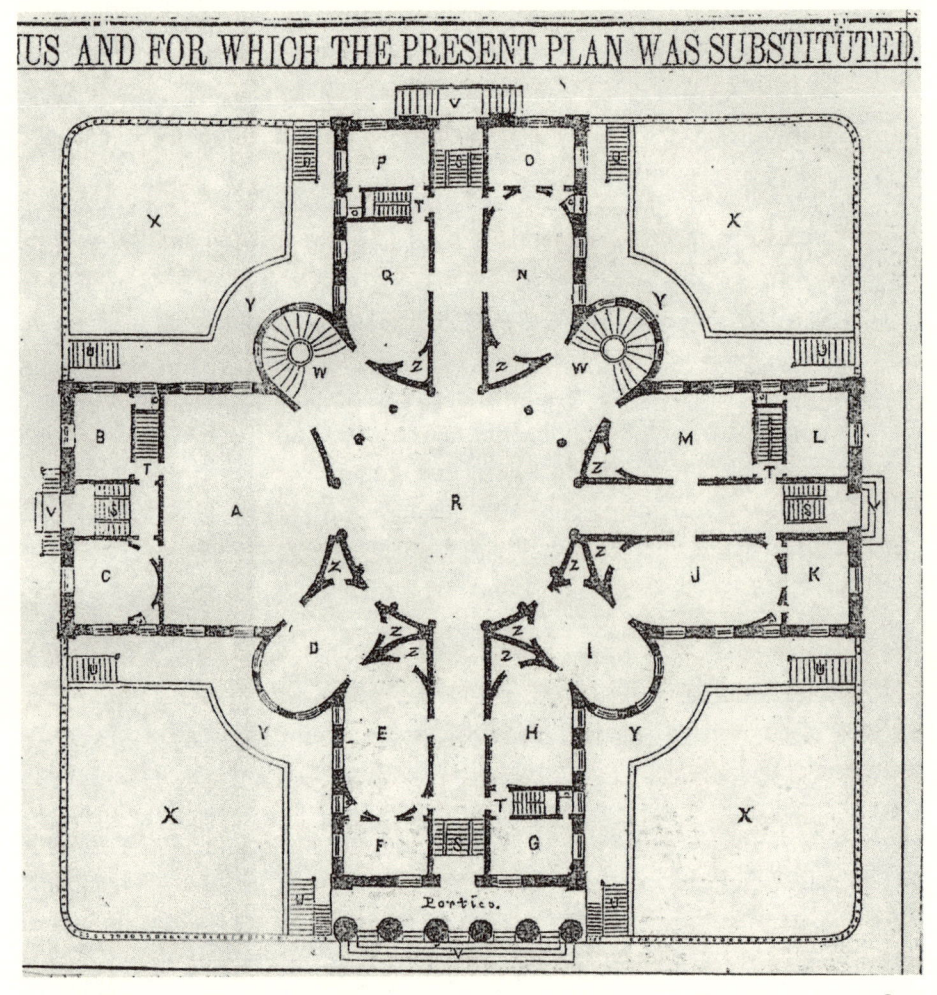

57. Unbuilt project for the Hamilton County courthouse, Cincinnati, Ohio, 1850–51. First-floor plan. *Daily Cincinnati Gazette,* May 8, 1855.

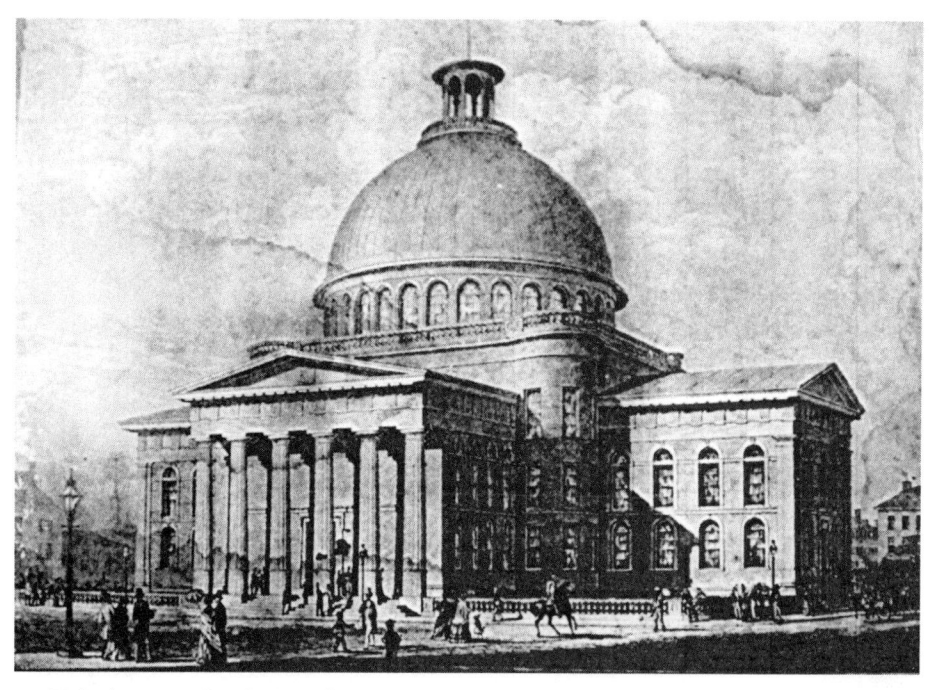

58. Unbuilt project for the Hamilton County courthouse, Cincinnati, Ohio, 1850–51. Perspective view. Photo of unlocated lithograph: photo from the files of Denys Peter Myers.

specifications cited by the paper called for all floors, roof, and dome to be made of cast and wrought iron "of various constructions for the different parts," all interior columns to be of cast iron, "all the ceilings to be constructed with cast-iron laths, secured to iron girders." In addition, "all doors and windows, frames and sashes," were "to be of wood, so arranged as not to communicate with any other woodwork of the building, rendering the whole about fire-proof." The interior as erected was primarily of iron construction, but it certainly looked very different from Rogers's original design.

The original plan might have worked better than what was built, but as the *Courier* maintained, had it been erected, its external appearance would have done little to enhance Rogers's reputation. The exterior, illustrated in a perspective of the building drawn by a local "lithograph man" on the architect's order between November and December 1851, is awkward, although Rogers liked it well enough to give one of the twenty lithographs to William Strickland. (Fig. 58) It shows that the central rotunda was intended to be encased in a cube with trabeated windows and rounded corners that was surmounted by a balustrade from which projected the narrower wings. Above rose the drum encasing the public hall, lighted by a ring of round-arched windows, on which rested a high-profile dome surmounted by an arcaded tholos. For all of Rogers's concern with fire safety, he proposed to place a huge crowd four stories in the air with only two winding stairs for exits.

The entrance wing took the form of a Grecian Doric hexastyle temple front, whose frieze of blank metopes continued around the round-arched walls of the other wings. The resulting structure would have been a hybrid that retained old-fashioned Grecian forms on an otherwise Italianate building.

The diary remains silent about the courthouse during the years of inactivity after 1851, but the *Courier*'s criticism must have had an effect. In December 1855 Rogers heard that he had been reappointed as architect of the county buildings and, a month later, as superintendent of the courthouse and jail. And so at the beginning of the end of this turmoil, what a later newspaper article referred to as the "ins and outs by turns of Isaiah Rogers and Jesse Timmanus,"[26] he received somewhat fuzzy instructions, at least as he recorded them in early February 1856, "to make estimates of cost of finish of court house according to original plans, and also cost . . . according to suggested changes in plan, also of jail according to original plan . . . [and] got from Walter & Wilson all plans in their possession" from (Thomas?) Bass, the foreman, not directly from the architects. Rogers was back on the job, but one way or another his original design had been importantly altered by his successors—there would be no going back to his cruciform scheme. The courthouse that was finally completed in 1861, at the staggering cost of about $695,000, lasted only twenty-three years. It was thought to be fireproof but burned to the ground during riots that occurred on the night of March 28, 1884, the result of an unpopular trial decision. All that remained was a hollowed-out shell. Postfire photographs show the twisted iron framework.

Behind the courthouse, facing away from it on Sycamore Street, the county erected a 152-cell jail, a completely separate building both in reality and in appearance (it was joined to the courthouse by an underground passageway). (Fig. 59) In his diary Rogers made a point of contrasting his penal design with G. J. F. Bryant's radial plan for the Charles Street jail in Boston, which followed the accepted arrangement for a prison initiated in the 1820s by John Haviland at the Eastern State Penitentiary in Philadelphia. His plan was T shaped, with double entrances added off Sycamore that led to wings parallel to the street and then to another straight ahead. It had a limestone exterior of Romanesque design, round arched openings, twin towers, and a tall chimney. Originally drawn in 1851, the jail was begun in 1859 and completed in 1861, by which time Rogers had again been replaced as superintendent by William Walter. It cost the taxpayers of Hamilton County another $226,500.

In January 1851, just when he learned of his appointment to build the Cincinnati courthouse and jail, Rogers received a summons from the hotel owner J. A. Slatter inviting him to New Orleans. What happened next added miles to his travels. In the city, the two men looked over Slatter's hotel, which had recently burned,[27] and Rogers traced the original drawings for it. He also looked in, without written comment, on some slave sales, visited the St. Charles Hotel to consult about a plan for its drying room, and called on former as well as future clients, such as R. D. Shepherd, with whom he had worked at the Newport cemetery and who had introduced him to Judah Touro, whose tombstone he would design in 1855. He also reconnected with Enoch Mudge, whose house in Massachusetts he had designed. He ran over to Mobile, all expenses paid, where he stayed at George Cullum's new Exchange Hotel, enjoying a meal of canvas-back duck with Cullum and his partner J. O. Bartels. He called on James Battle, a wealthy merchant, about plans for a hotel there. When shown a set of drawings already in hand, Rogers's bluntly appraised them as no good. He inquired about the intended new federal customhouse and was told that plans were expected from Washington, that is, from Robert Mills at the Treasury Department. Stopping at Louisville on the return journey, Rogers received a telegram from Mudge requesting that he report immediately to New Orleans to assist in remodeling the St. Louis Hotel.

Back in Cincinnati, Rogers set to work with Willard and Titus on drawings for Slatter's City Hotel, but by February 6 he found himself aboard the steamer *Peytona* for an eight-day trip back to New Orleans, in the company of his wife. He and Emily stayed at the St. Louis Hotel while he contemplated its renewal, looked at the ruins of the St. Charles, which had burned on January 18, and discussed with Slatter the work to be done at his hotel. He drafted his thoughts about the alterations to the St. Louis Hotel and, with Enoch Mudge, showed them to the director of the City Bank, who did not initially approve but eventually accepted one of two further schemes. Meanwhile, he worked on the City Hotel but told Slatter

59. Hamilton County jail, Cincinnati, Ohio, 1850–51, 1859–61. Sycamore Street front. Photo from the collection of Denys Peter Myers.

he could do nothing more until he returned to Cincinnati (where he also laid out a house for Slatter, intended for Common Street in New Orleans). Rogers then turned briefly to the St. Charles but was called back to Mobile, where he again stayed with George Cullum and inspected the site of the old Mansion House, also the victim of a blaze. He measured its foundation and remaining columns, all standing whole, then went to a theater performance. Did he recall his early effort at theater design in Mobile, now long gone? He did encounter "an old Negro" who recognized him from his stay twenty-eight years earlier. As he prepared to ship out, James Battle met him at the wharf and promised to send the dimensions for the site of the hotel to be built at Royal and St. Francis Streets. That structure would eventually become the Battle House.

Back in New Orleans, life on the treadmill continued. Rogers finished the plan of the St. Charles and discussed it with the committee, but nothing was decided. Having received the plot dimensions from Mobile, he finished the drawings for the Battle House as well as those for the Mansion House site there. He was so busy that he could not attend church on March 9, so he asked to be relieved of the St. Charles project. When his request was denied, he continued drawing in the evenings. He again begged to be released, and this time the committee agreed. Asked the price for his services, Rogers declined to name one because he considered what he had done of little use. The committee paid him $300, which he thought "pretty fair." In the subsequent rebuilding of the hotel by the architect George Purves, according to Gary Van Zante, "the most important design ideas came from Isaiah Rogers."[28] On March 12, 1851, Purves had called on Rogers "and talked over about management of the work of hotel and plans," and together they had looked over the ruins.

Rogers carried back to Cincinnati much work that chained him to the drafting boards for the next several months. When not superintending rising buildings, he and his assistants worked on drawings for the hotel in Mobile for George Cullum, a second hotel there that eventually became the Battle House, Slatter's hotel, improvements to Mudge's St. Louis Hotel in New Orleans, and the Louisville Hotel. Although it is difficult to untangle all this activity, it seems that just two projects came to fruition. Hewlett's Exchange, Slatter's fire-ruined old hotel at the corner of Camp and Common Streets, in the Second Municipality in New Orleans, was now to be the site of his new hotel, which Rogers calls the City Hotel throughout the diary. It is unclear what happened next, but it appears as if Slatter soon turned his hotel project over to Cullum and Bartels. By early May, Cullum had moved from Mobile to New Orleans, and in December 1851 the partners invited their friends to join them on December 18 in the new City Hotel's bar. The hotel opened the next month.[29] Accounts in the New Orleans *Times-Picayune* of the opening do not mention Rogers, although that is not unusual, and leave much else out. The paper did note the 130 private rooms and the usual complement of ladies' and gentlemen's parlors, all spacious, airy, and well lighted, as well as a barroom, dining room, and well-appointed kitchen. Revisions to the interior were necessary within less than two years, a fact not uncommon in the history of hotels in any age.

Perhaps the erection of the Battle House, a 240-room, four-story hotel with a fifth floor soon added, represented the most notable outcome of this Southern venture, although the building occasioned much negative criticism. Rogers's blocky exterior proved too severe for local taste, and a cast-iron veranda was even more quickly attached to the Royal Street front. "Without it," said the *Mobile Register*, "the house would look more like a cotton factory than the splendid hotel that it is." It opened under the direction of Messrs. Chamberlain in December 1852, a four-square box of a building with ground-floor shops fronting on Royal at the corner of St. Francis Street. The *Times-Picayune* of New Orleans scoffed that it had the architectural style in the "barracks or hospital order," which was hardly improved by adding the veranda. The Battle followed the lead of the Astor House in New York: it was austere on the outside and lavish on the inside. The paper's description of the layout must have been written by an interior decorator, for it dwells on furniture, furnishings, Brussels carpets, and portraits of Clay, Webster, and Washington while giving an unclear picture of the internal arrangement. In 1905 the building succumbed to fire, a familiar outcome in this story.

As busy as all that sounds, it does not cover Rogers's activities in the South. He had also talked to James Robb about a hotel in New Orleans, for example. Robb was a Whig and a leading financier with his fingers in many progressive building projects in the city and beyond; between 1844 and 1849, he owned acreage in Clifton, a developing suburb of Cincinnati, and then acquired land in Cheviot, a town just northwest of the city. He engaged Rogers to design a house "he intended to be built near Philadelphia," according to a diary entry. In 1851 the architect worked intermittently on that domestic project while in Cincinnati, until the client called at the office in late May to look at the drawings, declaring he would take them when he returned to the South in the fall. Robb then vanishes from the diary, but about this time he built in Cheviot a Gothic cottage of brick with stone facings containing thirteen rooms "finished in solid polished oak," and moved his mother and brother there from Pennsylvania. That "Robb house" stood until about 1935 at the corner of Lora and Francis Streets. Despite Rogers's giving Philadelphia as the intended location, this house may have been what Robb had in mind (Rogers does misstate locations from time to time). The cottage, known from a wretched copy of a lost photograph, appears to have been simpler than Rogers's residential design for Mudge of 1844, but both were designed in the mode of A. J. Davis.[30]

During his two trips to New Orleans, Rogers saw much of the architect James Dakin, and in February the two men went to talk to commissioners about the federal customhouse. The building had been designed in 1847 by Alexander J. Wood, recently released from prison for murdering a fellow architect; Wood had been dismissed in favor of Dakin in 1850.[31] While controversy over the dismissal raged, Dakin revised Wood's plan, seeking support for the changes from his colleagues. To Rogers, the commissioners appeared "to be in a bad fix with the building," and they wanted him to give them a written assessment of Dakin's work. Back in Cincinnati, Rogers wrote in support of Dakin, saying that "it certainly reflects severely on the architects of this country, if we cannot get Public Buildings designed with more fitness . . . than that of [Wood's] Custom House."[32] But Dakin soon found it preferable to resign than face the controversy. Back in New Orleans in March, Dakin and William Strickland, in town perhaps in conjunction with structural problems at his earlier U.S. Mint, called on Rogers, and the three professionals had a long talk about architecture and various subjects (once again a conversation the historian wishes he had been privy to).

Domestic work continued to enter the office in these early Cincinnati years while Rogers supervised the erection of the Davidson store and St. John's Church and as construction on the Hamilton County courthouse commenced. During 1849–51 Rogers's supervisory chores bounced him from the store to the church to the Commercial Bank; he also laid out houses for Messrs. Jason A. Gurley, George Hatch, Winthrop B. Smith, Robert B. Bowler, and Reuben Resor, the last three in Clifton. Meanwhile he drafted others—some alterations—for Slatter, McLean, Lawler, Lawson, Judge Short, Springer, Pierson, Scarborough, and Captain Strader, and drafted designs for cottages in Virginia and North Carolina. For the Cincinnatian Peter Thompson he designed in 1851 a boxy Grecian Revival house at Broadway and Sixth Streets in Richmond, Indiana.[33] Even away from the drawing board, his time continued to be filled. In one representative day—July 23, 1850— he oversaw the laying out of openings in the basement walls at Hatch's house, looked over the foundation of St. John's, checked the stonework at Davidson's store, looked in at Bowler's site, and discussed the project for the Phillips Hotel in Dayton. He kept up the pace even when word came in August that Emily had fallen gravely ill in Rhode Island on a visit to their daughter. Frantic telegrams flew back and forth between Cincinnati and Newport, and fortunately she recovered without interrupting his schedule.

A series of executed domestic works came out of this time as well. One such project was for Jason A. Gurley, a bookseller and the country's sole general agent for "French Catholicon" (a cure for spasmodic asthma, as plentiful contemporary ads proclaimed). Gurley had a wooden cottage erected outside town after he and his wife consulted with Rogers several times over the plans. Rogers and Emily visited the house in late October 1850, and Gurley would later commission a commercial building for Chicago. The house for George Hatch, erstwhile real estate entrepreneur, manufacturer of soap and candles, and mayor of Cincinnati in 1861–63, was on the boards by mid-February 1850 and stayed there a while, for Rogers found his client a hard man to please. After five tries at a plan, Hatch finally smiled, and Rogers began estimating the cost. By March 26 he could tackle the facade. By mid-April Hatch had approved the design "with few variations," and by the end of the month he knew what Rogers thought it would cost. The architect then bargained to superintend construction for 10 percent of that sum. As noted, it would seem that Rogers made his living superintending construction rather than designing—it's almost as if he "moonlighted" as an architect. In fact, he seems to have often been a general contractor *avant la lettre* more than an architect, practicing logistics rather than design. As we see him doing over and over, he had to find materials with which to build, hire workers both skilled and unskilled, and then trail after owners to get money to pay them, there being no system for doing so.

As foundations went in for Hatch's house, Rogers worked on framing plans. Construction progressed smoothly from spring into fall when, toward the end of November, the site was covered for the winter. Although construction ceased, stone cutters continued to work, and Rogers spent evenings at his drawing board considering more alterations to the design, which Hatch approved. Work recommenced in spring of 1851, and by early October the place was far enough along that the Hatches could inspect it; they "liked most of it very well," although they asked for a few more changes to the interior. By mid-October gas lines and plumbing were being installed. Drawings for interior finishes occupied some of Rogers's evenings for the rest of the month, but these had to be altered again in November. Late that month he received $2,000 from Hatch, but work continued as he designed interior balusters. In the end, Hatch must have been pleased with Rogers, especially his patience, for in December he asking for a house and stable to be built in another part of town. Rogers, always quick on the draw, produced pencil sketches overnight.

The Hatch House on Dayton Street, in the West End, is listed on the National Register of Historic Places. (Fig. 60) Despite later alterations, and its present sorry state, the original lines are fairly discernible.[34] Although an open site at the time of building, the area urbanized, making the house appear to have been designed for a city street. Its antecedents certainly were. With its double-barreled south front, it is a version of a common urban eighteenth-century type revived in the mid-nineteenth, especially in the northern and eastern states. To name just a few similar contemporaries, all designed around 1850, there are the Amon Bronson House in Rochester, New York; Henry Austin's Nelson Hotchkiss House in New Haven, Connecticut; the Perkins-Clark House, which once stood in Hartford; and the Henry Lewis House in Lynchburg, Virginia.

The fronts of these houses squeeze an entrance portal between two bulging curved bays, just as the Hatch does. The others may have bits of Gothic or other styles, but Rogers's overall reference is his usual Italianate with touches of Grecian.

The bays of Hatch House embrace a recessed semi-octagonal porch with half-rounded niches. It is capped by a ribbed vault and defined outwardly by two cast-iron fluted Corinthian columns in antis supporting a faceted bay window above. The curved walls of dressed sandstone, divided vertically by a pronounced belt course, stand flanked by paired fluted Corinthian pilasters (and another around the corner, the same articulation he had drawn for the president's house at Harvard seven years earlier, among other buildings). These have cast terra-cotta capitals based on those of the Temple of the Winds. Around this time, Rogers began using an early terra-cotta produced by Patrick Bannon in Louisville; whether these capitals were Bannon's work remains unknown. Terra-cotta was beginning to be produced in Cincinnati, but Rogers seems to have traveled to Louisville in search of such details. The whole facade is topped by a broad bracketed wooden eave, which was originally surmounted by a balustrade. Beyond that rises a cupola. The windows are large and double hung; those in the curved bays contain curved panes. Remnants of a reproduction of Rogers's custom-designed iron fence, of conventionalized vegetable forms, still define the edge of the terrace on the street. (Fig. 61)

The Hatch House is large in mass and in detail. From the four-by-ten-foot entrance door a hall runs back to what were dining and service rooms. This passageway divides a double parlor on the east from a parlor and what was the library, separated by sliding doors, on the west. Beyond a pair of three-centered arches supported on twin fluted Corinthian columns, the passageway broadens into the two-story top-lighted stairwell, probably added, with the porte cochere, by a later owner.

Rogers's other major domestic works in Cincinnati were to be found in the Clifton neighborhood. In 1844 Winthrop B. Smith, the well-known schoolbook publisher and stationer, had a house erected in that area, then a newly incorporated village north of the center of the city and now a part of it.[35] It became one in a string of other mansions, most long gone, that boasted extensively landscaped grounds, some laid out by Adolph Strauch. All had splendid views of the city and the river. In the evening of March 4, 1850, Rogers began working on alterations to Smith's house. Like Hatch, he was an exacting client, only more so. After nine different schemes, Smith finally approved a design more than a year later. Rogers spent much time traveling to the site or conferring with his client in town as the project rose into a two-story brick Italianate villa with cupola, piazza on three sides with slender cast-iron columns with "Egyptoid" capitals, and tall tower, the last two tied into the fabric of the house with iron bars. Smith seems to have been no less difficult with the builder than with the architect. A dispute with workmen erupted near the finish, and when in August 1852 Rogers urged promptness on Milton Cook, the builder "remarked . . . that they wanted to get finished as much as we wanted it, and be clear of it." Nonetheless, final touches dragged on

60. George Hatch house, Cincinnati, Ohio, 1850–51. Dayton Street front. Historic American Buildings Survey, Library of Congress.

61. George Hatch house, Cincinnati, Ohio, 1850–51. Reproduction of original front fence. Author photo, 2012.

into October, when long discussions were conducted about settling Cook's bill. Despite all the difficulty, Rogers would work for Smith again, designing a building for his publishing concern in 1854.

In July 1850 Rogers produced a sketch for a "new house" in Clifton for Reuben P. Resor, partner with his brother William in a stove factory. It was not until December that he returned in earnest to planning the project, and it is not mentioned again, which suggests he did not supervise its erection. The house was described in 1868, when it was the home of Robert Hosea, as a two-story brick villa painted a light color, with piazzas and an octagonal corner tower adjacent to the main entrance.[36] (Fig. 62) Its many windows are either trabeated or round arched, except for those at the top of the tower; the plan is a basic rectangle to which were added picturesque elements, such as a cast-iron veranda (now gone), a tower, and a quaint Tudor Revival arch. As is frequently seen in houses planned by Rogers, the broad central hallway led to a staircase, here a sweeping curved flying stair rising to the second floor. (Fig. 63) Today the Resor house survives in reduced circumstances.

Rogers's work for Robert B. ("R. B.") Bowler, a man described in 1851 in the *Ohio Statesman* as a "leading Pearl street merchant" of wholesale dry goods and the owner of the Cincinnati Bagging Factory, was certainly a remodeling; planning began in May 1849 with an estimate of $4,124. The present Mt. Storm Park, named for Bowler's estate, marks the site of the vanished mansion. By July, the client had purchased stone, but Rogers "made a stir about it" and Bowler sent it back. As the diary often proves, Rogers—like many an architect then and since—did not like clients to seek materials or advice beyond his control. A gap in the diary makes the story jump to January 1850, when Rogers and Bowler discussed the project with Milton Cook, whom Bowler subsequently hired. Two months later Rogers lent Bowler "two books on cottage architecture" and then sat down to design a gate lodge for the estate.

Alterations to the house began in April and proceeded through the rest of the year. In May, after a discussion about the Strauch-designed greenhouse, an important element of the seventy-acre estate that was to become famous for its landscaping and its horticulture,[37] construction of the gate lodge commenced. At the site in June, Rogers "laid out for window in foundation of octagon," then "laid out for oval windows into the conservatory." In July plastering began, Rogers received $250 from Bowler on account, and the brackets for the cornice began to go up; by early August the cornices and balustrades were completed. The gate lodge walls were partly constructed, ready for the roof. Presumably the remaining work was finished by the end of the year, after the last-minute repair of a badly leaking roof, for in early December Rogers began calculating hours to make out his bill. He soon had his money in hand. Here as elsewhere, Rogers records payment for services based on his working hours, not on a percentage fee.

62. Reuben Resor house, Cincinnati, Ohio, 1850. Exterior. Cincinnati Museum Center.

63. Reuben Resor house, Cincinnati, Ohio, 1850. Entrance hall. Cincinnati Museum Center.

In late summer of 1851 the architect returned from a trip east, and Bowler returned from London, where he had visited the Great Exhibition of the Works of Industry of All Nations. Client and architect talked about "further improvements" to the house, including alterations to the kitchen and greenhouse, and Rogers drafted the foundation for a brick tower that began to rise only in June 1852. A year later, we hear of Bowler again, Rogers having spent most of the intervening time in Frankfort, Kentucky, where he would immediately return. It was the end of July 1853 when he recorded making a plan of a fountain for Bowler's estate. The working drawings were turned over to Henry Whitestone, by then employed in the office, and fully paid for on August 12.

The original Bowler house is said to have been erected in 1846. Rogers's alterations produced a two-story brick Italianate mansion, whose exterior walls were stuccoed and scored to imitate stonework; its broad Corinthian piazzas looked north and west. Corners were edged with quoins, and the walls topped by a deep overhang supported by carved brackets and surmounted by a balustrade. A monitor that rose from the center of the roof suggests a domestic plan typical for Rogers, with central hall leading to a staircase. Handsome as the house was, its horticultural surroundings were even more imposing. Almost everything has vanished. The house was razed in 1917, and the only reminders of its splendor are a grottolike wine cellar and a "Temple of Love" standing isolated above a former cistern in Mt. Storm Park. Attributed by some to Strauch, the temple could equally have been part of Rogers's improvements; it is a domed open Corinthian tholos with a terra-cotta architrave and frieze that stood above a cistern that watered the grounds. When Edward, Prince of Wales, visited Cincinnati in the fall of 1860, he moved from one Rogers building to another: he stayed at the Burnet House, worshiped at St. John's, and visited the Bowler residence, where he enjoyed "the quiet, the society and some pears."[38]

Rogers's first years in Cincinnati proved to be busy ones. Both there and in the South, he filled a void in up-to-date architectural services. Despite his many frustrations, he managed to alter the course of his earlier career, adapt himself to the conditions of a new location, and work for many leading citizens in Ohio's major city and elsewhere. He achieved some remarkable successes, chief among them the famed Burnet House. The ensuing decade would be as fully occupied with the design and construction of buildings across what we now call the Midwest.

CHAPTER

5

Louisville and Cincinnati 1852–1861

THE IRISH-BORN Henry Whitestone joined Rogers's office by September 1852, having arrived in the United States early that year with much architectural experience already to his credit. He was first put to work on the Capital Hotel in Frankfort, Kentucky.[1] By November 1853 Whitestone had proven his worth, and Rogers offered him a partnership for "2/5 of the profit for his services. He to take charge of office in Louisville in my absence at Cincinnati and elsewhere. I am to make designs and he to finish them and to take charge of work in my absence." Rogers was clearly not giving up control of the products of the drafting boards, although he and Whitestone seem to have worked well together. Austin Whitestone, Henry's brother, also just over from Ireland, joined the office a little later, although it appears he was, like Theodore Washburn in Boston, a gofer who did not draw. Among his chores in 1855 was putting in order Rogers's correspondence and business papers, which have not been located. At the beginning of 1854, with Whitestone's acquiescence, Rogers's son Willard also became a partner. This expansion occasioned new "rates of proportions . . . myself 40%, Mr. Whitestone 35% and Willard 25%" of net income. Although Rogers and Whitestone were giving up higher shares to incorporate Willard, they must have hoped for expanded business.

The new firm of Rogers, Whitestone & Co. began flooding the Cincinnati and Louisville papers with advertising. In the *Louisville Daily Courier* in just one month, July 1855, an unillustrated ad listing twenty buildings designed and erected by Rogers—from Tremont House to the Capital Hotel—appeared at least twenty-two times. When Whitestone left the firm sometime in 1857, the name changed to Isaiah Rogers, Son & Co. These changes anticipated the general trend that began after the Civil War away from personal architectural practice and toward partnerships or corporate firms. (Whitestone established his own office in Louisville, and the present firm of Luckett & Farley, architects and engineers there, traces its origins to the Rogers and Whitestone contract.) Rogers may have felt a bit pressed by the volume of commissions when he decided to share responsibility for drawing and superintending, but his own schedule of work and travel hardly lessened in the ensuing years.

Work flooded into the firm's offices in Cincinnati and Louisville through the 1850s. Rogers continued his earlier pattern from the 1840s, spending much of his life on the road, riding the "cars" or buggy, and now more often sailing in riverboats. Besides Whitestone and Willard, also in the office were Titus and a Mr. Howe (briefly, apparently). The year 1852 found Rogers supervising houses under construction in or near Cincinnati for Winthrop B. Smith, George Hatch, and R. B. Bowler; among other commissions, he began planning houses for a Mr. Cook on Fourth Street (perhaps Milton Cook, his builder), David Griffin (alterations to a house on West Fourth Street), an Edgerton (in New Orleans), a Caldwell (in Mobile), a Hanna (in Frankfort, Kentucky), and others. On July 6 he went out to Joseph Longworth's house, which had been designed by Howard Daniels, "to measure for a tower" to give it the then-fashionable Italian villa look. He suggested several improvements, which Longworth "thought favorable," and then drew a measured plan of the existing building in his diary. He also recorded a view of the Daniels-designed house that remains his only known freehand perspective. It does not reveal him as an especially gifted sketch artist. (Fig. 64)

Then there were the stores and offices for Judge Hart and alterations for Henry W. Derby, a publisher and bookseller located on Main Street; an otherwise unidentified chapel and work at the St. Charles Hotel in New Orleans for Enoch Mudge, his former client in Massachusetts; tombs in Spring Grove Cemetery for A. B. Coleman, John P. Tweed, and Griffin Taylor (also to house the remains of his relatives, Stephen G. Brown and Elias H. Haines); a project for a building to contain the Literary Department at the University of Nashville; a store for a Mr. Cooper in the same city; a Universalist church on Walnut Street, Cincinnati; a church project for New Albany, Ohio; and, finally, almost total submersion in the work of designing and supervising the Capital Hotel in Frankfort. Such a catalogue suggests the busy pace of his practice. Not all these projects are easily identified or came to fruition, but each took an enormous amount of time in travel, discussions, drafting, and estimating. During these years the architect also continued trying to collect money owed for his work at St. John's Church.

A project for a building at the University of Nashville took Rogers to Tennessee in early March 1852. While there he inspected William Strickland's state capitol, then nearing completion, but "did not like the proportions of the building." It was, in his view, "all in bad taste." He handed out prints of his New York

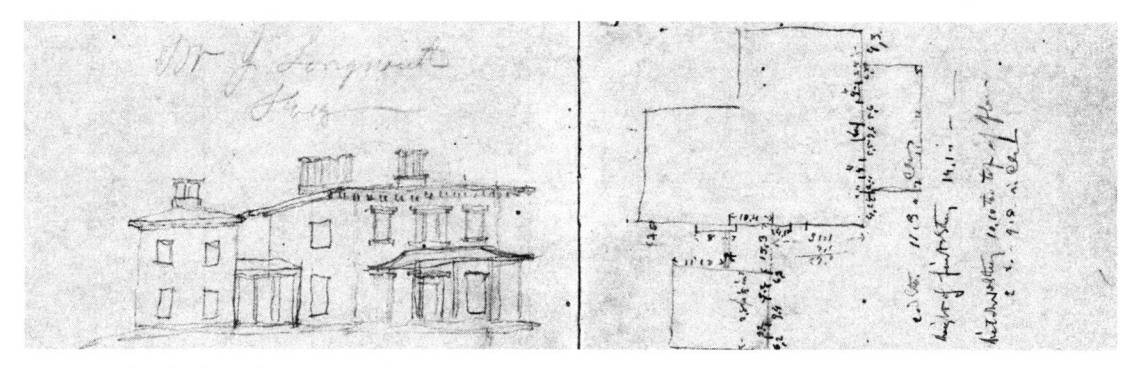

64. Sketch of Joseph Longworth house (Howard Daniels; architect) (before alteration), 1852. From Isaiah Rogers's diary. Avery Architectural & Fine Arts Library, Columbia University in the City of New York.

Merchants' Exchange and the proposed (and at that moment suspended) Hamilton County courthouse to Strickland and others. He also met with members of the building committee for the school and showed them his preliminary scheme. "They adopted it unanimously," he wrote, and instructed him "to make out plans and specifications as soon as" possible. Back in Cincinnati he and his assistants produced presentation drawings, a perspective, and specifications. These he took back to Nashville in April, the committee "appeared to like them very well," and they were put on view for builders to bid for the job. While Rogers waited for the results, Strickland introduced him to his friend and consultant, Major Adolphus Heiman, the other significant architect and engineer in town. Heiman had designed the 670-foot suspension bridge spanning the Cumberland River at Nashville that opened in 1850, but its erection had been put in the hands of others and he disassociated himself from the project.[2] Rogers probably took an interest in the bridge, although he does not mention it; he had begun to study a new system of spanning long distances, and as late as November 1861, in what must have been one of his self-generated problems, he laid out a design for a bridge to cross the same body of water.[3]

By the end of the month the school committee, with bids in hand, "adopted his design unanimously, and agreed to set about raising $20,000 to make up the amount of my estimate and commission" (a rare use of the word *commission* in the diary). He then began making alterations to his design: he "did away [with] the arches under portico and made portico full height of building, which gives more character to the whole." He redrew the elevations "with changes which have been suggested to me," and then agreed to wait six weeks while the committee arranged funding for a "contract at $72,000 including all old material and buildings on the grounds." This note sounds as if he intended to supervise construction. In early June the school asked for an extension to sign the contract. It apparently never arrived. Rogers's project was eventually rejected as being too expensive and "on too grand a scale," and the building was erected from a less expensive design by Heiman.[4] Rogers seems to have priced himself out of the job.

Little came of Rogers's Tennessee venture, but forays into Kentucky began to pay off. In September 1852 he received his expenses plus $100 to visit Frankfort, some fifty-five miles east of Louisville, to confer about a new hotel and inspect the site there, on which stood an old inn called the Weisiger House. He left the next day. The location, at the corner of Ann and Main Streets, turned out to be a "very fine" one, which he surveyed before heading home; on his return trip by boat, he finished reading a two-volume original edition of *Uncle Tom's Cabin* he had bought just two days earlier for $1. Drawings began immediately, as usual, on what was to be called the Capital Hotel; by September 20 he was back in Frankfort, with preliminary design and estimate in hand, to receive the approval of the building committee and directions to take down the old building. By October 1, Whitestone was at work on presentation drawings, and three days later the committee accepted the definitive design. Rogers signed an agreement to build the hotel as shown on the drawings for $41,000, plus all the salvageable material from the old building on the site. Reusing or selling used building materials was a common way for him (and others) to save money for the client or add to his own profit. Back in Cincinnati he prepared drawing boards with paper and cloth for the hotel plans, and set Whitestone to work.

Rogers soon established an office in Frankfort on the site of the new hotel and was drawing while demolition began. Over the next several weeks he and Whitestone drafted while a gang of laborers cleaned and sorted bricks and lumber from the demolished building. By the end of November the workmen had broken ground, and by mid-December Whitestone had completed all the "large" drawings and bound them together for Rogers to give the committee to sign the contract for what he was calling the New Weisiger House. That same month he wrote a contract for masonry with John Haly (sometimes written Hayley), who had worked in Cincinnati at the Hatch House and the vaults for A. B. Coleman and John P. Tweed. Stonework on the building seems to have gone along smoothly for a while, but, the job unfinished, Haly left the building site in August 1853 and sued over disputed payment. In April 1854 he won his case against Rogers for $832 and went on to a busy career, though he seems never again to have worked for the architect. Such was the kind of headache Rogers suffered during many building campaigns.

The speed with which these projects were designed and erected must astonish the modern architect, as does the fact that the draftsmen struggled to keep up with the builders. Designing was almost incidental and vastly less time-consuming than Rogers's supervisory work at the building sites or his forays to find men and materials. He was constantly complaining about slow progress. Although basically a kind man (except when he became architect of the Treasury, discussed in Chapter

6), he was all business, complaining once that the masons "were all off on a spree" on New Year's Day 1853 and telling Haly that it must be impressed upon them to work when they could so that the job progressed as quickly as possible. (This from a man who took off every Sunday.) With foundations begun and Whitestone onsite, Rogers could leave Frankfort for Cincinnati, where he sought bids from workers and suppliers, chores that continued in Louisville and elsewhere for both Rogers and Whitestone. He also need to constantly chase clients to pay him so that he could then pay the workers, a task that was not always easy.

Rogers interrupted his work in Frankfort for a swing through the East, stopping in New York, Boston, Philadelphia, Washington, D.C., and Pittsburgh. On his return to Cincinnati he shipped men, wood flooring, and ironwork for the hotel and headed via boat to Louisville and then by train for Frankfort. The laying of the cornerstone of the Capital Hotel on April 18, 1853, turned out to be "a very tame affair indeed," he wrote, "no speech or remarks made on the occasion." Next, he was off to New Orleans. Construction proceeded at the hotel, using workers from Ohio and Kentucky as well as inmates from the state prison; meanwhile, Rogers hopped between Frankfort and Cincinnati, and Whitestone became increasingly involved with the hotel, producing drawings for the "cupola," the erection of which was complete by year-end.

Like the Burnet House, the Capital Hotel departed from the single-block format of the Tremont and Astor hotels. A broad portico led the visitor into the lobby beneath the cupola, from which the mass of the building stretched right and left to perpendicular wings; straight ahead stood the dining room with kitchen beyond.[5] For the front of the building, Rogers and Whitestone produced a pronounced version of the former's usual Palladian quincunx. A raised, freestanding, hexastyle, pedimented portico of fluted, monolithic, colossal, Corinthian columns—rather more Roman than Grecian in proportion—projected boldly from the center wing; beyond it on the skyline, a sixteen-sided "domeless" drum, the cupola, surrounded by semicircular headed windows, rose awkwardly on a rectangular stone base. (Figs. 65–66) It was the smaller cousin of the one at the statehouse in Columbus, the work of William Russell West and his partner J. O. Sawyer of five years later, and the larger cousin of the belvedere at Rogers's domestic Highforest in Aurora, Indiana. Lower, flat-roofed, square-cut blocks of rooms flanking the portico were connected to the central block of the hotel by recessed hyphens. Trabeated windows cut directly through rugged ashlar walls. The result was one of Rogers's most original hotels. The question arises, but receives no definitive answer here, what Whitestone's influence was on Rogers's works of this period. In all cases the original sketch seems to have been Rogers's, but a reading of the diary suggests a mutual respect, and Whitestone certainly could have suggested ideas at any stage. The loss by fire of the Capital Hotel in April 1917 removed one of Rogers's major works.

65. Capital Hotel, Frankfort, Kentucky, 1852–53. Main Street front. Capital City Museum, Frankfort, Kentucky.

Rogers and Whitestone next turned to enlarging the Galt House in Louisville, originally built in 1835, at Second and Main Streets. In 1853–54 they added a story of round arched windows and a segmental pediment, a faint introduction of the coming Renaissance Revival in Rogers's work that may have been due to Whitestone's influence. It burned in 1865 and was replaced with a hotel by Whitestone on his own. The architects' attention then turned to the Galt's rival, the original Louisville Hotel, a concern that—as we have seen so often with Rogers—dragged on for years through many vicissitudes. It had opened in 1834 in a building designed by Hugh Roland with a front portico of ten colossal Grecian Ionic columns and a plan cribbed from the Tremont House.[6] Rogers had produced drawings for its remodel in the spring of 1850, and a year later, in March–April 1851, he again took up the project and sent drawings and explanation to L. L. Shreve, one of the owners, a man who had a finger in many local improvements. By July–August an addition was under construction, but in February 1852 the New Orleans *Times-Picayune* ran a piece detailing the hotel's enlargement and assigning it to the architect Elias E. Williams. It may be that Williams supervised a building of Rogers's design.

On January 20, 1853, the upper two floors of the Louisville Hotel succumbed to fire. Rogers's court case against St. John's in Cincinnati had been postponed, and with the alacrity of an ambulance-chasing lawyer he was in Louisville by January 25; that very day he got "instruments and drawing boards" and on the spot commenced sketching reconstruction documents. (These drawings are now at the Filson Historical Society in Louisville.) By the next day he had finished outlining plans and elevation for the front section of the building and estimated the cost. By January 28 he had propositioned Shreve to superintend the "improvements" for $1,500, spending four days a week in town, or had suggested that for 10 percent of the outlay he would build it for $25,000, so long as it was understood "out doors" (elsewhere?) that he was superintending. He received $50 for his sketches and left for Frankfort to tend to the Capital Hotel. A few days later he received a counteroffer from Shreve: come back, develop plans, and superintend four days a

66. Capital Hotel, Frankfort, Kentucky, 1852–53. Entrance portico. Capital City Museum, Frankfort, Kentucky.

week for four months for $1,000. He declined but sent from Frankfort, perhaps as bait, his sketch for the hotel. In April he was back in Louisville talking to Shreve and a Mr. Kean, "the gentlemanly proprietor," and in August he was designing improvements to the hotel, which opened with a grand banquet in December. Rogers does not mention being in that city for an extended period over the next months, being preoccupied with the hotel in Frankfort.

At this point Rogers also designed stores adjacent to the hotel and laid out a large house for Thomas H. Hunt. He showed a sketch of the house on Walnut Street to Hunt in April 1853, but we hear no more about the project. Rogers drafted the front elevation, and Whitestone produced the drawing for the portico. Erected by 1855, presumably without Rogers's supervision, the house no longer exists. As published by Samuel Thomas, the facade rose three stories to a deep overhang, supported by brackets, and stretched five bays across, with the central three slightly indented.[7] Built of stucco over brick, it showed round-headed windows set within recessed frames at the first and second levels. A rounded bay projected from an ell to the left of the main facade, and a trabeated portico stood at the top of the entrance stairs.

The Louisville Hotel seems not to have become an issue again until late in 1855, when Rogers talked to Kean "about the contemplated altering"; he then saw Shreve, who said he had abandoned his own plan and "was waiting on me to make him a plan of proposed changes." Rogers immediately retrieved his old drawings and started a new project of 220 rooms and a central courtyard with a covered passage leading to the water closets.[8] This was undoubtedly his patented cylindrical lattice bridge. If erected, it went unnoticed by the press. Back in Louisville he and Shreve agreed that he would superintend the alterations for 5 percent on cost, employing all the foremen and workmen and handling all business for the client. He returned to his drafting board, and the building was closed, as the *Ohio Daily Statesman* put it, for "repairs, additions, alterations, etc." On the morning of February 2, 1856, the four-story thirty-room east wing collapsed, killing a Hibernian workman and a neighborhood Irish lad. A young girl, playing nearby, "had her nose completely shattered" according to the *Louisville Democrat*. Rogers, in the city the next day, reported that he "examined all the premises" and concluded "that there was no fault from the work done" because none of the shoring structure had been removed. He believed that the "defect was in the original construction" and not in the process used to take down the work. A nice piece of side-stepping! Unfortunately, a gap of five and a half years occurs in the diaries here, so we cannot follow him through the aftermath of this disaster, but we know work proceeded on the hotel. The "really magnificent house," as the *Times-Picayune* described it, opened with a splendid dinner in mid-October.

The Renaissance Revival front of the Louisville Hotel dominated its block of Sixth Street, rising four solid stories above ground-floor shops to a bracketed cornice. (Fig. 67) A faint echo of the Palladian quincunx broke up the plane of the wall, as did the central feature, a somewhat attenuated Corinthian, two-story, distyle-in-antis recessed portico fronting the main entrance. Heavy cornices on equally heavy consoles topped the windows. A continuous iron balcony ran in front of the second-story rooms, providing a fine place from which to view passing spectacles, such as the arrival of Union troops in September 1861, as illustrated in *Harper's Weekly*. It may not have been Rogers's grandest hotel, but the *Louisville Journal* unblushingly thought it unrivaled in the country. It vanished in the mid-twentieth century.

As noted, the beginning of 1853 had found Rogers in Frankfort superintending the building of the Capital Hotel. While there, he set about designing a church for the Reverend George W. Quimby of the First Universalist Society in Cincinnati. The next few weeks were hectic with travel and work. Back in Cincinnati, he continued to draw details of the hotel, and on January 11 he had a discussion about his legal cases regarding St. John's Church and the Hamilton County courthouse.

67. Louisville Hotel, Louisville, Kentucky, 1850–56. Collection of Denys Peter Meyers.

The next day he drew the elevations for A. B. Coleman's tomb, then he received an inquiry about training the son of a friend. Learning that the St. John's case had been postponed, he returned to Frankfort on January 16; two days later he was back in Cincinnati to prepare for the trial, but again it was postponed. January 25 found him in Louisville drawing details of the hotel there. After two days back in Cincinnati, where he received $50 for making unidentified plans for his former client Winthrop B. Smith, at the end of the month he was back in Frankfort, continuing to draft details and secure bids for materials and labor for the that city's hotel. He was also working on drawings for fences on the grounds of Gideon Shryock's statehouse and the Presbyterian Church in Cincinnati, and he initiated the drawings for a jail in Hudson, New York. The man must have felt like a shuttlecock.

By March 1, 1853, Rogers was back in Cincinnati before boarding a train for New York on the fourth. While in the city he stopped at Astor House but mentions nothing about James Bogardus's new iron and glass covering for his courtyard. He visited the Crystal Palace, then under construction, studied funereal monuments in Green-Wood Cemetery in Brooklyn, and met with John Stanton Gould of Hudson, a Quaker, Whig, philanthropist, agriculturalist, and prison reformer. (Gould was born in Newport, Rhode Island, and may have been related to Rogers's son-in-law, Nathan Gould.) They looked over the architect's plans for a jail in Hudson, but it seems nothing came of that project. He left for Boston and his Tremont House on March 9. In the Hub he looked up family members and old friends, was asked to plan a new opera house (about which we hear nothing further), and dropped down to Plymouth, where he obtained a piece of Plymouth Rock and some brochures in preparation for entering the competition for the Forefathers' Monument, for which he sketched a design in November 1854 but may not have entered it. Even though Rogers gathered influential endorsers, he is not listed among the entrants, and the prize was awarded to the design for a baldachin over Plymouth Rock and a colossal statue of *Faith,* both designed by his former brief helper, Hammatt Billings of Boston.[9] Rogers also visited Marshfield for a few days. Back in Boston he was met with drama: arrested for an unpaid board bill from 1846, he settled the account under protest. In Newport he visited his daughter and son-in-law, criticized several new houses, which he thought mostly badly arranged despite some good ideas, and had himself daguerreotyped for $3.

Again in New York by March 23, Rogers looked at the new "good and elegant" St. Nicholas and Metropolitan hotels but found them badly arranged also, though he would later stay in both. Just two days later he was walking around Philadelphia with John Notman, then he moved on to Washington, D.C., where he found nothing striking at the Washington Monument—and rightly so, for it was only a stump. At the Capitol he found a great waste of material in the new work, but probably did not mention his opinion to T. U. Walter, who received him gladly. At the Treasury Office, Ammi B. Young gave him the drawings for various federal customhouses in progress, and Rogers suggested improvements in iron construction to his friend. He talked to the Patent Office about advancements in cast-iron laths, part of his constant quest for fireproof building methods, although no patent ensued. The return west took him quickly through Baltimore, Pittsburgh, and Cleveland.

Back in Cincinnati by early April 1853, Rogers had a discussion about superintending the Ohio statehouse, then shipped out for Frankfort aboard a boat loaded with ironwork for the hotel there. By April 7 he was again at his drafting board, working on plans for Reverend Quimby of the First Universalist Society. On April 16 he woke up with a severe pain in his chest, perhaps an early sign of the heart ailment that would eventually kill him, but he was soon drafting plans for the house on the farm he had acquired at Goshen, northeast of the city. In Louisville on April 21 he and Emily boarded the *Eclipse* heading for New Orleans. Back in Cincinnati by May 5 he had some conversations about the St. John's case and was advised to settle without going to trial. At Frankfort, work on the Capital Hotel progressed while he and Whitestone drafted designs for iron storefronts west of the Burnet House; Rogers also worked on elevations for Thomas Gaff's "Hillforest" in Aurora, Indiana. In Cincinnati again on May 14 he talked to Jason Gurley, for whom he had designed a country house, about a Chicago building, and again to Reverend Quimby about the design of the First Universalist church. Back at Frankfort the next day, he set Whitestone to drawing an iron front to a store for Tweed and Andrews, wholesale grocers, and he commenced a design for Gurley's "hall and store for Chicago." An article on Rogers's "doings," written by "Quimby," appeared in what he called, in his entry of June 16, 1853, the *Artists Journal,* a Cincinnati publication now exceedingly rare (alas, no copy of that issue has come to light). Cincinnati city directories suggest that nothing came of Rogers's project for Quimby's church. The reverend had left that congregation by 1856 to become editor and publisher of the *Star of the West,* a Universalist periodical, and then apparently left the city.

In Cincinnati on May 21, 1853, Rogers contacted Jesse Timanus, his former nemesis from the Hamilton County courthouse (and who had not yet been indicted for fraud), asking for men who would work in Frankfort. His need for laborers was great, and he sought them from anyone who might help. In Frankfort two days later he continued to work on Gurley's Chicago project, made an estimate of cost for a Mr. Hanna, who wanted a building on the same Frankfort corner as the Capital Hotel, and began to design the stone front for an existing house and store at 120 East Fourth Street, in Cincinnati, for James C. Hall, president of the new Ohio & Mississippi Railroad Company. Whitestone, meanwhile, kept working on the Thomas Gaff house. Rogers also sketched a tomb for John P.

Tweed and worked on framing plans for his own house in Goshen. After a day in Cincinnati he returned via Louisville to Frankfort, where he continued to work on Gurley's building and heard that Hall had accepted his design for the front of his store.

Again heading upriver through Louisville, always looking for workers willing to go to Frankfort, Rogers stopped briefly in Cincinnati on June 16 on his way to Ironton, Ohio, to inquire about the cost of fabricating iron storefronts; he then headed for Portsmouth, where he walked along the riverbank and found some flint used, he said, by the Indians for arrows. He continued back to Cincinnati, staying long enough to talk to John P. Tweed about the Tweed and Andrews store, then was bound for Louisville on the *Scioto* (these river craft must have been to him what the subway is to modern commuters) and from there on to Frankfort. He was soon working on drawings for a schoolhouse for Ironton, and Whitestone applied himself to the Gurley project. Rogers next turned to drawings of stonework for James Hall's house in Cincinnati and estimated the cost of Gurley's Chicago building.

Back in Cincinnati by early July, Rogers discussed his design for the Tweed and Andrews store with Miles Greenwood at Greenwood's Eagle Iron Works before taking his drawings upriver to Ironton, a settlement just four years old but quickly growing into an immense pig-iron works. Thanks to the boom in ferrous construction, the town was at the beginning of a period in which it claimed to be one of the world's foremost producers of iron.[10] Back in 1849 the fronts Rogers had designed for the Commercial bank and the Davidson store combined iron with stone. It appears he was now calling for nothing but iron. His trip ended in vain, however, for the company he visited refused to estimate the cost. The building front in question was to be one of three stores for lots west of the Burnet House, which Rogers first mentions on May 10, 1853. Another is eventually identified as being for Charles G. Springer, also a wholesale grocer. When Rogers found it impossible to get a bid on the first scheme for Tweed's in July, he and Whitestone drafted a second design. In August, Tweed decided to award the contract to the local firm of Horton & Macy for "all the iron work of the stores on Third Street next to Burnet house." On May 16 Rogers got Benjamin Horton's proposition for the ironwork, then left for a long stay in Frankfort as hotel construction heated up. He mentions nothing about the stores during a few trips back upriver. On September 1 he sent out bills for his plans and, two days later, received the balance due for designing "stores next [to the] Burnet House." Then all is silence. In 1858 Tweed and Andrews were located on Pearl Street, according to the city directory, not next to the Burnet House, so these stores were never built or were built for rental.

Such was just a half year, much condensed here, in the oscillatory life of Isaiah Rogers at the height of his career out West. Among the residential projects cited, perhaps the most original (for Rogers) and eye-catching is "Hillforest" (originally called Forest Hill) in Aurora, Indiana, commissioned in 1853 and inhabited in 1855. It is sufficiently different from his other domestic work to suggest that Whitestone had an important hand in its design and acted as draftsman. But according to the formula for their partnership, and in particular here, it is clear that Rogers designed, often in pencil sketches, and Whitestone (or sometimes Willard) helped execute presentation and working drawings. This does not mean, of course, that Whitestone could not offer suggestions during the design process.

Drawings for Hillforest were finished by mid-May, and Rogers appears not to have supervised construction. The client was Thomas Gaff, a distiller, brewer, financier, industrialist, and steamboat owner. His wood-frame house sits on ten acres, some originally landscaped, overlooking the Ohio River.[11] The structure is basically a low hip-roofed two-story Italianate box augmented in front by a semicircular, double-layer piazza. (Figs. 68–71) The smooth exterior walls are edged with wooden quoins, opened through round-arched windows, and are topped by deep eaves resting on carved brackets. The half-round entry is extended by the delicate, half-circular two-story porch defined by thin fluted columns of wood resembling cast iron; it is surmounted by a circular belvedere opened by a ring of round-arched windows. The belvedere is a smaller and rounded variation on the theme of Rogers's cupola at the contemporary Capital Hotel in Frankfort. Gaff's connection to the shipping industry has led some Romantics to describe the double-layered porches as steamboat decks. (The same allusion confuses discussion of Mark Twain's Hartford house as well.) The axial entrance leads into a hall between lateral parlors that sweeps back to a flying staircase, an arrangement typical of Rogers's domestic planning. The building is remarkably well preserved, retaining the hall floor's original marquetry, or geometrical patterning through the use of different-colored woods. The house is open to the public and listed on the National Register of Historic Places.

Hillforest is one of the few works by Rogers to survive. Many from this decade are gone, including Jason Gurley's commission for a multipurpose building in Chicago. Erected for $70,000, Metropolitan Hall was named for its imposing third-floor concert room. In March 1854 Rogers spent several days in the city giving instructions to workmen, and the building was dedicated on September 26. It was a crisp Italianate pile. Shops lined the ground floor around the corner of La Salle and Randolph Streets.[12] According to the *Chicago Daily Tribune,* the hall was approximately one hundred by sixty feet, with a thirty-foot-high ceiling for which Whitestone had drawn a centerpiece. Light came in through fifteen slender, east- and south-facing, round-arched windows twenty feet tall. The walls were furred to prevent disturbances caused by echoes; the floor was likewise treated to dampen footfalls. Some thirteen hundred listeners could be seated comfortably on settees, each holding four people, or two thousand if crowded. At the "New

68. "Hillforest," the Thomas Gaff house, Aurora, Indiana, 1853–55. View of the estate. From *Atlas of Dearborn County, Indiana,* 1875.

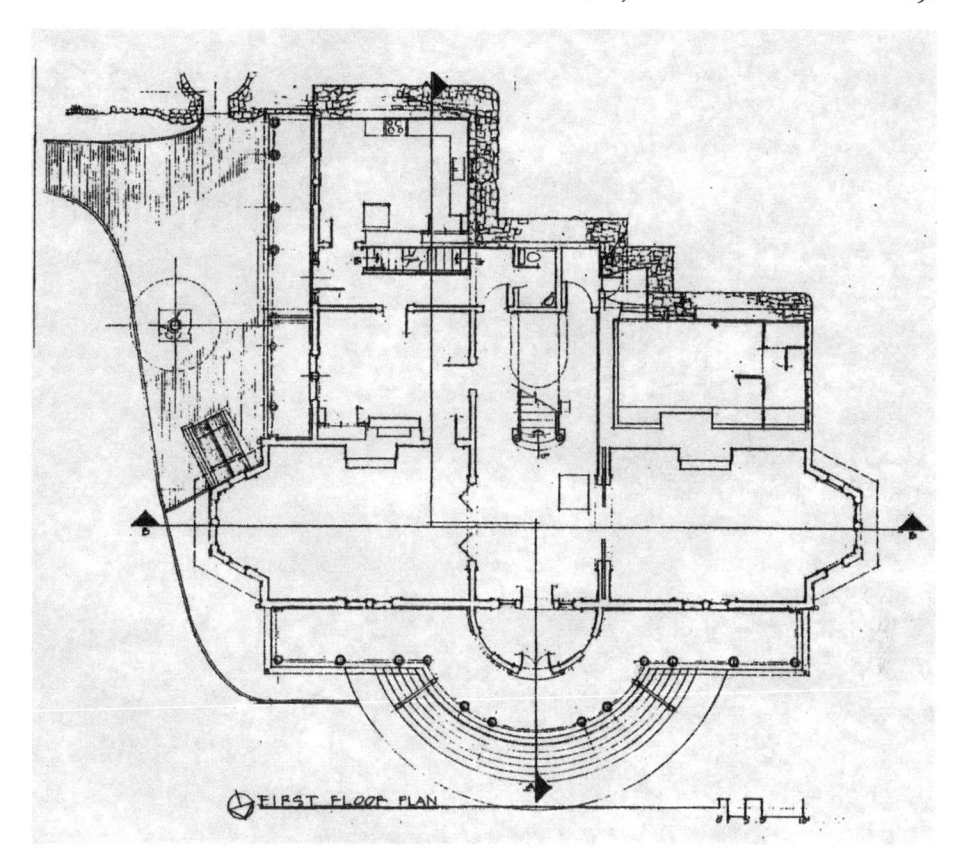

69. "Hillforest," the Thomas Gaff house, Aurora, Indiana, 1853–55. First-floor plan. Courtesy Hillforest Victorian House Museum.

Hall of Mr. Gurley" in November 1854, Rogers attended a performance by Ole Bull, the famed Norwegian violinist whose music he had enjoyed in New York, and found it a "very good room to sing in."

In Louisville on July 1, 1853, Rogers looked at a lot to accommodate a residence for Colonel William Preston, soldier, politician, and member of Congress from Louisville, who in November paid him $25 for plans and elevations of a three-story house. The next May, Rogers was working on a cottage for the same client, and the following March he was again sketching a house for him. Rogers then headed for Aurora, where he explained his design to Thomas Gaff. Back in Goshen he took a moment for himself and hunted quail and larks. Back to work in Chicago he explained the design of Gurney's building to that client. He also advised R. B. Bowler about his work and discussed designing the stone front for James Hall's house. By the evening of July 8 he was headed downriver on the steamer *Sam Snowdon.* At Frankfort he worked on designs for both Tweed and Hall as well as plans for Colonel Preston's house, all the while attending to the rising Capital Hotel (New Weisiger House). In Louisville on July 22 Colonel Preston looked over

70. "Hillforest," the Thomas Gaff house, Aurora, Indiana, 1853–55. Exterior. Historic American Buildings Survey, Library of Congress.

his sketches and said he would get back to him. Back in Cincinnati Rogers found his office door broken open but nothing missing; he delivered Hall's plans and, as usual, went looking for men to send to Frankfort. After a quick trip to Goshen he was again on his way downriver. In Frankfort he found a partition at the hotel badly built and had it taken down and replaced with a truss. He then planned the fountain for Bowler and, after a quick trip to Louisville, started working on improvements at the hotel there. Back in Cincinnati he received $10 for his design of Bowler's fountain, shipped more materials to Frankfort, went out to Goshen and staked out the cellar for his own house, and again caught the boat downriver.

In Louisville in August 1853 he noted that his fifty-third birthday found him "in good health and spirits and plenty to do," a vast understatement. T. T. Shreve, brother of the proprietor of the Louisville Hotel, ordered drawings for altering his house. Rogers said he would do a pencil sketch for $50 (his rates had risen as his availability shrank) and commenced it two days later. The work was completed and the design paid for by mid-February 1854. On August 25, 1853, in Cincinnati, Rogers finished a sketch for Coleman's icehouse and had it approved. Back in Louisville four days later he consulted about the Shreve house and then moved on to Frankfort. With materials for the Capital Hotel pouring into town, he learned that the money had run out, but he was authorized to go on with building anyway. If he remembered his ordeal after H. H. Dexter vanished from Boston in 1846 and left him deep in debt, he must have quickly put it out of his mind, for work did indeed continue. In Cincinnati for two days in mid-September there was much discussion about materials and new projects, including the prospect of a hotel for Chicago. Supplies for the Capital Hotel continued to arrive in Frankfort, and work progressed with the help of prisoners, all while Rogers drew new plans for Coleman's wooden icehouse and details for the Shreve house. Money again began to flow at the Frankfort hotel, and he worked on finishing drawings while Whitestone drew up the plans for Hanna's store across the way.

By mid-October 1853 Rogers was showing visitors around the nearly finished hotel in Frankfort while Whitestone attended to the drawings for Coleman's tomb at Spring Grove Cemetery. Rogers was back in Cincinnati on October 24, talking to suppliers, paying bills, and hearing rumors of yet another hotel to be designed. In Louisville he talked about improvements to the local courthouse, which he

71. "Hillforest," the Thomas Gaff house, Aurora, Indiana, 1853–55. Central hall and stairway from entrance. Courtesy Hillforest Victorian House Museum.

promised to plan for $250, discussed the Shreve house, and moved on to Frankfort, where money continued to arrive and progress to be made. In Cincinnati on November 5 he ordered locks and ironwork for what was still called the Weisiger House. Back downriver the next day, he looked at a site for a cottage in Louisville for a Mr. Bullitt, worked on sketches for the Galt House, and continued them at Frankfort, where he found the hotel "well advanced toward completion." He worked on drawings for Bullitt's house and delivered them in Louisville, and at this time he officially formed the partnership with Whitestone. In Frankfort he packed up his furniture ready to go home to Cincinnati, where on November 21 he was hanging pictures in the parlor. But he was mistaken if he thought he would stay off the boats, for two days later he was back in Louisville showing his plans for improving the Galt House and picking up a commission for a house from a Mr. Adams, one of the proprietors. Prentice paid him for his sketch of a house made the summer before (and would soon return for more drawings). He looked for an office for the Louisville branch of Rogers and Whitestone and then caught the *Blue Wing* for Frankfort, where he talked to a Mr. Taylor about a cottage. Back in Louisville to discuss with Adams the plans for the Galt house, he was requested to go east to look at hotel improvements.

Trips farther afield occasionally broke up these back-and-forth river runs. Rogers returned to Cincinnati from Louisville by the last day of November 1853, but within a week he was again at the Astor House in New York, where he visited the exhibitions at the Crystal Palace, which he found very fine, before moving on to the Tremont in Boston. At Quincy he called on Solomon Willard and requested an estimate for granite to be used in the Coleman tomb. He was asked to study improvements to his exchange building in Boston. In Marshfield he visited his eighty-five-year-old mother, other family members, and friends. Back through Boston and on to Newport to see Emily Jane and family, he then set off for New York by the steamer *State of Maine*. While there he sought depositions regarding his suit about the Hamilton County courthouse from several people, including the architect Martin E. Thompson, and studied the Taylor House for possible improvements. He visited in Philadelphia and then headed for Washington, D.C., where he talked to Ammi B. Young at the Treasury and J. J. Greenough at the Patent Office, fraternized with several senators, looked at the site of a prospective hotel southwest of the Capitol, and found the work at James Renwick Jr.'s Smithsonian Institution "very inferior and badly constructed" and the stone at the Washington Monument "flaking at the joints." Willard's Hotel charged him nothing for room and board (a kindness he sometimes enjoyed during his travels). He had returned to Cincinnati by Christmas Day, resuming his frantic catch-as-catch-can routine.

In his travels, Rogers often visited cemeteries and studied funereal vaults and monuments.[13] Back in September 1844, in conjunction with his design for the

Henshaw vault at Mount Auburn Cemetery, he had bought a "book on tombs." Several such works came from his drawing board over his long career, and some remain to be identified in Newport, Rhode Island; New Haven, Connecticut; and New Orleans. In Cincinnati he designed vaults for Spring Grove Cemetery, which like Mount Auburn was among the first of the rural gardens of graves. Founded in 1844 by Salmon P. Chase, Griffin Taylor, and others, Spring Grove was originally laid out by John Notman, although it was soon altered by others, including Adolph Strauch. Vaults were discouraged in favor of monuments, but of the former Rogers did provide a few. As early as June 1849 he mentions one for a "Mr. G. Taylor," presumably Griffith Taylor. In May 1852 he measured "Mr. Taylor's tomb" and "made a plan for alteration of it"; drawings seem to have carried through to July. A lithograph by Ehrgott & Forbinger, published in *The Cincinnati Cemetery of Spring Grove* in 1862, shows the square facade of Griffin Taylor's vault formed of deeply drafted masonry punctuated by a round-arched doorway edged with delicate carving, the whole flanked by *ressauts* composed of paired thin fluted columns supporting the entablature, frieze, and cornice that ran between them at the face of the wall. (Fig. 72)

That delicate published design suggests the hand of Whitestone rather than of Rogers. However, a trip to Spring Grove today reveals that the vault now listed as Griffin Taylor's is far less elegant than the one pictured in the lithograph, and it bears the names of his two relatives who were to have been buried with him, Stephen Brown and Elias Haines, but not his own.[14] Its rectangular front is flanked by planar triangular walls and framed by broad paneled pilasters that support a heavy entablature dotted with rosettes. The doorway is round headed, with an oversized carved keystone. Since the diary does not mention that Rogers supervised the erection of the improvements he drew, it is possible the front shown in the 1862 publication never materialized. Yet what is there now surely looks like a work from Rogers's pencil.

On February 2, 1852, Rogers had gone out to Spring Grove in the "funeral train" of A. B. Coleman's wife, but the burial he mentions must have been a temporary arrangement, for two days later the hotelier asked Rogers to design a vault for him at the cemetery. In January 1854 Coleman decided that his should have a granite front. And so it did, with stone from Quincy, Massachusetts, put in place in early July. As shown in a Middleton, Strobridge & Co. lithograph in *The Cincinnati Cemetery of Spring Grove* for 1857, it was a chunky Renaissance Revival facade flanked by paneled piers supporting a flat roof, with a round-arched doorway surrounded by heavy moldings and surmounted by an oversized decorative keystone in the form of a console. A paneled, stone or iron door closed the vault. "A. B. Coleman" in raised block letters marched across the architrave. (Fig. 73) When he died in Utica in 1879, Coleman presumably joined the remains of his wife in that vault. Although management staff of Spring Grove reports that

72. Griffin Taylor tomb, Spring Grove Cemetery, Cincinnati, Ohio, 1849–52. From *The Cincinnati Cemetery of Spring Grove*, 1862.

no such mausoleum exists, it—or more likely its twin—does indeed still stand. Near the Griffin Taylor tomb is another containing the remains of one Alfred Marsh that is an exact copy of Coleman's, without his name.[15] We know from the diary that Rogers simultaneously produced and saw erected a tomb "same as Mr. Coleman's" for John P. Tweed. It would seem possible that what is now Marsh's vault was originally Tweed's. At various times in the past, bodies were moved from their original resting places to new locations in the cemetery. That is true of Isaiah Rogers's own remains there.

Such a year says much about the man's energy despite persistent bouts of illness, the constant demands on his time, his wide-ranging interests, and his high reputation as an architect and builder. It should be noted too that in Rogers's criticism of the work of others, planning and construction usually took precedence over the niceties of architectural style. It is probably no accident that throughout his diary he describes his work as planning, not designing.

The next year, 1855, saw the office of Rogers, Whitestone & Co. as crowded with work as the year before and the one to come. Rogers continued his frequent hundred-mile to-and-fro between Cincinnati and Louisville, as well as many trips to Niagara Falls about the hotel there, for which drawings were promptly begun. On the second trip to the town, he found nothing attractive in an architectural way among the public buildings. On a quick run over to Albany, he looked at the recently dedicated Gothic Cathedral of the Immaculate Conception, still lacking its towers, one of many ecclesiastical designs of the Tipperary-born Patrick Charles Keeley. Rogers found it imposing but displaying nothing original. Back in Niagara he had himself daguerreotyped standing in front of the falls. On a third trip there he was approached about an orphan's asylum and picked up some projects for Milwaukee as well. On a fourth trip, in September, he met with clients about the hotel and heard that it was not to cost more than $100,000, but should be designed to be enlarged. He then went to look at the "wire bridge" over the Niagara River and found the workmanship "very good, but . . . [did] not like the suspension principle." From the edge of the river, however, in a rare statement of aesthetic pleasure he found it "a most sublime sight to look up and see the bridge suspended 230 feet above." This was John A. Roebling's nearly finished 825-foot railroad bridge, although Rogers never mentions the engineer's name. He had seen Adolphus Heiman's bridge at Nashville, which had encountered difficulties, and if he also knew of the contemporary failure of the deck of Charles Ellet Jr.'s Wheeling Suspension Bridge, this knowledge might have led him to suspect the hanging structural system.

On the way home from his third Niagara trip, he stopped in Milwaukee. On a hot August 24, 1854, an arsonist set the Second Great Fire that destroyed a large swath of the young city, including the United States Hotel.[16] Two days later Rogers received a dispatch from John Lockwood of that city, with whom he had earlier

73. A. B. Coleman tomb, Spring Grove Cemetery, Cincinnati, Ohio, 1852–55. From *The Cincinnati Cemetery of Spring Grove*, 1857.

corresponded, to come immediately. His first reaction to the architecture there was to note that he saw some good buildings, "but most of them partook too much of the New York tawdry style of sickly ornament of the most grotesque style." Rogers's buildings of both early and later dates were chaste, with applied ornament held to a minimum. But he had come as an architect, not a critic, and quickly met with the new hotel's board of trustees, a group that included the civic developers John Lockwood and James Ludington, "leading spirits in the enterprise." Rogers noted their desire for a brick hostelry that would contain a bank, and he left with assurances of future friendship. Back in Louisville he commenced to draw through October and into November while superintending the erection of work there. As usual Rogers sketched plans and elevations in pencil and Willard inked them. During this time the Milwaukee architect George W. Mygatt also paid him a visit. On November 11 back in Milwaukee he supped and smoked a "segar" with Ludington, then showed the drawings to Lockwood, who did "not speak very encouragingly of the success of the Hotel until next spring." Two days later he made the rounds of investors, bankers, and Mygatt, all of whom were well pleased with the design, but only one more entry appears in the diary about the project. It mentions a letter of early January 1855 from Lockwood in Milwaukee questioning Rogers's bill.

James Buck's history of early Milwaukee quotes the local newspaper's description of what was to have been called the Shepardson Hotel. Sometime after Rogers's meeting with the board, the reporter saw the drawings for the proposal "at the room of Mr. Mygatt." This was obviously Rogers's design, one for an L-shaped building at the corner of East Water and Michigan Streets with an extension to Main (mentioned in the diary), measuring 60 by 254 by 120 feet. There were to be six stories above ground-floor shops and banks, to be built of brick with iron caps and sills. It was probably intended that Mygatt would superintend the erection. Buck reported the fate of the project: it fell through for want of money. During this period John Lockwood also asked Rogers to design a house for him; at a meeting on November 11 he took away Rogers's sketches, nothing more is heard about them. In 1857 Lockwood did erect a "lavish Italianate house" of brick costing an astounding $20,000 in North Point, a new development he had had laid out. It was razed in 1889. Only deeper research and some luck will uncover whether that building was what Rogers designed for him. James Ludington, the other "leading spirit" of the hotel, commissioned one or more stores from Rogers, perhaps the postfire replacements at 341 and 343 East Water Street.[17]

Back in Cincinnati, the office had on the boards the usual run of commercial designs. These included Winthrop B. Smith's book concern and George W. McAlpin's intended building on Fourth Street, both in the city; Horatio Dalton Newcomb's five-story Italianate block on the corner of Main and Bullitt Streets in Louisville; and the adjacent Alexander building. The architects were also working on houses, including one, now apparently gone, for Rogers's daughter and son-in-law in Newport; the couple was living at 3 Fir Street the next year. The trio of Rogers, Whitestone, and Willard worked on alterations to the Galt House and the Louisville and Burnet hotels. Rogers sketched a department store in Cincinnati for Ellis, McAlpin & Co. in early April and was encouraged to develop the scheme in a set of plans. McAlpin had little to say when shown the set, but Rogers must have assumed he had a green light because he and Whitestone moved on to developed drawings. In early July, McAlpin said he wanted to talk about the project with Milton Cook, the builder. In mid-August, Rogers received $100 on account, and then the project vanishes from his accounts. City directories list the company as located on Vine Street before it moved to Fourth in 1880, occupying a building designed by James K. Wilson.

In Louisville in June 1854 the office began work on a building for Horatio Dalton Newcomb, a whiskey merchant and manufacturer. Born and raised on a Massachusetts farm, he shared a common background with Rogers. On June 19 Whitestone commenced outlining the Newcomb Banking House–Second National Bank at Bullitt and Main Streets, and the client liked the drawings when he saw them on June 27. Two days later in Cincinnati, Rogers took Newcomb "to look at several buildings in reference to a plan . . . I had made for him." He would do this kind of inspection with other clients as well. Newcomb authorized the taking of bids in mid-July, and the production of drawings of sections and stonework continued as excavation for the cellar began at the end of the month. Bids for stonework, brickwork, cast iron, and timber were discussed by architect and client as Whitestone prepared working drawings. To save money, Newcomb decided to have the foundation of brick set in cement rather than stone, which he thought too expensive. A finished drawing of the main elevation (now in the collection of the Filson Historical Society in Louisville) shows the tall narrow block with three bays on each street.[18] Openings were round arched at each floor; the columns were Ionic at the second level and Corinthian above. Toward late August, Whitestone set himself to drawing capitals for the cast-iron columns, to be supplied by the Snead & Co. architectural foundry. A month later he produced drawings for safes for the building to be bid on by Horton & Macy in Cincinnati.

Meanwhile, Rogers laid out the plan for the iron-fronted Alexander's store, adjacent to Newcomb's, and soon received an order to build it. A small fire in the latter building barely slowed production. Well into 1855, workmen applied the finishing touches at Newcomb's: soldering the tin roof, putting up the tin dentil cornice, laying floors and stone entrance stairs, putting in gas pipes, installing partitions on the fifth floor for a porter's room, glazing, preparing lath for the plastering after the winter by Patrick Bannon, painting and graining, setting plate glass for the banking room, tiling the entrance, and so on. By May the banking room was ready for Francis Pedretti's mural decoration. Whitestone eventually had his office in the building. It came down in 1948.

Newcomb's satisfaction was so great that he introduced Rogers to several clients and asked Rogers and Whitestone (or perhaps Whitestone alone[19]) to design his Broadway house. That structure was a five-bay, two story plus attic, stuccoed Italianate palazzo with rustic base and quoins and a Corinthian portico surmounted by balusters. It was later remodeled as St. Xavier High School and eventually demolished.

In fall of 1854 Rogers commenced drawings for the orphanage in Niagara Falls and the hotel in Milwaukee. Back east he traveled from Boston to Plymouth to promote his project for the Forefathers' Monument, then moved on to Marshfield, Boston, Newport, and the Astor House in New York. There he visited Appleton's bookstore to look over works on architecture. In Philadelphia he again called on John Notman and went to an indifferent play at the Walnut Street Theatre. Back in Louisville by December 9 he caught up with works in progress, looking through his drawings of public buildings for one to lithograph for an advertising card. Whitestone drew up an ad for papers in various cities, but when it appeared it was not illustrated.

Buildings from the offices in Cincinnati and Louisville continued to rise during this period. Sometime before the end of September 1854, Rogers and Whitestone produced fifteen sheets of drawings for "Rosewell," the home of the fur dealer Philatus S. Barber located in Harrods Creek, Kentucky.[20] The commission is barely mentioned in the diary, suggesting that Whitestone had the upper hand in the design. The builder was J. N. Breeden & Co.; when Rogers visited the site in mid-January the next year, he found "the carpenter work badly executed. Roof very faulty." Perhaps because of Rogers's criticism, Breeden was not paid in full and had to sue the owner for $896.50. The house rose as a two-story, three-bay block with Italianate bracketed overhanging eaves and a tetrastyle Corinthian portico. It still stands as restored.

Back in Cincinnati, Rogers turned his attention to the five-story building designed for Winthrop B. Smith & Company, educational publishers and producer of the McGuffey Readers for children. It stood on the corner of Baker and Walnut Streets. When it opened toward the end of 1856, it had been on the boards for some time. The ground story of its "chaste and elegant" front was Gothic in style and entirely of iron; the rest of the building was of iron and stone ornamented with elegant columns, according to the *Cincinnati Daily Gazette,* which credited it to "Rogers, Whetstone, & Co." Rogers fitted it with A. Livingston Johnson's patented rolling shutters, "which render it alike Fire and Burglar proof," the first building in the city to have them, according to the paper. Rogers had talked to Johnson in New York about the shutters in April 1855, and they had another long discussion in Louisville in May. He was to use them again at the Commercial Bank in Paducah. Smith's plan was ultimately to connect his building to another, planned for the north side of Baker Street, "by an iron tunnel." Although this description sounds as if it could have been an example of Rogers's patented lattice bridge, it was later called a "subterranean tunnel" by the *Christian Advocate* when that paper described the three-building complex into which the plant evolved. Whether Rogers's office designed the additional blocks is unknown—they were built during a gap in the diary, and their erection went unnoticed by the local papers.

Rogers welcomed 1855 by complaining that the workers on Newcomb's building in Louisville were "off frolicking." Two weeks later he was "reading descriptions of different styles of architecture in different parts of Europe," but he does not say which sources he consulted (James Fergusson's *Handbook of Architecture,* long the standard for that sort of research, appeared that year, but Rogers was in New York too early for Appleton's to have imported it for stock). With several buildings in various stages of construction, as well as a new store for W. B. Reynolds and storefronts in Louisville on the boards, he turned to still more tasks: the Judah Touro monument for the Newport cemetery, whose design was requested by his son-in-law, Nathan Gould, as heir to Touro's wishes; a cottage on Long Island for A. B. Coleman and a visit to the site where it was going up in June; another cottage for a Mr. Pratt in New York State, for which the two of them pored over reference books; a sketch for a house for Colonel Preston and another for T. S. Kennedy in Louisville; the fifth plan for the Niagara hotel; and some nibbles.

With onsite work temporarily slow, and unquestionably stimulated by the recent visit to Roebling's Niagara span and a conversation with Adolphus Heiman, Rogers returned in mid-February to his ongoing study of bridges, a pursuit he followed when work slackened, talking at length to Whitestone about the principles of arches. Since early in 1852 he had been rethinking his approach to bridging systems and was mulling things over when he met with Heiman in Nashville; he certainly looked at that architect's suspension bridge over the Cumberland. Rogers turned his attention to designing a bridge to cross the Ohio River at Cincinnati, at the site where Roebling's suspension span, which opened in 1867, still brightens commuters' daily crossings.[21] He rejected the Roebling, Ellet, and Heiman suspension systems, however. Rogers's proposed bridge was especially suited for the railroad-employed arches of cast-iron tubular sections. Lateral bracing resulted from narrowing the distance between arches toward the center of the span. His approach to the problem was methodical. In Cincinnati he thoroughly researched his project—seeking information about the average and maximum weight of freight cars, inquiring about the width and depth of the Ohio at the city, acquiring a section through the river at the foot of Main Street, studying tables of the strength of cast iron—and by mid-March 1855 he was ready to send drawings to Washington for a caveat, or application for temporary protection, preparatory to applying for a patent. That patent—for a bridge obviously intended as a conservative alternative to the suspension system—was granted on September 30,1856.[22] (Figs. 74–75)

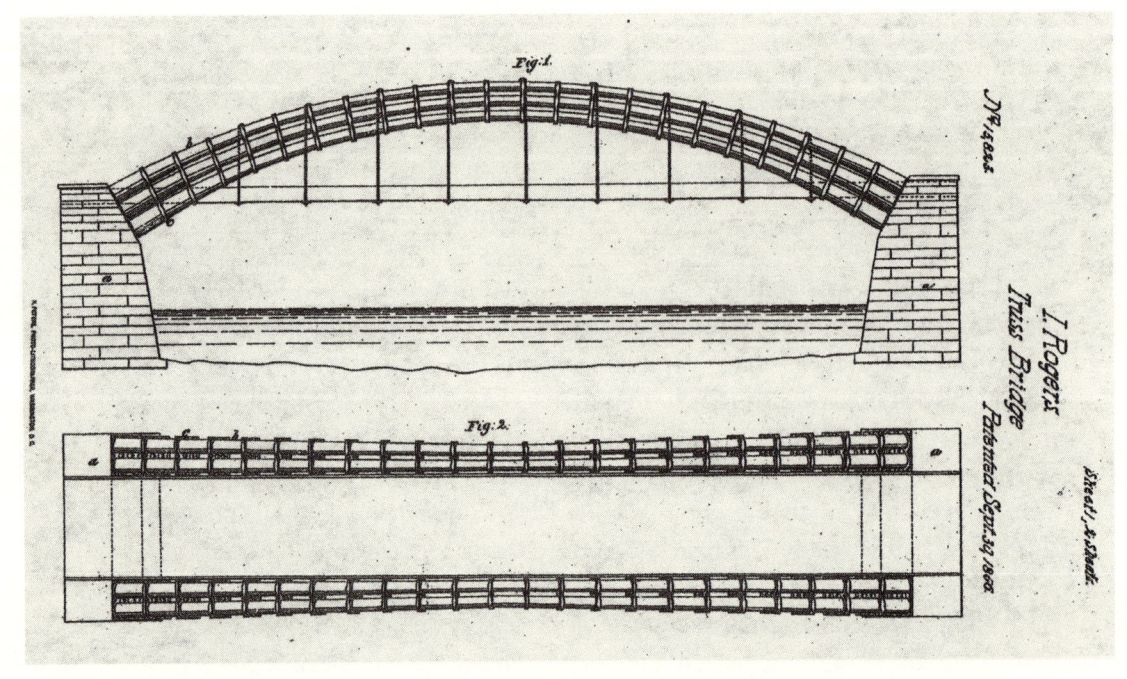

74. Tubular arch bridge. Lithograph after drawing from U.S. Patent No. 15,823, granted September 30, 1856.

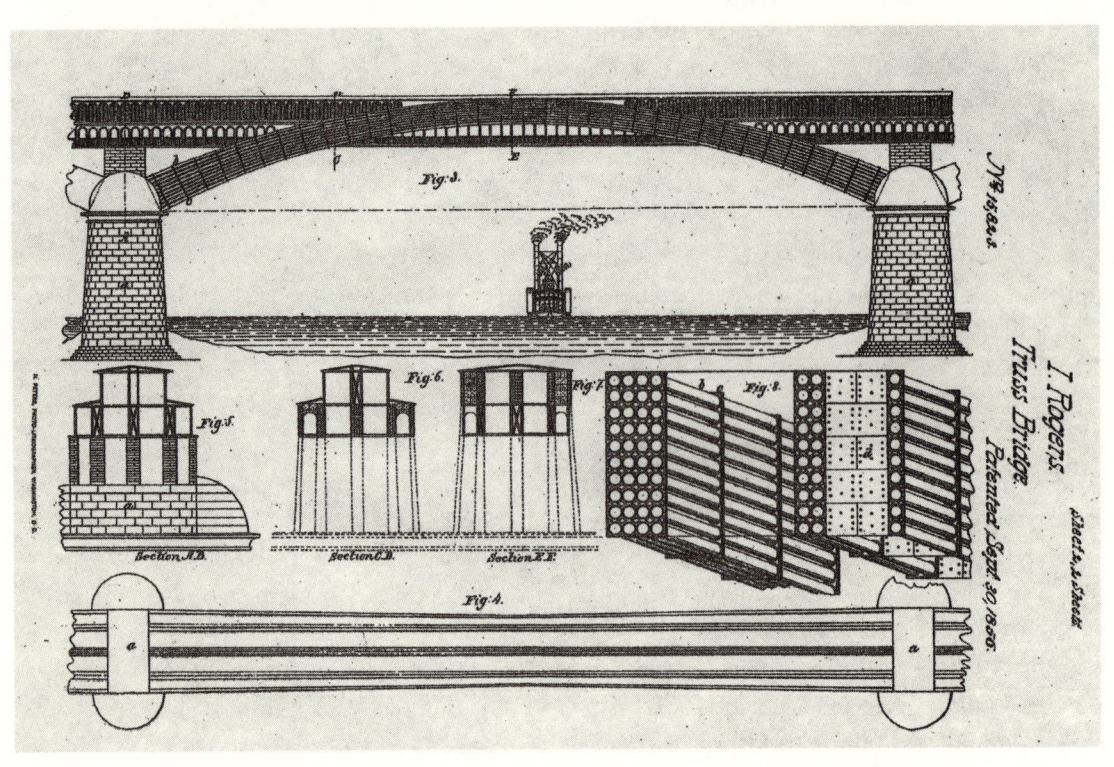

75. Tubular arch bridge. Lithograph after drawing from U.S. Patent No. 15,823, granted September 30, 1856.

Meanwhile, Whitestone worked on a stone-dressing machine, which ultimately functioned "pretty well," according to Rogers. New work arrived in the form of improvements to the Louisville Hotel. A more important commission appeared for a bank in Paducah, Kentucky, for which Rogers produced a penciled design and an estimate of cost overnight, as usual. In Albany, New York, in April he consulted about remodeling Congress Hall, a venerable and prestigious hotel frequented by legislators; working with a local architect named Smith, he drafted a plan for changes. He visited Newport and Boston, where he tried and failed to get information about the intended public library project, a building that was erected on Boylston Street in 1858 from a design by Charles Kirk Kirby and replaced by McKim, Mead & White's landmark on Copley Square. In April he stayed at the Willard Hotel in Washington and had a lawyer apply for the caveat for his "new principle of constructing an arch of cast-iron." He called on T. U. Walter and Ammi Young and then went to Wheeling, West Virginia, where he walked over Ellet's "wire suspension bridge," probably to freshen his memory of that system, again noting he did not approve of it for permanent structures.

Back in Louisville, Rogers's client Horatio Newcomb seems to have become thought of as an authority on planning commercial buildings. When Rogers took W. B. Reynolds to interview other storeowners preparatory to embarking on his Main Street edifice, they received nothing worthwhile except from Newcomb. Indeed, when Reynolds inspected the drawings, he said he "could not determine if he liked them without Mr. Newcomb and others looking at them." After extended negotiations over schemes begun in late 1854 or early 1855, with the client worrying about cost, Reynolds asked for a detailed estimate. Rogers declined at once, "as it has always led to unpleasant feelings and remarks." He also complained about the client showing the drawings to mechanics without consulting the architect first, something Rogers forbade or at least tried to avoid. In late December 1856 Reynolds finally gave instructions to begin construction as soon as the drawings were finished. An extended gap in the diary leaves us in the dark about details, but the four-story, limestone-fronted building was erected and still stands.[23]

Rogers also worked during April and May 1855 on a design for the Washington Monument and then he had a long talk with Whitestone "about publishing a series of structures on architecture of this country." That most likely did not happen. A commission on May 8 to design the tower and spire for William Keeley's 1850–52 unfinished Roman Catholic Cathedral of the Assumption on Fifth Street, in Louisville, sent him to the books for precedent.[24] This was a religion Rogers often heard scourged by the preachers whose sermons he attended, and among his usual Sunday tracts, in January he had read *The Great Red Dragon,* "an exposé of Catholicism" by Anthony Gavin, which had been trumpeted in the daily press throughout the previous year. Perhaps that is why when we next hear of the church, the Irish-born Whitestone was finishing the plans, although Rogers priced it. When called by Bishop Martin John Spalding on May 26, Rogers took Whitestone with him, got the drawings approved, and scheduled construction to begin within the week. Whether news of this intended flaunting of the presence of Romanism in town had anything to do with "Bloody Monday," August 6—when antiforeigner and anti-Catholic rioters led by Know-Nothings left twenty-two dead and scores injured—these were clearly fraught times in a fraught place for such a defiant gesture. Roger was in Paducah at the time and says nothing about the tragedy, though mention of current affairs is rare in his diary. In any event, through all the negative energy Rogers stayed true to the first rule of the successful architect: get the job and hold it. The tall terminal, one of his few Gothic efforts, was completed in 1858; its style was dictated by Keeley's church, on which it stands, and perhaps in detail owed more to Whitestone than to him.[25]

Besides this endeavor, the new bridge design, for which Rogers made drawings for a model, and the Washington Monument continued to hold his attention into May. In July, Rogers and Whitestone took time to write a "communication" about the winning design for the national monument to Henry Clay, who died in 1852, which was intended for the cemetery in Lexington. Although there is no record that the pair entered that competition, they paid a borrowed $1 to have their opinion inserted in the *Louisville Journal,* then owned by the controversial Know-Nothing George Dennison Prentiss. The competition produced the leading contender, J. R. Hamilton of Cincinnati, who proposed an elaborate, all cast-iron Gothic dome that proved to be too expensive to build.[26] It has been characterized by William Blair Scott Jr. as resembling "a gothic arch shaped bird-cage with stain glass windows all around and a museum to Clay on the second floor. It was greatly out of scale for the site."[27] It was rejected at the end of the month. (A statue on a tall column was eventually erected.) The partners' insert was to be an "advertisement of criticism," but it is no longer possible to say what bothered them. Although during the month much ink was spilled over the subject in the local papers, none has as yet been identified as coming from Rogers's office.

Back in Paducah, Rogers heard about a commission for a stable for his old Cincinnati client Winthrop B. Smith, of the publishing company, and he made preparations for Gardner Lathrop to begin making a model of his arched bridge. Through July he worked on the design of the Fifth Ward School in Louisville, and by the twenty-fifth he had finished "plans, elevations and sections" for the building, perhaps the first of the rare times that he mentions such drawings by name rather than lumping them together as "plans."

We lose sight of Rogers due to a lacuna in the diary between August and November 1855. In Cincinnati on November 14, he was awarded by arbitration a settlement of $7,000 for his work on the Hamilton County courthouse. He then called on Lathrop, who had begun casting the tubes for his bridge model, that being a necessary part of his application for a patent; he also began studying alterations and improvements to the Unitarian Church, worked on plans for the Pearl Street dry-goods store of King, Corwin & Co.; attended to Robert Bower's fountain, gate, and tower; and had himself daguerreotyped yet again. He then discussed completing the Hamilton County courthouse, wondered about the relationship of his original plans to those of Walter & Wilson, and again went to see Lathrop about fitting the cast tubes together. While supervising the Commercial Bank in Paducah, he worked on the Louisville Hotel and the Unitarian church. In Louisville he heard he had been (re)appointed architect of the Hamilton County courthouse, and back in Cincinnati he began to study the problem of finishing that structure while working on drawings for another courthouse in Louisville. He continued to fuss with details of Bowler's house, including the reservoir, a necessary feature of his extensive horticultural site; he agreed to superintend the work on the Louisville Hotel; and he began working on new proposals for the courthouse in Cincinnati as well as designs for a house there for a Mr. (John S.?) Chenoweth. These and several other projects continued into the next year, when he also turned to his own property, sketching a house for his farm at Goshen that proved too expensive. But mostly he dealt with the myriad problems of the revitalized work at the Hamilton County courthouse. Finally, he sketched a store for John Shillito & Co. on Fourth Street in Cincinnati, work that eventually went to a rival, James W. McLaughlin. At year's end he had to rush off to Louisville when the wing of the hotel crashed.

In March 1855 Rogers had been asked for sketches for the design of the Commercial Bank building in Paducah, one scheme with and one without a dwelling attached. The original charge was to remodel the existing building, but that was eventually pulled down, and the site on the corner of Broadway and Locust Streets was reused for the new fireproof structure. After a convivial mint julep, the architect discussed the project with James L. Dallam and the other directors. They requested a written explanation of the design, work, materials, and construction, which they then signed, with slight additions, the whole to cost $24,600. Rogers hired a local foreman, looked over the available building materials, and in early June began work on the drawings back in Louisville. In May he had discussed rolling iron shutters with the patentee, A. L. Johnson of Baltimore, which he subsequently installed in the building; he finished the presentation drawings, signed the contract, and began the inevitable search for workmen and materials. The construction drawings followed, and building commenced in June while he sought bids for the job. Freemasons officiated at the laying of the cornerstone on the Fourth of July 1855 "in a very impressive manner." By December, with work nearing completion, L. M. Flournoy, the bank president, asked Rogers to design a counter and have it made.

Terra-cotta was among the materials Rogers specified for the Paducah bank. The decorations in this material was supplied by Patrick Bannon, whom Rogers had used at Newcomb's store. Newly arrived in Louisville in 1850,[28] the Irish-born Bannon had established by 1852 the P. Bannon Pipe Company and, a few years later, the Falls' City Terra-Cotta Works, a company producing "Designs of Ornamental Work For the exterior and interior decoration of Buildings, embellishment of Gardens, &c." at Fifth Street near Walnut, as proclaimed in a handsome lithograph by Hart & Mapother of 1859.[29] In 1855 Rogers ordered terra-cotta capitals and base moldings for the portico, specified by full-size drawings, for which Bannon charged $100. This would seem to be an early use of terra-cotta in American architecture, if that is what it really was. According to William R. Black Jr., a restorationist in Paducah who has examined pieces of Bannon manufacture, the material is "chalky and soft like the brick of the period . . . more like plaster."[30] Indeed, Bannon was a plasterer by trade.

For the front of the bank, Rogers resorted to a familiar formula, at least in part. The central feature was a Corinthian hexastyle temple. This was flanked by a residential wing to the left and a right rear wing, which housed the banking room behind an entrance and round-arched windows that could be shuttered with iron. The brick exterior side walls were covered with stucco and scored to resemble stone. The Commercial Bank of Kentucky stood in Paducah until the 1880s; today, part of it remains embedded in later structures.

There is a long gap in the diary from early February 1856 to May 1861, but it is possible to follow some of Rogers's activities during these years. The school on Fifth Street in Louisville, originally called the Fifth Ward School and then the Monsarrat School, a work credited to Whitestone by Elizabeth Jones, still stands as converted into apartments.[31] The diary shows that Rogers drew the original plans, and Whitestone, as usual, produced finished drawings. In 1855 Rogers and Whitestone were sued for damages while taking down the ruins of the old building, a fact that Rogers uncharacteristically fails to mention. Nine-foot-tall, round-arched windows set into shallow reveals provided maximum daylight into the classrooms at the second and third levels. The minimal exterior ornament consists of a brickwork dentil course above the ground floor, a protruding two-brick belt course between the classroom floors, another connecting the imposts of the window arches, and two more between those arches and the cornice. Early views indicate that the exterior was either painted or stuccoed. The school opened in 1857.

The degree of Henry Whitestone's influence on the school is unknown, but he left Rogers sometime in 1857 to set up his own office in Louisville. He alone is credited in a document dated the end of November with the second building of the Louisville Medical Institute (now part of the University of Louisville), although that could mean he simply supervised the work on the ground.[32] The original 1837 building by Gideon Shryock burned in December 1856 and was replaced by the end of 1857.

With Whitestone on his own in Louisville, Rogers's presence in Kentucky predictably waned, although another reason may explain the fall off in commissions from south of the river: growing tensions in the region. We cannot let Rogers leave the state without mentioning a strange, and at this distance, inexplicable occurrence that befell members of his family in Frankfort four years after the completion of the Capital Hotel. The gap in the diary means that we do not have his take on the episode (if he had one), but the *Cincinnati Daily Gazette* carried the story on October 16, 1857. It refers to Rogers's son Willard ("S. W. Rogers"), identified as an "architect of this city," and his brother-in-law Nathan H. Gould ("N. H. Gold") of Newport, Rhode Island. The headline read "Two Gentlemen Driven out of Frankfort, Ky., by a Mob." What happened is clear enough, but the why remains speculative. In town on private business, the pair was accosted by a crowd of men outside the Capital Hotel shouting "Drive the cussed Cincinnati Abolition brokers out of the town!" They were suspected, said the paper, of being money-brokers who crossed the river to redeem for specie bills issued by Frankfort banks. According to the paper, their visit in fact referred to the "performance of a sacred duty, and had no connection with money matters." Perhaps the reason given is correct, if vague. Nationally, however, the failure of the Ohio Life Insurance and Trust Company led to the Panic of 1857, during which specie payments were temporarily suspended, although such was not the case in either Ohio or Kentucky. Perhaps Willard was helping his Rhode Island brother-in-law obtain cash as well as showing him the hotel.[33]

The shouted word *abolition* also raises the possibility that slaveholding might have played a factor. The Ohio River was an active fault line between free and slave states (remember *Uncle Tom's Cabin*), although Kentucky never left the Union, and the mob—being a mob—may have decided without cause that a pair of abolitionists from across the river had come to interfere with the local workings of their "peculiar institution." Perhaps Gould, a Quaker, was overheard to say something critical of that institution. The altered name "Gold" given by the paper might suggest still a different motive, a racial one. One wonders if a misconception played into the ruckus. Crowds of Know-Nothing roughnecks rarely asked questions before starting a riot. For whatever reason, these were nervous times between northern and southern states, although that sense never seeps into Rogers's matter-of-fact diary. Rather than be insulted or worse, the pair retreated to the train, escorted by the excited crowd. Such an ugly experience might have made it easier for the Rogers firm to leave further business in Kentucky to Whitestone.

During the late 1850s the office of Isaiah Rogers, Son & Co. remained in Cincinnati, and sometime in 1857, the twenty-three-year-old Alfred B. ("A. B.") Mullet replaced Whitestone. By 1860 he had been named a partner and, by 1861, had left to travel in Europe. His influence on the work of the Rogers office during his three-year tenure is unknown, although a descendent of the architect has attempted to assess his contributions.[34] He would reenter Rogers's life in 1861 in Washington, D.C., with negative impact.

Over the years, Rogers had resisted requests that he take over superintendence of the statehouse in Columbus, but in 1858 he finally gave in. The design and erection of this structure had been unfolding by fits and starts since the 1830s. Rogers's participation in that history began with his losing entry in the competition of 1838. Yet he continued to record conversations with interested parties, including one in 1853 that took place as he was building the Capital Hotel in Frankfort; it concerned his supervising the ongoing construction, during which architects-in-charge came and went in large numbers. In June 1855 Nathan B. Kelley, then the onsite architect, guided him through a structure he found on the whole "badly arranged and constructed." With the work of seven different architects nearing completion, Rogers finally agreed to the thankless task of overseeing the finishing stages, including the interiors and dome. T. U. Walter, then engaged at the U.S. Capitol, seems also to have been previously consulted about the dome but declined in favor of Rogers, whom he knew well from back east. In a letter dated June 22, 1858, Walter wrote to General James T. Worthington, the advisory commissioner for the statehouse, that it was unlikely any (eastern) architect would want to go out to Ohio, where he expected there was not enough work to make it worthwhile. (One can imagine the harrumph from out west!) He went on to explain that "there used to be a Mr. Isaiah Rogers there, who is one of the safest builders in the world, and who is well skilled in his profession." In a second letter, this one to William A. Platt, the acting commissioner for the statehouse, Walter says he heard from Worthington that Rogers had been appointed to the job (on July 22, 1858, to be exact): "I am very much pleased that you have obtained the services of so able and excellent a man—in *his* hands you are safe" (his emphasis). (Walter's wording in these statements suggests that he thought of Rogers as a builder rather than designer, just as William Jervis Hough had during the judging of the Smithsonian Institution competition entries. Although, to be fair, Walter was probably asked directly about Rogers as a superintendent of building.) Walter goes on to say that he has half finished a study of the dome "as a matter of friendship," not professionally, and his chief draftsman, Augustus Schoenborn, was drawing it, but he adds that it was "useless for me to proceed; Mr. Rogers is on the spot, he needs no aid from me."[35]

To the existing statehouse, Rogers first proposed the addition of a Doric decastyle entrance portico and a crowning peripteral Corinthian tholos. (Fig. 76) Both were unrealized. Among completed work, according to the official report, Rogers was responsible for superintending the main stairways, the pattern of the contrasting tiles of the rotunda floor (a cousin to the flooring of the rotunda at

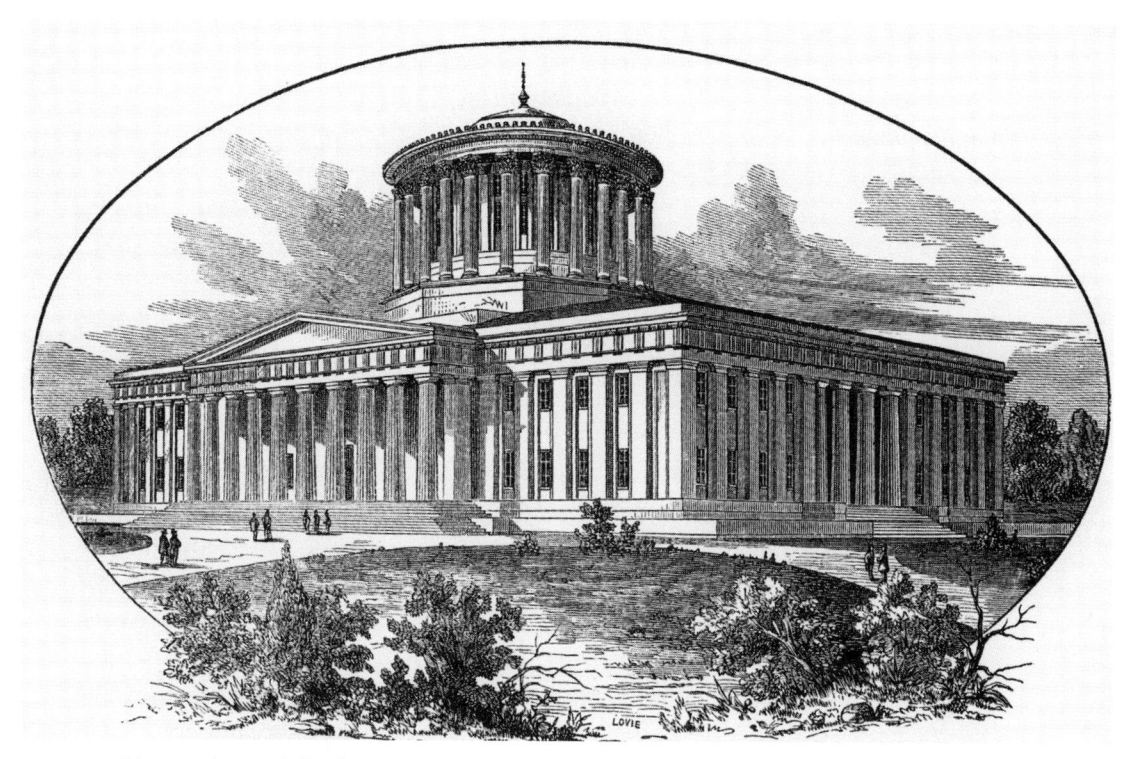

76. Ohio statehouse, Columbus, 1838–61. Unrealized proposed additions. From *Annual Report of the State House,* 1863. Courtesy Ohio Historical Society Library.

Rogers's slightly later Longview Asylum), gas fixtures, brick arches, stone flagging, and grading and planting of the grounds.[36] He may also have added windows to light the north and south corridors of the second floor in 1860. More important, he finalized the look of the "domeless drum" of the cupola, reverting to an earlier design but reflecting the one that crowned his Frankfort hotel. That thankless chore ended under his direction in 1861, long after the sun had set on the Grecian years. Rogers's attitude toward this task is perhaps best recorded in a laconic diary entry. He mentions just one perfunctory stop in Columbus while traveling east on August 21: "Walked over to the Capitol—saw it."[37]

These last prewar years also saw the design of at least three more hotels, one for Memphis, Nashville, and Toledo. Back in 1842 James Dakin had designed a hotel named the Gayoso House in south Memphis for Robertson Tropp, a wealthy planter.[38] In 1857 Tropp engaged the Rogers firm to design a hundred-room addition in the form of a stark quadrangle of three stories above ground-floor shops fronted by wrought-iron balconies that overlooked the Mississippi. That structure burned in 1899. Nashville's "immense" brick 240-room Maxwell House, at Church Street and Fourth Avenue North, commissioned by Colonel John Overton Jr., reverted to a subtle quincunx on its main five-story facade. A shallow portico marked by a Corinthian colonnade formed the men's entrance on Fourth Avenue.

Although designed in 1859, it stood unfinished through the war, when it was appropriated as a Union military hospital, barracks, and prison; it opened for its intended use only in 1869 and burned in 1961.[39]

The Oliver House in Toledo opened in June 1859 with the usual glittering celebration, and the local press hailed the accommodations as the grandest in the land.[40] Shifting populations in the city reduced the building to a rooming house in the 1890s, after which it became an industrial plant. Its shell survives, however, as one of two remaining examples of the type designed by the "father of hotels" (the other is in Bangor, Maine; neither is used for its original purpose) and was recorded in its reduced condition by the Historic American Buildings Survey in 1971. It has been converted for reuse. Perhaps because of the oddly shaped site, at the intersection of Ottawa and Broadway Streets, Rogers created an original variation of his Palladian quincunx, one that is bent around an obtuse angle and whose center is the curved exterior bay of an elliptical lobby, planned to be topped by a never-executed dome. (Fig. 77) The intended result would have been an angled and reduced variation of the Burnet House. The building stands three stories above a basement and is made of brick with sandstone trim and capped by a wooden Grecian cornice. The ground-floor windows in the center are headed with half-circular arches; other openings are trabeated. One entered the lobby at the center; the rest of the establishment had the usual complement of rooms, from dining to sleeping. Interior structural walls were of brick, and the original cast-iron columns remain at ground level. Evidence suggests that the rooms were heated by stoves rather than fireplaces. The *Cleveland Plain Dealer* reported that a "snug fortune" was spent on the furnishings.[41]

The antebellum years ended with one of Isaiah and Willard Rogers's major accomplishments: Longview Asylum on the Miami and Erie Canal at Carthage, Ohio. It opened in 1860 with four hundred inmates, plus a proposed separate building for "colored." Yet the story of this commission begins even earlier, with Cincinnati's city hospital. Called Commercial Hospital, that structure had opened in 1823 with four divisions: medical, surgical, obstetrical, and "lunatics." By 1853 the place was in deplorable condition. In 1859 the city council considered a design for a new building by the Rogers firm, but the local newspaper accused that civic body of acting on the supposition that the "monetary resources of the city are inexhaustible."[42]

Although the paper did not favor the project because it was too expensive, it thought the plan of the proposed building "magnificent" and was convinced it would produce a hospital more complete than any in the world. Rogers projected an Italianate structure quite different from other hospital layouts of the period. In Boston, for example, the 1861 competition's winning design by Gridley J. F. Bryant was guided by the theories of Dr. Henry Clark: a "pavilion plan" based on

Pierre Gauthier's Lariboisière Hospital in Paris (1846–53), in which the institution was broken into individual building blocks focused on a central administration building.[43] Rogers, by contrast, proposed a contained, four-story-plus-base hollow square building enclosing a courtyard 210 by 248 feet, in the center of which would stand an ornamental "campanile" 180 feet tall containing ventilation and smoke flues. From this stack, three-story wings would extend to the center of each

77. Oliver House, Toledo, Ohio, 1858–59. Broadway front. Photograph taken 1971 by Allen Stross for the Historic American Buildings Survey, Library of Congress.

side of the square, subdividing it into four courts—representing the hospital's four divisions—that would communicate with the street through carriageways. Ventilation was to be as complete as in any existing building; there would also be elevators in each section. (In 1853 Rogers had visited New York's Crystal Palace, where Elisha Graves Otis first demonstrated the safe passenger elevator; however, he did not mention that particular exhibit in his diary.) The outside dimensions of Commercial Hospital were projected to be 322 by 282 feet. After receiving the construction bids, the lowest at over $500,000, the city decided instead to renovate and expand the existing hospital. Rogers's proposal was not erected, although he was to be involved in planning and overseeing some work on the building in May 1867.

Out of this background came the 1859 Longview Asylum design by Isaiah Rogers & Son. It was a version of what was then considered the ideal plan for a mental hospital, as championed and first published in 1854 by Dr. Thomas Kirkbride in *On the Construction, Organization, and General Arrangements of Hospitals for the Insane,* with architectural drawings by Samuel Sloan.[44] Rogers might have discussed such a problem with John Notman on one of his visits to Philadelphia. The latter's New Jersey State Lunatic Asylum of 1848 was modified by Sloan in 1850; it could well have been in Rogers's mind as he first sketched a project for an asylum in 1852 and, more probably, when he turned his attention to Longview. Like so many other asylums that were abandoned or demolished when treatment of the mentally ill advanced in the mid-twentieth century, Longview no longer exists. However, a detailed contemporary description does.

In a stretch of building 612 feet long, a domed five-story central block (eventually fronted by a high-roofed three-story pavilion) contained a forty-four-foot-wide rotunda reaching eighty-eight feet tall to the skylighted dome.[45] (Figs. 78–79) On the interior of the rotunda, balconies with glass floors marked each of the levels, which were defined by ornamental cast-iron railings. (Fig. 80) For the underside of the dome Francis Pedretti, a frequent Rogers collaborator, created four allegorical figures. The three-story wards stretched right and left, interrupted by four-story pavilions; those closest to the center were also domed. The exteriors of these ranges were opened with a multitude of half-round arched windows. The hospital was supplied with water pumped from the Miami Canal into tanks at the top of the main building, lighted by gas, and heated by steam. It contained 600 rooms and 56 water-closets. This was the refuge dedicated to white inmates. There was also to be a small, separate building on the grounds for people of color: an eight-bay, two-story-plus-attic box fronted by a two-story porch defined by columns supporting segmental arches. This structure may or may not have been the work of the Rogers & Son.

During the last decade before the war Rogers's firm, which employed Henry Whitestone, Willard Rogers, and A. B. Mullett, straddled Cincinnati and Louisville

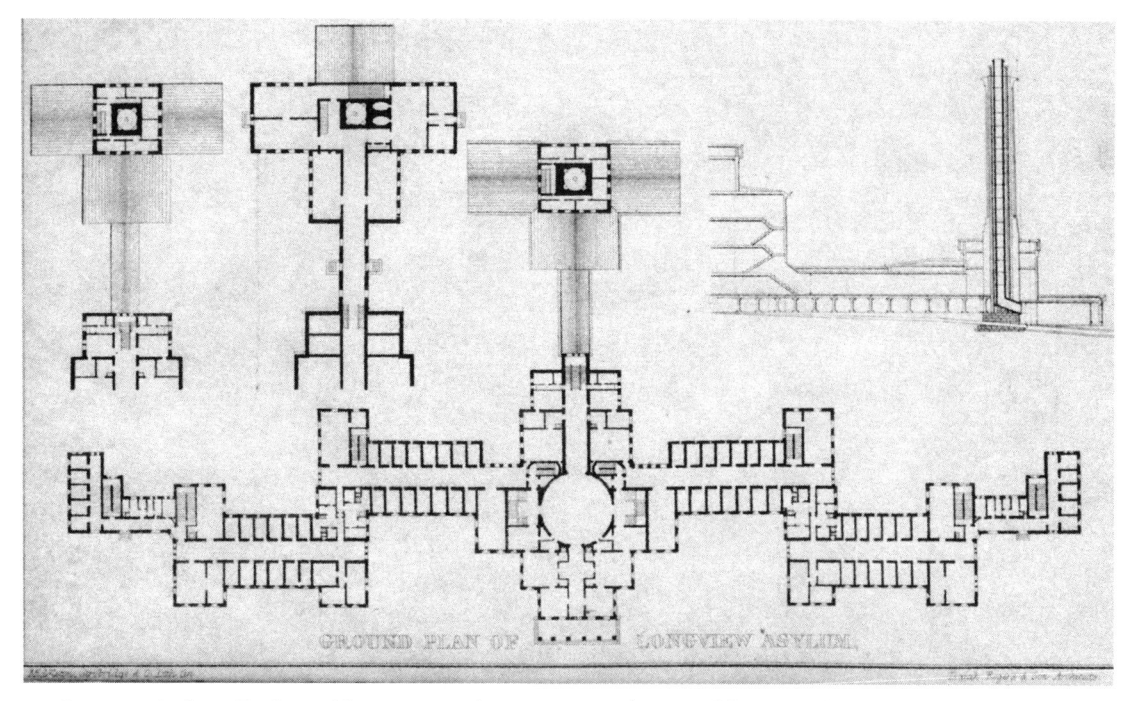

78. Longview Asylum, Carthage, Ohio, 1859–61. Plan. From *Annual Report of the Board of Directors and Officers of Longview Asylum,* 1860. Courtesy Ohio Historical Society Library.

79. Longview Asylum, Carthage, Ohio, 1859–61. View from the Miami and Erie Canal. From *Annual Report of the Board of Directors and Officers of Longview Asylum,* 1860. Courtesy Ohio Historical Society Library.

while reaching from Chicago to New Orleans. Hotels remained a specialty, but domestic and commercial work continued to emerge from the drafting boards and require onsite supervision. The impressive Longview Asylum was a fitting capstone to this period of significant achievement that ended with the Civil War. With the exception of Rogers's appointment as architect of the Treasury, the ensuing years were aftermath to his prolific career.

80. Longview Asylum, Carthage, Ohio, 1859–61. Detail of the rotunda. Photo taken 1978 by Steve Gordon, collection of Denys Peter Myers.

CHAPTER

6

Cincinnati and Washington, D.C.
1861–1869

AFTER THE lacuna from 1856 into 1861, Rogers's diary picks up again about three weeks after the bombardment of Fort Sumter. He turned down a commission from the U.S. Army but assisted in arranging tents at Camp Dennison, which had been laid out near the Ohio River northeast of Cincinnati. Business had obviously sagged. While overseeing the finishing touches on the Hamilton County jail, drafting details and complaining about the increasingly sluggish progress as funds dwindled, he had time to look over a book on bridge construction borrowed from a Mr. Stacey, perhaps George Stacey of the Stacey Manufacturing Company of Cincinnati, producer of structural ironwork. He was sketching a bridge to cross the Ohio River at Cincinnati and the Cumberland River at Nashville. In the office a Mr. Young developed his penciled design; this was perhaps the architect J. B. Young, to whom Rogers would soon give a handout, despite his own precarious finances, so that the man could get home. Rogers designed a steam-powered gunboat for the Ohio, although he did not think anything would come of it. He used his influence to get his son-in-law Samuel Hatch the position of sutler to the Seventh Regiment, Ohio Volunteer Infantry, and set him up in business at the camp. Willard Rogers returned from Nashville, where he had been supervising construction of the Maxwell House, which was put on hold until after the war. The episode of St. John's Church lingered, and Rogers found it difficult to borrow money on a mortgage he held on the building. He was constantly searching for payments of long-overdue bills; he was earning almost nothing. On a quick trip to Louisville in July he ordered chimney pots, presumably for the jail, from Patrick Bannon, his proven source for terra-cotta even though such architectural details had long been available in Cincinnati. On August 17 he noted his sixty-first birthday without further comment. A series of aliments interrupted his days.

A journey east with Emily followed. They traveled through Columbus and New York to Newport, stopping to visit his folks, and on to Philadelphia, where he inspected the famed Greco-Roman waterworks on the Schuylkill River at Fairmount, walked around the city, and then headed home, little in the way of business having transpired. Back in Cincinnati on September 10, 1861, he penciled a rare outburst of emotion: "I feel very discontented, a great change, which I have always been so much occupied. It is difficult to become accustomed to be idle." (Fig. 81) His health was not all that good, with several medical procedures concerning his urinary tract suggesting an enlarged prostate. He moved his office to smaller quarters in the courthouse as he and Willard spent a few hours a day drafting directions for work at the jail. One weekday he recorded doing nothing

81. Isaiah Rogers. From *American Architect* 99 (May 3, 1911).

but picking tomatoes and gathering elderberries to make some wine. He often found himself "miserable and [in] some pains."

In early October 1861 Rogers again took up the problem of spanning the Ohio at Cincinnati and went over to Covington to look at existing plans for a new bridge over the river. He took notes because he thought to use the piers being built for John A. Roebling's long-delayed span. The project for the bridge dated back to 1846, when the Kentucky general assembly granted a charter for it, but not until 1856 was Roebling engaged to build it. Construction began, was immediately halted by the Panic of 1857, and recommenced during the war. It opened in 1867.[1] On October 22 Rogers started to draw a design that incorporated Roebling's piers, presumably after having studied the engineer's plans. In early November he made another scheme and an estimate of cost "of the center arch 1005 feet span $900,000," revising it a week later. This scheme improved on the tubular arch design he had patented in 1856, and he proceeded to discuss preparing a caveat for a new patent. Rogers described this second arch design in U.S. Patent No. 37,642, granted February 10, 1863, while he worked at the Treasury department. (Figs. 82–83) According to *Scientific American,* he "tendered the use of the plans for this bridge to the Government, without compensation" while he remained in office;[2] no record of its use has surfaced. Rogers's two later patented bridge designs, intended for loads heavier and spans longer than those of his earlier cylindrical lattice design, may be viewed as a response to the suspension technologies used by Roebling, Ellet, and Heiman, which he knew from visits in early 1852, September 1854, and April 1855. (He saw his first example, Ellet's ground-breaking "wire bridge," in Philadelphia in August 1842.) He found them "sublime" to look at, but disapproved of them as permanent structures.

In late October–early November 1861, Rogers received a severe blow when he was nudged off the job at the jail in favor of William Walter, one of the architects who had replaced him on the very same job ten years earlier. Spending most of a day "about town," he endured "hearing the various remarks of my being turned off of the superintendency." Although chagrined, he met his successor "pleasantly and kindly," showed him about the work, and told him that he "would at all times give him such information" as he possessed. By then Rogers must have been tired of his labor on the county buildings, which seems to have paid well but lasted more than a decade and caused him much trouble. Newly idle, he sketched a design for a military hospital "to keep my mind . . . engaged." This design may have been a version of the layout he had proposed for the Cincinnati Commercial Hospital in 1859; when finished, he thought it "hard to beat." He went to Washington, D.C., in November to dig up interest in its use but was informed that it was too expensive, only temporary hospitals were wanted. At the beginning of the war, Northerners generally believed that hostilities would end quickly and that no special medical installations would be needed. The year closed with Rogers engaged in

82. Improved tubular arch bridge. Broadside datable ca. 1859. Visualization of its use as a railway bridge. U.S. Patent No. 37,642, granted February 10, 1863. American Antiquarian Society, Worcester, Massachusetts.

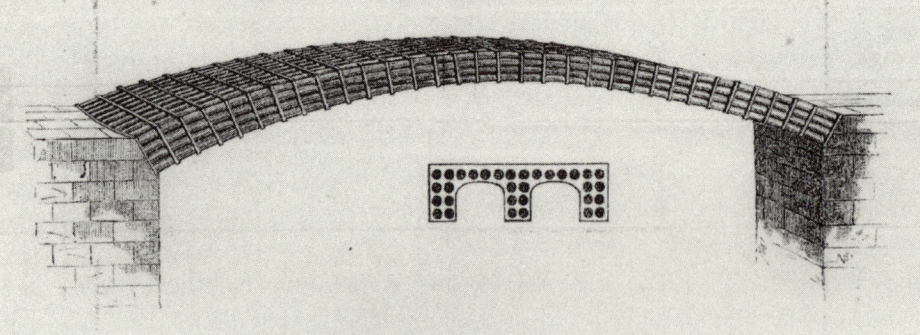

sketching a hotel "on the English plan of keeping" for one of the Willard brothers of Washington, well-known local hoteliers.

The trip east began by rail on November 26, 1861, while Rogers was still thinking about spanning the rivers at Covington and Nashville. On his way to Washington, he stopped in New York to visit the construction site of the Second Harlem (or Third Avenue) Bridge, being supervised by William J. McAlpine, a student of John B. Jervis. Begun in 1860 and finished in 1865, it was the first iron bridge in New York and incorporated new building techniques. "All to be of iron," Rogers noted, "piers cast iron 6 foot diameter, sunk 27 foot below bed of river. A fine job." McAlpine's method of using compressed air to sink cast-iron cylinders into the riverbed was innovative. Rogers failed to describe that process, but inspired by what he saw, he went to Appleton's, the publishers and booksellers, to look in vain for a basic yet authoritative guide. He may have had in mind *Griswold's Railroad Engineers' Pocket Companion* of 1855.

In Washington he took out preliminary papers to submit a patent for his second tubular arched bridge. He also thought his 1856 patent was being infringed on with a bridge thrown over the Potomac by Montgomery C. Meigs, then supervising engineer for the Washington aqueduct. Rogers was probably referring to what is now the Rock Creek Bridge, begun in 1858, which used two cast-iron

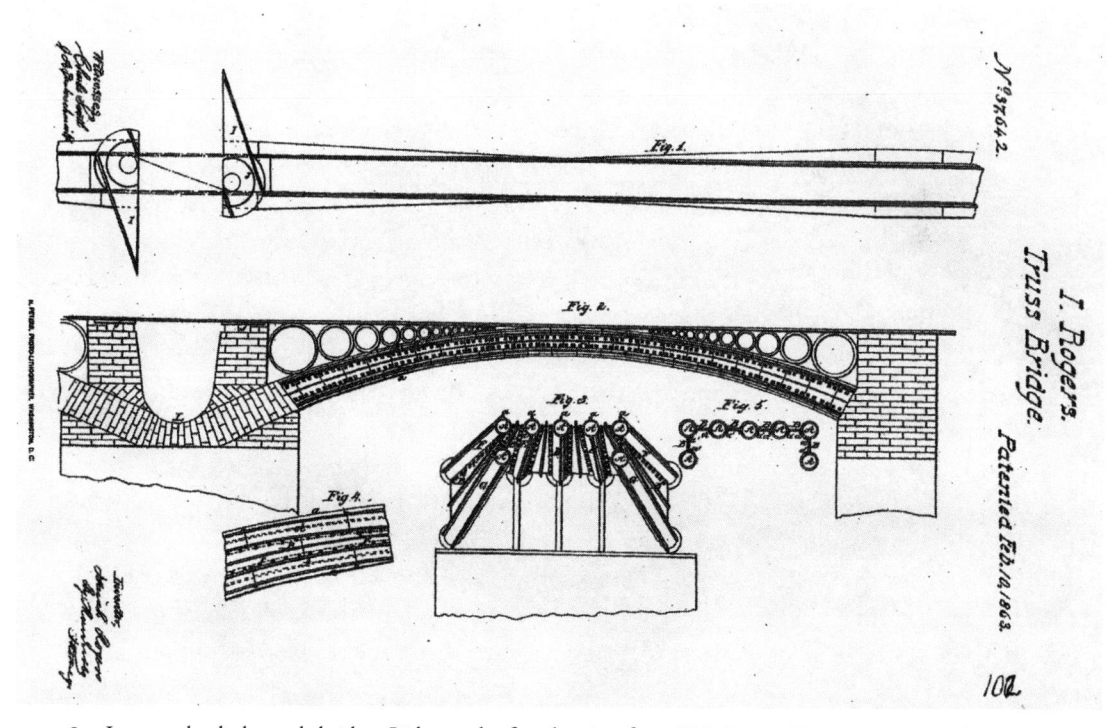

83. Improved tubular arch bridge. Lithograph after drawing from U.S. Patent No. 37,642, granted February 10, 1863.

arches composed of seventeen pipe sections forty-eight inches in diameter to carry not only traffic but also the aqueduct's water over a span of two hundred feet.[3] It was the second, and much longer, iron arch bridge to be erected in the United States, after the Dunlap Creek Bridge in Pennsylvania. Rogers consulted George H. Pendleton, his Ohio representative, and a Mr. Knight, probably a patent lawyer, about the infringement, but the outcome of his chagrin is unrecorded. The diary breaks off in early December, and the gap continues through his tenure at the Treasury department. While serving in that office, he offered the government free use of his improved 1863 patent, so it is doubtful he went to the expense of challenging Meigs in court.[4]

Given the history of Rogers's attempts to work for, and get paid by, the federal government, it might surprise that he spent the war working at the Treasury department. But after the kind of year Rogers had in 1861—with his spirit low, his health shaky, and few prospects for commissions as the conflict raged—he needed only a brief moment of reflection to reply favorably to an "unexpected" letter in July 1862 from the Ohioan Salmon P. Chase, Lincoln's secretary of the Treasury. In it, Chase offered him the position that Rogers called supervising architect in the Treasury department. In fact, he first served as "Engineer in Charge of the Bureau of Construction."[5] The position nominally made him director of all federal building except the ongoing work on the Capitol, which continued under the direction of Meigs. With a war on, projects would be limited beyond the work on the Treasury building. In his acceptance letter to Chase, Rogers wrote modestly, "I do not know clearly the duties but presume they are to plan, arrange plans and superintend such buildings as may be required by the Government . . . if so I feel myself competent to the duties."[6] Rogers replaced his old friend Ammi B. Young, who had run the office since 1852 but was now forced out. Less than a year after arriving in the nation's capital, Rogers did become "Supervising Architect of the Treasury Building," earning $3,000 a year, a post he held until conflict with A. B. Mullett, his former employee and partner in Cincinnati and now his assistant in Washington, made life intolerable. In the absence of the diary, we must rely on outside sources to reconstruct these years.[7] Fortunately, given his position with the government, such sources are plentiful.

The announcement of Rogers's appointment called forth at least three letters to Secretary Chase, one to warn him that the architect "needs close watching to prevent *friendly understandings* between him and Contractors" and another to say that his contractor friends would immediately start for Washington to grab the spoils.[8] Such abuses were probably common when architects also acted as builders, before general contractors separated them from the day-to-day responsibility for construction, and Rogers did have a reputation for litigation against clients, supplies, and builders, especially in Ohio and Kentucky. As we have also seen, the unstructured methods of doing business in the building trades led to many misunderstandings and, yes, probably some shady deals before the establishment of order in the architectural ranks imposed by the American Institute of Architects. On his own in a tough world, Rogers was probably no better or worse than most of his competitors. He had certainly made enemies along the way.[9] Chase may have been disgruntled to hear reports of such shenanigans, but these were countered by a third letter from A. B. Coleman, Rogers's client and friend in Cincinnati, who reported in June 1862 (without Rogers's knowledge) that the architect was "intelligent & liberal in his views, and a man of the most strict honesty & integrity."[10] The appointment stuck.

As head of the bureau responsible for designing, supervising the construction of, and maintaining all federal buildings, Rogers oversaw work within as well as beyond Washington. Two examples of his outside activities will suffice to paint the picture of his time in that office. In 1863 he designed the rebuilding of the exterior east and west stairs of Young's Boston Custom House, a structure Rogers had known well from its inception.[11] Gridley J. F. Bryant superintended the work. According to the *Boston Daily Advertiser,* "the new steps and buttresses, with the handsome candelabra at the top, are certainly a great improvement to the architectural appearance of the building." They were later replaced. In 1864 the architect's office designed a new customhouse for Portland, Maine. The *Portland Daily Press* for July 11 noted that the plans exhibited at the Merchants' Exchange, a building designed nearly thirty years earlier by Rogers's estranged former partner Richard Bond, were drawn by the "Government Architect." The new structure would be of granite, extending from Fore to Commercial Streets, and "will be one of the most beautiful buildings in the city." Requests for bids from builders were published in September, calling for proposals "to be either for the whole building, or separate for different kinds of work," a statement that recognized the tentative emergence in these years of the general contractor.[12] In November the government awarded the contract "at about $140,000" to Sargent, Whidden and Coburn of Boston, and appropriations were approved, but the building never materialized. Instead, the Second Empire customhouse of 1866–72 now standing on the site is the work of Mullett, his defiant successor. Rogers's drawings do not survive.[13]

Rogers's tenure at the Treasury and the acrimony surrounding his departure have been well laid out in the history of the supervising architect's office by Antoinette Lee and in the context of the long and complex history of the erection of the Treasury Building by Pamela Scott. They may be summarized here. Among his main responsibilities was to carry on the work on that building, begun in 1836 by Robert Mills and erected piece by piece under the direction of, before Rogers, T. U. Walter and Ammi B. Young and, after Rogers, A. B. Mullett.[14] Such was the confused and confusing story of the "ongoing evolutionary process" of the building's erection, according to Scott. By summer of 1863 Rogers had ordered a large model of the whole building, with his proposed additions, and displayed it in his office. But the history of his stay in Washington, D.C., like that of the other architects, reflects the lot of talented designers trying to do good work at the center of the political (and, in Rogers's case, militarily preoccupied) maelstrom that was—and remains—the nation's capital. Much of what Rogers accomplished on the building was altered by Mullett after his departure.

However, it was Rogers, always the inventor, who patented the Treasury's system of safety vaults wherein vast sums of money were stored.[15] In April 1863 he called for bids from manufacturers for supplying fire- and burglar-proof safes, bids that were to include a "description of the safes they propose . . . , accompanied by drawings showing the mode of construction, and full-size sections of the material used."[16] Surreptitiously instructed by these detailed samplings of the latest technology in a changing industry, he designed his own system with linings of iron balls in two layers between wrought-iron and steel plates; the balls, with their rotation, made it impossible to drill through the walls. In December he obtained U.S. Patent No. 40,947 for his "Burglar Proof Safe." Four such vaults, built by George R. Jackson of Burnet and Company of New York, were installed in 1864 in the northwest corner of the building behind the cast-iron wall embossed with Grecian ornament and Treasury symbols. One still stands.[17]

Rogers proved to be a "stern taskmaster."[18] His restrictive rules for workers and controversial work hours led to a labor strike in fall of 1863. He had always expected much of his laborers, but now he was fighting increasing rebellion in his office as well. By fall of the next year, he and Mullett were on bad terms, and the latter was repeatedly sent out of Washington. How this feud has been understood depends on whose side the commentator is on, but what caused Mullett to change from being Rogers's partner to his adversary remains something of a mystery. An ambitious, supercritical man with powerful political friends, Mullett began a campaign of vicious attacks on Rogers, referring, for example, to "the disgraceful management of affairs" at the Treasury in 1865; other letters accused his boss of incurring unnecessary expenditures. Such criticism had its effect, and as late as 1876 the architect Peter B. Wight could state that Rogers had lost his federal office because of "some irregularities in the management of it."[19]

Rogers and Mullett had a falling-out over alterations to the federal building in, of all places, Cincinnati, when Rogers tried to remove Mullett as supervisor there. According to Rogers in a letter of November 1864, "ever since my disapproval of his management of the . . . Cincinnati Custom House . . . Mr. Mullett has been greatly incensed at me and has been treating me in such a manner that both of us cannot be retained in the positions we now occupy." If he were to stay, Mullett had to go. The situation worsened as Mullet continued to undermine Rogers's authority. On August 28, 1865, according to Mullett's own diary, he was in Louisville setting aside Rogers's plans for the customhouse there and commencing to draw his own.[20] Three weeks later, on September 20, Rogers resigned after little more than three years in the post and returned to Cincinnati. He could take no more of the hubbub in the capital. He had just passed his sixty-fifth birthday and suffered from recurrent ailments; Mullett at least thought his state of health affected his work. Given all the stress and unfulfilled accomplishments, in his grave Rogers might have nodded thanks at Montgomery Schuyler's later statement that he "was about the best" architect at the Treasury in those years.[21]

The fragment of Rogers's surviving diary written after he left the Treasury department does not begin until the first day of 1867, but we might guess that in the meantime he visited Marshfield. After his days at the Treasury, he resumed working with his son Willard in Cincinnati and returned to his home, then in Mount Hope, a community west of the city center. He kept busy for a while but found time to twice visit the "Apocalyptic Programme of the Illustrious or Moving Representations of the Book of Revelation; or, Visions of St. John" at Mozart Hall.[22] Such rolling panoramas were the mid-nineteenth-century equivalent of twentieth-century movies and just as popular. But there would also be a few major projects.

In 1866 Rogers designed the city's second opera house for the businessman Samuel N. Pike of Cincinnati and New York, who then owned the Burnet House; as his diary recommences, he is drawing revisions and working documents and supervising its construction. This activity continued throughout the year as the building progressed. He was also looking for V.I.P. endorsements for his competitive plans for the statehouse in Albany, New York, having paid someone else to draw statuary (suggesting that no one in his office could handle the human figure). In addition, he sketched a bridge across the East River, also for New York; worked on improvements for Nathan H. Gould, his son-in-law, who had just bought a house at Catherine and Fir Streets in Newport, Rhode Island[23] (apparently not building the house Rogers had sketched for him earlier); worked on improvements to the Odd Fellows Hall in Lexington, Kentucky, in the form of an added theater;[24] worked on ultimately unbuilt plans for another Cincinnati opera house containing an art gallery and studios, intended to rival Pike's, commissioned by "wild" Truman S. Handy, the builder and speculator (James W. McLaughlin also produced a design for the building). He continued to study plans for the hotel in Washington for one of the Willard brothers and went off to New York to lobby for projects entered in competitions for the Manhattan post office and the Albany statehouse. Although not recorded in the diary, he produced a hotel for Springfield, Ohio, that opened a few months after his death.

The history of Pike's Opera House, erected on Fourth Street in Cincinnati, is complex. It was designed and constructed in 1857 by John M. Trimble for Samuel N. Pike, a man made wealthy distilling whiskey—his brand was Magnolia—and investing in real estate.[25] The original structure rose five stories on Fourth Street, the upper part of its facade decorated with "allegorical busts of poets and musicians and bas-reliefs of garlands of flowers and musical instruments." The locals found the theater inside grand and beautiful, but the *Architect's and Mechanic's Journal* of 1859 was unimpressed.[26] On April 14, 1866, with "A Mid-Summer's Night's Dream" on the stage, a "great fire," caused by a gas explosion, it was thought, completely destroyed the building, "the most splendid structure of the kind in the West," according to *Harper's Weekly.*[27] The "Moloch of Flame" also took out stores to each side along Fourth Street and to the rear, on Baker Street, consuming the stables of the Adams Express Company and the home of the *Cincinnati Enquirer.*[28] There was, astonishingly, no loss of life. Although the house had proven itself a slim profit maker, Pike's "public spirit," manifesting itself in his "cultural asset for the city," led him in a little over a year to rebuild and reopen the building from the design of Isaiah Rogers, Son & Co. As completion neared, the *Cincinnati Daily Gazette* published a description in June 1867 that located the building on Fourth Street between Walnut and Vine. (Fig. 84) The ground floor contained six stores. The reporter found the five-story freestone front "a grand achievement . . . [of] beauty, grace and imposing dignity," and especially admired the huge bronzed American eagle with outstretched wings that capped the whole. In fact, Rogers's front—and eagle—closely resembled those of the original (and he may have reused some of the earlier facade). It was a grid of seventy-six trabeated windows, arranged tier upon tier and centered on the axial bay with portal at ground level and, rising above, a stack of ornate quasi-Palladian windows terminating in a low triangular pediment.

The newspaper mentioned the main stair of the opera house mounting from the central entrance flanked by stone goddesses, it said, of music and oratory (Euterpe and Polyhymnia?), which led to one hundred offices, those on the second and third floors supplied with water closets. At the second level a corridor, which Rogers described as skylighted, ran parallel to the facade and led to stairways. At the second level was the concert hall, as opposed to a theater, measuring 70 by 128 feet and 43 feet high; it was lighted and ventilated by six immense round-arched windows. The gallery, we know from the diary, was supported not by columns but by iron girders, as requested at the last minute by Pike. Rogers also mentions a second gallery on girders, these also belatedly ordered by Pike, but images of the room do not show them. The original stage, only twenty feet wide, was "sufficient . . . only for concerts and public exhibitions and speaking," meaning that, oddly enough given the name of the building, "there is to be no opera-house there." That theater was much admired, its frescoes particularly praised. They were executed by Francis Pedretti, the roving decorative artist whom Rogers mentions visiting at this time and who had worked for the architect at the Burnet House, Longview Asylum, and elsewhere. Four years later, and some two years after Rogers's death, the concert hall was transformed into one suitable for opera, and it opened with a series of Offenbach's works.[29] The decoration was now overseen by Giuseppe Guidicini, another roving decorator from New York.[30]

84. Pike's Opera House, Cincinnati, Ohio, 1866–67. South side of Fourth Street between Walnut and Vine, ca. 1871. Ehrgott, Forbriger & Co. lithograph. Cincinnati Museum Center.

Admitting that the building was not strictly fireproof, the newspaper reported that if fire broke out, the flames would not pass speedily from one room to another because of the construction of floors and partitions of a kind Rogers had used at the Tremont House and Burnet House. The roof was of heavy painted tin, another common feature of Rogers's works, and opened with skylights. These measures notwithstanding, the second Pike's Opera House in turn fell to the flames in 1903.

Other work came into the office during these last years, but little was accomplished. By the end of February 1867 Rogers was writing specifications and estimating his design for the Odd Fellows' Lexington Theater and sketching the post office for New York City, a design finished by May. In March he had a talk with James K. Wilson, probably the most important local architect after the war and the designer of the recently finished, astonishing Plum Street Temple, executed for Rabbi Isaac Mayer Wise. They agreed to think about joining forces, but never did. In May, Rogers's son Willard did join Wilson's office—little was going on in Rogers's—although he continued to work with his father when needed. In New York, Rogers found that the deadline in the post office competition had been extended because of an error in the survey of the lot, and he needed to redraw his design. While in Manhattan then and later, he did not stay at his Astor House. On this trip he booked into the St. Nicholas, a million-dollar hotel opened in 1853 that exceeded the Astor in luxury. He took in a performance at Niblo's Garden of *The Black Crook,* considered to be the first Broadway musical. His delight in the "most magnificent" scenery he had ever seen must have eased the five-and-a-half-hour showing. At one memorable point, as reported in the papers, a rocky grotto transformed before the audience into a fairyland throne. He stopped in

Washington to explain his project for the hotelkeeper Willard. Back home again, he took to the boards on his third plan for the post office, and by May 1 his office help, Augustus Eichhorn, a draftsman apparently on loan from Wilson, and Willard commenced a perspective view of his design.

On May 22 the drawings for the New York statehouse were returned from Albany without comment. The search for an architect had begun competitively in 1865, with the commission receiving thirty entries by 1867, none of them satisfactory. After a brief association with Arthur D. Gilman, the Canadian architect Thomas Fuller received the appointment, although he was dismissed after a few years because of cost overruns, and the building was redesigned by Leopold Eidlitz and H. H. Richardson (and, nominally, Frederick Law Olmsted). On May 29, Rogers packed up his plans, specifications, estimates, and letters of support for the post office and customhouse competition and sent them to New York City by Adams Express to arrive by the June 1 deadline. His was one of fifty-two entries, and again none earned the commission. The project was taken over by Mullett in 1869, and he produced—for a staggering sum of taxpayer money—a powerful French Second Empire building called locally "Mullett's Monstrosity."

By June 12, 1867, Rogers was fiddling with make-work "to pass time, as [I] have nothing to do" except to watch Pike's Opera House slowly (too slowly for him) move toward completion and to oversee structural improvement at the local gas house. As usual in such downtime, he studied a design for an iron bridge over Mill Creek, at the foot of Sixth Street, to replace the old one, raising the roadbed above the high-water mark; this was a far cry from projecting a span across the Ohio. His ever shorter diary entries contain frequent mention of ailments, doctors, and fatigue. En route in July through New York and Boston to Marshfield, he and Emily stayed at Coleman's Hotel at Twenty-seventh and Broadway, again avoiding the Astor, and in Boston they dined with the Newport Goulds at the Tremont House, then nearly forty years old, but took a room at William Washburn's Parker House, which opened in 1855 and, by 1867, had stolen some of the Tremont's luster. The Saturday Club now called it headquarters, and Charles Dickens lodged there that year. Both Rogers and his major work were fading. On a rainy day he walked about the city, perhaps revisiting early memories and early buildings. An extended visit of more than two months followed at Marshfield.

The stay in the Rogers homestead, where he first saw the light of day and which he had remodeled in 1842, took him back to his beginnings. As always when there, he fished, hunted, picked berries, and sailed, this time attending the Hingham agricultural fair and a cattle show; he also visited with friends and family. To fill his active mind he began to design a bridge over the East River at Blackwell's (now Roosevelt) Island (having purchased a chart of the river while in New York), studied the plan of a stone house for a local site, and designed a gateway for a neighbor. Up to Boston for the day, he got Gridley J. F. Bryant to set one of his draftsmen to copying at a large scale his design for the East River bridge. This was to span from Manhattan to Queens at the site of the present Queensboro Bridge. Talk of erecting a similar structure had gone on since the 1830s, and in 1856 Roebling proposed two 800-foot suspension bridges at the site. Rogers—always looking to challenge Roebling, if only on paper—must have gotten wind that a company had been chartered the previous April to finance it. Nothing came of his study, of course, and nothing was accomplished at the site until 1909, when the Queensboro Bridge began carrying traffic over the river. The diary ends on October 7, 1867, as Isaiah and Emily headed for Boston and home. A stop at Bryant's office found the drawings for his latest bridge proposal "not quite finished."

Although it is not mentioned in the diary as it survives, Rogers had one last hotel in him, the Lagonda House in Springfield, Ohio, which began receiving guests on September 30, 1869, more than four and a half months after his death. "The famous hotel architect" visited Springfield in April 1868, according to the local paper, and quickly bagged the commission: "the committee . . . have been so fortunate as to secure . . . that eminent artist, Mr. Isaiah Rodgers, after whose plans have been built several of the finest hotels in America. . . . [He] is pre-eminently a hotel architect . . . [and will remain in town] for some time—until a definite plan, with full specifications, in every particular, is decided upon, and the entire work is ready to be let out to the builders." By midmonth the paper had gotten his name right.

A description of the opening in the *Springfield Daily Republican* assigned the design of the Lagonda House to "the late Isaiah Rogers."[31] It was funded by the Champion Hotel Company, a coalition of businessmen led by William N. Whitely, as a credit to the citizens' "good taste and public spirit." It was, as well, a fitting finale to the career of the "father of the hotel." Its 140 rooms rose in a five-story block on a footprint 160 by 115 feet on the corner of South Limestone and East High Streets. (Fig. 85) The basement contained billiard and refreshment rooms, a laundry, a pastry room, a steam boiler, "and engine by which the water is pumped to all the rooms." The main floor contained the "grand reception room" with entrances from both streets. The flooring here and in the rest of the hotel was of three layers, the upper one composed of narrow strips of pine and walnut, oiled. The reception room counter was of ash, "most tastefully ornamented with black walnut carvings and mouldings." Behind that was one of Joseph L. Hall's patented burglar- and fireproof safes. On this floor was also found the washing room, reading room, gentlemen's parlor, barber shop, bath room for gentlemen, and six "business rooms" or shops, following the model of the Astor rather than the Tremont. The upper floor was occupied by a dining hall seating 150, the kitchen, "three beautifully furnished parlors . . . with immense, plate glass mirrors," and thirty sleeping rooms and a bath room for ladies. The upper two floors also contained thirty rooms each, all connected to the clerk's desk by an annunciator.

The Lagonda House sat on a slightly sloping site so that the facades read as four planar stories slightly articulated as a Palladian quincunx, as is usual in Rogers's later hotel work. It wore its Italianate style lightly, while a recessed distyle-in-antis Corinthian portico centering the main facade recalled Rogers's earlier work. Its effective exterior relied on reticent brickwork. The principal story was set off from the upper floors by a pronounced molded belt course. The two floors above consisted of segmental-arched windows set within shallow recesses topped by half-circular arches, while the windows of the top floor were segmental-headed and set within the plane of the wall. A bold bracketed cornice crowned the walls, and above that in the center of each public skyline rose a low, broad pediment bearing the name of the establishment in raised letters. It stood a worthy provincial descendent of Rogers's great hotels in Boston, New York, and Cincinnati until October 1895, when it became "the largest single structure ever destroyed by fire in the city's history."[32] The site is now occupied by a small park.

We know of other, minor works of these last years, such as stores for Miller & McRoberts at Second and Yeatman Streets in Cincinnati, for which Rogers advertised for proposals "most beneficial to the owners" in February 1868. But Pike's Opera House and the Lagonda House seem to have been his last significant efforts.

85. Lagonda House, Springfield, Ohio, 1868–69. Limestone and High Street facades. Clark County Historical Society.

On April 14, 1869, the *Cincinnati Daily Times* regretted to inform its readers that the "distinguished architect" had died the night before of heart disease at the residence of his daughter Cornelia.[33] It listed some of his most important buildings, as did papers across the East, but wrongly credited him with T. U. Walter's dome of the U.S. Capitol (an understandable mistake since he was the architect of the Treasury during part of its erection, although Montgomery Meigs supervised the Capitol job). "In his profession," said the *Times,* "he was, perhaps, better known than any other person in the country." It added: "In private life, he was a man of the purest character, steadfast in his attachments, true to his professions of friendship, always guided by principles of honor and justice."

Such inflated rhetoric was characteristic of an obituary, but as far as one can tell from Rogers's diary, it was not wildly incorrect. According to his entry in the *Biographical Encyclopaedia of Ohio,* published just seven years after his death (and also not without the purple prose of the time): "although afflicted from an early age by violent physical prostrations, his mental caliber was never perceptibly impaired by such visitations, while his willpower and untiring perseverance have been rarely excelled. His nature was as impulsive as it was benevolent, while his unasumed [*sic*], frank and cordial bearing ever banished all doubt . . . of his entire sincerity of purpose." Rogers's remains were interred at Spring Grove Cemetery, later joined by those of his wife, Emily, who died in Chicago in late February 1878, and other family members. His son Solomon Willard Rogers, whose remains also lie near his father's, was said to rank among the leading architects of Cincinnati in 1876 and continued to practice well into the twentieth century.

Afterword

IN THE PREVIOUS pages, I have described in available detail and specific context much of what we know of the life and work of one American architect and builder in the years before the Civil War. We ought now to ask how that career fits into the general history of architectural practice during this period, that is, to summarize how Isaiah Rogers's working life appears next to those of some of his peers.[1] The short answer is that it was both typical and distinctive. What follows will expand briefly on that dichotomy.

As a man who began his career in the building trades, Rogers was similar to any number of his Stateside contemporaries. Unlike the status of architects in Britain and on the Continent, the profession of architecture did not yet exist in the United States at the time of his birth in 1800. The early years of the first major American-born architects show at least three major options for training: serve an apprenticeship to or study with one of the established immigrant architects, move into building from the visual arts, or emerge from the skilled trades. (The older Charles Bulfinch, educated at Harvard and finished on the European grand tour, was the exception to the usual course.) Robert Mills trained under Benjamin Henry Latrobe, an English immigrant, and James Hoban from Ireland; William Strickland learned his profession under Latrobe, and under Strickland, Gideon Shyrock served as apprentice. But Strickland was also an artist, as was the "architectural composer" A. J. Davis, while Hammatt Billings combined apprenticeships with the artist Abel Bowen and the architect Asher Benjamin and then drafted for Ammi B. Young. Those were somewhat unusual tracks. More common was the move from laboring at a building site to sitting at a drafting board.

Among eighteenth-century names, the most prominent is William Buckland of Virginia and Maryland. In early nineteenth-century New England, Young, Solomon Willard, Alexander Parris, Asher Benjamin, Richard Bond, Henry Austin, and the little-known Aaron Morse of New Hampshire all began life as "mechanics" (in the terminology of the time). So too did Martin E. Thompson, T. U. Walter, Ithiel Town, John McComb Jr., Minard Lafever, Calvin Pollard, and a host of others down the coast. Rogers went from an apprenticeship with the housewright Jesse Shaw to working with or for Willard, the architect-builder, and eventually, as did others of his generation, he occasionally took on "pupils" in his own office. As their careers developed, these mechanics slowly abandoned the hammer and trowel in favor of architectural drafting instruments. Rogers emerged from the trades to become one of the leading architects of his generation, but his early training and subsequent experience qualified him to superintend the construction of his designs as well. (The same can be said of Strickland and others.) This identity as both architect and builder was something Rogers retained until his death. Some of his peers established a single identity. They tried to separate design services from the detailed overseeing of construction, that is, to sharpen the definition of *architect*.

With no university training in architecture available in the early nineteenth century (that would come after the Civil War), an architect's education depended for the most part on apprenticeship to an established architect or builder, self-instruction from published sources, or attendance at one of the first occupational schools established for the trade in New England and Philadelphia, among other cities. Early on, English publications stemming from the Georgian era could be found in private collections of the gentry and, after 1809, for example, at the Architectural Library in Boston, of which Willard was a founder. The establishment of that library formed an early stage in the evolution of the architectural profession in the United States.[2] Some architects began to publish their own books, and their titles alone track the evolution of these men from onsite to on the boards. Asher Benjamin was the first American-born author to publish pattern books diagramming the classical orders and standard building types, such as residence and meetinghouses. His *American Builder's Companion,* the first of seven titles, beginning with carpentry and ending with architecture, appeared in 1797. His last, *Elements of Architecture,* came out in 1843.

Throughout the period of Rogers's career, several of his contemporaries augmented Benjamin's efforts. Minard Lafever's *Young Builder's General Instructor* appeared in 1829, and his *Beauties of Modern Architecture* in 1835. By 1852 Samuel Sloan, in *Model Architect,* advocated the division between design and construction to establish the independent identity of the architect.[3] At one point Rogers seems to have toyed with some sort of published work on architecture, although nothing came of that attempt. His early rural education had not prepared him to be a writer. But design in his day was a bookish business, and we find that he referred to publications at least as early as his work on the Tremont House in 1828. Often in his career he leafed through his books to find ideas for specific architectural problems, and at times he huddled with clients over pattern books, especially for domestic work. It should also be noted that William Eliot's most influential *A Description of Tremont House* was a precedent-establishing first in a long line of American building monographs.

Given the scarcity of public architectural libraries, architects acquired their own. At his death, Ithiel Town's collection of some eleven thousand volumes was anything but typical; the top private collection in the country, it was open to qualified readers. There is no record that Rogers used either that or any other such collection or the Architectural Library in Boston, but throughout his career he did educate himself in design and engineering. He acquired publications by purchase or swap (from Town, for one). What little we know of his architectural library, pieced together from scattered references in his diary, suggests that it may have been more or less commensurate with those of Latrobe, Henry Austin, or T. U. Walter. His interest in the remains of Native American cultures in the Ohio Valley, witnessed by his reading of several histories on the subject and visits to Native sites, sets him apart from his peers, although it seems not to have directly affected his work. Of course he had the advantage of prolonged residence in the middle of the country, while for the most part other architects hugged the Eastern Seaboard or Gulf States, with only occasional inland forays. Such reading would have been unusual among his colleagues, although one exceptional predecessor, Thomas Jefferson, had anticipated him by several years.[4]

Given his background, Rogers, like many of his peers, was skilled at supervising construction as well as judging workmen and valuing the worth of labor and materials. Henry Austin, for example, became the inspector of buildings for the city of New Haven. Rogers's death in 1869 more or less coincided with the birth of general contracting in America, a development that eventually relieved the architect from constant attendance at building sites, supplying materials and hiring workers, and keeping accounts. But Rogers never did establish an identity as a designer separate from that of builder. His drafting, although fundamental, was often done at night and took up much less time than did his onsite work during the day. By the 1840s he had begun to complain about clients like the Mr. Ward in Boston who wanted him onsite all the time, but he never managed to break completely free. By the 1870s university- or foreign-trained professional architects could spend most of the daylight hours in their offices conceiving design solutions while a specially trained staff member, general contractor, or both monitored the builder's process on location. In the office of H. H. Richardson, for example, that role was filled by T. M. Clark, author of *Building Superintendence,* among many such works. Today it is frequently said that an architect "built" or "erected" a building but in fact only produced the drawings for it. That erroneous assumption is a carry-over from a time when such a statement was true.

The shift from work in construction to designing on paper required more than just book learning. It required skill in drawing. Several early drawing schools operated in New England, Philadelphia, and elsewhere. In New England, Asher Benjamin, Alexander Parris, and Solomon Willard taught students, and Ammi B.

Young advertised for pupils. Owen Biddle, John Haviland, William Strickland, T. U. Walter, and others taught at the Franklin Institute in Philadelphia beginning in 1824.[5] Rogers, however, presumably learned to draw outside such schools, probably during his apprenticeship with Shaw or Willard. Architectural draftsmanship in this era took on a standard form. James Dakin said Rogers was a good draftsman, but the drawings that survive from his hand or his assistants' are largely indistinguishable from those of his peers, with the exception of artist-trained men like Davis or Billings.

Design began with pencil sketches and a cost estimate. If the project progressed, those sketches would be transformed into inked lines, dimensioned, and infilled with various colored washes indicating different materials or surfaces, all laid out on standard-size wove paper that was often manufactured by Whatman. Plans, elevations, and sections—which Rogers lumped together under the simple term *plan*—with perhaps a perspective rendering, made up the lot. Printed specifications followed; Rogers's set for the Astor House seems to be a rare early survivor. Working details came later and were usually quick full-scale sketches on rough paper.[6] They rarely survive. Such a process, standard for the period, describes what we know of Rogers's working method from his few existing drawings. Not having been trained in a school or as an artist like Strickland, Davis, or Billings, he seems to have left perspective presentations to others. Such colorful views, of course, are what sell designs to clients. So do models of buildings, the use of which was common in Rogers's practice, as in those of his peers, but apparently none by him survive. Models were also used by most architects, including Rogers, to study both structural and decorative parts of buildings.

One could learn how to draw, and study books on the various architectural styles and engineering principles, but to put all that learning to use, one needed clients. And since the idea of hiring an architect was new at the beginning of the century, clients had to be taught the value of the architect's services. To attract customers, one needed to establish a reputation. Some architects, including Strickland, Bryant, and McComb, were born into the métier because they were sons of well-respected builders; others, like Rogers and Willard, did not have that advantage. Rogers participated in most of the major competitions of his time, winning some early ones, and that set his name before the public. In his youth he also had a certain quality, as well as the backing of Willard, that appealed to important people in Boston. His unprecedented Tremont House proved their judgment correct in hiring him to design it at a young age, and Eliot's *Description* of the building broadcast those skills. His Astor House and other work in New York and elsewhere built on that achievement, and Rogers made sure it was noticed through the distribution of engravings or lithographs, in the same way that Bryant and others promoted their works. At some point his reputation reached Baltimore, despite the lack of a record that he worked there.

By the time he arrived in Cincinnati, Rogers had achieved a large body of important buildings, an achievement he advertised through newspaper ads in the spirit of entrepreneurship that Mary Woods identified as part of the workings of architectural offices from midcentury onward. His work was generally praised in the popular press. He was among the few of his peers (others were Bryant and Haviland) whose work caught the attention of foreign publishers. His appointment to the Treasury department in Washington proved that his reputation could attract political patronage. Throughout his career, Rogers's clients came from the leadership of the communities he served. Such good press and the character of past accomplishments carried a host of diverse clients to his office through the 1850s, but in his last years his practice trailed off, as did those of Davis, Walter, and others. His Cincinnati obituary nonetheless declared the former mechanic to be perhaps the best-known architect in the country.

His clientele and thus his reputation ranged over territory vaster than any of his peers, for Rogers was probably the most mobile, the best-traveled among them. The new industrial means of transportation, the steamboat and railway, made it possible for him to work across the whole of the built-up part of the country east of the Mississippi. In his peripatetic practice, he took advantage of that fact far more than most of his contemporaries. In this sense it might be said that he was the first modern architect, for his practice anticipated the international, high-flying, city-hopping creative lives of such late twentieth- and early twenty-first century architects as Zaha Hadid, Frank Gehry, and Rem Koolhaas. But his practice was "modern" in other ways too—for his early embrace of the daguerreotype, for example, not only to preserve his likeness but to record his buildings. Within eight months of Samuel F. B. Morse's first Manhattan demonstration of the new wonder, Rogers had acquired an image of his Merchants' Exchange in New York. He also anticipated the later incorporation of architectural offices, founding an early version with Henry Whitestone and his son Willard in 1853 that survives to this day in Louisville as Luckett & Farley Architects and Engineers.

By the time he was called to Cincinnati, Rogers's reputation as a designer of broad architectural and engineering skills had been established, but recognition of the value of those services still proved tentative among the commissioning public. Men calling themselves architects were something new in early nineteenth-century American society. As a group they had a difficult time convincing clients that their services were worth paying for and persuading builders that their drawings and specifications should be followed. Potential clients had to be taught to understand what skills the practicing architect brought to the building process and what those skills were worth. Fees were commonly established by the client rather than the architect, and collecting them was often a problem. So it was with Rogers, who seems to have usually received compensation based on a percentage of the cost of a building, as is common among architects today, only when he completely supervised its erection. He often worked for hourly wages. The word *commission* in regard to payment for a design seems to occur only once, during negotiations for the unexecuted building at the University of Nashville in 1852.

Although he never mentions the words *profession* or *professionalism* in his diary, Rogers nevertheless fought in his own way for the rightful recognition of those services and how they should be regarded and, hence, rewarded. Latrobe brought the concept to the United States and struggled for professional stature until the day he died. His protégé Mills carried on the cause. Custom-designing for a client, whether private or corporate, is now at the core of architectural practice. This means more than adequate financial compensation—it means control of the worksite and control of the quality of materials. Latrobe and other immigrant architects from Britain and Europe found it incredible that the concept of professionalism did not exist in the United States, that they had to fight for the right to see work executed according to their plans without intervention from client or builder. Rogers often records disagreements with clients over payment for his efforts and with clients and workers for control of the site. His struggles with both at buildings such as the Boston Merchants' Exchange (where he noted that it seemed he could say little about the work without giving offense), the Bank of America in New York, St. Paul's Church in Cincinnati, and elsewhere were often matched by those of his colleagues.

Rogers's attendance at the inaugural meeting of the short-lived American Institution of Architects in 1836 indicates that he joined forces with his colleagues in trying to establish the practice of architecture as a profession. So did his meetings with those architects who protested the unfair handling of the competition for the Smithsonian Institution, although he failed to show up twenty years later at the founding of the American Institute of Architects in New York in 1857. Perhaps it is because he was living in Cincinnati, and the organization looked at first like a local affair. Litigation took up a significant amount of Rogers's time. His disputes over payment, such as his claim against George Griswold in 1840, like those of Richard Upjohn and others, led to lawsuits against some of his clients. These predated the landmark 1861 New York trial of Richard Morris Hunt versus Eleazer Parmly, which helped establish that the architect, like lawyers and other professionals, sold concepts rather than the drafts that illustrated them.[7] They were, in other words, professionals. Recognition by the pubic came slowly, however, and Rogers continued to fight for his financial due. It was not until near his death that the American Institute of Architects recommended a standard, graduated fee schedule and tried to have it followed.

Rogers worked for a broad spectrum of clients on a wide range of building types, perhaps more than many of his peers. When the Smithsonian regent William Jervis Hough said that Rogers could not plan a building but only erect it, a statement reflecting Rogers's dual identity, he was voicing what might have been a generally held but certainly mistaken assessment of Rogers's strength. T. U. Walter's later letter to the committee at the Ohio state capitol seems to echo that assessment. But from early on, Rogers was an innovator in both planning and building. He was in his mid-twenties when he created the layout and complex infrastructure of the dramatically influential Tremont House. He and those who followed went on to accommodate that plan to a host of later hotel commissions east of the Mississippi and as far away as England. He seems to have had a recognized gift for hiding the quirks in irregular sites, such as those of the Tremont House, the New York Merchants' Exchange, and the Exchange Hotel in Richmond. His planning skills applied to a host of other building types characteristic of his era as well: urban and rural residences, ecclesiastical structures, hospitals, banks, theaters, libraries, monuments, commercial buildings, shops, schools, observatories, a department store, asylums, civic buildings, government offices, Masonic halls, synagogues, and customhouses. Some were built, some were not. He was independent enough to reject John Haviland's most influential radial plan for penitentiaries, as he knew it from Gridley J. F. Bryant's Charles Street Prison in Boston, in favor of his own T-shaped plan for the Hamilton County jail in Cincinnati. His unrealized enclosed-block plan for the Commercial Hospital in Cincinnati diverged sharply from the dispersed pavilion plans then in vogue.[8]

The harsh treatment of some of Rogers's works by critics and younger architects, such as Henry R. Cleveland and Arthur D. Gilman, was aimed at stylistic details rather than planning and points up the fact that he often strayed from the tried and true. The same can be said of the savage attacks he suffered publicly in the 1830s and 1840s at the hands of journalists such as *Putnam*'s dyspeptic critic, and privately from Thomas Cole. His own terse comments about the works of his peers often focus on arrangement, workmanship, or materials rather than style. The majority of contemporary journalistic comments about his buildings praised their innovation and functionality. The Cincinnati *Gazette,* for example, lauded his "magnificent" layout for the Commercial Hospital, calling it, a bit hyperbolically, more complete than any other in the world, although it also advised its rejection because of cost.

Rogers, like his peers, worked in some but not all of the revival styles of the nineteenth century. He entered history near the beginning of the Boston Granite Style and, over the next few years, contributed some of its outstanding examples. As we have seen, Grecian work in that city was characterized by large-scale granite details. One of the canonical examples is Ammi B. Young's Boston Custom House of 1837–47, a work that was certainly influenced by the presence of Willard's granite works at Quincy and Young's conversations with Rogers. For the structure, Young designed a huge Doric order of fluted granite columns on four temple fronts, unexpected only in the rare size of the monolithic supports (and, for Grecian purists, its dome). Like most of his peers and the hovering critics, Young was concerned with the accuracy of reproduced antique forms to express the assumed democratic values of the men who had created them. Rogers seems to have been much less interested in such precise repetition of historical precedent (hence, the heavy blows of his critics). His approach was often less dogmatic. Where is the equal of his austere granite gridwork facade for the Brazer's Building in Boston, a building, like many of A. J. Davis's paper projects, so admired by later history-denying modernists? His entry in the competition for Girard College showed the same boldness of approach, as compared to T. U. Walter's winning and executed design.

Although it is precarious to generalize about the character of lost architectural works based on prints, photographs, and descriptions, the design for Rogers's major Boston building, his Merchants' Exchange of 1840–43, seems to have given extraordinary variety to the standard parti of the time. He chose colossal piers rather than columns. Piers were used by others, of course, but a search for as impressive a composition among his contemporaries proves fruitless. John Haviland's Franklin Institute, of about fifteen years earlier, a building Rogers knew from trips to Philadelphia, offers one of the useful if not close comparisons. Rogers's individuality is especially evident. The one thing the facades of these urban buildings shared was the range of four piers—Rogers's fluted, contained by antae and capped by a pediment; Haviland's four equally plain piers without pediment or lateral closure. But what otherwise distinguished Rogers's architecture in such a comparison was the recognizable size and heft of his monolithic granite supports. Haviland's piers were erected of smooth limestone blocks stacked one atop the other. Not even Young's customhouse so expands on Rogers's parti. Compared to the muscular, Charles Atlas–like piers of the Boston Exchange, Haviland's uprights seem to be ninety-eight-pound weaklings.

Among other major qualities that characterized Rogers's work was this exploitation of the effects achieved from a particular material, and the ease with which he carried that to new locations and new materials when he left the East Coast. His communications with peers often concerned new materials. In later work in the West, in partnership with Henry Whitestone, Rogers switched to the round-arched early Romanesque Revival or Italianate styles executed in materials different from the trabeated granite of his Grecian works, while he continued to show an unusual use of decorative touches garnered from that ancient source. Those details were frequently achieved in cast iron and, on occasion, molded in terra-cotta, a material revived from antiquity, in whose use Rogers, Renwick, and Upjohn were among the earliest pioneers in this country.

Rogers was not a stylistic innovator, but within the prevalent styles he managed to produce exceptional works. For him, materials generated forms arranged by following function, perhaps more strictly than anything later intended by Louis Sullivan. In what used to be called "The Battle of Styles" he seems to have taken little interest. Throughout the diary he describes his work as planning rather than designing. His mind was practical rather than theoretical. He found the architecture lectures by the university-educated Arthur Gilman of small interest, and he does not mention that architect's advocacy of the Renaissance Revival. By contrast, he does refer to a communication by Alexander Parris on heating and ventilating. The only publication he notes (without comment) that concerned the meaning of historical details is Ruskin's *Stones of Venice,* which he probably read as a travelogue. His use of the revived Gothic did not produce buildings worthy of much consideration. He tacked crockets and finials onto a church in Cambridge, incised Tudor arches onto such works as the Henshaw tomb, used Tudor windows on the facade of the Tyler Davidson Hardware Store in Cincinnati, as he had for the Howard Athenaeum. Except for this last building, whose pointed arches formed an unprecedented statement for a theater (and may have been suggested by the theater that his own Howard replaced), these were expected superficial touches, not essential forms. He was mainly concerned with large or small building blocks, as witnessed by any one of his many hotels and even his Dutch Reform Church in New York and St. Paul's in Cincinnati. He left the ecclesiastical Gothic to peers such as Minard Lafever, Richard Upjohn, and James Renwick Jr. He gave the Egyptian Revival scant attention, using it only for cemetery gates, where it seemed appropriate, and a few unrealized projects. He probably thought of Henry Austin's use of exotic Islamic-inspired details on his Connecticut houses—if he knew them—as sheer nonsense.

We find the word *chaste* often used by Rogers's contemporaries in describing his works. In all cases, details were subordinate to the overall "plan" (as Rogers used the word) of the building. He relied on a limited vocabulary of decorative details. Issues of style concerned him less than they did his contemporaries, because he was a practical man who first sought practical solutions to practical problems. He concentrated on the building at hand. There is no indication that he ever thought beyond the architecture to design the landscape, as did John Notman, for example. After the layout of a building, uppermost in his mind was structural design, as well as consideration for so-called fireproofing. In this he kept abreast of his contemporaries and at times forged ahead of them. Wood frames as well as brick and stone arches and vaults gradually gave way to a mix of stone and cast iron and then all-iron construction in his work, as in that of others, as the century progressed. He paralleled the trajectory of his peers, especially Robert Mills, in their search for "fireproof" methods of building, because blazes threatened—and frequently occurred—in that time of wood construction and open-flame lighting. His use of plaster fire stops in floors and walls was not unique, but he looked beyond that. He discussed with Young the possibilities of iron laths, which he used in place of wooden ones, although his contemplated patent never materialized. He specified Johnson's patented rolling iron shutters for security and fire protection in commercial work. His patented vault design for the Treasury building extended fireproofing into the realm of burglar-proofing.

The U.S. Treasury Building's bank vault and his three patents for bridging systems were seemingly unequalled by other architects of his day. Just as they gradually separated themselves from builders, so did they gradually separate themselves from engineers (and the engineers from them). Until the end of his career Rogers embraced both architecture and engineering—Horatio Greenough assigned both to him—so it seems fitting that the firm he and Henry Whitestone originated currently bills itself as "Architects and Engineers." His imaginative exploration of bridge construction, especially his early cylindrical spans, and the occasional reference in the diary indicate that his perusal of books was not limited to those on architecture. Over at least thirty years his mind ranged beyond the confines of architecture, strictly speaking, to study the engineering problem of spanning distances beyond those of roofing standard buildings. He occasionally mentions an engineering text, but he went out of his way to inspect onsite the bridges of Charles Ellet Jr., John Roebling, Adolphus Heiman, Montgomery Meigs, and other engineers. In this he followed—and went well beyond—Ithiel Town, whose patented lattice truss bridge of 1825 probably inspired Roger's own patented cylindrical lattice bridge of 1841. Although that design never materialized in a long-span road or railway bridge, he did erect several footbridges according to this system. Seemingly as a conservative alternate to the suspension systems of Roebling and Ellet, he next turned his attention, in two subsequent patents, to tubular iron arched bridges. In this he was abreast of Richard Delafield or Montgomery Meigs. He projected designs to span the Mississippi, the Ohio, the Harlem, and other rivers, and one of his last self-generated projects was to span the East River in New York. Such extra-architectural studies went beyond bridges and safes. In 1861, at the beginning of the Civil War, he drafted a steam-powered patrol boat for the Ohio.

These projects remained on paper, and undoubtedly had little impact on the emerging engineering profession, but here again Rogers stands apart from the majority of his fellow architects. Knowledge of his career as a whole adds yet another dimension to the history of the evolving architectural profession in nineteenth-century America.

APPENDIX

Chronological List of Buildings and Projects

THIS LIST is a chronology of the buildings and projects (unbuilt designs) undertaken by Isaiah Rogers from 1822 to 1868. Based largely on his diary, it is not a complete account of his career and excludes many alterations and works that are poorly identified. Because Rogers was writing for himself and not for the twenty-first-century historian, many names are illegible or inaccurate, requiring some necessary guesswork to fill in details, although facts have been checked against available evidence and sources. This is not a complete list of his career, something that will probably never be achieved.

Date	Location	Work
1822	Mobile, Ala.	theater (attribution)
1824	Boston, Mass.	six houses on Pond Street ("front view")
1824	Boston, Mass.	house on Pleasant Street
1824	Boston, Mass.	three houses on Purchase Street
1825	Boston, Mass.	Smith building at Merrimac, Portland, and Market Streets
1825	Boston, Mass.	house in Nassau Court
1825	Boston, Mass.	six houses in Federal Court
1825	Boston, Mass.	two houses at Pond and Cooper Streets
1826	Boston, Mass.	two houses with storefronts at Prince and Salem Streets

Date	Location	Work
1826	Boston, Mass.	two stores at State Street and Merchants Row
1826	Boston, Mass.	house on Pond Street
1826	Boston, Mass.	two houses on Winter Street
1826	Boston, Mass.	house in Provence House Court
1826	Cambridge, Mass.	interior decorative work, Christ Church
1827	Augusta, Ga.	Masonic hall (facade)
1827	Boston, Mass.	Tremont Theatre (converted to church, 1842–43)
1827	Boston, Mass.	Pine Street Trinitarian Church
1827	Boston, Mass.	North Bennet Street Methodist Church
1828	Boston, Mass.	three stores on Marginal Street
1828	Boston, Mass.	two town houses (no location recorded)
1828	Boston, Mass.	Tremont House
1829	Boston, Mass.	house at May and Grove Streets
1829	Albany, N.Y.	city hall (competition entry)
1829	Lowell, Mass.	town hall
1830	Lancaster, Mass.	Joseph Andrews house
1830	Boston, Mass.	Masonic temple
1830	Boston, Mass.	Old State House (alterations)
1831	Boston, Mass.	Massachusetts statehouse (additions)
1831	Charlestown, Mass.	Philip McGrath house
1831	Nahant, Mass.	Village Church (enlarged, 1845–46)
1832	Worcester, Mass.	Lincoln Square houses
1832	Philadelphia, Pa.	Girard College (competition entry)
1832	Cambridge, Mass.	First Parish Meeting House
1832	Boston, Mass.	Commercial Wharf

Chronological List of Buildings and Projects

Date	Location	Work
1832	New York City	Astor House
1833	New York City	federal customhouse (competition entry)
1833	Milton, Mass.	Robert Bennet Forbes House and barn
1833	Bangor, Maine	Bangor House
1833	Salem, Mass.	St. Peter's Episcopal Church
1833	Boston, Mass.	Suffolk Bank
1835	New York City	Halls of Justice ("The Tombs") (competition entry)
1835	New York City	Bank of America, Wall Street
1835	New York City	Merchants' Exchange
1836	Worcester, Mass.	Stephen Salisbury house (attribution)
1836	New York City	Middle Dutch Reformed Church
1837	Boston, Mass.	Custom House Block (attribution)
1838	Columbus, Ohio	Ohio statehouse (competition entry)
1838	New York City	City Bank (project?)
1838	New York City	George A. Jarvis house (project?)
1838	New York City	United States Bank of New York
1838	Brooklyn, N.Y.	houses and hotel for Red Hook (project)
1838	New York City	Merchants' Bank
1838	New York City	Church of the Messiah (attribution)
1838	Philadelphia, Pa. (?)	hotel for Pierce Butler (project)
1838	West Point, N.Y.	barracks for the U.S. Military Academy (projects)
1838	(none)	studies for a cylindrical lattice bridge (U.S. Patent No. 2347)
1838	New York City	Harlem River Aqueduct (private proposal)
1839	West Point, N.Y.	observatory for the U.S. Military Academy (project?)

Date	Location	Work
1839	New York City	Bank of New York (project?)
1839	New York City	Brandegee houses (project?)
1839	New York City	Benjamin L. Swan house (attribution?)
1839	New York City	Andrew B. Glover house (project?)
1839	Staten Island, N.Y.	Davis cottage
1839	Boston, Mass.	city hall (project)
1839	Troy, N.Y.	unidentified church (project?)
1839	New York City	New National Theatre (project or private proposal)
1839	Boston, Mass.	Old Granary Burying Ground gateway and fence
1839	Washington, D.C.	hotel for Enoch Redington Mudd (project)
1839	Richmond, Virginia	Exchange Hotel
1839	New York City	"jobbing" for John Jacob Astor
1840	New York City	Astor Library (project)
1840	near Cape Girardeau, Mo.	bridge to span the Mississippi River (personal project)
1840	New York City	Masonic Hall (alterations)
1840	New York City	Union Bank & Federal Trust Company
1840	Richmond, Va.	Exchange Bank
1840	Newport, R.I.	Jewish cemetery gateway and fence
1840	Newport, R.I.	Touro Synagogue gateway and fence
1840	Boston, Mass.	Merchants' Exchange (alterations, 1854)
1841	Cambridge, Mass.	John Thornton Kirkland cenotaph, Mount Auburn Cemetery
1841	Boston, Mass.	cylindrical lattice bridge for the Massachusetts Charitable Mechanic Association Fair

Chronological List of Buildings and Projects

Date	Location	Work
1841	Boston, Mass.	Western Railway depot
1841	Cambridge, Mass.	Lee monument, Mount Auburn Cemetery (project?)
1841	outside Richmond, Va.	Duval house (alteration)
1841	Richmond, Va.	Dudley house (project?)
1841	New Haven, Conn.	Woolsey monument, Grove Street Cemetery (?)
1841	Brooklyn, N.Y.	city hall (project)
1841	Boston, Mass.	cylindrical lattice bridge in courtyard of Tremont House
1841	Brookline, Mass.	Theodore Lyman House (project)
1841	Richmond, Va.	Horace L. Kent house (project)
1841	Richmond, Va.	orphan asylum for girls (project)
1842	Cambridge, Mass.	Mount Auburn Cemetery gatehouse (personal proposal or project?)
1842	Boston, Mass.	Brazer's Building
1842	Boston, Mass.	two houses on Paris Street
1842	Marshfield, Mass.	Rogers homestead (remodeling)
1842	Newport, R.I.	tombstone for Mrs. J. H. Easton
1842	Boston, Mass.	offices for Mr. Gray (project?)
1842	Boston, Mass.	Lowell Lecture Room building (project)
1843	New York City	Braman's Baths (project)
1843	Cambridge, Mass.	Walker house
1843	Swampscott, Mass.	Enoch Redington Mudd House
1843	Cambridge, Mass.	astronomical observatory, Harvard University
1843, 1845	Cambridge, Mass.	president's house, Harvard University (projects)

APPENDIX

Date	Location	Work
1843	Cambridge, Mass.	Dana Hall, Harvard University (alteration; project)
1844	Boston, Mass.	bridge for Massachusetts Charitable Mechanic Association Fair (project)
1844	Boston, Mass.	sixteen houses on Washington Street
1844	South Boston, Mass.	house on Washington Street
1844	Newport, R.I.	David Sears House (project)
1844	Newport, R.I.	Ocean House hotel
1844	Quincy, Mass.	town hall (facade)
1844	Boston, Mass.	Mills house (project?)
1844	Boston, Mass.	Armstrong house (alterations)
1844	Lynn, Mass.	Phillips house
1844	Boston, Mass.	Washington Street houses for Kimball and Company
1844	Boston (?), Mass.	Fleming house
1844	Roxbury, Mass.	church (project?)
1844	Boston, Mass.	Samuel Henshaw house (alterations)
1844	Richmond, Va.	Horace L. Kent House
1844	Nahant, Mass.	T. W. Ward cottage
1844	Watertown, Mass.	Mrs. Heard or Hurd (?) house
1844	Boston, Mass.	Shawmut House (alterations)
1844	Lynn, Mass.	Enoch Redington Mudge cottage
1844	New York City	hotel for Mr. Howard (project?)
1844	Boston, Mass.	Rose house
1844	Boston, Mass.	Female [Orphan] Asylum
1844	Norfolk, Va.	Farmers' Bank (attribution)
1844	undefined location	athenaeum (project; perhaps intended for the Boston Athenaeum competitions of these years)

Date	Location	Work
1844	Cambridge, Mass.	Samuel Henshaw tomb, Mount Auburn Cemetery
1844, 1845	Washington, D.C., and/or New York	Washington Monument (projects)
1844	Washington, D.C.	War and Navy Offices (competition entry)
1844	Boston, Mass.	stores for Dr. George C. Shattuck
1845	Brookline, Mass.	cottage for Mrs. William H. Eliot
1845	Taunton, Mass.	Mills machine shop
1845	Boston, Mass.	hall for Massachusetts Charitable Mechanic Association (competition entry)
1845	Newport, R.I.	Ocean House
1845	Boston, Mass.	Merchants' National Bank (alteration)
1845	Boston, Mass.	Sargent house
1845	Boston, Mass.	Eastern Extension Railroad Depot
1845	Boston, Mass.	Hooper house
1845	New York City	Chinese Museum (project)
1845	Boston, Mass.	alterations to Boylston Hall for a theater (project)
1845	Boston (?), Mass.	Eldridge cottage
1845	Boston, Mass. (?)	Waterman cottage
1845	Brookline, Mass.	Samuel Eliot house (alterations)
1845	Nantasket Beach, Mass.	hotel (project?)
1845	New York City	New Waverly House (personal project?)
1845	Boston, Mass.	theater for James Henry Hackett (project)
1845	Groton, Mass.	work for Lawrence Academy
1845	Roxbury, Mass.	Nichols cottage

Date	Location	Work
1845	Boston, Mass.	Howard Street Theatre (Howard Athenaeum)
1845	Boston, Mass.	stores for Long Wharf
1845	New York City	St. Charles Hotel (attribution)
1846	New Bedford, Mass.	bowling alley (project?)
1846	Boston, Mass.	H. Gray house
1846	Cambridge, Mass.	William Lawrence tomb, Mount Auburn Cemetery (project)
1846	Boston, Mass.	Ward house
1846	Roxbury, Mass.	city hall (alterations; project)
1846	Boston, Mass.	town houses for H. H. Dexter (project)
1846	unknown location	mill workers' housing for Enoch Redington Mudd (project?)
1846	Bangor, Maine	addition to the Samuel Farrar house
1846	Washington, D.C.	Smithsonian Institution (competition entry)
1847	Washington, D.C.	Heise house
1847	New York City	Astor Place Opera House
1847	Marshfield Hills, Mass.	Second Meeting House (alterations)
1848	Madison, Ind.	unnamed church (project?)
1848	Cincinnati, Ohio (?)	Market House for Reuben P. Resor (project?)
1848	St. Louis, Mo.	theater (project)
1848	Cincinnati, Ohio	Burnet House
1848	Madison, Ind.	Madison House
1848	Niagara Falls, N.Y.	various hotel projects
1849	Cincinnati, Ohio	theater (project)
1849	Cincinnati, Ohio	public assembly room (project?)

Chronological List of Buildings and Projects

Date	Location	Work
1849	Cincinnati, Ohio	stores for Griffin Taylor
1849	near Cincinnati, Ohio	McLean house
1849	Cincinnati, Ohio	Commercial Bank
1849	Cincinnati, Ohio	Tyler Davidson & Company store
1849	Cincinnati, Ohio	Robert B. Bowler estate (alterations)
1849	Cincinnati, Ohio	St. John's Episcopal Church (unfinished)
1849	Cincinnati, Ohio	Griffin Taylor tomb, Spring Grove Cemetery
1849–61	Cincinnati, Ohio	Hamilton County courthouse and jail
1850	Cincinnati, Ohio	medical college for Dr. Baylis (?)
1850	Cincinnati, Ohio	synagogue (project?)
1850	Cincinnati, Ohio	buildings for Dr. John T. Shotwell (project?)
1850	Cincinnati, Ohio	Lawler house
1850	Cincinnati, Ohio	Jason A. Gurley house
1850	Cincinnati, Ohio	Winthrop B. Smith house (alterations)
1850	Cincinnati, Ohio	Waverly House (alterations)
1850	Cincinnati, Ohio	fire department watchtower
1850	Cincinnati, Ohio	market house for Conrad Fox
1850	Cincinnati, Ohio	J. W. Coleman house (alterations)
1850	Cincinnati, Ohio	house for Judge Short
1850	Cincinnati (?), Ohio	Pierson house
1850	Cincinnati, Ohio	building (temporary?) for appearance by Jenny Lind (project)
1850	Cincinnati, Ohio	restaurant and office for George (?) Selves
1850	Louisville, Ky.	library (project)
1850	Louisville, Ky.	Masonic Hall (project)

Date	Location	Work
1850	Louisville, Ky.	Exchange and Reading Room (project?)
1850	Cincinnati, Ohio	George Hatch house
1850	Dayton, Ohio	Phillips House
1850	Cincinnati, Ohio	Reuben P. Resor house
1850–56	Louisville, Ky.	Louisville Hotel
1851	New Orleans, La.	City Hotel
1851	New Orleans, La.	St. Louis Hotel (alterations)
1851	New Orleans, La.	St. Charles Hotel (project and consultation)
1851	Mobile, Ala.	unnamed hotel (project)
1851	Mobile, Ala.	Battle House
1851	Cheviot, Ohio (?)	Mrs. Robb house
1851	Richmond, Indiana	Peter Thompson house
1851	Boston, Mass.	unidentified clubhouse
1851	Cincinnati, Ohio	monument for Milton H. Cook, Spring Grove Cemetery
1851	Cincinnati, Ohio	William W. (?) Scarborough house
1851	Cincinnati, Ohio	John P. Tweed tomb, Spring Grove Cemetery
1852	Cincinnati, Ohio	Joseph Longworth house (addition)
1852	Nashville, Tenn.	Literary Department building, University of Nashville (project)
1852	Nashville, Tenn.	store for Mr. Cooper
1852	Cincinnati, Ohio	Milton H. (?) Cook house (project?)
1852	Cincinnati, Ohio	block of houses for Milton H. (?) Cook
1852	Illinois (town unknown)	chapel for Colonel (Enoch Redington?) Mudge
1852	Cincinnati, Ohio	building for Judge Hart

Chronological List of Buildings and Projects

Date	Location	Work
1852	Cincinnati, Ohio	bridge across the Ohio River (personal project)
1852	Dayton, Ohio	lunatic asylum (project?)
1852	Cincinnati, Ohio	Smith's icehouse (project?)
1852	Mobile, Ala.	Caldwell house
1852	Cincinnati, Ohio	bookstore for Henry W. Derby (alteration?)
1852	New Albany, Ind., or Ohio	church
1852	New Orleans, La.	Edgerton house
1852	Frankfort, Ky.	Hanna house (alterations)
1852	Frankfort, Ky.	Capital Hotel
1852–55	Cincinnati, Ohio	A. B. Coleman tomb, Spring Grove Cemetery
1852–56	(none)	studies for a cast iron tubular arch bridge (U.S. Patent No. 15823)
1853	Cincinnati, Ohio	First Universalist Society church (project?)
1853	Frankfort, Ky.	fence for statehouse grounds
1853	Hudson, N.Y.	jail (project?)
1853	Goshen, Ohio	Rogers farmhouse (alterations?)
1853	Cincinnati, Ohio	Tweed and Andrews store (project?)
1853	Cincinnati, Ohio	Coleman's icehouse (project?)
1853	Cincinnati, Ohio	J. C. Hall house
1853	Ironton, Ohio	schoolhouse
1853	near Louisville, Ky.	Bullitt cottage
1853	Cincinnati, Ohio	Springer and Whiteman store
1853	Louisville, Ky.	Galt House (alterations)

Date	Location	Work
1853–56	Louisville, Ky.	Louisville Hotel
1853	Chicago, Ill.	Metropolitan Hall
1853	Louisville, Ky.	William Preston house (project?)
1853	Louisville, Ky.	T. T. Shreve house (alterations)
1853	Cincinnati, Ohio	Masonic Hall
1853	Louisville, Ky.	Thomas H. Hunt house
1853	Aurora, Ind.	Thomas Gaff house
1854	Plymouth, Mass.	Forefathers Monument (project)
1854	Milwaukee, Wisc.	Shepardson Hotel (project)
1854	Milwaukee, Wisc.	John Lockwood house (project?)
1854	Milwaukee, Wisc.	Ludington stores (project?)
1854	Niagara Falls, N.Y.	orphanage (project?)
1854	Louisville, Ky.	Estes Store (project?)
1854	Louisville, Ky.	Duffield Warehouse (project?)
1854	Louisville, Ky.	Zane Cottage (project?)
1854	Foster's Crossing, Ohio	Simpson house
1854	Newport, R.I.	Nathan Gould house (project?)
1854	Cincinnati, Ohio	bookstore for Uriah P. (?) James
1854	Cincinnati, Ohio	Fielder cottage
1854	Cincinnati, Ohio	McAlpin store
1854	Cambridge, Mass.	monument to Hosea Ballou, Mount Auburn Cemetery (personal project?)
1854	Harrods Creek, Ky.	Pilatus S. Barber house
1854	Louisville, Ky.	Newcomb Banking House
1854	Louisville, Ky.	Alexander's store
1854	Louisville, Ky.	Hunt store
1854	Louisville, Ky.	W. B. Reynolds store

Chronological List of Buildings and Projects

Date	Location	Work
1854	Cincinnati, Ohio	Winthrop B. Smith Publishing Company building
1855	Louisville, Ky.	Hilton house
1855	Louisville, Ky.	T. S. Kennedy cottage
1855	Newport, R.I.	Judah Touro monument, Jewish Cemetery
1855	Long Island, N.Y.	A. B. Coleman cottage
1855	Paducah, Ky.	Thomas Smith Kennedy house (alterations)
1855	Paducah, Ky.	Commercial Bank
1855	Albany, N.Y.	Congress Hall hotel (alterations)
1855	Cincinnati, Ohio	King, Corwin & Company store (project?)
1855	Cincinnati, Ohio	John S. (?) Chenoweth house (project?)
1855	Louisville, Ky.	Alexander house (alterations)
1855	Louisville, Ky.	courthouse (project?)
1855	Cincinnati, Ohio	John Shillito & Company store (project)
1855	Cincinnati, Ohio	Unitarian church (project?)
1855	Louisville, Ky.	Fifth Ward School
1855	Louisville, Ky.	spire for the Cathedral of the Assumption
1857	Memphis, Tenn.	addition to James Dakin's 1842 Gayoso Hotel
1858	Louisville, Ky.	Horatio Dalton Newcomb house
1858	Washington, Ind.	M. L. Brett house
1858	Toledo, Ohio	Oliver House
1858	Columbus, Ohio	completion of the Ohio statehouse
1859	Cincinnati, Ohio	Commercial Hospital (project)
1859	Carthage, Ohio	Longview Asylum

Date	Location	Work
1859	Nashville, Tenn.	Maxwell House
1860	Cincinnati, Ohio	John P. (?) Tweed house
1860	Cincinnati, Ohio	Reuben Resor house
1861	(none)	improved design for cast-iron tubular arch bridge (U.S. Patent No. 37,642)
1861	Nashville, Tenn.	bridge across the Cumberland River (personal project)
1861	(none)	Mississippi River gunboat (personal project)
1861	(none)	design for a military hospital (personal project)
1861	Washington, D.C.	hotel for Willard brothers (project)
1862–65	Washington, D.C.	work on the West Wing of the Treasury Building
1863	Washington, D.C.	burglar-proof safes for Treasury Building (U.S. Patent No. 40,947)
1863	Boston, Mass.	customhouse (alteration; repairs)
1864	Portland, Maine	customhouse (project)
1864	Cincinnati, Ohio	customhouse
1864	Louisville, Ky.	customhouse (project)
1865	Bangor, Maine	enlargement of the customhouse (project)
1866	Cincinnati, Ohio	Pike's Opera House
1866	Albany, N.Y.	statehouse (competition entry)
1866	New York City	East River bridge (personal project)
1866	Newport, R.I.	Nathan H. Gould house (alterations)
1866	Lexington, Ky.	theater for the Odd Fellows' Hall (project?)
1866	Cincinnati, Ohio	opera house for Truman S. Handy (project)

Date	Location	Work
1867	New York City	post office and customhouse (competition entry)
1867	Washington, D.C.	hotel for Mr. Willard (project?)
1867	Cincinnati, Ohio	Commercial Hospital (alterations)
1868	Cincinnati, Ohio	Miller & Roberts store
1868	Springfield, Ohio	Lagonda House

NOTES

Introduction

1. Leah Upton, "The Boston Artists' Association, 1841–1851," *American Art Journal* 15 (Autumn 1983): 45–57.

2. Henry-Russell Hitchcock, *Architecture: Nineteenth and Twentieth Centuries* (Baltimore: Penguin, 1958).

1. Marshfield and Boston, 1800–1834

1. L. Vernon Briggs, *History of Shipbuilding on North River, Plymouth County, Massachusetts* (Boston: Coburn Bros., 1889), ch. 12.

2. J. H. Drummond, *John Rogers of Marshfield and Some of His Descendents* (West Hanover, Mass.: R. B. Ellis, 1898).

3. *The Biographical Encyclopaedia of Ohio of the Nineteenth Century* (Cincinnati: Galaxy Publishing Co., 1876), 182–83. Could this be the equivalent of a creation myth? Minard Lafever, two years Rogers's senior, is said to have walked 50 miles at age 18 to buy his first book on architecture; Jacob Landy, *The Architecture of Minard Lafever* (New York: Columbia University Press, 1970), [1].

4. See Jack Quinan, "Some Aspects of the Development of the Architectural Profession in Boston between 1800 and 1830," *Old-Time New England* 68 (July–December 1977): 32–37.

5. Martha J. McNamara, "Defining the Profession: Books, Libraries, and Architects," in *American Architects and Their Books to 1848,* ed. Kenneth Hafertepe and James F. O'Gorman (Amherst: University of Massachusetts Press, 2001), 73–89.

6. See John Morrill Bryan, "Boston's Granite Architecture, c. 1810–1860" (PhD diss., Boston University, 1972).

7. The original map is in the collection of the Library of Congress.

8. *Biographical Encyclopaedia of Ohio,* 182–83.

9. Robert Gamble, e-mail message to author, ca. 2012.

10. Elizabeth Barrett Gould, *From Fort to Port: An Architectural History of Mobile, Alabama* (Tuscaloosa: University of Alabama Press, 1988), 30, 39–41. Gould writes that Rogers's diary "seems to verify the attribution," but the surviving diary does not cover the 1820s, nor does the Myers article she cites mention it.

11. Horatio Greenough, *The Travels, Observations, and Experience of a Yankee Stonecutter* (1852; repr., Gainesville, Fla.: Scholars' Facsimiles & Reprints, 1958), 133.

12. See Talbot Hamlin, *Greek Revival Architecture in America* (New York: Oxford University Press, 1944), ch. 5.

13. William W. Wheildon, *Memoir of Solomon Willard* (Boston: Monument Assoc., 1865).

14. The documents are in the Robert L. Raley Collection at the Athenaeum of Philadelphia. One, dated May 8, is marked "paid" by his brother Jotham Rogers; the other, a request for the remainder of his bill, is dated June 17 and signed by Isaiah. The writing on the first was probably Jotham's, too; spelling and penmanship on the second are more assured and certainly by Isaiah. Rogers apparently did additional work at the church as late as 1857; Keith N. Morgan, ed., *Buildings of the United States: Massachusetts: Metropolitan Boston* (Charlottesville: University of Virginia Press), 341.

15. Gardiner M. Day, *The Biography of a Church: A Brief History of Christ Church, Cambridge, Massachusetts* (Cambridge: Riverside Press, 1951), 38–39.

16. *Autobiography of James Gallier, Architect* (1864; repr., New York: Da Capo Press, 1973), 20.

17. Earle G. Shettleworth Jr., comp., "An Index to Boston Building Contracts Recorded in the Suffolk County Registry of Deeds," 1820–1829, 1830–1839, 1840–1844, 1845–1849, and 1995–1997, Historic New England.

18. James F. O'Gorman, ed., *Drawing toward Home: Designs for Domestic Architecture from Historic New England* (Boston: Historic New England, 2010), 66–67. The large number of individual units cited for Rogers was not exceptional. In one year alone, 1845–46, Roath turned out at least 26 townhouses.

19. Richard Stoddard, "Isaiah Rogers' Tremont Theatre, Boston," *Magazine Antiques* (June 1974), 1314–19; this article is based on Stoddard's "Architecture and Technology of Boston Theatres, 1794–1854" (PhD diss., Yale University, 1971), 106–43. For a contemporary description, see *American Traveller,* August 26 and 28, 1828. Besides the views of the facade mentioned in the text, Abel Bowen published a woodcut in his *Picture of Boston* (Boston: Otis, Broaders and Co., 1838), 108.

20. Rogers not only designed buildings but often acted as a kind of general contractor long before that term and that occupation came into being. See Sara Wermiel, "The Rise of the General Contractor in Nineteenth-Century America," *FMI Quarterly* 3 (2008): 117–29.

21. Review of *The American Builder's Guide General Price Book, North American Review* 43 (October 1836): 364–65. See Roger Reed, *Building Victorian Boston: The Architecture of Gridley J. F. Bryant* (Amherst: University of Massachusetts Press, 2007), 18.

22. Roger Hale Newton, *Town & Davis, Architects* (New York: Columbia University Press, 1942), 54. The drawing was exhibited at the National Academy of Design in New York.

23. That plate survives in the collection of the Bostonian Society.

24. "Copied from Nature and drawn on stone by A. J. Davis," 1828; copies are at the Metropolitan Museum in New York, the Boston Athenaeum, and the American Antiquarian Society. Stoddard, "Isaiah Rogers's Tremont Theatre," *Antiques,* fig. 3.

25. For the resulting facade, see Stoddard, "Isaiah Rogers's Tremont Theatre," fig. 6.

26. Arthur Gilman, "Architecture in the United States," *North American Review* 58 (April 1844): 447–48.

27. *Daily Georgian,* November 22, 1827, 2.

28. Joseph M. Lee III, *Images of America: Augusta and Summerville* (Charleston, S.C.: Arcadia, 2000), 18 and 54.

29. Pine Street Church Records, Subgroup II, Series I, Congregational Library, Boston. This source gives no further mention of the southern church.

30. Bowen, *Picture of Boston*, 154; N. Dickinson, *Boston Almanac for the Year 1843* (Boston: Thomas Groom & Co., 1843), 104; Caleb H. Snow, *A History of Boston, the Metropolis of Massachusetts*, 2nd ed. (Boston, 1828); and *Sketches and Business Directory of Boston for 1860 and 1861* (Boston: Damrell & Moore and George Coolidge, 1861), 34. In addition to these publications, there are documents at the Congregational Library, Boston.

31. Documents at the School of Theology Library, Boston University; Bowen, *Picture of Boston*, 132–34, channeling the *Brief Account of the Dreadful Occurrence at the Laying of the Corner Stone of the Methodist Church in North Bennet Street, Boston, April 30, 1828; Sketches of Boston, Past and Present* (Boston: Phillips, Sampson and Co., 1851), 84.

32. Molly W. Berger, *Hotel Dreams: Luxury, Technology, and Urban Ambition in America, 1829–1929* (Baltimore: Johns Hopkins University Press, 2011), 32.

33. Jack Quinan, "The Boston Exchange Coffee House," *Journal of the Society of Architectural Historians* 38 (October 1979): 256–62. See also Jane Kamensky, *The Exchange Artist* (New York: Penguin, 2009).

34. The fundamental source is [William H. Eliot], *A Description of Tremont House, with Architectural Illustrations* (Boston: Gray and Brown, 1830). A contemporary account is in *American Traveller*, January 2, 1829. See also Bowen, *Picture of Boston*, 204–6. Among myriad later discussions, see Henry Lee, "Boston's Greatest Hotel," *Old-Time New England* 55 (Spring 1965): 97–106. For an excellent study of the building's place in the history of American society in general and of hotels in particular, see Berger, *Hotel Dreams*, chs. 1–3. The strength of Berger's richly detailed study is that it is not limited to architecture narrowly defined, but this approach occasions some misstatements about the building. The scene she illustrates on p. 55, for example, cannot be the original Tremont dining room, for the space shown is vaulted wall to wall, which would make the use of free-standing columns in the original layout odd if not impossible. The section given in Eliot's *Description* clearly shows a flat ceiling (see Fig. 7). The columns were later removed (and are now at the Greenfield Historical Society in Mass.) but the ceiling remained flat. For a view of the room in 1852, see Lee, "Boston's Greatest Hotel," 100.

35. *Boston Weekly Messenger*, June 26, 1828, 4; *Christian Watchman*, July 18, 1828.

36. An 1830 *Catalogue of Pictures* from the Athenaeum Gallery in Boston, in the archive at the Boston Athenaeum, says Harvey's view was taken "from the model."

37. Although the formats are parallel, the quality of production is not. Wyatt's book contains fold-out plates, some of which are beautifully shaded sections.

38. Berger, *Hotel Dreams*, 41. The copy of Eliot's extraordinary publication owned by the Boston Athenaeum is inscribed by both Eliot and Rogers "with the respects and friendly salutations" to Thomas W. Sumner Esq. Sumner led an important Boston life as politician, housewright, and architect of the recently constructed East India Marine Hall in Salem, among other works.

39. Statistics are from a series of contemporary accounts in *Trumpet and Universal Magazine*, January 3, 1829, 107, and March 7, 1829, 143; and *Christian Secretary*, March

7, 1829, 27. After the demolition of the hotel, the columns were moved to Industrial Park, Worcester, across from the American Antiquarian Society.

40. There exists a second version of Kidder's view, engraved by J. Archer, that eliminates the cupola.

41. Thomas Hamilton, *Men and Manners in America* (Philadelphia: Carey, Lea & Blanchard, 1833), as quoted in Hamlin, *Greek Revival*, 113–14.

42. James F. O'Gorman, "Pure Water for Boston," *Nineteenth Century* 29 (Spring 2009): 19–25.

43. Berger, *Hotel Dreams*, 19–28.

44. *Boston Evening Transcript*, September 30, 1834; *Portland Evening Advertiser*, March 19, 1835. The early attribution to Charles C. Bryant and Lyman Seavey in James H. Mundy and Earle G. Shettleworth Jr., *The Flight of the Grand Eagle* (Augusta: Maine Historic Preservation Commission, 1977), who superintended construction and probably made some changes, was corrected by Denys Peter Myers in his entry on Rogers in the *Biographical Dictionary of Architects in Maine* (Augusta: Maine Historic Preservation Commission, 1986). He lists a few other minor works by Rogers in the state. The building stands, but altered.

45. Mary Raddant Tomlan, ed., *A Neat Plain Modern Style: Philip Hooker and His Contemporaries, 1796–1836* (Amherst: University of Massachusetts Press, 1993), 262–79.

46. Bruce Laverty, Michael J. Lewis, and Michele Taillon Taylor, *Monument to Philanthropy: The Design and Building of Girard College, 1832–1848* (Philadelphia: Girard College, 1998), 28–29, 55, 129, and passim.

47. For Lowell, Mass., 1829. Struggling to say something positive about this work, Denys Peter Myers wrote in a draft fragment of his unpublished study: "Plain, simple and minimalist . . . in its original state, [the town hall] was redeemed from dullness by its excellent proportions and from the commonplace by its classical restraint."

48. William D. Stratton, *Dedication Memorial of the New Masonic Temple, Boston* (Boston: Lee and Shepard, 1870), 14–15, 23; "Proceedings of the Grand Lodge of Massachusetts," 1826, 241, 245, Masonic Temple, Boston; *Ballou's Pictorial Drawing-Room Companion*, 1859, 169; *Boston Daily Globe*, May 18, 1902, 46.

49. The Nutting print may have been the connection between this Boston building and the Mormon Temple in Salt Lake begun in 1853, if there was one. See David S. Andrew and Laurel B. Black, "The Four Mormon Temples of Utah," *Journal of the Society of Architectural Historians* 30 (March 1971): 61.

50. Henry R. Cleveland, "American Architecture," *North American Review* 43 (October 1836): 364.

51. *Report of the Connection at Various Times between the First Parish in Cambridge and Harvard College* (Cambridge: Metcalf and Co., 1851), 29–39; Cambridge Historical Commission, *Survey of Architectural History in Cambridge*, vol. 4 (Cambridge: Cambridge Historical Commission, 1973), 136–37.

52. In 1830–31 Rogers worked on alterations to Boston's venerable Old State House and additions to Bulfinch's statehouse. Donlyn Lyndon, *The City Observed: Boston* (New York: Vintage, 1982), 4–6. The former were erased by subsequent restorations; the latter were completely enclosed by alterations by G. J. F. Bryant in 1853–54.

53. Mrs. Samuel Hammond, *Nahant Church, 1832–1932*, n.d.; and Andrew P. Peabody, *A Sermon Preached in Commemoration of the Founders of the Nahant Church . . . 1877*, 2nd ed. (Cambridge: John Wilson and Son, 1892), 18–19, 22–25.

54. Bryan, "Boston's Granite Architecture," 80–86; Roger Reed, *Building Victorian Boston* (Amherst: University of Massachusetts Press, 2007), 82.

55. Lyndon, *City Observed*, 58–59.

56. Charles H. Sawyer and Louisa Dresser, "The Salisbury Houses," *Worcester Art Museum Annual*, 1946 (repr., Worcester, Mass.: Worcester Historical Museum, 1980): 43n.

57. Documentation of the building of the 1830s and remodeling of the 1870s is in the archive of the Forbes House Museum.

58. Bryan, "Boston's Granite Architecture," 80–86; Reed, *Building Victorian Boston*, 82.

59. Bowen, *Picture of Boston*, 151.

60. A contract dated May 1833, now in the Peabody and Essex Institute in Salem, records the agreement between Loamme Coburn and William Roberts, stonemasons, and the proprietors of St. Peter's Church, in which they agree to build "according to the plan or draft of the same, prepared & drawn by Mr. Rogers . . . of Boston"; Bryant F. Tolles Jr., *Architecture in Salem* (Salem, Mass.: Essex Institute, 1983), 113–14.

61. "Director's Records," Suffolk Bank, Baker Library, Harvard Business School, Cambridge, Mass.; *The American Magazine of Useful Knowledge*, August 1, 1836, 501.

62. This illustration broadens the proportions of the front as compared to the photo reproduced in Hamlin, *Greek Revival*, pl. 26, perhaps improving them a bit.

63. National Archives, Records of the U.S. Senate, Commission of Claims, RG46-Sen-23A-C1. U.S. Congressional Serial Set online. In some entries in the journals of the House and Senate, Rogers and Bond are joined in seeking payment by Calvin Pollard, Lafever and Gallier, and Seth Greer.

2. New York and Boston, 1834–1841

1. A readable account of the man and his hotel is Justin Kaplan, *When the Astors Owned New York* (New York: Viking, 2006), ch. 1; a more thorough and recent discussion set within the history of the type is Molly W. Berger, *Hotel Dreams: Luxury, Technology, and Urban Ambition in America, 1829–1929* (Baltimore: Johns Hopkins University Press, 2011), chs. 1–3.

2. *New York Commercial Advertiser*, July 7, 1834.

3. Between 1834 and 1841 Rogers moved his offices from Broadway to Amity Street to 13th Street to the Merchants' Exchange; Dennis Steadman Francis, *Architects in Practice in New York City, 1840–1900* (New York: Committee for the Preservation of Architectural Records, 1979), 65.

4. *Charleston Courier*, January 28, 1831. The New-York Historical Society holds a collection of Pollard's architectural drawings as well as his memorandum books for 1841 and 1842. An inventory of the drawings is available online.

5. Amelia Peck, ed., *Alexander Jackson Davis* (New York: Rizzoli, 1992), pl. 21.

6. Rhodri Windsor Liscombe, "T. U. Walter's Gift of Drawings to the Institute of British Architects," *Journal of the Society of Architectural Historians* 39 (December 1980); 308.

7. *Hampden Whig* (Springfield, Mass.), October 17, 1832.

8. *Specifications and Description of the Work and Materials to Be Contracted for in Building, According to Plans Exhibited a New Hotel in Broadway, to Extend from Vesey*

Street to Barclay Street for J. J. Astor, f. 4, box 9, John Jacob Astor Papers, Baker Library, Harvard Business School, Cambridge, Mass. A detailed study of the history of specifications in this country is yet to be written. A brief introduction to the subject by Roger R. Reed appears in his facsimile edition of *Specifications of Masons' Work* and *Specifications for Carpenters' Work* for the Jarvis Williams house by Ware and Van Brunt in Boston in 1869 (Champaign, Ill.: Published by the Small Homes Council-Building Research Council of the University of Illinois, 1989). The earliest examples he cites date from the 1840s.

9. *New York Commercial Advertiser,* July 7, 1834.

10. Montgomery Schuyler, "The Old 'Greek Revival'—Part IV," *American Architect* 99 (May 3, 1911): 161–68.

11. Margot Gayle and Carol Gayle, *Cast-Iron Architecture in America: The Significance of James Bogardus* (New York: W. W. Norton, 1998), 117–20.

12. "Visit to the Astor Hotel, in New York," *Parley's Magazine,* January 1, 1836, 4.

13. "Ollapodiana," *New Yorker,* June 25, 1836, 1.

14. Kaplan, *When the Astors Owned New York,* ch. 1.

15. Berger, *Hotel Dreams,* 63.

16. Kaplan, *When the Astors Owned New York,* ch. 1.

17. A project drawing exists for the facade of the Astor Library signed by A. J. Davis and dated 1843; Peck, *Alexander Jackson Davis,* 53–54.

18. As quoted in the *Albany Evening Journal,* November 23, 1841.

19. Copied in the *Jamestown Journal,* May 4, 1836.

20. *New York Spectator,* October 18, 1838. Basham later received $30 "for model of truss," presumably for the exchange building.

21. *The Daily Picayune,* September 30, 1840.

22. Stephen Jerome, "Richard Bond," *A Biographical Dictionary of Architects in Maine* (Augusta: Maine Historic Preservation Commission, 1988); and James F. O'Gorman and Earle G. Shettleworth Jr., *The Maine Perspective: Architectural Drawings, 1800–1980* (Portland, Maine: Portland Museum of Art, 2006), 71–72 and pl. 6.

23. The Charleston Hotel in South Carolina has been attributed to Rogers, in association with Charles F. Reichardt of New York, according to Talbot Hamlin, *Greek Revival Architecture in America* (London: Oxford University Press, 1944), 199n18 and pl. 27. Designed in 1837, built by (Jacob?) Small (Jr.?) of Baltimore, and opened in 1839, the building burned to the ground and was rebuilt as modified by Reichardt. It reopened in October 1839 and fell to the wreckers in 1960. The parti of the front facade echoes somewhat that of the New York Exchange, but there is no mention of the building in Rogers's diary, which does not survive for 1837. The building appears without comment as the work of Reichardt alone in W. Barksdale Maynard, *Architecture in the United States, 1800–1850* (New Haven: Yale University Press, 2002), 192.

24. Contemporary descriptions and views include those in *Gleason's Pictorial Drawing-Room Companion,* December 11, 1852, 369, and many other sources.

25. Solomon Willard, *Plans and Sections of the Obelisk on Bunker's Hill* (Boston: Chas. Cook's Lith., 1843), 25 and pl. 14. This description contradicts such secondary accounts as that given in the *New York Tribune,* November 17, 1841, which says the stones were hauled by railroad.

26. *Philadelphia Public Ledger,* September 3, 1840. See also "Pillars for the New York Exchange," *Philadelphia North American,* August 19, 1839.

27. Montgomery Schuyler, "Federal Buildings," *Art and Progress* 1 (March 1910): 115–18.

28. William Wilder Wheilden, *Memoir of Solomon Willard* ([Boston], Monument Association, 1865), 235.

29. "New-York Daguerreotyped," *Putnam's Monthly* 1 (February 1853): 1–17; this is the first of three articles on New York architecture published in the magazine. It should be noted that all the illustrations were engraved and not necessarily derived from daguerreotypes.

30. Wheilden, *Memoir of Solomon Willard*, 235.

31. Hamlin, *Greek Revival Architecture in America*, 151–53.

32. The book contains no text beyond minimum identification. The other American buildings are the U.S. Capitol (by many architects), the U.S. Custom House in New York (by Town and Davis), and the St. Charles Theatre in New Orleans (by Antonio Mondelli). The *Bilder-Atlas* is hard to find in print, but a digitized version is available online. The New York Merchants' Exchange appears in plate 405, "Public Buildings in the Neo-Classical Style," of S. G. Heck, *The Complete Encyclopedia of Illustration*, trans. Spencer F. Baird (New York: Park Lane, 1979).

33. *Washington Post*, November 4, 1888.

34. Abbott Lowell Cummings, "The Ohio State Capitol Competition," pt. 1, *Journal of the Society of Architectural Historians* 12 (May 1953): 15–18; pt. 2, *Journal of the Society of Architectural Historians* 14 (March 1954): 28.

35. Cole to William A. Adams, May 26 and October 31, 1838, Cole Correspondence, New York State Library, Albany.

36. "J. S." might have been James Savage, a builder who worked on the New York Merchants' Exchange and the Bunker Hill Monument. He appears often in the diary of these years, although there is no indication that he drafted or worked on this church. At the end of Rogers's diary for 1838 is a series of such pew sketches by Savage recording the dimensions of those in several unnamed churches.

37. S. A. Warner, "Description of the Architecture of the Middle Reformed Dutch Church on Lafayette Place," in *A Discourse Delivered in the North Reformed Dutch Church, in the City of New York, on the Last Sabbath in August,* ed. Thomas Dewitt (New York: By request of the Consistory, 1856), 88–91.

38. *New York Evening Star*, as reported in the *Alabama Intelligencer and States Rights Expositer*, August 15, 1835; and *New York Commercial Advertiser*, September 15, 1836.

39. On November 27, 1838, Rogers "Made a plan of City Bank in evening," and two months later he made another for its Wall Street lot. He also planned some work at the Bank of New York in February 1839, for which he was paid $75 in April. Apparently nothing came of either project, unless they were built without his supervision. The Farmer's Bank of 1844–45 in Norfolk, Va., has been attributed to Rogers as well. It is another echo of his Bank of America.

40. *Connecticut Herald*, January 2, 1838; *Connecticut Courant*, January 9, 1839; *New York Commercial Advertiser*, January 14, 1839.

41. A copy of the letter (not in Rogers's hand) is in the John B. Jervis Papers at the Jervis Public Library in Rome, N.Y. Other than Rogers's letters preserved at the National Archives, this is the only example of his correspondence uncovered to date.

42. *Biographical Sketches of Hezekiah Jarvis, Noah Jarvis, George A. Jarvis and William Jarvis from Encyclopaedia of Contemporary Biography of New York* (New York: Atlantic Publishing and Engraving Co., 1887), 5:7.

43. In his entry on Rogers, Denys Peter Myers listed the Benjamin L. Swan house in New York as his work, but I can identify no such mention in the diary; Adolf K. Placzek, ed., *Macmillan Encyclopedia of Architects* (New York: Free Press, 1982), 3:599–602.

44. Mrs. D. T. Davis, "The Daguerreotype in America," *McClure's* 8 (November 1896): 8. The image is now in the National Museum of American History (acc. no. 72.72.B155), where it is dated ca. 1840. The stony crenellated tower is clearly visible.

45. Apparently no churches were erected in Troy between 1839 and 1844; Peter D. Shaver, New York preservationist, letter to Denys Peter Myers, May 23, 1994. Only the First Baptist Church on Third Street, built in 1846, seems to be a possible work by Rogers.

46. *Southern Patriot*, November 16, 1839. See also *National Gazette*, October 1, 1839; and *Boston Courier*, October 7, 1839. For Wallack, see *A Sketch of the Life of James William Wallack (Senior)* (New York: T. H. Morrell, 1865).

47. *New York Commercial Advertiser*, October 12, 1840.

48. A published report, undated but from this period, relates an example of the mistreatment of slaves; while working in the South "superintending the building of a rice machine," Rogers was ordered by a plantation owner to take a hammer and knock out the tooth of an enslaved man who complained of a toothache; see Theodore Dwight Weld, *American Slavery as It Is: Testimony of a Thousand Witnesses* (New York: American Anti-Slavery Society, 1839), 13; and "The Condition of Slaves," *Emancipator* 3 (November 4, 1839): 200. Rogers was working in Virginia, a state that produced little rice, if any. True or not, and given the man we know from the diary, it is impossible to think that Rogers carried out such an order; he must have known of the mistreatment of slaves, if not specifically Butler's, but worked for the slaveholder as he worked for other Southern clients.

49. Mary N. Woods, *From Craft to Profession* (Berkeley: University of California Press, 1999), 95.

50. *Richmond Whig*, June 5, July 17, and December 22, 1840.

51. "More Light!—Give Us Light!!" *Richmond Whig*, July 5, 1841; and "Greenough's Chemical Oil," *Alexandria Gazette*, July 7, 1841.

52. In an entry for January 15, 1842, Rogers noted that he had written a letter "to Mr. Boyden about drawing [a] perspective for [the] Exchange Hotel." One naturally first thinks of his Worcester contemporary Elbridge Boyden, but that architect is not known to have drawn any perspectives for his own buildings.

53. "The Opening Dinner," *Richmond Whig*, July 5, 1841.

54. Theodore J. Crackel, *The Illustrated History of West Point* (New York: Harry N. Abrams, 1991), 128–35; and Theodore J. Crackel, *West Point, A Bicentennial History* (Lawrence: University of Kansas Press, 2002), 110–15. Crackel's discussions omit much of the history of Rogers's work for the military and are not always accurate with dates. See also Aloysius A. Norton, *A History of the United States Military Academy Library* (Wayne, N.J.: Avery Publishing, 1986), 16–18.

55. For Robert Mills's intervention in the library design, see Rhodi Windsor Liscombe, *Altogether American: Robert Mills, Architect and Engineer* (New York: Oxford University Press, 1994), 222–23.

56. Some of these details are taken from "Heart & Soul of the U.S. Military Academy, 1822–1900," a paper on the history of the academy's library that was sent to the author by Alan Aimone, the reference librarian. Until I contacted him, he had never

heard of Isaiah Rogers and knows of no documents at the academy related to the architect's work there. The online image library ARTstor has a Wayne Andrews photograph of the library (minus its domes) that assigns the building to Rogers. He may have confused the library with Rogers's castellated project for the barracks, although the differences are marked.

57. Roger Reed, *Building Victorian Boston: The Architecture of Gridley J. F. Bryant* (Amherst: University of Massachusetts Press, 2007), 29.

58. See Richard G. Carrott, *The Egyptian Revival* (Berkeley: University of California Press, 1978).

59. *New York Commercial Advertiser,* October 14, 1839.

60. The specifications also requested one "Egyptian Baisltor pedestal with sunk panels." I have yet to learn to what that refers.

61. *Newport Mercury,* February 4, 1854.

62. See James Hildreth, *Notes of the Buckingham Lectures Embracing Sketches of the Geography, Antiquities, and Present Condition of Egypt and Palestine: Compiled from the Oral Discourses of the Hon. J. S. Buckingham* (New York: Leavitt, Lord, & Co., 1838).

63. See George R. Gliddon, *Otia Aegyptiaca: Discourses on Egyptian Archaeology and Hieroglyphical Discoveries* (London: James Madden, 1849).

64. Calvin Pollard diary, January 25–29, 1842, New-York Historical Society; William J. Conklin and Jeffery Simpson, *Brooklyn's City Hall* (New York: Dept. of General Services, 1983).

3. Boston and New York, 1841–1848

1. Cole to William A. Adams, May 26, 1838, Thomas Cole Papers, New York State Library, Albany. In another letter, dated October 31, 1838, in reference to the competition for the Ohio statehouse, Cole wrote that he was "inclined to think that my nephew executed the . . . design for Mr Rogers of N York." A later newspaper notice reported that Chamberlain, "architect of the New York Exchange," fell from the cornice and was considerably injured; *Baltimore Sun,* October 22, 1840, 2. The incident, which Rogers reported as Chamberlain's "narrow escape of losing his life . . . did not prove very bad," is noted in the diary on October 21, 1840. Chamberlain, although probably not an architect but rather an expert on masonry, worked closely with Rogers during these years.

2. Mary Sayre Haverstock et al., *Artists in Ohio, 1787–1900* (Kent, Ohio: Kent State University Press, 2000); Elwood Parry, *The Art of Thomas Cole* (Newark: University of Delaware Press, 1988), 199, 207–10.

3. See Roger G. Reed, "Theodore Voelckers," *The Architects of Winchester, Massachusetts* (Winchester Historical Society, 1996).

4. For more on the Washburn brothers, see Rochelle S. Elstein, "William Washburn and the Egyptian Revival in Boston," *Old-Time New England* 70 (1980): 63–81.

5. According to Elstein, members of the Washburn family were not good with money; three went bankrupt (Elstein, "William Washburn," 63–81).

6. William W. Wheildon, *Memoir of Solomon Willard* (Boston: Monument Assoc., 1865), 235.

7. Blanche M. G. Linden, *Silent City on a Hill* (Amherst: University of Massachusetts Press, 2007), 190, fig. 9.32.

8. A brief notice of the event appeared in the *Baltimore Sun,* August 8, 1840.

9. *Baltimore Sun,* January 8, 1841.

10. Although no work in Baltimore has yet come to light, Rogers was known in the city in the 1840s. According to a notice in *The Anglo-American, a Journal of Literature, News, Politics* for November 21, 1846, 116, houses there "have been erected with much taste, the proprietors have been apparently reckless of expense both in building and in fitting them up . . . and the name of Isaiah Rogers of Boston is in most mouths as connected with architecture."

11. "The New Exchange," *Christian Watchman*, August 6, 1841.

12. "Opening of the New Exchange Reading Room," *Boston Courier*, May 1, 1843.

13. See *King's Handbook of Boston* (Cambridge, Mass.: Moses King, 1885) for a succinct description of the building.

14. Arthur Gilman, "Architecture in the United States," *North American Review* 58 (April 1844): 448–50.

15. "Gilman's Second Lecture on Architecture," *Daily Evening Transcript*, October 31, 1844.

16. Who invented what remains undecided. A rough sketch on a diary page from August 1840 shows one of the derricks Young used to raise the columns at the Boston customhouse. Rogers is listed among those, including Young, endorsing the "Improved, patented Boom Derrick" of James S. Savage in the Boston *Daily Atlas*, June 8, 1841.

17. Douglass Shand-Tucci, *Built in Boston* (Amherst: University of Massachusetts Press, 2000), 16.

18. *Trumpet and Universalist Magazine*, August 6, 1842.

19. In fact, the view published in (John) *Hartshorn's Commercial Tables* (Boston, 1852) does show the cupola, but it is clearly based on Voelckers's perspective.

20. R. I. Ridgely [David Pulsifer], *Sights in Boston and Suburbs; or, Guide to the Stranger* (Boston: John P. Jewett & Co., 1856), 17. The book is illustrated by four artists named on the title page, one of whom is Hammatt Billings. Although this view is not credited, Billings did work on construction drawings for the building while on loan to Rogers by Young.

21. *King's Handbook of Boston*, 318–20.

22. See Winston Weisman, "Philadelphia Functionalism and Sullivan," *Journal of the Society of Architectural Historians* 20 (March 1861): 3–19.

23. Years ago Denys Peter Myers published an unsigned drawing of the facade of a decidedly Rogersian hotel-like building dated August 6, 1841, in Boston but could find no record of a Rogers hotel in the city for that period. The drawing may have been just a drafting exercise by someone in the office. "An Unidentified American Hotel, Boston, 1841," *Journal of the Society of Architectural Historians* 23 (December 1964): 210.

24. Drawings and documents are at Historic New England, Boston.

25. For views of bridges not by Rogers that were erected for later triennial fairs, see Christopher P. Monkhouse, *Faneuil Hall Market: An Account of its Many Likenesses* (Boston: Bostonian Society), 1968.

26. *Niles' National Register*, October 9, 1841; also, the Amherst (New Hampshire) *Farmer's Cabinet*, October 1, 1841.

27. Rogers would presumably be delighted to see Bernard Tschumi and Hugh Button's 2008–10 steel footbridge at La Roche sur Yon in western France, a long-span latticework cylinder.

28. Tom F. Peters, *Building the Nineteenth Century* (Cambridge: MIT Press, 1996), 93. See also John Weale, *Theory, Practice, and Architecture of Bridges,* 4 vols. (London: John Weale, 1839–43).

29. *Boston Evening Transcript,* September 3, 1844.

30. This information comes from a letter dated March 19, 1981, and written by Victor C. Darnell, an M.I.T.-trained civil engineer and historian, to the Boston Athenaeum, where it is preserved. Darnell inquired about a lattice bridge erected over Oliver Street during the demolition of Fort Hill in 1869 that is pictured in fig. 104 of Walter Muir Whitehill's *Boston: A Topographical History,* 2nd ed. (Cambridge: Harvard University Press, 1968). The Athenaeum could provide no specific information, but that bridge was probably an example of Thomas Moseley's "Wrought Iron Lattice Girder Bridge," patented in 1857. Moseley reappears in ch. 4, n22.

31. Nor does Benjamin F. Stevens, "The Tremont House: the Exit of an Old Landmark," *Bostonian* 1 (January 1895).

32. S[olomon]. Willard, *Plans and Sections of the Obelisk on Bunker's Hill* (Boston: Charles Cook's Lith., 1843); Wheildon, *Memoir,* chaps. 9–29; George Washington Warren, *The History of the Bunker Hill Monument Association* (Boston: James R. Osgood and Co., 1877).

33. Willard, *Plans and Sections,* 23 n. The steam elevator lasted just two years.

34. After its dedication, Rogers worked on a design for the fence around the monument.

35. Calvin Pollard diary, March 16–18, 1842, and end note for the year ("Plans for a Grecian or Gothic orphan asylum at Richmond VA."), New-York Historical Society.

36. Franklin Fire Insurance Company (Philadelphia), policy 6807, June 26, 1846, copy in the collection of Denys Peter Myers, now at Historic New England, Boston.

37. The history of this house is told in great detail by Laura G. Carr, "Creating the Kent-Valentine House: A History of Change, 1845–1995" (master's thesis, Virginia Commonwealth University, 1995).

38. Earle G. Shettleworth Jr., comp., "An Index to Boston Building Contracts Recorded in the Suffolk County Registry of Deeds, 1840–1844" (1996), Historic New England, Boston.

39. Robert Mills designed two versions of a permanent shelter for the statue; neither was executed. See Rhodi Windsor Liscombe, *Altogether American: Robert Mills, Architect and Engineer, 1781–1855* (New York: Oxford University Press, 1994), 229–30.

40. Nathalia Wright, *Letters of Horatio Greenough* (Madison: University of Wisconsin Press, 1972), 332–42.

41. Nathalia Wright, *Horatio Greenough: The First American Sculptor* (Philadelphia: University of Pennsylvania Press, 1963), 150.

42. *Quincy Aurora,* February 2 and April 8, 1844; *Quincy Patriot,* February 10, April 20, and May 11, 1844.

43. Harvard College Papers, 2nd ser., vol. 13, 228 and 189; from an unpublished paper by Harold Kirker, copy the collection of Denys Peter Myers.

44. Examination of the drawings also suggests that they are the work of two different draftsmen, or of a draftsman in the process of development, perhaps the "James" mentioned often the diary during these years. They are approximately 19½ x 27½ inches on Whatman paper, drawn in graphite, ink, and various washes; the letterforms improve from one to the other, and only the later drawings are back-lined (albeit inconsistently). Rogers signed the first set, but the second is unsigned and undated.

45. Filed with Rogers's drawings for the president's house in the Harvard Archives are two drawings for trusses identified by a later hand as for that building. Those trusses

were intended for a longer span, however, and may have been the ones drawn by Rogers for Dana Hall on May 30, 1844.

46. F. O. Vaille and H. A. Clark, *The Harvard Book* (Cambridge: Welch, Bigelow, and Co., 1875), 1:305–8, with illus.

47. Bainbridge Bunting and Margaret Henderson Floyd, *Harvard: An Architectural History* (Cambridge: Harvard University Press, 1985), 54–55.

48. *Reminiscences of the Boston Female Asylum* (Boston: Eastburn's Press, 1844), 62–68.

49. Morrill Wyman, *A Practical Treatise on Ventilation* (Boston: James Munroe & Co., 1846).

50. *Boston Courier,* October 23, 1845. See also *Boston Evening Transcript,* August 22, 1846.

51. "Improvements in Boston," Amherst, New Hampshire, *Farmer's Cabinet,* October 9, 1845, 2. The names of Dexter, Bryant, Billings, Upjohn, and Bond are cited, but not those of Young or Rogers.

52. *The American Architect and Building News,* February 14, 1880, 7. For a view of the original building, see William Robinson, *A Certain Slant of Light* (Boston: New York Graphic Society, 1980).

53. Support for this paragraph comes from the diary as well as the daily newspapers in Boston, New York, and elsewhere.

54. *Commercial Advertiser,* September 11, 1845.

55. Th title remains unidentified, but one possibility is George Maliphant, *Designs for Sepulchral Monuments* (London: J. Taylor, 1835), a portfolio that can be found in the collection of Richard Bond now at the Amherst College library. Many of the designs took the form of sarcophagi.

56. Linden, *Silent City on a Hill,* 203–4.

57. Nathan Hammett Gould (1815–1895), born to Isaac Gould and Sarah Hammett, died in San Antonio at the house of his son Stephen. Emily Jane's fate is unknown.

58. *Daily Evening Transcript,* September 14, 1846, 2; October 3, 1846. John H. Woodruff, "America's Oldest Living Theatre: The Howard Athenaeum," *Theatre Annual* 8 (1950): 71–81; Roger Stoddard, "The Architecture and Technology of Boston Theatres, 1794–1854" (PhD diss., Yale University, 1971), 182–98.

59. *Daily Evening Transcript,* June 29, 1846.

60. Shettleworth, *Boston Building Contracts,* app. 1.

61. See also the supplement to the *New York Herald,* June 16, 1846 (available through fultonhistory.com).

62. Pamela Scott, "Robert Mills's Washington National Monument" (master's thesis, University of Delaware, 1985).

63. 28th Congress, 1st sess., Rep. No. 434, April 12, 1844.

64. Jacob Landy, "The Washington Monument Project in New York," *Journal of the Society of Architectural Historians* 28 (December 1969): 291–97; and Jacob Landy, *The Architecture of Minard Lafever* (New York: Columbia University Press, 1970), 140–46. On the last page of the Book 14 diary, opposite the entry for August 12, 1845, Rogers sketched a series of obelisks with shafts ranging from 19 to 26 feet between bases and caps. The surrounding text gives no indication what these were intended for, although the size suggests funereal monuments.

65. For Mills's proposal, see Liscomb, *Altogether American,* 241–46.

66. Background for my reading of Rogers's diary here comes from the chapter on the Smithsonian in the manuscript of the third volume of the late William H. Pierson Jr.'s *American Architects and Their Buildings* (hopefully soon to be published). I thank Michael J. Lewis for his kind permission to read this thorough history of the building's design.

67. Kenneth Hafertepe, *America's Castle* (Washington, D.C.: Smithsonian Institute, 1984), 50, fig. 18; 54–56.

68. *Portland Tribune and Bulletin,* January 12, 1847; *New York Evangelist,* January 14, 1847, 7.

69. Hafertepe, *America's Castle,* 58.

70. Smithsonian Institution Board of Regents, Minutes, 20 February 1847, available at siarchives.si.edu.

71. Denys Peter Myers, "Isaiah Rogers," *A Biographical Dictionary of Architects in Maine* (Augusta: Maine Historic Preservation Committee, 1986), n.p. A sketch plan of the original Grecian Revival Farrar house appears in a diary entry dated August 17, 1846.

72. "City Hall, Roxbury," *Boston Daily Atlas,* June 22, 1846.

73. None appears in Shettleworth, *Boston Building Contracts.* The story told here is based on the diary, augmented by contemporary newspaper accounts.

74. "Lawrence Academy, Groton," *Boston Recorder,* December 22, 1848.

75. "Death of Mr. Lawrence," *Boston Evening Transcript,* October 16, 1848.

76. A sketch plan of entrance stairs in the diary account dated August 25, 1846, could relate to the remodeling of Lawrence's front porch.

77. *American Architect and Building News* 42 (November 18, 1893): 82.

78. *Boston Evening Transcript,* November 17, 1847.

79. Montgomery Schuyler, "The Old Greek Revival—Part IV," *American Architect* 99 (May 3, 1911): 161–68.

80. *The Classical Language of Architecture* (London: Methuen & Co., 1964).

81. Edwin G. Burrows and Mike Wallace, *Gotham: A History of New York City to 1898* (New York: Oxford University Press), 762.

82. Cynthia Hagar Krussel and Berry Magoun Bates, *Marshfield, a Town of Villages, 1640–1990* (Marshfield: Historical Research Assoc., 1990), 165.

4. Cincinnati, 1848–1852

1. "To the Queen of the West, / In her garlands dressed, / On the banks of the Beautiful River." Although Rogers enjoyed an occasional glass of wine, he never mentions the city's viniculture.

2. *Milwaukee Sentinel,* January 14, 1848. See Blanche M. G. Linden, "Inns to Hotels in Cincinnati," *Cincinnati Historical Society Bulletin* 39 (Summer 1981): 139–50.

3. Walter E. Langsam and Alice Weston, *Biographical Dictionary of Cincinnati Architects, 1788–1940* (Cincinnati: Cincinnati Architectural Foundation, 2008); and Glenn Patton, "James Keys Wilson (1828–1894)," *Journal of the Society of Architectural Historians* 26 (December 1967): 115–18.

4. For an overview of Rogers's local work in Cincinnati, see Denys Peter Myers, "Isaiah Rogers in Cincinnati," *Bulletin of the Historical and Philosophical Society of Ohio* 9 (April 1951): 121–32. It should be recognized, however, that this early work has been corrected in several ways.

5. *Cincinnati Chronicle and Atlas,* January 22, 1850.

6. Quoted in the *Trenton State Gazette,* May 7, 1850.

7. *New Orleans Picayune,* May 3, 1850.

8. *Cincinnati Gazette,* January 23, 1850; *Chronicle,* January 22, 1850.

9. Linden, "Inns to Hotels," 149.

10. See Ann Deborah Michael, "The Origins of the Jewish Community of Cincinnati, 1817–1860," *Cincinnati Historical Society Bulletin* 30 (Fall–Winter 1972): 154–82. The article includes a document signed by Moses Heidelbach, a partner of Jacob Seasongood who is mentioned by Rogers, but it is difficult to identify the congregation to which they belonged.

11. *Daily Ohio Statesman,* April 1, 1851.

12. Rogers's use of hoisting shears may hark back to his family boatbuilding at Marshfield. They were often used for masting and demasting ships as well as hoisting other heavy loads, according to *Webster's Third New International Dictionary.*

13. For another view of the facade, see Charles Cist, *Sketches and Statistics of Cincinnati in 1851* (Cincinnati: W. H. Moore & Co., 1851).

14. "The Suburbs of Cincinnati V: Clifton," *Cincinnati Daily Gazette,* June 19, 1868; Sidney D. Maxwell, *The Suburbs of Cincinnati* (Cincinnati: George E. Stevens & Co., 1870), 27–52; Alice Weston and Walter E. Langsam, *Great Houses of the Queen City* (Cincinnati: Cincinnati Historical Society, 1997).

15. *Daily Ohio Statesman,* September 22, 1852. The daguerreotype is unlocated.

16. *Laws of the State of New-York Passed at the Seventy-First Session of the Legislature* (Albany: E. Croswell, 1848), ch. 118.

17. Clay Lancaster, *Antebellum Architecture of Kentucky* (Lexington: University of Kentucky Press, 1991), 291.

18. *Daily Ohio Statesman,* February 9, 1850.

19. Pre–Civil War general contracting would be a rarity; see Sara E. Wermiel, "The Rise of the General Contractor in 19th-Century America," *FMI Quarterly* 3 (2008): 121–29.

20. One of the 40 pocket books ("the diary") at the Avery Library is a small notebook with, in some cases, slighted altered excerpts from other entries between January 30, 1850, to November 11, 1851, related to Rogers's schedule and supervision of the courthouse and adjacent jail. He must have prepared them as a consequence of this November interruption of work, perhaps for handy reference should questions arise about the timing and focus of his work. The same notebook contains a few measured sketches and a rough section of a Gothic church.

21. "Supreme Court of Ohio in Banc: March Term, 1852," *Western Law Journal* (June 1852): 385.

22. *New Albany (Indiana) Daily Ledger,* August 29 and December 21, 1854.

23. "Supposed Defalcation of Jesse Timanus," *Ohio State Journal,* January 3, 1855.

24. *Report of the Committee (Appointed by the County Commissioners) to Investigate the Books of the New Court House Building, under the Superintendence of Jesse Timanus* (Cincinnati: Moore, Wilstach, Keys & Co., 1855), 20.

25. Myers, "Isaiah Rogers in Cincinnati," 126–28.

26. *Cincinnati Daily Gazette,* June 14, 1875.

27. Slatter thanks the fire department for saving his building; *Daily Picayune,* February 23, 1851.

28. Gary A. Van Zante, *New Orleans, 1867* (London: Merrell, 2008), 171.

29. *Times-Picayune,* January 9, 1852.

30. Robb is buried at Spring Grove Cemetery in Cincinnati. His obituary (*New York Times,* August 2, 1881) tells us that his brother, William H. Robb, occupied a seat among the Hamilton County commissioners during the tenure of Jesse Timanus. Further unpublished information from the research of Greg Kissel conveyed by Betty Ann Smiddy. In 1853–55 Robb had a house erected in New Orleans that was begun by Morris Smith, a Philadelphia architect, and revised by Gallier and Turpin.

31. Arthur Scully, *James Dakin, Architect* (Baton Rouge: Louisiana State University Press, 1973), 177–79; Van Zante, *New Orleans,* 92–100.

32. Daniel Bluestone, "Civic and Aesthetic Reserve: Ammi Burnham Young's 1850s Federal Customhouse Designs," *Winterthur Portfolio* 25, nos. 2/3 (Summer–Autumn 1990): 131–56.

33. Mary Raddant Tomlan and Michael A. Tomlan, *Richmond, Indiana* (Ithaca: Cornell University Press, 2003), 41. Robert Morrison bought it in 1853 for $8,000.

34. Weston and Langsam, *Great Houses.* For more detail, see the registration form for the National Register of Historic Places prepared by Walter E. Langsam and Margo Warminski (contact nr_reference@nps.gov).

35. Maxwell, *Suburbs of Cincinnati,* 28, 37–38; D. J. Kenny, *Illustrated Cincinnati* (Cincinnati: George E. Stevens & Co., 1875), 306–12.

36. Maxwell, *Suburbs of Cincinnati,* 33. Brother William's mansard still stands in the Clifton area; it is listed on the National Register of Historic Places.

37. Maxwell, *Suburbs of Cincinnati,* 35.

38. *New York Times,* October 1, 1860.

5. Louisville and Cincinnati, 1852–1861

1. Elizabeth Fitzpatrick Jones, "Henry Whitestone: Nineteenth-Century Louisville Architect" (master's thesis, University of Louisville, 1974); Elizabeth Fitzpatrick Jones, "Hotel Design in the Work of Isaiah Rogers and Henry Whitestone," *Victorian Resorts and Hotels* (Philadelphia: Victorian Society in America, 1982), 33–37. Jones is working on a definitive study of Whitestone's career.

2. John G. Frank, "Adolphus Heiman: Architect and Soldier," *Tennessee Historical Quarterly* 5 (March 1946): 35–37.

3. This design preceded the destruction of Heiman's bridge by Confederate troops in 1862 but followed the collapse of the bridge floor in 1855. Rogers presumably returned to Nashville in 1859 to work on the Maxwell House, but no diary exists for that year.

4. Sara Sprott Morrow, "Adolphus Heiman's Legacy to Nashville," *Tennessee Historical Quarterly* 33 (Spring 1974): 5.

5. Apparently no original plan survives. This general description is based on the plot plan given in the 1896 Sanborn map of Frankfort.

6. Samuel L. Thomas, *The Architectural History of Louisville, 1778–1890* (Louisville: Filson Historical Society, 2009), 52–53, 96.

7. Ibid., 119. The same study notes that Rogers concurrently worked on the domestic duplex inhabited by the brothers Shreve (60).

8. Drawings for the Louisville Hotel are in Roll 490 of the Records of D. X. Murphy & Bros., Architects, Filson Historical Society, Louisville, Ky.

9. James F. O'Gorman, *Accomplished in All Departments of Art: Hammatt Billings of Boston, 1818–1874* (Amherst: University of Massachusetts Press, 1998), ch. 9.

10. See the ads at the end of D. J. Kenny, *Illustrated Cincinnati* (Cincinnati: George E. Stevens & Co., 1875).

11. Although the design of the grounds does not seem particularly Downingesque, there is in the house a copy of A. J. Downing's *Rural Essays* (New York: G. P. Putnam, 1853) that may date back to the original owner.

12. The building is illustrated in Harold M. Mayer and Richard C. Wade, *Chicago: Growth of a Metropolis* (Chicago: University of Chicago Press, 1969).

13. Book 30 of the diary, covering the last half of 1852, contains a sketch of what appears to be a funereal monument: a column surmounted by a winged head or orb on a pedestal, the whole rising some 8 feet. It is not identified, but Rogers admired "some very fine monuments" in the Frankfort cemetery in September 1852, and this may be one of those. It is unlike his other known funereal work. (He also visited Green-Wood Cemetery in Brooklyn in March 1853.)

14. The grave is on Lot 62, Section 57.

15. The grave is on Lot 58, Section 57,

16. James S. Buck, *Under the Charter,* Vol. 4: *From 1854 to 1862* (Milwaukee: Swain & Tate, 1886), 45–46.

17. Buck, *Under the Charter,* 116, 45. Rogers described his design for Ludington as two story, whereas those on East Water rose to four, "with an arched wall from the basement to attic through the center." *Wisconsin Free Democrat,* December 12, 1855.

18. Thomas, *Architectural History of Louisville,* 69. This could be the work of Rogers or Whitestone. Other drawings can be found in Rolls 512–514, 538, and Folder 588 of the Records of D. X. Murphy & Bros., Architects, Filson Historical Society, Louisville, Ky.

19. Whitestone was on his own by 1857. The house may have been discussed earlier; Rogers mentions a Newcomb house in his diary. See Jones, "Henry Whitestone," 225–26.

20. Thomas, *Architectural History of Louisville,* 7.

21. See D. J. Kenny, *Illustrated Cincinnati* (Cincinnati: George E. Stevens & Co., 1875), 120–21.

22. Rogers was not the only one in Cincinnati designing tubular iron arched bridges in the 1850s. Charles Cist's *Sketches and Statistics of Cincinnati in 1859* contains a full-page ad for "Moseley's Tubular Wrought Iron Arch Bridge and Roof," with a wood engraving of a railroad bridge crossing a river occupied by a steamboat, rather like the drawing Rogers used in his patent of three years earlier. Thomas W. H. Moseley was an engineer, bridge builder, and designer in Cincinnati from ca. 1858 until he moved to Boston. Rogers makes no mention of him in the diary.

23. Drawings for the W. B. Reynolds building are in Roll 531 of the Records of D. X. Murphy & Bros., Architects, Filson Historical Society, Louisville, Ky.

24. Diary entries in May 1855 make it clear that Rogers drafted plans for remodeling Thomas Smith Kennedy's "Fairview," now gone. Thomas, *Architectural History of Louisville,* 99.

25. Ibid., 77–78.

26. Entry for John R. Hamilton in Walter E. Langsam and Alice Weston, "Biographical Dictionary of Cincinnati Architects, 1788–1940," Architectural Foundation of Cincinnati, http://oldsite.architecturecincy.org.

27. William Blair Scott Jr., e-mail message to the author, ca. 2012.

28. Zachariah F. Smith, *History of Kentucky* (Louisville: Prentice Press, 1892), 890; Thomas, *Architectural History of Louisville,* 65, 67–68.

29. Copy is in the Prints and Photographs Division, Library of Congress. By the mid- to late 1850s Rogers could have found terra-cotta in Cincinnati. The *Williams' Cincinnati Directory* for 1855 lists the Steinauer, Henzler & Co. terra-cotta works. Cist's *Sketches and Statistics of Cincinnati in 1859* carries a full-page ad for the Queen City Terra Cotta Works, supplier of ornamental features for buildings. The terra-cotta work at the George Hatch house could have been ordered locally.

30. William R. Black Jr. to Denys Peter Myers, April 28, 1998; telephone conversation with the author, June 25, 2012. James Renwick used terra-cotta extensively in 1853 on his Tontine Building in New York; in 1852 Richard Upjohn had used terra-cotta keystones at his Trinity Building in New York; Susan M. Tindall, "How to Prepare Project-Specific Terra-Cotta Specifications," *Bulletin of the Association for Preservation Technology* 21 (1989): n. 1.

31. Jones, "Henry Whitestone," 104; Thomas, *Architectural History of Louisville,* 119–20.

32. "Minutes of the Faculty Meeting," November 27, 1857, University of Louisville Medical Department; Clay Lancaster, *Antebellum Architecture of Kentucky* (Lexington: University Press of Kentucky, 1991), 198–99; Jones, "Henry Whitestone," 102–4.

33. It may have been at this time that Willard presented Nathan with a copy of William Wells, *Western Scenery* (Cincinnati: Otto Onken, 1851). Around 2012 a copy of this now rare example of early Cincinnati lithography, inscribed by S. W. Rogers to N. H. Gould, appeared in a book dealer's catalogue.

34. D. Mullett-Smith, *A. B. Mullett: His Relevance to American Architecture* (Washington, D.C.: Mullett-Smith Press, 1990).

35. Walter sent a bill to the commission for Schoenborn's drafting services, so he must have been asked in some official way to study the problem before Rogers arrived on the scene. I thank Jhennifer Amundson, who is writing a monograph on Walter, for this information from Walter's letter books at the Philadelphia Athenaeum.

36. *Annual Report of the State House to the Governor of the State of Ohio for the Year 1863* (Columbus: Richard Nevins, 1864), 27–29. A letter from "Tax-Payer" to the *Daily Ohio Statesman,* June 15, 1859, commended the diligence of Rogers and the acting commissioner "in defeating what appear to be grossly exorbitant charges" by a painter working at the statehouse.

37. According to Denys Peter Myers, I. Rogers, Son & Co. erected a house on Elm St., Cincinnati, for a Capt. Tweed in 1860; Denys Peter Myers, "Isaiah Rogers in Cincinnati," *Bulletin of the Historical and Philosophical Society of Ohio* 9 (April 1951): 128.

38. Arthur Scully, *James Dakin, Architect* (Baton Rouge: Louisiana State University Press, 1973), 105–6; Blythe Semmer, "Gayoso Hotel," *Tennessee Encyclopedia of History and Culture,* 2010, http://tennesseeencyclopedia.net.

39. *Memphis Daily Avalanche,* February 19, 1869. The broadside published ca. 1859 for Rogers's second tubular arch bridge design (see Fig. 82) lists an office for him in Nashville.

40. *Cleveland Plain Dealer,* March 30, 1859; and *Toledo Blade,* June 30, 1859.

41. The *Hinkle, Guild & Co.'s Plans of Buildings* (Cincinnati: Hinkle, Guild & Co., [1862]), fig. 17, illustrates the M. L. Brett residence in Washington, Ind., attributed to J. [or S., in another edition] Rogers & Son. It is close to vernacular, with a center-hall

plan and central gable with Victorian exterior touches. Denys Peter Myers's files show that Brett built his house in 1858 and duplicated it in 1865. Both houses were standing but altered in 1986. Rogers is said to have entered the competition for the original building of the University of Tennessee, Suwannee, announced in August 1860, but I have been unable to confirm that.

42. *Cincinnati Gazette,* December 19, 1859. See also *Cincinnati Daily Inquirer,* June 20, 1861, and *Cincinnati Gazette,* August 7, 1862.

43. Roger G. Reed, *Building Victorian Boston: The Architecture of Gridley J. F. Bryant* (Amherst: University of Massachusetts Press, 2007), 70–75.

44. See Carla Yanni, *The Architecture of Madness* (Minneapolis: University of Minnesota Press, 2007). Yanni does not mention Longview.

45. See *Annual Report of the Board of Directors and Officers of Longview Asylum* (Columbus, Ohio: Richard Nevins, 1861), 8–15, and the next report, of 1862; as well as *Longview Asylum* (1869), at www.davidrumsey.com. See also Sue Ann Painter, *Architecture in Cincinnati* (Athens: Ohio University Press, 2006).

6. Cincinnati and Washington, D.C., 1861–1869

1. For details, see Joseph S. Stern Jr., "The Suspension Bridge: They Said It Couldn't Be Built," *Bulletin of the Cincinnati Historical Society* 23 (October 1965): 211–28.

2. "Improved Cast-Iron Tubular Bridge," *Scientific American* 9 (August 15, 1863): 104. The article reproduces the view of a bridge datable ca. 1859; it mentions a Rogers office in Nashville when he was presumably there working on the Maxwell House.

3. "Pennsylvania Avenue Bridge, Spanning Rock Creek & Potomac Parkway," survey no. DC-21, Historic American Engineering Record, Library of Congress, Washington, D.C., www.loc.gov/pictures. For a photograph of the bridge taken about this time by A. J. Russell, see Susan Danly, "Andrew Joseph Russell's 'Great West Illustrated,'" in *The Railroad in American Art,* ed. Susan Danly and Leo Marx (Cambridge: MIT Press, 1988), 95.

4. A search of Montgomery Meigs's papers revealed nothing.

5. Because of this appointment, Rogers turned down an offer to design and supervise the construction of the new building for Centre College at Danville, Ky; "Building Committee Minutes," 1861–67, Centre College Board of Trustees.

6. Record Group 121, National Archives, Washington, D.C.

7. Original documents for this unhappy interlude in Rogers's career are in the National Archives. These have been well mined by Antoinette J. Lee, *Architects to the Nation* (New York: Oxford University Press, 2000), 66–72 and passim; and Pamela Scott, *Fortress of Finance: The United States Treasury Building* (Washington, D.C.: Treasury Historical Society, 2010), 192–242 and passim.

8. Scott, *Fortress of Finance,* 195.

9. Recall Andrew Eliot Belknap's 1847 letter to the Smithsonian Board of Regents defending Rogers's professionalism.

10. Record Group 121, National Archives, Washington, D.C.

11. *Boston Daily Advertiser,* August 4, 1863, and January 14, 1864. Letters related to this work, dated June and November 1863 and February 1864, are in the National Archives, Washington, D.C. Margaret Henderson Floyd, *The Custom House and Tower:*

Boston, vol. 1, *Architectural History,* Historic Structure Report for the Beal Companies (Cambridge, Mass., 1988), 54, available at https://openlibrary.org.

12. *Portland Daily Press,* September 2, 1864; *New York Times,* September 24, 1864.

13. "Various Reports of the Office of the Supervising Architect," 1862–65, National Archives, Washington, D.C. *Portland Daily Press,* May 4, 1864–March 2, 1866. Rogers also drew plans for the enlargement of Young's customhouse in Bangor, Me. (*Bangor Daily Whig,* November 8, 1865) and seems to have been overseeing completion of Young's prewar customhouse in Dubuque, Iowa, when he left the office.

14. For a succinct outline, see Pamela Scott and Antoinette Lee, *Buildings of the United States: Buildings of the District of Columbia* (New York: Oxford University Press, 1993), 154–58.

15. *Salt Lake Daily Telegraph,* June 10, 1868 (channeling the *New York Gazette*).

16. *New York Times,* April 19, 1863.

17. Among myriad smaller chores, Rogers estimated the cost of rebuilding the White House stables after a fire on February 10, 1864; Herbert R. Collins, "The White House Stable and Garages," *Records of the Columbia Historical Society,* 1966, 376–81.

18. Scott, *Fortress of Finance,* 196.

19. *American Architect and Building News,* March 18, 1876, 91.

20. Lawrence Wodehouse, "Alfred B. Mullett and His French Style Government Buildings," *Journal of the Society of Architectural Historians* 31 (March 1872): 22–37; Suzanne Mullett Smith, ed., *A. B. Mullett Diaries* (Washington, D.C.: Mullett-Smith Press, 1985); and D. Mullett Smith, *A. B. Mullett: His Relevance in American Architecture* (Washington, D.C.: Mullett-Smith Press, 1990). For an unflattering account of Mullett in Washington—to put it mildly—see "Little Mullett's Career," *New York Sun,* October 7, 1876.

21. Montgomery Schuyler, "Federal Buildings," *Art and Progress* 1 (March 1910), 115–18.

22. *Cincinnati Daily Gazette,* January 28, 1867.

23. *Newport Mercury,* March 31, 1866.

24. There is an Odd Fellows' Hall in Lexington, erected in 1870; whether it was designed by Rogers is still to be determined.

25. Joseph E. Holliday, "Notes on Samuel N. Pike and His Opera Houses," *Bulletin of the Cincinnati Historical Society* 25 (July 1967): 164–83.

26. Sue Ann Painter, *Architecture in Cincinnati* (Athens: Ohio University Press, 2006), 32.

27. *Harper's Weekly* 10 (April 14, 1866).

28. *Cincinnati Daily Gazette,* June 25, 1867.

29. Denys Peter Myers, "Isaiah Rogers in Cincinnati," *Bulletin of the Historical and Philosophical Society of Ohio* 9 (April 1951): 131; the view of the theater's interior reproduced in the article would seem to be that of the post-Rogers remodeling.

30. Incorrectly spelled "Guidecini" in Holliday, "Samuel N. Pike," 171.

31. *Springfield Daily Republican,* September 30, 1869.

32. *Springfield Republican,* October 30, 1895.

33. Other obituary notices were much shorter but reflect the national character of his career: *Cincinnati Commercial Tribune,* April 14, 1869; *New York Herald,* April 16, 1869; *Memphis Daily Avalanche* April 20, 1869; *Mobile Register,* April 30, 1869.

Afterword

1. The fundamental study of nineteenth-century architectural practice in the United States is Mary N. Woods, *From Craft to Profession* (Berkeley: University of California Press, 1999). Woods seems not to have known of Rogers's diary, and her emphasis is largely directed to the later 1800s.

2. See Martha J. McNamara, "Defining the Profession: Books, Libraries, and Architects," in *American Architects and Their Books to 1848*, ed. Kenneth Hafertepe and James F. O'Gorman (Amherst: University of Massachusetts Press, 2001), 73–90.

3. Elspeth Cowell, "Samuel Sloan, Pattern Books, and the Question of Professional Identity," in Hafertepe and O'Gorman, *American Architects*, 95–128.

4. Roger Kennedy, "Jefferson and the Indians," *Winterthur Portfolio* 27, nos. 2/3 (Summer/Autumn 1992): 105–21.

5. See Jeffery A. Cohen, "Building a Discipline: Institutional Settings for Architectural Education in Philadelphia, 1824–1890," *Journal of the Society of Architectural Historians* 53 (June 1994): 139–83.

6. For more, see Lois Olcott Price, *Line, Shade and Shadow: The Fabrication and Preservation of Architectural Drawings* (New Castle, Del.: Oak Knoll Press, 2010), esp. "Fabrication of Architectural Drawings Prior to 1860," 1–55.

7. Paul R. Baker, *Richard Morris Hunt* (Cambridge: MIT Press, 1980), 82–84.

8. Roger G. Reed, *Building Victorian Boston* (Amherst: University of Massachusetts Press, 2007), 69–75.

INDEX

Adams, Dudley G., 109–10
Adams, John, 14
Adams, John Quincy, 22
Adams Express Company, 224
Aikin, Edmund, 17
Albany city hall, 63
Albany Evening Journal, 159
Alcott, Bronson, 42
Alexandria Gazette, 77
All Souls Church, 66
Alsop, Richard, 70
Altes Museum, 59
American Architect, 66
American Builder's Companion (Benjamin), 232
American Institute of Architects, 2, 9, 38, 63, 83, 99, 101, 221
American Institution of Architects, 4, 63, 236
American Magazine of Useful and Entertaining Knowledge, 48
Ancient Monuments of the Mississippi Valley (Squier and Davis), 8
Anderson, Lars, 160
Andrews, Joseph, 39–40
Antiquities of America (Delafield), 8
Antiquities of Athens (Stuart and Revett), 7, 17, 23, 26, 31, 33, 45
Antiquities of Herculaneum and Pompeii (Pistolesi), 7–8
Appleton, William, 43
apprenticeships, 14–17, 231, 234
Aqueduct, Croton, 71
Archer, John, 58
Architect's and Mechanic's Journal, 224
Architectural Library, 232–33
architecture: American difference of, 30–31, 38, 52–53, 63; apprenticeships and, 14–17, 231, 234; competitions and, 2–4, 6, 10–11, 21, 23–24, 38, 50, 52–53, 57, 59, 89, 122, 129–35, 154, 169–70, 208, 221, 234, 236, 265n1; design processes and, 10–12; fires and, 2, 10, 16, 24, 29, 35, 60–61, 75, 110, 121, 128, 148, 168, 181–83, 197, 224; histories of, xv–xvi; national practices and, 90–93, 235; payment norms and, 9; professional relationships within, 4–6, 9, 12, 18–19, 46, 63, 72, 83, 99, 134–35, 169–70, 220–21, 225, 231, 236; role of, in building practices, 9, 12, 20–21, 40, 231–34, 236, 258n20. *See also* American Institute of Architects; American Institution of Architects; general contractors; *specific architects, buildings, and firms*
Arnot, David Henry, 4, 7, 63, 133–35
Artists Journal, 187
Ashley, Timothy, 28
Ashton (Smith), 9
Astor, John Jacob, 52, 54, 56–57, 87, 92
Astor House, 53, *55*, 56–57, 59, 63, 78, 121, 144, 147, 169, 234
Astor Place Opera House, 125, 139–40, *140*, 141, *141*, 142
Astor Place Riot, 141
Augusta, Georgia, 1–2, 24, *25*
Austin, Henry, 231, 233, 239
Ayling, W. L., 124

Ballard, John P., 78
Ballou, Hosea, 8, 19, 124
Ballou, Maturin, 19
Baltimore City Hotel, 35
Baltimore Sun, 93
Bangor, Maine, 1, 35, 136, 210
Bank of America, 67, *68*, 236

Index

Bank of Louisville, 67
Banner, Peter, 15, 38, 82
Bannon, Patrick, 171–72, 205–6, 215
Barber, Philatus S., 200
Barnes, Joseph, 71
Bartels, J. O., 167
Bass, Thomas, 166
Bates, John, 150–51
Battle, James, 167
Battle House hotel, 16, 168–69
Bayless, William Henry, 10, 58, 63, 89–90, 161
Beard, Duke, 125
Beauties of Modern Architecture (Lafever), 232
Beecher, Henry Ward, 9, 143
Beecher, Lyman, 26, 46
Belknap, Andrew Eliot, 29, 82, 91, 94, 97, 134
Benjamin, Asher, 15, 18, 29, 42, 48, 63, 231–33
Bennett, Emerson, 9
Berger, Molly, 28, 31, 56
Bernard, Henry, 7
Bey, Amen, 149
Biddle, Owen, 234
Bigelow, Jacob, 86, 138
Bilder-Atlas zum Conversations-Lexikon, 62
Billings, C. Hammatt, 58, *58*, 59, 95, 121, 186, 231, 234, 266n19
Billings, John, 9
Biographical Encyclopaedia of Ohio, 16, 229
Bisbee, Albert, 158
Black, William R., Jr., 206
Bogardus, James, 56, 186
Bond, Richard, 6, 42, 48, 50, 59, 94–95, 111–12, 231
Bond, William C., 115, 118
Boston, Massachusetts. *See specific buildings, organizations, and people*
Boston Almanac, 26
Boston Architectural Library, 18
Boston Common Council, 82
Boston Courier, 4
Boston Custom House, 4–5, 132, 221, 237, 266n16
Boston Daily Advertiser, 221
Boston Daily Atlas, 91, 118, 122
Boston Directory, 20, 48
Boston Evening Post, 94
Boston Evening Transcript, 122, 126–27, 137
Boston Globe, 42

Boston Granite Style, 15–24, 26, 28–29, 38, 43, 45, 48, *49*, 54, 73, 97–99
Boston Merchants' Exchange, 1–2, 9, 43, 67, 83, 88–100, 236, 238; images of, *96*
Boston Recorder, 134
Boston Weekly Messenger, 29–30
Bosworth, Hiram, 26
Bowen, Abel, 22, 26, *27*, 28, 33, 46, 50, 231
Bower, Robert, 205
Bowler, Robert B., 170, 174, 176, 178, 192, 205
Boyd, J. M. W., 125
Boyden, Simeon and Frederick, 56, 78
Brackett, Edward A., 19
Bradlee, N. J., 121
Bragaldi, Mario, 139, 142
Braman, Jarvis, 107–8
Brandegee, Jacob, 72–73
Brazer's Building, 99, *100*, 238
bridge designs, 2, 5, 71–72, 90–92, 101–5, 147–48, 156, 201–4, 217–27, 240, 272n22; images of, *103–4, 202, 218*
Brimmer, George Watson, 46
Brimmer, Martin, 87
Brodie, Lewis Dunbar, 103
Bronson, Amon, House, 171
Brookline, Massachusetts, 1, 43, 92, 100, 121
Brooks, Peter Chardon, 43
Brown, Stephen G., 178, 195
Brunel, I. K., 87–88
Bryan, John, 43
Bryant, Gridley J. F., 5, 71–72, 82, 110, 121, 166, 210, 221, 226, 234–35, 237
Buckingham, James Silk, 87, 198
Building Superintendence (Clark), 233
Bulfinch, Charles, 12, 14–15, 17–18, 20, 30, 42–43, 231
Bunker Hill Monument, 18–19, 30, 92, 105–6, 129
Bunting, Bainbridge, 118
Burnet, John Jacob, 144
Burnet House, 11, 67, 104–5, 143–62, 176, 181, 187–88, 199, 223; images of, *146, 148*
Butler, Pierce, 75

Cabot, E. C., 114, 122
Cambridge, Massachusetts, 1, 18–19, 42–50, 62–64, 86, 109, 123–24, 142, 239; images of, *44, 116–17*
Camp Dennison, 3, 215

Capital Hotel, 177–78, 180–81, *182*, 183, *183*, 185–94, 207–8
Carter, Elias, 45–46
"Catawba Wine" (Longfellow), 143–44
Cathedral of the Immaculate Conception, 197
Catherwood, Frederick, 87
Catholicism. *See* Roman Catholics
Céleste, Céline, 93
Champion Hotel Company, 227
Chapman, Jonathan, 82–83
Charles Street prison, 5, 237
Charleston Hotel, 262n23
Chase, Salmon P., 195, 220–21
Chatham Street Chapel, 87
Chicago, Illinois, 1, 36, 91, 142, 170, 187–93, 214, 229
Chicago Daily Tribune, 189
Choate, Rufus P., 132, 134
Choragic Monument of Lysicrates, 23, 50, 66
Christ Church, Cambridge, 18, 29, 62
Christian Advocate, 201
Church of the Messiah, 73–74, *74*
Cincinnati, Ohio. *See specific buildings, organizations, and people*
The Cincinnati Cemetery of Spring Grove, 195
Cincinnati Chronicle and Atlas, 145, 147
Cincinnati Custom House, 222–23
Cincinnati Daily Gazette, 152, 162–63, 200, 207, 237
Cincinnati Daily Times, 229
Cincinnati Enquirer, 145, 224
Cipriani Club Residences, 59
Cist, Charles, 152, 272n22
City Hotel (City Tavern), 35
Civil War, 3, 150, 207, 215
Clark, Henry, 210
Clark, T. M., 233
Clay, Henry, 204
Cleveland, Henry R., 21, 42, 237
Cleveland Plain Dealer, 158, 210
Coburn, Loamme, 261n60
Cogswell, Joseph, 57
Cole, Thomas, 3, 10, 63, 89, 161, 237
Coleman, Abraham B., 144–50, 162, 178, 180, 186, 192–95, *197*, 201, 221
Coleman, John W., 157–58
Columbian Centinel, 39–40
Columbian Lodge of Masons, 24

Columbus, Ohio, 1, 181, 208, *209*, 216. *See also* Hamilton County courthouse; Ohio statehouse
Commercial Advertiser, 70, 76
Commercial Bank, 151–52, 170, 205–6
Commercial Hospital, 210, 217, 237. *See also* Longview Asylum
Commercial Wharf building (Boston), 43, 83
Conant, Kenneth John, xi
Congress Hall, 203
Connecticut Courant, 70
Cook, Milton H., 162, 172, 174, 178, 199
Cooper, James Fenimore, 9
Costigan, Francis, 156
Country Builder's Assistant (Benjamin), 15
Cox, Richard K., 161–62
Crane, John, 24
Croton, John Jervis, 139
Crystal Palace, 186, 194, 212
Cullum, George, 167–68
Currier, Nathaniel, 57
Cushing, Levi L., 30, 131

Daily Courier, 156
Daily National Intelligencer, 70
Daily Ohio Statesman, 89, 161
Dakin, James, xv, 5, 10, 35, 38, 67, 169–70, 209, 234
Dallam, James L., 205
Daniels, Howard, 134, 161, 178
Darnell, Victor C., 267n30
Davis, Alexander Jackson, 7, 22, 38, 53–59, 63, 96, 99, 107, 154, 169, 231, 234, 238
Davis, Jefferson, 56
Dayton, Ohio, 1, 6, 158, *159*, 161–62, 170–72, *173*
Delafield, John, 8
Delafield, Richard, 79–80, 82, 87, 115, 240
Democratic Vistas (Whitman), 66–67
Derby, Henry W., 178
Description and Historical Account of Hydraulic and Other Machines for Raising Water (Ewbank), 7
Description of Haviland's Design for the New Penitentiary (Haviland), 31
Description of Tremont House (Eliot), 23, 30–33, 40, 103–4, 232, 234, 259n34
Dewey, Orville, 73
Dexter, George Minot, 110, 114

Dexter, H. H., 136–37, 193
Dickens, Charles, 3, 36, 56, 149, 226
distyle-in-antis, 45, 54, 67, 70, 102, 107, 185, 228
Doric features, 17–26, 31–32, 38, 53–54, 59–63, 102, 129, 166, 208, 237. *See also* Greek Revival; *specific buildings*
Douglas, Stephen A., 62
Draper, John W., 74
Driaper, Frederick, 80
Drury Lane Theatre, 23, 30
Dunlap Creek Bridge, 220
Durand, Jean-Nicolas-Louis, 7
Duveneck, Frank, 143

Eads, James B., 101
Eastern State Penitentiary, 166
Eaton, Asa, 40
Egyptian Revival, 57, 83, 86–87, 129, 239
Eidlitz, Leopold, 226
Elements of Architecture (Benjamin), 232
Eliot, Samuel A., 29, 31, 33, 40, 43, 82, 113–15, 122
Eliot, William, 30, 43, 103, 121, 232, 234, 259n34
Ellet, Charles, Jr., 5, 101, 197, 203, 240
Elliot, William, 135
Elmwood (house), 106–7, *108*, 109
Elssler, Fanny, 93
Emerson, Ralph Waldo, 36
Endicott, George, 78
Erechtheion, 53–54
Essay on the Doric Order of Architecture (Aikin), 17
Everett, Edward, 114
Ewbank, Thomas, 7
Exchange Bank of Richmond, 67, 69, *69*, 76
Exchange Coffee House, 18, 29–30, 35
Exchange Company (New York), 57–62, 94
Exchange Hotel in Richmond, 33, 69, 76–78, *79*, 89, 91, 237

Falls' City Terra-Cotta Works, 206
Faneuil Hall Market, 38, 92, 101, 132
Farrar, Samuel, 136
Federal Hall National Memorial, 50
Federal Street Theatre, 20
Fergusson, James, 201
Filson Historical Society, 183

fires, xv, 2, 10, 16, 24, 29, 35, 60–61, 75, 110, 121, 128, 148, 168, 181–83, 197, 224
First Parish Meeting House, 42, *44*, 50, 63–64, 113, 142
Fitz, Henry, 80
Flournoy, L. M., 205
Floyd, Margaret Henderson, 118
Forbes, Robert Bennet, 45, *46*, 50, 75
Forbes House Museum, 45, 115
Forbriger, Adolphus A., 145, *146*
Forefathers' Monument, 186, 200
Forrest, Edwin, 141
Frankfort, Kentucky, 1, 176–94, *182–83*, 207–9
Frank Leslie's Illustrated Weekly Newspaper, 24
Franklin, Benjamin, 8, 77
Franklin Institute, 77, 88, 234, 238
Free Will Baptists, 26–27
Frost, Richard K., 71
Fry's Counting Room, 76
Fuller, Seth, 35
Fuller, Thomas, 226
Furness, Frank, 12

Gaff, Thomas, 187, 189
Gallier, James, xv, 19, 35
Galt House, 182, 199
Gamble, Robert, 17
Gauthier, Pierre, 211
Gavin, Anthony, 203
Gayoso House, 209
Gazetteer of Massachusetts, 99
Gehry, Frank, 235
general contractors, 9, 12, 48, 99, 170–71, 258n20
George Washington Statue, xv, 111–12, 131
Gerry, Elbridge, 43
Geschiedt, Morris, 135–36, 139
Gilbert, Cass, 99
Gilman, Arthur D., 6, 24, 97–99, 226, 237, 239
Girard College, 6, 38, *39*, 88, 238
Gleason's Pictorial, 33
Gliddon, George Robins, 87
Glover, Andrew B., 73
Goater, Walter, 24
Gore Hall, 51
Gothic Architecture Applied to Modern Residences (Arnot), 7
Gothic forms, 2, 40–46, 80, 107–10, 122, 126, 146, 152–55, 239; images of, *41*, *133*

"Gothick" style, 42, 46, 50
Gould, Elizabeth Barrett, 257n10
Gould, Isaac, 84
Gould, John Stanton, 186
Gould, Nathan, 84, 86, 124, 201, 207, 223
Grace Lee (Kavanagh), 9
Grant, Ulysses S., 150
The Great Red Dragon (Gavin), 203
Greek Revival: Myers and, xi–xii; Rogers's uses of, 16–26, 31–33, 38–40, 45, 48, 53–63, 66, 78–80, 87, 102, 113, 129, 140, 147, 164–66, 171–72, 182, 199, 208, 237; textbooks on, 7, 17, 23, 26, 31, 33, 45. *See also* Boston Granite Style
Greek Revival Architecture in America (Hamlin), xi
Greeley, Horace, 8, 142
Greenough, Horatio, xv, 17, 26, 111–12, 131, 240
Greenough, John James, 112, 194
Green Street Church, 50
Greenwood, Miles, 188
Griswold, George, 70
Griswold's Railroad Engineers' Pocket Companion, 219
Groton Academy, 138
Guidicini, Giuseppe, 224
Gurley, Jason A., 170, 187, 191

Hackett, James Henry, 124–27, 139, 150
Hadid, Zaha, 235
Haines, Elias H., 178, 195
Hall, James C., 8, 151, 187–88, 192
Hall, Joseph L., 227
Haly, John, 180–81
Hamilton, John R., 154, 204
Hamilton County courthouse, 3–5, 10–11, 150, 161–65, 179, 185–87, 204–5, 270n20; images of, *164–65*
Hamilton County jail, *167,* 215–16, 237, 270n20
Hamlin, Talbot, xi, 16, 62
Handbook of Architecture (Fergusson), 201
Handy, Truman S., 223
Hanover Street Church, 40
Harper's Weekly, 56, 185, 224
Harrison, Peter, 18, 86
Harrison, William Henry, 3
Harry, Philip, 22, 37

Harvard College, 42, 51, 113–15, *116–17,* 118, *119,* 120–21, 137, 142
Harvey, George, 30, 33
Haselton, Daniel, 64
Hatch, George, 170–71, 178
Hatch, Samuel, 144, 215
Hatch House, 171–72, *173,* 180
Haviland, John, 31, 38, 57, 63, 133–34, 166, 234–35, 237–38
Hayward, John, 99
Heiman, Adolphus, 5, 179–80, 197, 201, 240
Henshaw, Samuel, 109, 123, *124,* 195, 239
Herald of the Times, 84
High Bridge, 72
"Hillforest" (house), 187, *190–93*
Historic American Buildings Survey, xi–xii
"The Historic Architecture of Maine" (Myers), xi
History of Boston (Snow), 15
History of the Indian Tribes of North America (McKenney and Hall), 8
Hitchcock, Henry-Russell, 7, 99
Hoban, James, 231
Holmes, Oliver Wendell, 36
Hooker, Philip, 38
Horton, Benjamin, 188
Hosea, Robert, 174
Hotchkiss, Nelson House, 171
hotels. *See* Rogers, Isaiah; *specific hotels*
Hough, William Jervis, 132, 135, 208, 236
Howard Athenaeum, 124–27, *127,* 128, *128,* 132, 137, 139, 142, 239
Howe (assistant), 178
How(e), Hall J. and James, 19
Hugh W. Fry & Sons, 76
Humboldt, Alexander, 9
Hunt, Richard Morris, 12, 236
Hunt, Thomas H., 184
Huxtable, Ada Louise, 67

Imbert's Lithography, 57
Incidents of Travel in Central America, Chiapas, and Yucatan (Stephens), 7
Independent Order of Odd Fellows, 3, 123, 225
Ingram, James, 7
Ionic forms, 22–25, 33, 40–48, 54–59, 66, 78–80, 87, 113, 129, 140, 182, 199. *See also* Greek Revival; *specific buildings*

Irving, Washington, 8–9
Isaac Gould & Sons, 84
Isaiah Rogers, Son & Co., 177–78, 224
Italianate influences, 2, 78, 100–101, 134, 146–47, 156, 176, 198. *See also* Romanesque influences

Jackson, George R., 222
Jackson, J. D., 149, 156
Jacobs, Jane, 96
James (assistant), 113, 120–21, 132, 138, 267n44
James, George, 9
James, William, 56
Jarvis, George A., 72
Jefferson, Thomas, 233
Jenkins, Joseph, 40
Jervis, John B., 219
Jewish cemetery, *85*, 86
J. N. Breeden & Co., 200
Jones, Elizabeth, 206
Jones, W. G., 93
J. Washburn & Brothers, 91

Kaplan, Justin, 56
Kate Cluredon (Bennett), 9
Kavanagh, Julia, 9
Keeley, Patrick Charles, 197
Keeley, William, 203
Kelley, Nathan B., 208
Kemble, Fanny, 75–76
Kennedy, T. S., 201
Kent, Horace L., 92, 108–9,
Kent, Horace L. House, *110–11*
Kimball, Benjamin W., 110
King, Charles Bird, 8, 134
King, Daniel P., 129
King, Gamaliel, 87
Kirby, Charles Kirk, 203
Kirkbride, Thomas, 212
Kirkland, John Thornton, 92
Knickerbocker's History of New York (Irving), 8–9
Know-Nothings, 149, 163, 204, 207
Koolhaas, Rem, 235
Kossuth, Lajos, 62, 149
Kutts, John, 38

The Lady of the Lake (Scott), 9
Lafever, Minard, 6, 63, 231–32, 239, 257n3

Lagonda House, 12, 227–28, *228*
Lane Theological Seminary, 143–44
Langham Hotel, 36
Lariboisière Hospital, 211
Latrobe, Benjamin Henry, 11–12, 17, 97, 231, 233, 236
lattice-work bridge designs, 102, *103–4*, 147–48, 156, 184, 201, 217, 240. *See also* bridge designs
Lawrence, Amos, 105, 118, 137–38
Lawrence, William, 136
Layard, Austen, 8
Lee, Antoinette J., xv
Lefever, Minard, 38
Leonard, George, 142
Lewis, Henry, House, 171
Lewis, Michael J., 38–39
Lexington Theater, 225
Liberator, 90
Lincoln, Abraham, 2–3, 36, 56
Lincoln, Levi, 22
Lind, Jenny, 3, 56, 149, 151
Linden, Blanche, 149
lithographs and lithography, 11, 22, 30, 40, 57, 90, 95, 145, 195. *See also specific buildings and images*
Little, Edward Preble, 14
Little, George, 14
Lobell, Thomas J., 110
Lockwood, John, 197–98
Longfellow, Henry Wadsworth, 36, 143–44
Longview Asylum, 147, 209–10, 212, *213–14*
Longworth, Nicholas, 143–44, 178, *179*
Louisville, Kentucky, 1, 10, 67, 146, 151, 156, 160–61, 167, 172, 177–215, 222, 235
Louisville Democrat, 184
Louisville Hotel, 10, 161, 168, 183–85, *185*, 199, 203, 205
Louisville Journal, 185, 204
Lowell, Massachusetts, 1, 6, 87
Lowell Institute, 6
Luckett & Farley, 178, 235
Ludington, James, 198
Lyceum lectures, 23–24
Lyell, Charles, 9
Lyman, Theodore, 90, 92, 100

Macready, William Charles, 141
Madison House, 156, *157*

Maine Catalogue of the Historic American Building Survey, xi
Maine Historical Society, 64
Mandeville, William, 64
Mann, Levi, 6
Mansion House, 157–58, 168
Mansions of England (Nash), 7
Marcy, William L., 131, 134
Marlboro Chapel, 122–23
Marsh, Alfred, 196
Marshfield, Massachusetts, 13–21, 28
Masonic Grand Lodge of Massachusetts, 40, 42
Masonic Temples and Masonry, 3, 24, *25*, 40, *41*, 42
Massachusetts Charitable Mechanic Association, 3, 101, 121, 123
Massachusetts General Hospital, 17
Maury, Matthew Fontaine, 115
Maxwell House, 209, 215
McAlpin, George W., 198
McAlpine, William J., 219
McComb, John, Jr., 231, 234
McKenney, Thomas, 8
McKim, Mead & White, 59
McLaughlin, James W., 144, 149, 154, 205, 223
McLellan and Ambrose, 77
Mechanics' Hall, 121, 123
Mechanics' Institute, 57
Mechanics' Magazine, 52
Meigs, Montgomery C., 219–20, 229, 240
Memorials of Oxford (Ingram), 7
Memphis, Tennessee, 1, 209
Methodists, 26–27
Metropolitan Hall, 189
Mexican War, 3, 62, 131
Middle Reformed Dutch Church, xii, 11, 63, *65*, 66–67, 70, 73, 88, 239
Middleton, Charles, 30
Miller, William B., xi, 125
Miller & McRoberts store, 228
Mills, Robert, 6, 35, 60, 93, 129, 131–32, 167, 221, 231, 236, 239
Milton, Massachusetts, 1, 45, *46–47*, 50, 115
Milwaukee, Wisconsin, 1, 3, 6, 142, 197–200
Mobile, Alabama, 1, 16–17, 21–22
Mobile Register, 169
Model Architect (Sloan), 232
models (architectural), 11–12

Monument of Thrasyllus, 45, 50
Moore, Charles, 91
Morgan, Matthew, 139
Morison, Samuel Eliot, 37
Morse, Aaron, 231
Morse, Elijah, 40
Morse, Samuel F. B., 74, 98, 235
Moseley, Thomas W. H., 272n22
Mount Auburn Cemetery, 19, 86–87, 92, 109, 123, *124*, 138, 195
Mt. Storm Park, 174, 176
Mudge, Enoch Redington, 106–7, 109, 136–37, 167–68
Mullett, A. B., 5, 10, 51, 131, 207–8, 212–13, 221–22, 226
Murphy, Henry C., 87
Myers, Denys Peter, xi–xvii, 129, 260n47, 266n23, 273n41
Mygatt, George W., 6, 198
Mysteries of the Heath (Sue), 9

Nahant Church, 122
Nahant Village Church, 43
Nash, John, 66
Nash, Joseph, 7
Nashville, Tennessee, 1, 5, 178–79, 197, 201, 209, 215, 236
National Archives, 79
National City Bank, 59
National Hotel, 35
National Theater, 75, 150–51
Native Americans, 8, 233
Newcomb, Horatio Dalton, 198–201, 203, 206
New Jersey State Lunatic Asylum, 212
New Orleans, Louisiana, 5, 35, 106–7, 121, 151, 166–70, 178, 181–82, 195
New Orleans Times-Picayune, 168–69, 182
Newport, Rhode Island, 1, 83–92, 110, 124, 167, 170, 186, 194–207, 216, 223, 226
Newport Mercury, 83
New South Church, 43
Newton, James, 7
New York City. *See specific buildings, organizations, and people*
New York Herald, 73
New York Journal of Commerce, 122
New York Merchant's Exchange, 4, 48, 57–63, 70, 89–97, 105–6, 235, 237; images of, *58, 61*

New York Mirror, 54
New York Tribune, 57, 61
Niagra Falls House Company, 158–60
Nicholson, W. R., 154
Norcross Brothers, 12
Norfolk County Courthouse, 18
Norman influences, 133, 154–55
Notman, John, 6, 131, 133, 135, 186, 200, 212, 239
Nutting, B. F., 40, *41*

Oakwoods (house), 154
Oberlin College, 51
Observations on the Design for the Theatre Royal, Drury Lane (Wyatt), 16, 30
Ohio Daily Statesman, 145, 147, 174, 184
Ohio Life Insurance and Trust Company, 207
Ohio Mechanic Institute, 161
Ohio statehouse, 39, 63, 147, 208, *209*, 237, 265n1
Old Granary Burying Ground, 37, 82–83, *84*, 92
The Old Oak Chest (James), 9
Oliver House, 210, *211*
Olmsted, Frederick Law, 226
On the Construction, Organization, and General Arrangements of Hospitals for the Insane (Kirkbride), 212
orphan asylums, 5, 38, 92, 108–9, 118, 120
Otis, Elisha Graves, 212
Overton, John, Jr., 209
Owen, David, 132–33
Owen, Robert, 9, 131–32, 134–35

Paducah, Kentucky, 1, 200–206
Palladian quincunx, 118, 147, 156, 181, 185, 210, 228
Palmer, Seneca, 144
Panic of 1857, 207
Panorama of Thebes (Catherwood), 87
Parker, Daniel P., 136
Parker House, 36
Parmly, Eleazer, 236
Parris, Alexander, 4, 15, 17–18, 23, 29, 63, 231, 233, 239
P. Bannon Pipe Company, 206
Pedretti, Francis, 149, 199, 212, 224
Pelby, William, 20
Pendleton, George H., 220

Perkins, Thomas Handasyd and James, 29, 43, 45, 95
Perkins-Clark House, 171
Peters, John R., Jr., 122
Phillips, J. D., 158
Phillips House, *159*, 170
Pickering, Loring, 110
Picture of Boston (Bowen), 26, *27*
Pierson, Isaac, 73
Pike, Samuel N., 223
Pike's Opera House, 223, *225*, 226, 228
Pine Street church, 25–27, *27*, 33
Pistolesi, Erasmo, 7–8
Plans, Elevations, and Sections of the House of Correction for the County of Middlesex (Middleton), 30
plan(s), 10–11, 20
Platt, William A., 208
Plum Street Temple, 225
Polk, James K., 131
Pollard, Calvin, 6, 52–53, 75–76, 87, 109, 122, 129, 231
Portland, Maine, 6, 19–20, 50, 59, 134, 221
Portland Daily Press, 221
Power, Tyrone, 88
Practical House Carpenter (Benjamin), 15
Pratt, Enoch, 129
Pratt, Thomas Willis, 102
Prentiss, George Dennison, 204
Prescott, William, 43
Preston, William, 191–92, 201
Principles of Geology (Lyell), 9
Probasco, Henry, 143, 152, 154
Pugin, A. W. N., 155
Purves, George, 168
Putnam's Monthly, 62–63, 73, 237

Queensboro Bridge, 227
Quimby, George W., 185, 187
Quincy, Josiah, 22
Quincy, Josiah, III, 42, 113
Quincy granite, 2, 4–5, 15, 18, 31–32, 54, 59–60, 82–84, 91–92, 105, 121, 146
Quincy Market, 17, 29, 92, 101
Quincy Patriot, 113
Quincy Town Hall, 112–13, *114*

Recueil et parallèle des édifices (Durand), 7
Red Hook Company, 72

Reichardt, Charles F., 262n23
Renaissance Revival, 182, 184, 239
Renwick, James, Jr., 6, 122, 133–35, 194, 238–39
Resolves of the Town of Marshfield, 13
Resor, Reuben, 170, 174, *175*
Revett, Nicholas, 17, 23, 26, 31, 33, 45
Reynolds, W. B., 201, 203
Richards, Lawrence, 110
Richardson, H. H., 118, 149, 226, 233
Richmond, Virginia, 1, 3, 6, 33, 66–69, 76–79, 88–92, 108–10, *111*, 118, 237
Richmond Compiler, 69, 77–78
Richmond Whig, 76–78
Roath, Charles, 20
Robb, William H., 271n30
Roberts, William, 261n60
Rock Creek Bridge, 219
Roebling, John A., 197, 201, 217, 227, 240
Rogers, Cecilia, 71
Rogers, Cornelia (daughter), 93, 144, 229
Rogers, Emily (wife), 19, 124, 150, 170, 216
Rogers, Emily Jane (daughter), 86, 93, 124, 194
Rogers, Frederick, 71
Rogers, Isaac, 13–14
Rogers, Isaiah: assistants and partners of, 10, 48, 50, 58, 63–64, 67, 71, 86, 89–91, 94–101, 120, 161, 177–79, 226, 231–32, 235, 238; asylum designs of, 19, 124, 147, 150, 170, 209–12, *213–14*, 216; bridge design and, 2, 5, 12, 71–72, 90, 92, 101–2, *103–4*, 105, 147–48, 156, 179, 184, 197, 201, *202*, 203–4, 217, *218*, 219–20, 226–27, 240, 272n22; building practices and, 40, 52–54, 59–61, 63, 76–77, 92, 95, 99, 109, 123, 144, 170–71, 214, 222, 231–33, 236–37, 258n20, 270n20; business practices of, 11, 18–19, 57–58, 80, 112–13, 136–37, 170–71, 177–80, 196–97, 206–8, 222, 234–36; cemeteries of, 37, 90, 92, 109, 123, 138, 146, 167, 194–96, 239; churches of, 24–27, 40, 42, *44*, 46–48, 50, 62–64, *65*, 66–67, 73–74, *74*, 75–76, 144, 154, *155*, 163, 170, 183–86, 215, 236, 239; competitions and, 2–4, 6, 10–11, 21, 23–24, 38, 50, 52–53, 57, 59, 82, 89, 121, 129–35, 154, 169–70, 208, 221, 234, 236, 265n1; death of, 229, 235; Denys Myers and, xi–xii; education of, 6–7, 13–17, 20, 23–24, 29–30, 36, 93, 231, 233–34; family life of, 4, 18–19, 70–71, 93, 123–24, 144, 150, 194, 216; federal government work and, 111–12, 115, 129, 131–36, 167, 170, 220–22, 235, 240, 275n13; Gothic influences and, 42–43, 51; Greek Revival and, 2, 15, 17–26, 31–33, 38–40, 45, 48, 53–63, 66, 78–80, 87, 97–98, 102, 113–15, 129, 140, 146–47, 164–66, 171–72, 182, 199, 208, 237; hotels of, 1, 15, 20, 28–31, *32*, 33, *34*, 35–37, 39–40, 51–56, 69, 75, 77–78, 89, 94, 121, 145–50, 155–56, 158–59, 167, 178–82, 214, 227–28; materials-consciousness of, 2, 95–100, 112–13, 146, 205–6, 237; national reach of, 1–3, 91–93, 177–215, 235; portraits of, *126, 216*; reading habits of, 3, 6–9, 88, 203; religious life of, 2–3, 9, 24–26, 124, 150, 203–4; residential jobs of, 19–20, 45–46, *46, 47, 47,* 50, 72–73, 92, 100, 106–10, 121, 135–37, 143–44, 146–48, 157–58, 174, *175,* 176, 178–79, 184, 187–88, 191, 205, 210, *211*; work habits of, 10–11, 159–61. *See also specific assistants and competitors*
Rogers, Isaiah, Jr., 144
Rogers, Isaiah Augustus (son), 70–71
Rogers, Jotham, 14
Rogers, Peleg, Jr., 13
Rogers, Phoebe Mann, 71
Rogers, Solomon Willard, 10, 18, 120, 139, 167, 177, 207, 212–15, 223–29, 235
Roland, Hugh, 182
Roman Catholics, 3, 19, 25–26, 163, 203–4
Romanesque influences, 2, 15, 17, 43, 166, 238. *See also* Italianate influences
Ropes, Hardy, 26
Ropes, William, 26
"Rosewell" (house), 200
Royal Institute of British Architects, 53
Rundbogenstil, 57
Rural Residences (Davis), 7, 107
Ruskin, John, 7, 239

Saeltzer, Alexander, 57
St. Charles Hotel, 35, 121, 166, 168, 178
St. John's Church, 154, *155*, 163, 170, 183, 185–86, 215, 236, 239
St. Louis Hotel, 167–68
St. Nicholas Hotel, 149, 225
St. Paul's Church (Cincinnati). *See* St. John's Church
St. Paul's Episcopal Cathedral (Boston), 17–18, 40

St. Peter-in-Chains Church, 144
St. Peter's Episcopal Church, 46, 48, *49*, 73
Salisbury, Stephen, II, 45
Salisbury House, 46
Sargent, Whidden and Coburn, 221
Saturday Club, 36
Savage, James, 71, 105–6, 263n36
Sawyer, Joseph C., 161
Sawyer, Joseph O., 181
scagliola, 60, 77, 98–99
Schinkel, Karl Friedrich, 59
Schmidt, Frederick, 89–90, 145
Schoenborn, Augustus, 208, 273n35
School Architecture (Bernard), 7
Schuyler, Montgomery, 37, 54, 57, 60, 63–64, 66, 223, 237
Scientific American, 217
Scott, Walter, 9
Scott, Willliam Blair, Jr., 204
Scott, Winifield, 149
Sears, David, 110
Second Great Awakening, 2
Second Meeting House, 142
Shand-Tucci, Douglass, 97
Shattuck, George C., 120
Shaw, Edward, 38, 231, 234
Shaw, Jesse, 10, 14–17, 30
Shaw, Robert Gould, 43, 94–95
Shawmut House, 110
Shelden, Richard A., 89–90
Sheldon, Henry, 107
Shepardson Hotel, 198
Shepherd, R. D., 167
Sherman, William Tecumseh, 150
Shettleworth, Earle G., Jr., xi–xii, xv
Shreve, L. L., 182, 184
Shreve, T. T., 192
Shryock, Gideon, 186, 206, 231
Simpson, M. H., 122
Sketches and Statistics of Cincinnati in 1859 (Cist), 152, 272n22
Slatter's City Hotel, 167–68, 170
slavery, 75–76, 166, 207, 264n48
Sloan, Samuel, 232
Small, William F., 35
Smith, Benjamin, 40
Smith, Ebenezer, 20
Smith, John Frederick, 9

Smith, Winthrop B., 170, 172, 174, 178, 186, 198, 204
Smithsonian Institution, 6, 10, 129, 132, *133*, 134–35, 194, 208, 236
Snell, George, 121
Snow, Caleb, 15
Society of Architectural Historians, xi, 1
Soule, H. B., 8
Soule, John, 142
Spalding, Martin John, 204
Sparks, Jared, House, 46
Sparrow, Thomas J., 6
Spencer, Frederick, 102
Spencer, John C., 112
"Spiral Cylinder Bridge" (Rogers), 101–2
Springer, Charles G., 188
Springfield, Ohio, 1, 12, 223, 227, *228*
Springfield Daily Republican, 227
Spring Grove Cemetary, 146, 193, 195, *196*, 229
The Spy (Cooper), 9
Stacey, George, 215
Standish, Lemuel M., 125
Star of the West, 187
The Star Papers (Beecher), 9
Stearns, R. H., 42
Stephens, John Lloyd, 7
Stoddard, Richard, 24, 125
Stones of Venice (Ruskin), 7, 239
Stowe, Caleb, 143
Stowe, Harriet Beecher, 9, 143
Stradler, Jacob, 151
Strauch, Adolph, 172, 174, 176, 195
Strickland, William, xv, 5, 38, 63, 129, 165, 170, 178, 231–32, 234
Stuart, Gilbert, 20–23, 26, 31, 33, 45
Stuart, James, 17
Sue, Eugene, 9
Suffolk Bank, 48, *49,* 59
Suffolk University, 33
Sullivan, Louis, 238
Summerson, John, 140–41
Swampscott, Massachusetts, 1

Tappan, Charles, 26
Taylor, Griffin, 144, 151, 178, 195, *196*
Taylor House, 194
terra-cotta, 2, 205, 215–16, 238
theaters, 15–17, 21–22

Thomas, A. C., 8
Thomas, Samuel, 184
Thomas, Thomas, 6
Thompson, Martin E., 6, 21, 57, 60–61, 194, 231
Thompson, Peter, 170
Thompson, William, 24
Timanus, Jesse, 162–63, 166, 187, 271n30
Tinsley, William, 144, 154
Titcomb, Robert, 110
Titus (assistant), 145, 158, 161–63, 167, 178
Tobey, Emily Wesley, 19, 124, 150, 170, 216
Toledo, Ohio, 1, 209–10, *211*
The Tombs, 57
Totten, J. G., 129, 132, 134
Touro, Judah, 83–84, 86, 90, 92, 105, 124, 167, 201
Tower of the Winds, 67
Town, Ithiel, 21, 38, 53, 59, 63, 89, 101–2, 231, 233, 240
Treasury Department, 5, 221–22, 235, 240
Treatise on the Theory and Practice of Landscape Gardening (Downing), 107
Treatise on Ventilation (Wyman), 7, 120
Tremont House, 12, 15, 20, 23, 28–40, 51–54, 67, 77–82, 94, 102–5, 237; images of, *32, 34, 36–37*
Tremont Theatre, Boston, *21,* 23, 25–26, 28, 48
Trinity Church, 46, 76
Trollope, Frances, 9, 143
Tropp, Robertson, 209
Trumbull, John, 8
Twachtman, John Henry, 143
Twain, Mark, 189
Tweed, John P., 178, 180, 187–88, 196
Tyler, John, 131
Tyler Davidson & Company, 152, *153,* 239

Uncle Tom's Cabin (Stowe), 9, 143, 180, 207
Unitarian Universalism, 9, 19, 25–26, 73, 150, 178. *See also specific meeting houses*
United States Hotel, 36, 197
Upjohn, Richard, 6, 25, 43, 47, 76, 87, 100, 236, 238–39
U.S. Branch Bank, 17–18, 121
U.S. Capitol, xv, 6, 14, 18, 229
U.S. Custom House, 59–60

Vail, Alfred, 98
Van Buren, Martin, 3
Vandenhoff, George, 93
Van Zante, Gary, 168
Vitruvius, 7
Voelckers, Theodore, 10, 64, 67, 86, 90–91, 95–100, 120
The Voyage of Life (Cole), 3

Walker, Samuel, 58
Wallack, James, 75
Walter, Henry, 144
Walter, Thomas Ustick, 6, 8, 19, 38–39, 63, 187, 203, 208, 221, 229–38, 273n35
Walter, William, 144, 166, 217
Walter & Wilson, 163–64, 166
Warren, Owen G., 6, 133
Wasburn, Theodore, 90–91, 101
Washburn, Theodore, 101, 177
Washburn, William, 24, 36, 90–91, 101, 120, 177, 226
Washington Monument, 93, 122, 129, *130,* 186, 194, 203
Waterman, Isaiah, 26
Watriss, George E., 121
Waverly House, 121, 158
Webster, Daniel, 13, 56, 62
Weed, Joseph H., 122
Weisiger House, 180
Weisman, Winston, 99
Wells, Charles, 40, 133
West, William Russell, 181
Western Art Journal, 163
West Point Military Academy, 1, 79–82, *81,* 87, 115
Wheeling Suspension Bridge, 197
Whieldon, William, 106
Whig party, 3, 90, 94, 98, 105, 169
Whitely, William N., 227
Whitestone, Austin, 177
Whitestone, Henry, 10, 51, 160, 176–89, 194–95, 199–207, 212–13, 235, 238, 240
Whitman, Walt, 66–67
Whitney, Jocelyn & Annin, 66
Wigwam Quarry, 59
Willard, Solomon: Boston Merchants' Exchange and, 1–2; Bunker Hill Monument and, 18–19, 30, 92, 105–6, 129;

Willard, Solomon (*continued*)
  collaborations with Rogers and, 10, 71, 91, 95, 97, 105–6, 112–13, 118, 121, 132, 194; Gothic style and, 46–47; Quincy quarry and, 59–60, 69, 83–84, 91, 97, 237; Rogers's mentorship and, 5, 15, 17–18, 20, 23, 29–30, 62, 82, 231, 233–34
Williams, Elias E., 160, 182
Williams' Cincinnati Guide, 144
Wilson, James K., 144, 199, 225
Winslow, Edward, 13
Winthrop B. Smith & Company, 200
Wise, Mayer, 225
Wood, Alexander J., 170
Woodbury, Charles, 125
Woods, Mary, 76, 235
Worcester, Massachusetts, 1, 45–46, *218*
The Working-man's Cottage Architecture (Thomas), 6
Worthington, James T., 208
Wren, Christopher, 1
Wright, Frank Lloyd, 1
Wyatt, Benjamin, 16, 23, 30
Wyman, Morrill, 7, 120

Young, Ammi B., 4, 58–63, 72, 95, 132, 187, 194, 203, 220–21, 231–37, 266n16
Young, J. B., 6, 215
Young Builder's General Instructor (Lafever), 232

JAMES F. O'GORMAN, Grace Slack McNeil Professor of the History of American Art Emeritus at Wellesley College, concentrates on the architecture of nineteenth-century America. He is the author of monographs on H. H. Richardson, Frank Furness, Hammatt Billings, and Henry Austin, as well as studies of the work of Charles Bulfinch, Louis Sullivan, Frank Lloyd Wright, and Bertram Goodhue, and of architects' libraries, architects' portraits, and architectural drawings from New England, Maine, Boston, Philadelphia, and New Orleans. A past president and fellow of the Society of Architectural Historians, he has twice won the Henry-Russell Hitchcock Award of the Victorian Society in America.